NATIONAL PARKS BY DATE
OF ESTABLISHMENT

1872	Yellowstone
1890	Sequoia
	Yosemite
	General Grant (later Kings Canyon)
1899	Mount Rainier
1902	Crater Lake
1903	Wind Cave
1906	Mesa Verde
1910	Glacier
1915	Rocky Mountain
1916	Hawai'i Volcanoes
	Haleakala
	Lassen Volcanic
1917	Mount McKinley (Denali)
1919	Grand Canyon
	Acadia
	Zion
1921	Hot Springs
1924	Bryce Canyon
1929	Grand Teton
1930	Carlsbad Caverns
1934	Great Smoky Mountains
1935	Shenandoah
1938	Olympic
1940	Isle Royale
	Kings Canyon
1941	Mammoth Cave
1944	Big Bend
1947	Everglades
1956	Virgin Islands
1962	Petrified Forest
1964	Canyonlands
1968	North Cascades
	Redwood
1971	Capitol Reef
	Arches
1972	Guadalupe Mountains
1975	Voyageurs
1978	Badlands
	Theodore Roosevelt
1980	Channel Islands
	Biscayne
	Katmai
	Glacier Bay
	Gates of the Arctic
	Kenai Fjords
	Kobuk Valley
	Lake Clark
	Wrangell–St. Elias
1986	Great Basin
1988	National Park of American Samoa
1992	Dry Tortugas
1994	Death Valley
	Saguaro
	Joshua Tree
1999	Black Canyon of the Gunnison
2000	Great Sand Dunes
	Cuyahoga Valley
2003	Congaree

One learns that the world, though made, is yet being made. That this is still the morning of creation. That mountains, long conceived, are now being born, brought to light by the glaciers, channels traced for rivers, basins hollowed for lakes.

When we try to pick out anything by itself, we find it hitched to everything else in the universe. . . . The whole wilderness in unity and interrelation is alive and familiar . . . the very stones seem talkative, sympathetic, brotherly. . . .

Everybody needs beauty as well as bread, places to play in and pray in, where Nature may heal and cheer and give strength to body and soul alike.

This natural beauty-hunger is made manifest . . . in our magnificent National Parks—Nature's sublime wonderlands, the admiration and joy of the world.

JOHN MUIR

THE NATIONAL PARKS

THE NATIONAL PARKS

AMERICA'S BEST IDEA

An Illustrated History

by **DAYTON DUNCAN**

Based on a film by **KEN BURNS**
Produced by **DAYTON DUNCAN** and **KEN BURNS**
Written by **DAYTON DUNCAN**

With a preface by **KEN BURNS**
Picture research by
SUSANNA STEISEL and **AILEEN SILVERSTONE**

ALFRED A. KNOPF
NEW YORK
2009

FOR OUR CHILDREN AND
OUR CHILDREN'S CHILDREN

This Is a Borzoi Book
Published by Alfred A. Knopf
Copyright © 2009 by The National Parks Film Project,
LLC

All rights reserved. Published in the United States by
Alfred A. Knopf, a division of Random House, Inc.,
New York, and in Canada by Random House of
Canada Limited, Toronto.
www.aaknopf.com

Knopf, Borzoi Books, and the colophon are registered
trademarks of Random House, Inc.

A portion of this book originally appeared in *Reader's
Digest.*

Library of Congress Cataloging-in-Publication Data

Duncan, Dayton.
   The national parks: America's best idea: an illustrated
history/by Dayton Duncan; with a preface by Ken
Burns.—1st ed.
        p.   cm.
   "Based on a Ken Burns film produced by Ken Burns
and Dayton Duncan, written by Dayton Duncan."
   Includes bibliographical references.
   ISBN 978-0-307-26896-9
   1. National parks and reserves—United States—
History. 2. National parks and reserves—United
States—History—Pictorial works. 3. United States—
History, Local. 4. United States—History, Local—
Pictorial works. 5. Nature conservation—United
States—History. 6. United States. National Park
Service—History. 7. Interviews—United States.
I. Burns, Ken, 1953–   National parks. II. Title.
   SB482.A4D85   2009
   333.78'30973—dc22   2009020880

This book is printed on paper containing a minimum of
40 percent recovered fiber, manufactured by Newton
Falls Fine Paper, Newton Falls, New York.

Manufactured in the United States of America
First Edition

Preceding pages:
Hawai'i Volcanoes National Park
An early visitor to Yosemite
    National Park admires Half
    Dome from Glacier Point.
A tourist wanders through a
    geyser basin, Yellowstone
    National Park.
Two hikers rest after reaching the
    Colorado River at the bottom
    of Bright Angel Trail, Grand
    Canyon National Park.
Right: A family pauses in the giant
    trees of Sequoia National Park.
Following pages:
Contemplating reflections, Mount
    Rainier National Park
Bison herd, Wind Cave National
    Park
John Muir on the banks of the
    Merced River, Yosemite
    National Park

CONTENTS

OUR BEST SELVES

This book was born in the process of producing a documentary film series on the history of our national parks. That series, in turn, grew out of experiences and emotions and attitudes formed and shaped by more than three decades of trying to get to the heart of a deceptively simple question: Who are we? That is to say, who are those strange and complicated people who like to call themselves Americans? What can an investigation of the past tell about not only where we have been as a people, but also where we are and where we are going? The various films and books we have made over those thirty-plus years have often tried to explore the central issue of *race* in America, the great sin and stain of slavery and its ennobling as well as bedeviling consequences, in works on the Statue of Liberty, the Civil War, baseball, jazz, Thomas Jefferson, Mark Twain, and the first African-American heavyweight champion Jack Johnson, among others.

But we have also been drawn inexorably to a question of *space*; that is, the way in which the sheer physicality of this great continent has molded us as a people, for better and for worse. From book and film projects on the history of the American West—that strange and dangerous intersection of cultures where so much of our national character and mythology has emerged—to the Lewis and Clark expedition and its own decidedly bittersweet lessons; from a lighthearted look at the first cross-country automobile trip made a century after Meriwether Lewis and William Clark began theirs to the wonderful and unforgiving landscape that would inspire a young Samuel Clemens to take on the central themes of both race and space that his complicated young nation seemed unable to avoid, we too have been captivated and directed by a sense of possibility and promise in the magnificence of our land.

That interest has reached its apotheosis for us in the story of our national parks. For in the narrative of their creation, in the evolution of their clean and stunningly influential ideal, we have been able to engage and join themes that transcend the political or military or social elements that have traditionally passed for American history and have at times, we believe, touched on or at least glimpsed the intimate, indeed, spiritual themes that bind us—and that complicated past—together. We have found in our life-long love and curiosity for the still-wild places of America an animating spirit that has renewed our passion as filmmakers and writers, his-

torians and friends. We cannot imagine a better subject to continue to pursue the questions that have propelled us for so long.

It is not as if the national parks haven't been done before in both book and film form. They have. But it was our intention to make first a documentary film series and then this book on the *history* of the parks. This would not be a tour guide, a travelogue filled with pretty pictures of wildlife or spectacular natural scenery (though our projects in the end would have some of both), nor would this be a list of which inn or lodge to stay at when on vacation. We were most interested in following the individuals and ideas that have created this uniquely American thing called the national parks, an invention we now take for granted like the air that we breathe, the water we drink. (In the course of the production, we learned to our dismay that most people think the parks have always been there, that there has always been an agency charged with their care, and that—and nothing could be further from the truth—they will always be there.) We were principally drawn to the fact that, for the first time in human history, land—great sections of our natural landscape—was set aside, not for kings or noblemen or the very rich, but for everyone, for all time. We liked the fact that we Americans had invented such a wonderful thing, that this idea, like our articulation of universal political freedom in the Declaration of Independence, should be so widely admired and copied throughout the world.

Three decades of continually brushing up against this amazing and surprisingly little-known story during the course of producing our other projects, "meeting" and getting to know historical figures who were important to the evolution of the park idea, spending time out in these transformative and restorative places, only heightened our interest in the subject. Nearly ten years ago, therefore, we committed to making a documentary series and a book about our national parks. Over the many years it has taken to complete these projects, we have found in the story of the parks quite simply a reminder of our best selves, a connection to the most primitive impulses we human beings have, and an appreciation of the value of commonwealth that these parks represent on both a spiritual as well as material level.

During the course of our investigation, we began to gain a new, intimate awareness of the flabbergasting and nearly incalculable geological forces at work and on display in the parks. "One of the things I think we witness when we go to the parks," the historian William Cronon told us in an interview for our film, "is the immensity and the intimacy of time. On the one hand, we experience the immensity of time which is the creation itself. It is the universe unfolding before us. And yet it is also time shared with the people that we visit these places with. . . . We remember when our parents took us for the first time. . . . And then we as parents passing them on to our children, a kind of intimate transmission from generation to generation to generation of the love of place, the love of nation, that the national parks are meant to stand for."

———— • ◆ • ————

Walking quietly and awestruck within a grove of huge sequoia trees that like sentinels have borne silent witness to this immense passage of time, standing next to the rim of an unfathomably deep canyon, or in the spray and roar of a thousand-foot waterfall, gazing in wonder at the nighttime roost of tens of thousands of birds in a "dismal swamp," walking in a cathedral of stone more impressive than any made by man, stepping gingerly around geysers and fumaroles and boiling and spitting mudpots in "God's Laboratory," watching clouds clear off the crown of the most massive mountain on our continent, we have come to want to know *more* about that "intimate transmission" Cronon spoke of. Our film series and this book are our attempt at an answer.

For nearly seven years, we have made trip after trip from our home in New Hampshire out into the national parks looking, scouting, filming, interviewing, *asking*; delving into their origins and mythology, recovering their long-neglected stories and archives, searching for some sign or guidepost that would illuminate our way, getting to know the remarkable people who continue to protect this fragile inheritance. In the course of our work, we were awakened daily by the life-changing power these saved and sacred places exert. Stumbling among the ruins of Chaco Canyon in New Mexico and Mesa Verde in Colorado, we breathed the dry air of a civilization that vanished hundreds of years ago, yet in the eerily silent ruins, the warren of now deserted rooms and kivas and passageways of a once flourishing culture, we came to know the fragility of our own existence. In the crisp air of the pines and maples and in the thunder of the surf at Acadia in Maine, we found an unusual sustaining tranquility and reveled in the contradiction that much of that place had been saved by the son of the richest and most hated man in America. In northwestern Montana and later on a mountain near Seattle, we hiked up to living but now threatened and disappearing glaciers, while still marveling at the "floral Elysium," the riot and jumble of brightly colored wildflowers joyously blooming on the alpine slopes. It was hard to leave these protected places and the grief that fell over some of us,

as the built world reclaimed its supremacy, was palpable and long lasting.

In Hawaii, the hellish landscapes of Maui's Haleakala and the Big Island's Hawai'i Volcanoes provided us a glimpse back—it seemed—into the moment of creation itself, while the colorful, windswept canyons of southern Utah were mesmerizing, sometimes forbidding, museums of patient erosion. Down in the grandest canyon on earth in northern Arizona, we braved the chilly rapids of a still-insistent and dangerous Colorado River and wondered again at the layers of history, grand geological history, that river has revealed to travelers over the eons. Back on its south rim, we felt the insignificance of our own lives, the sense of one's smallness in the larger scheme of things that the view from the canyon's edge continually promotes, and in the inscrutable contradictory ways of our national parks, felt bigger in that knowledge. Like privileged visitors to some sacred shrine or cloistered monastery, Alaska took us in and permitted us moments with mountains and fjords and tundra, brown bear and caribou and moose, whale and seal and puffin we will never forget. We saw wolves, too.

In northwestern Wyoming, we found a kind of second home among the wildlife and wild eruptions of the many stunning otherworldly thermal features, fell silent at an overlook that afforded a view of the inspirational multihued canyon of the Yellowstone, and had the sense there that the forces which had created the earth were still operating just below the brittle, sometimes hollow-sounding ground we were walking on, a cosmic laboratory of startling beauty and majesty. We've come back to this place again and again, in every season, at every time of day and night; and from every vantage, we have struggled and strained to catch a view of the primeval, to reconnect ourselves to the natural world that *was* our home at the beginnings of our dimmest memories as a species. At one glorious moment, a magnificent bison walked out of a cloud of steam and into our shot, a refugee—a cautionary emissary—from some prehistoric age, a creature only recently saved from extinction because Americans had the foresight to permanently set aside this wild place as a national park.

And in the Sierra Nevada of California, we found our sanctuary and our church. If the genius of America has been to liberate humankind by permitting its citizens to govern themselves, it has also helped to free them in another perhaps more important way by permitting its believers to worship God as they saw fit. Where our European ancestors required a formalized dogmatic devotion in cathedrals made by men, we Americans would more easily find God—or Science or Art, if that is your way—in Nature. And on the western slope of those same Sierras, where the Ahwahneechee Indians once made their home, is a valley of incomparable transcendent beauty that the white men who first "discovered" it called

Yosemite. It is the first great natural park in history and it contains towering waterfalls and thundering cataracts, polished granite rocks of unusual and unique architecture, majestic trees of almost supernatural size, dense forests and alpine meadows, bald eagles and hermit thrushes, deer and black bears. But an inventory of its treasures does not come close to describing its power. In Yosemite, the whole is always greater than the sum of its parts, and we as filmmakers and writers, cinematographers and editors, have struggled these many years to comprehend the nearly cosmic calculus that continually recommends that special valley to us. A final accounting will not come, of course, our arithmetic will always fail; the glories of Yosemite, indeed of all the national parks, will be impossible to articulate with any precision by mere mortals.

Interestingly, those mortals have been, in many ways big and small, the glue that holds the story of the national parks together. It was people, after all, who failed to find the words to express the emotions they felt in these places but who nonetheless moved fearlessly into that "unknowing"; it was people, who in fits and starts, and up against powerful and relentless opposition, first tried to set aside these parks; it was people who saw the danger to wildlife and scenery and rescued some threatened species from extinction; it was people who drew up the laws and fought the bureaucratic fights to create an agency charged with overseeing these spectacular parks; and it was—and is—people who have dedicated their lives to the ongoing work of protecting, expanding, and now restoring the best idea we've ever had.

They include an energetic and idealistic young president, a man with a nearly unquenchable thirst for knowledge of the natural world, who would do more for parks and conservation than any other politician of his day by emphasizing "the essential democracy" at the heart of the park impulse and by insisting that these locations be saved for "our children and our children's children." "We are not building this country of ours for a day," he once said. "It is to last through the ages." But they also include a young boy from Kansas, who after reading in the newspaper that had wrapped his lunch about an exquisite lake out west would dedicate the next thirty-one years of his life to saving one of the most beautiful spots in the country. They include a restless housewife from Lincoln, Nebraska, who, with her photographer husband, would tour the national parks each summer in their car, creating a loving scrapbook and a journal of startling poignancy and artistry, filled with timeless memories of the unforgettable places the childless couple had adopted. They include a brilliant Hispanic biologist who would do more than anyone else to turn the Park Service's attention toward the preservation of wildlife and the correct stewardship of the many species that called the parks their home. They include two tireless and enterprising brothers who in the first decades of

the twentieth century made photographing and filming the grandest canyon on earth their life's work, who brought back some of the finest pictures ever made of that region, and who also made a living taking photographs of the equally awestruck tourists who rode mules into the canyon. They include a fisherman's guide, the son of a slave living on a small key off the coast of Miami, who refused to sell his land to a developer planning to despoil his beloved paradise, and then happily turned his island over to the people of the United States who had decided, in their wisdom, to preserve forever his pristine sanctuary.

Over the course of our film and this book, you will meet several dozen people, most of them unsung or unfamiliar, who found in the parks salvation of one kind or another. They include a talented but troubled alcoholic who fell in love with the wildwoods of western North Carolina and eastern Tennessee, rehabilitated himself in the isolation of nature, and then sacrificed everything to see the region transformed into a park. He was aided by an equally dedicated Japanese immigrant who would with his camera help insure the preservation of the wilderness that was so close to and so threatened by the major population centers of the east. They include a family of Colorado cowboys, Quakers, who transformed themselves into archaeologists and helped save the dwindling and often vandalized relics of ancient American cultures, and a Minnesota boy who stepped off a train in Alaska, near the nation's highest peak, and became one of the fiercest protectors of predators nearly everyone else wanted eradicated.

They include the millionaire businessman with seemingly limitless enthusiasm for the expansion of parkland in America, who would spearhead the creation of the National Park Service and then benefit from its calming and peaceful resources as perhaps no one else has; and his young assistant, who would be forced to take over during his boss's mysterious absences, and who would also help an invalid president expand the very notion of what a national park could be. They include an iconoclastic crusader from Florida, a woman with her own unique relationship to the swamp at her doorstep, who would help lead the fight to save that swamp from a relentless tide of development and commercial exploitation.

And they also include a Scottish-born wanderer who walked clear across California and into the Ahwahneechees' magical valley in the middle of the high Sierras and was utterly transformed, finding in Nature's exquisite lessons an alternative to the harsh religious discipline of his father, and who would articulate his new creed of Nature in writings so transcendent that millions of Americans are still beguiled and inspirited by the rapture flowing from his words. For John Muir, Yosemite, indeed any wild place, revealed a design and an intelligence more permanent, more valuable than anything made by man, and man would be wise to submit to that natural world. He was certain, too, that a genuine and authentic relationship with Nature would help to forge a special "kinship" between all lovers of the mountains, and this kinship, in turn, required us—each of us within ourselves—to work to become better people. For this new human evolution to take place, Muir insisted that we had to go out into nature. But by going out, he said, we were "really going in." This is the journey, the journey of self-discovery, we all can make as we embrace our national parks. "This is still," John Muir wrote assuredly, "the morning of creation."

In many ways, they are hard to get to. The siren call of civilization is nearly impossible to resist; its enervating rhythms discordant yet seductive; the promise of wealth or position too engrained a reward for most of us to ignore. Though human *beings*, we seem compelled relentlessly to *do*. Yet we are beset by discontinuity; people quarrel, get sick, die, fall away. Rarely does the momentum of things permit repair or reconciliation; rarely do we throttle back. Even in nature, even in our beloved national parks, that momentum has a way of distracting us. We are now used to and come to expect a windshield experience, a quick drive through, and anything else is a bit frightening, time-consuming, other. The intimate specificity of nature, seen in the highest of mountains or a speck of lichen on a rock, its ever-enlarging vastness, is lost in the control we seek to superimpose over the chaos, the random chaos, of events. For many of us, we just don't have the time to submit, to enroll, as it were, as students in the great classroom our natural world provides, its curriculum endless and varied, sustaining and vital. In short, we have ignored the extraordinary commonwealth that is waiting just outside the city limits, ready to end the poverty of spirit that afflicts us all from time to time.

A traveler leaving San Francisco's airport by car and heading east out of the Bay Area has to negotiate a maze of interstate highway exchanges, and it is easy to forget, despite the "progress" one sees everywhere—the random overlap and seeming endlessness of our built environment—that it was and still is a beautiful place. Unlike a walk, which makes every place infinitely big, air travel makes the country small, impersonal, a few hours to get from one side to the other. As a result, we become impatient; even in a car after a flight, the sameness of things, whether man-made or natural, can erode our precious but often squandered attention.

But civilization does relent and the highways become less crowded, the multilane swaths of the city turn into smaller two-lane ribbons that cut through rather than consume landscape. If you are heading to John Muir's Yosemite, as I was near the beginning of this project, to catch up with my partners for several days of

filming, I-80, I-580, I-205, and I-5 eventually yield, west of Manteca in the vast inland valley, into California Route 120. Now the shopping centers and malls give way to smaller towns and farms and fields and orchards. The land reclaims its primacy, but all of that is just preliminary, decompression, compared to what awaits the traveler on his first visit to Yosemite. The road begins to climb, even the farms now fall away, and 120 becomes Big Oak Flat Road, and eventually California Route 140, which leads the traveler (in the car now nearly as long as in the plane) into Yosemite National Park.

There is no preparation for it. A turn in the road and suddenly the valley unfolds before you. I have never in my life felt the way I felt at that moment. The crisp air and high altitude made the mountains and waterfalls, trees and road look almost like a backdrop you could roll up and store away. But it was something more. Like Muir, though I was physically outside, I was actually going in, transforming the old generic question once again into "Who am I?" The view was an anchor and a beacon; it held me gently but firmly in its grip (a grip I don't think I have ever completely lost) and it pulled me directly into the heart of the park.

When I caught up with the rest of our crew, who had all been to Yosemite before, they grinned when they saw my face. Like the loss of one's virginity or the fresh intimacy of parenthood, I had entered a new world, one I would find hard to forget or relinquish. For the next few days, we worked dawn to dusk filming the surrounding valley floor, hiking up past Vernal and Nevada falls to spend a night outdoors, each step a further surrender to the forces that had held John Muir so closely, to the forces that were changing my life. Each of us felt it, especially my co-producer and writer Dayton Duncan (whose love of the parks had initiated this project and this journey for me), and it only took a sideways glance or a quick exchanged smile to realize that each of us felt the same, each of us was hearing the same great symphony. The Park Service sells a small booklet they call a passport to those who wish to keep a permanent record of their trips into the parks; you can get this passport stamped with the date and location of each park you enter. The symbolism then was not lost on me. I had been permitted entry into a new country, not just a country of physical space and time, but of meaning and memory. I felt born again as we walked back into the valley.

That last night before we would head back to San Francisco and our busy, compelling lives, I lay awake unable to sleep. Memories were stirring and I suddenly realized that this was not the first natural national park I had ever been to, as I had thought and as I had confessed to my friends and colleagues. And then it all rushed back, a memory so long forgotten that it had ceased to be a part of my "history." In 1959, as a six-year-old boy, my father had taken me on our first and last road trip together. My mother was slowly

Ken Burns with his father, Robert, late 1950s

dying of cancer and our household was a grim and demoralized place. And he had not been the best father, either; baseball catches in the backyard were few and far between, attendance at my games nonexistent. He was moody and distracted by my mother's illness and by inner demons none of us—my mother, younger brother, or me—fully understood, demons that would consume him for most of his too-short life.

But one Friday after school, he and I drove from our home in Newark, Delaware, to my grandparents' house, the place he had grown up in, in Baltimore. We went to bed late (I slept in his old bedroom, in his old bed under his old chenille comforter) and it seemed like only a second later that my father was leaning over me in the dark, gently touching my shoulder, urging me to get up quickly. I had never been up so early in my life. It was still dark as we left the house and I can still remember nearly fifty years later all the things we talked about (butterflies and baseball, the route we were taking, the battlefield of the Civil War we passed) as the sun came up and we made our way, pre–interstate system, to Front Royal, Virginia, and the north entrance of Shenandoah National Park.

The Skyline Drive runs along the spine of the ridge that makes up the relatively small park and that morning there was still fog and mist and cloud hugging the road. I had never been in a cloud before. We went through short tunnels carved through the mountains (!) and we saw a handful of deer standing stock-still before us on the road before my dad scattered them with his car horn. After what seemed like hours in this new world, we turned off the drive and checked into a small cabin just big enough for the two of us. It was chilly and my dad insisted on my putting on a jeans jacket with red lining we had just bought and we set off down a trail that led eventually to a waterfall. It was an impossibly long hike for my young legs—probably all of a mile and a half—but I held my father's hand and I can still remember his grip to this day.

We saw a bear, I think. We turned over rotting logs and caught a bright-red salamander and my father named every butterfly and tree we saw. I don't remember what or even where we ate that night, but I do remember lying awake, as I would do years later alone in Yosemite, thinking how great this was to be in this magical place, with memory and emotion attached so securely, this time with my dad. The next day we had more hikes and more adventures before we headed home; my dad sang to me songs like "Wolverton Mountain," "Silver Threads and Golden Needles," "Scarlet Ribbons," and other folk songs that are permanently on my hard drive, though when I had later sung them to my children I had forgotten when I learned them. Later, after my epiphany at Yosemite, my then thirteen-year-old middle daughter, Lilly, was dragged down the same Skyline Drive, as I attempted to re-create what a distracted father and his desperately young son had experienced as the 1950s came to a close. This time we most definitely saw bears.

When that memory-stirred night in Yosemite came in May of 2003, my father had been gone for more than a year and a half, and I suppose it is reasonable to ask, confronting such an epic story as that of the national parks, what purpose these personal stories serve. But the narrative of the parks is not just in their spectacular scenery, the waterfalls and big trees and wildlife, or even the complicated sagas of the charismatic individuals who saved these places. It is also about who we see these sacred places with, whose hand we are holding at the rim of the Grand Canyon (or in Shenandoah National Park), what intimate transmissions, as Cronon would say, occur between the generations as we instill this love of the parks, our parks, to our posterity. We *are* beset by discontinuity; people do quarrel, get sick, die, fall away. Rarely does the momentum of things permit repair or reconciliation. But I have found, in places where the narrative of human lives and those of their "brotherly" rocks seem just as important, that some inexpressible something is retained, repairs are made, and we are all, as John Muir so fervently wished, kindred spirits.

KEN BURNS
Walpole, New Hampshire

A TREASURE HOUSE OF NATURE'S SUPERLATIVES

They are a treasure house of nature's superlatives—84 million acres of some of the most stunning landscapes anyone has ever seen: including a mountain so massive it creates its own weather, whose peak rises more than 20,000 feet above sea level, the highest point on the continent; a valley where a river disappears into burning sands 282 feet below sea level, the lowest, driest, and hottest location in the country; a labyrinth of caves longer than any other ever measured; and the deepest lake in the nation, with the clearest water in the world.

They contain trees, dead for 225 million years, that are now solid rock. And trees, still growing, that were already saplings before the time of Christ, before Rome conquered the known world, before the Greeks worshipped in the Parthenon, before the Egyptians built the Pyramids—trees that are the oldest living things on earth. And the tallest. And the largest.

They encompass a mile-deep gash in the ground where the Hopis say the first people emerged from the underworld, and where scientists say a river has patiently carved its way to expose rocks that are 1.7 billion years old—nearly half the age of the planet itself; and an island where a goddess named Pele destroys everything in her path while she simultaneously gives birth to new land.

A moving rock on the Racetrack, Death Valley National Park

They preserve cathedrals of stone, gaily ornamented by cascading ribbons of water; arctic dreamscapes, where the rivers are made of ice; and a geological wonderland with rivers that steam, mud that boils, amidst the greatest collection of geysers in the world.

They became the last refuge for magnificent species of animals that otherwise would have vanished forever. And they remain a refuge for human beings seeking to replenish their spirit; geographies of memory and hope, where countless American families have forged an intimate connection to their land—and then passed it along to their children.

But they are more than a collection of rocks and trees and inspirational scenes from nature. They embody something less tangible yet equally enduring—an idea, born in the United States nearly a century after its creation, as uniquely American as the Declaration of Independence and just as radical. National parks, the writer and historian Wallace Stegner once said, are "the best idea we've ever had."

Mount McKinley viewed from Wonder Lake, Denali National Park

Like the idea of America itself, full of competing demands and impulses, between individual rights and those of the community, between idealism and exploitation, between the sacred and the profitable, between the immediate desires of one generation and its obligation and promise to the next, the national park idea has been constantly debated, constantly tested, and is constantly evolving, ultimately embracing places that also preserve the nation's first principles, its highest aspirations, its greatest sacrifices—even reminders of its most shameful mistakes.

Most of all, the story of the national parks is the story of people. People from every conceivable background—rich and poor; famous and unknown; soldiers and scientists; natives and newcomers; idealists, artists, and entrepreneurs. People who were willing to devote themselves to saving some precious portion of the land they loved—and in doing so, reminded their fellow citizens of the full meaning of democracy.

From the very beginning, as they struggled over who should control their national parks, what should be allowed within their boundaries, even why they should exist at all, Americans have looked upon these wonders of nature and seen in them the reflection of their own dreams.

Left: Ancient bristlecone pines, Great Basin National Park
Overleaf: View of the Colorado River from the South Rim, Grand Canyon National Park

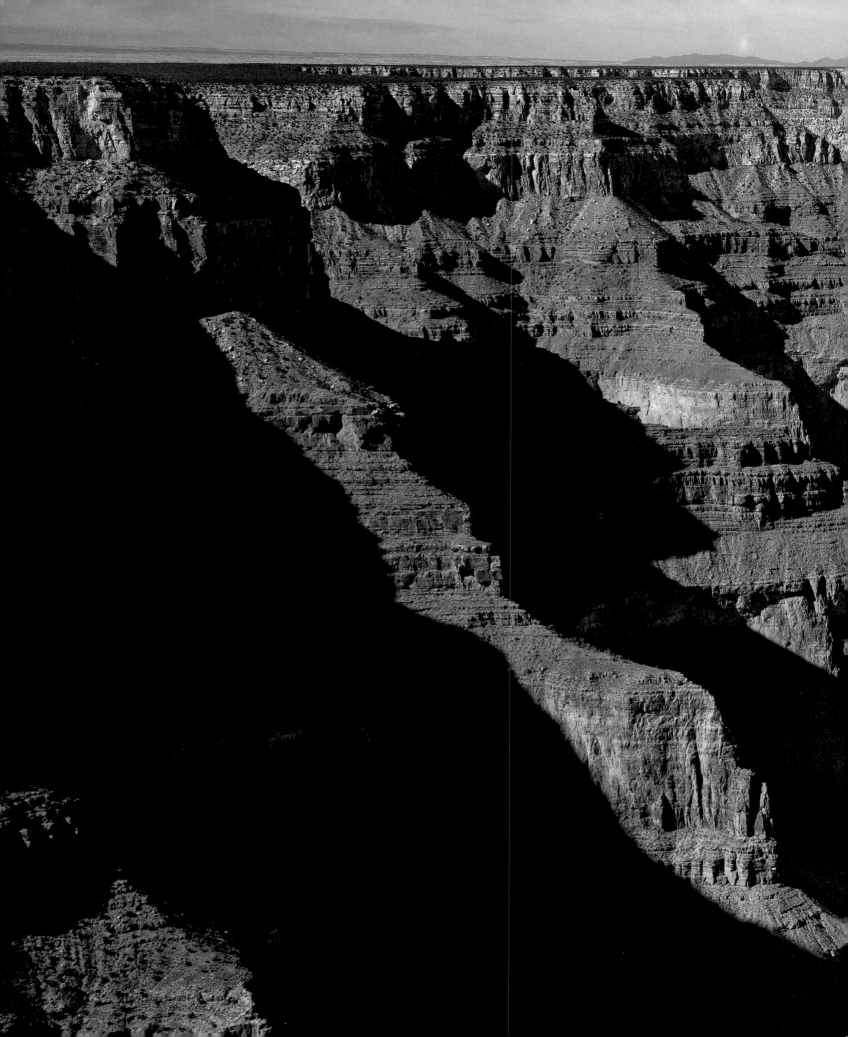

CHAPTER ONE

THE SCRIPTURE OF NATURE

EARLY IN 1851, during the frenzy of the California Gold Rush, an armed group of white men was scouring the western slopes of the Sierra Nevada. They called themselves the Mariposa Battalion, and they were searching for Indians, intent on driving the natives from their homelands and onto reservations.

Late on the afternoon of March 27 the battalion came to a narrow valley surrounded by towering granite cliffs, where a series of waterfalls dropped thousands of feet to reach the Merced River on the valley's floor. One of the men, a young doctor named Lafayette Bunnell, found himself transfixed by the vista. "As I looked, a peculiar exalted sensation seemed to fill my whole being," he wrote, "and I found my eyes in tears with emotion."

> *I said with some enthusiasm . . . "I have here seen the power and glory of a Supreme Being; the majesty of His handy-work is in that 'Testimony of the Rocks.' "*

Bunnell's enchantment with the scenery was not shared by the rest of the Mariposa Battalion. Its commander, a hardened Indian fighter named James D. Savage, was angered that the natives had somehow disappeared into the mountains. He ordered his men to set fire to the Indians' homes and their storehouses of acorns, in order to starve them into submission.

But before the battalion moved on, Bunnell convinced the others that, as the first white men ever to enter the valley, they should give it a name. He suggested "Yosemite," based on Savage's information that this was the name of the tribe they had come to dispossess. Long after the tribe was finally located and forced from their beloved valley, scholars would learn that in fact the natives called the valley *Ahwahnee*, meaning "the place of a gaping mouth," and that they called themselves the Ahwahneechees, in honor of the valley they had considered their home for centuries. "Yosemite," it was learned, meant something entirely different. In the native language, "Yosemite" refers to people who should be feared. It means "they are killers."

Preceding pages: Yosemite Valley, with Bridalveil Falls on right, Half Dome in the middle distance, El Capitan on left
Right: An early picture of the valley from the Mariposa Trail by Charles L. Weed, the first photographer to enter Yosemite

Descending towards the Yo-Semite Valley, we came upon a high point clear of trees, from whence we had our first view of the singular and romantic valley; and as the scene opened in full view before us, we were almost speechless with wondering admiration at its wild and sublime grandeur.

JAMES MASON HUTCHINGS

In 1855, a second group of white people arrived in Yosemite Valley—this time as tourists, not Indian fighters. They were led by James Mason Hutchings, an energetic Englishman who had failed miserably as a prospector during the Gold Rush and decided instead to seek his fortune as a publisher.

His broadsheet, *The Miner's Ten Commandments,* had already sold 100,000 copies. Now he planned on

Three Brothers and the Merced River, photographed by Carleton E. Watkins, c. 1861

expanding his business by promoting California's scenic wonders through an illustrated magazine. When a report about the Indian campaign in the Sierras briefly mentioned a waterfall "nearly a thousand feet high"—six times the height of Niagara's—Hutchings determined to see it for himself.

The first difficulty was simply finding the valley Bunnell had described with such rapture. At the nearby town of Mariposa, few residents had ever heard of Yosemite; even veterans of Savage's battalion were no longer sure how to get there. After securing two Indian guides and enduring three days of rough going through thick underbrush and dense forests, Hutchings and his group finally emerged at what is now called Inspiration Point.

"It is beyond the power of language to describe the awe-inspiring majesty of the darkly-frowning and overhanging mountain walls of solid granite that here hem us in on every side," Hutchings wrote, once they had entered the valley itself. Farther on, they came upon Yosemite Falls, the highest waterfall on the continent.

Although this stream shoots over the margin of the mountain . . . it falls almost in a body—not in a continuous stream exactly, but having a close resemblance to an avalanche of snowy rockets that appear to be perpetually trying to overtake each other in their descent, and mingle the one into the other, the whole composing a torrent of indescribable power and beauty.

James Mason Hutchings

Painter Albert Bierstadt, seated on a log, at work in a Miwok village

Huge boulders and large masses of sharp, angular rocks, are scattered here and there, forming the uneven sides of an immense, and apparently ever-boiling cauldron. . . .

If man ever feels his utter insignificance at any time, it is when looking upon such a scene of appalling grandeur.

In his zeal to put his own stamp on the valley, Hutchings decided that one waterfall, which Bunnell had said the Indians called *Pohono,* needed a different name, something more likely to draw tourists. Since it looked to Hutchings like a bride's veil caught by a breeze, he dubbed it Bridalveil Falls, "by far the most musical and suitable of any of all others yet given."

To make the most of the visit for his publishing business, Hutchings had brought along Thomas A. Ayres, an aspiring young artist, hired to draw pictures of everything he saw, which Hutchings would sell as lithographs and use to illustrate his new magazine. They would be the first artistic representations of Yosemite ever to reach the public.

Four years later, in 1859, Hutchings made his second visit to the valley, this time with Charles L. Weed, a practitioner of the young art of photography. Weed's photographs were soon on display in San Francisco and copied as engravings in Hutchings's magazine, meant to feed the growing public appetite for more descriptions and views of a place Hutchings predicted "will serve to immortalize the natural features of California, and draw from all parts of the world admiring tourists to visit them."

Other artists and photographers quickly followed. Carleton E. Watkins launched what would become a fifty-year career as one of the West's most renowned landscape photographers by lugging thousands of pounds of equipment into the valley in order to capture Yosemite's sweeping majesty on his mammoth glass plate negatives, weighing four pounds each. Back East, his photos would be collected by Oliver Wendell Holmes and Ralph Waldo Emerson and exhibited in art galleries in New York City.

In 1863, the celebrated painter Albert Bierstadt arrived and produced a series of masterpieces that would cement his fame as one of the founders of what came to be called the "Rocky Mountain

School." One of his paintings, *The Domes of the Yosemite*, nine and a half feet by fifteen feet, would command a price of $25,000, equal to the highest amount ever paid for an American work of art at the time. While Bierstadt painted, his friend Fitz Hugh Ludlow wrote glowing dispatches to *The Atlantic Monthly*, the nation's most prestigious magazine:

> *We did not so much seem to be seeing from that crag of vision a new scene on the old familiar globe as a new heaven and a new earth into which the creative spirit had just been breathed.*
>
> *I hesitate now, as I did then, at the attempt to give my vision utterance. Never were words as beggared for an abridged translation of any Scripture of Nature.*

Meanwhile, other tourists had begun showing up to see Yosemite's beauty firsthand. They were a trickle at first, fewer than eighty-five a year. The trip required a two-day journey from San Francisco to the nearest town and then, with no wagon road into the valley, a grueling two- to three-day trek by foot or horseback, up and down steep mountainsides on narrow, rocky paths.

Most found the scenic reward worth the hardship, and in their struggle to describe their experience, early tourists usually resorted to either religious terms or glowing comparisons to the churches and antiquities of Europe. Looking at the majestic Cathedral Rocks and Cathedral Spires, wrote Samuel Bowles, editor of the Springfield *Republican* in Massachusetts, made it "easy to imagine . . . that you are under the ruins of an old Gothic cathedral, to which those of Cologne and Milan are but baby-houses." Upon seeing Yosemite Falls, another visitor began quoting the Bible and praising "the glorious works of

Sunset in the Yosemite Valley, 1868, one of Albert Bierstadt's many dramatic interpretations of the valley that made people want to visit

In the early years, the upstairs rooms in James Mason Hutchings's hotel (top) were separated only by cloth partitions, to the embarrassment of many female visitors. Other tourists (above) complained that Hutchings seemed more interested in talking about Yosemite than in serving them proper meals.

he departed the next day over yet another torturous mountain trail for the Mariposa Grove of giant sequoias—the largest living things on earth, trees that survive for nearly three thousand years. There, in the midst of what he called "the mammoths of the vegetable world" that were of "very substantial size when David danced before the ark," Greeley was not disappointed at all.

> If the village of Mariposa, the county, or the state of California does not immediately provide for the safety of these trees, I shall deeply deplore [it]. . . .
>
> I am sure they will be more prized and treasured a thousand years hence than now, should they, by extreme care and caution, be preserved so long, and that thousands will then visit them, over smooth and spacious roads, for every one who now toils over the rugged bridle-path by which I have reached them.

A few years later, the Mariposa Grove was visited by Frederick Law Olmsted, a frail and melancholic New Englander who had recently made a name for himself as the designer of New York City's Central Park, the nation's first major urban park. It was a *man-made* space in which, Olmsted boasted, "every tree and bush . . . has been fixed where it is with a purpose." He knew, because he had fixed them there himself. Among the giant sequoias—and later in Yosemite Valley itself—far from the city park he had so meticulously designed, Olmsted found instead a natural landscape of grace and charm that seemed to soothe his mind and spirit. Yosemite, he wrote, was "the greatest glory of nature . . . the union of the deepest sublimity with the deepest beauty."

By 1864, as famous as it had become, Yosemite had been visited by a total of only 653 tourists since James Mason Hutchings's first trip in 1855. But Hutchings still had faith in the future of tourism for the place he had now been promoting for nearly a decade—enough faith that he had given up his publishing business to buy one of the valley's two hotels, which he promptly renamed the Hutchings House.

With his sickly wife and his strong-willed mother-in-law, Hutchings confidently tried to make a go of it as Yosemite's unofficial host. His skills as an innkeeper, however, fell short of his enthusiasm for

God." "Now let me die," he told his companions, "for I am happy."

Horace Greeley, the influential editor of the *New York Tribune* on his well-publicized trip to the West in 1859, was in such a rush to see Yosemite that he refused to make the usual overnight stop on his way into the valley and instead rode from sunrise to midnight on what he later called "the hardest trotting horse in America." Yosemite Falls, diminished to a trickle in midsummer, was a "humbug," he wrote, so

his surroundings. He enjoyed lecturing his guests and leading them on sightseeing tours, yet he sometimes failed to provide them with knives and forks at dinner or filled their coffee cups with cold water. "Guests would be better served," one of his early customers wrote, "if the proprietor paid less attention to describing the beauties and more to providing comfortable beds and properly prepared meals."

Another complained that people changing clothes in the upstairs rooms, separated only by sheets of cotton, sometimes found their silhouette projected onto the cloth partition "hugely magnified, for the amusement of one's neighbors." When a friend dropped a piece of soap at the wash basin, she added, it ended up in the downstairs parlor "because the floor and the outside wall didn't quite meet." Hutchings seemed oblivious to it all. He liked the increased attention Yosemite was attracting. And he also liked the attention the valley brought to him.

EDEN

On May 17, 1864, in the midst of the Civil War, the junior senator from California, John Conness, rose in the Senate chamber in Washington, D.C., to explain a bill he had just introduced. Ulysses S. Grant's invasion of Virginia had bogged down in the Wilderness campaign, and Union forces were averaging two thousand soldiers wounded a day. William Tecumseh Sherman's troops had just entered Georgia, aiming at a well-fortified Atlanta. In Arkansas, Joseph Shelby's Confederates took the town of Dardanelle that day. But Conness's bill had nothing to do with the war that threatened to destroy his nation.

I will state to the Senate that this bill proposes to make a grant of certain premises located in the Sierra Nevada mountains, in the State of California, that are for all public purposes worthless, but which constitute, perhaps, some of the greatest wonders of the world.

SENATOR JOHN CONNESS

Conness's bill proposed something totally unprecedented in human history: setting aside, not a landscaped garden or a city park, but a large tract of natural scenery for the future enjoyment of everyone. More than sixty square miles of federal land, encom-

passing the Yosemite Valley and the Mariposa Grove of Big Trees, were to be transferred to the care of the state of California, on the condition that the land never be opened for private ownership and instead be preserved for "public use, resort, and recreation."

He was acting, Conness said, at the urging of some of his constituents—"various gentlemen of California," he explained, "gentlemen of fortune, of taste, and of refinement," though he did not name them. To this day their names are still unknown, except for that of Captain Israel Ward Raymond, the California representative of the Central American Steamboat Transit Company, who had sent a letter on their behalf to Conness, suggesting the legislation. Included with the letter was a set of Carleton Watkins's large-format photographs of the sequoias and the valley.

Exactly how Raymond's group had come up with such a radical proposal is not known, but precursors of the idea had been surfacing off and on since the beginnings of the nation itself. In 1767, nine years before drafting the Declaration of Independence, Thomas Jefferson had come across what he described as "the most sublime of Nature's works"—Virginia's Natural Bridge, a limestone arch 215 feet high spanning a gorge carved by a tributary of the James River. "The rapture of the Spectator is really indescribable," Jefferson wrote, before attempting nonetheless to describe it. At the top, "you involuntarily fall on your hands and feet, creep to the parapet and peep over it. Looking down from this height about a minute gave me a violent headache." But from the bottom, "it is impossible for the emotions, arising from the sublime, to be felt beyond what they are here: so beautiful an arch, so elevated, so light, and springing, as it were, up to heaven."

Jefferson paid King George 20 shillings for the bridge and 157 surrounding acres. "I view it in some degree as a public trust," he wrote a friend later, "and would on no consideration permit the bridge to be injured, defaced or masked from public view."

In Jefferson's mind, America was closer to Eden—pure and unspoiled, nearer to what the world had been at the time of creation—than the jaded Old World whose monarchies the infant United States so firmly rejected. The wild, bountiful continent and the new nation being born upon it were inextricably

Senator John Conness

Right: To demonstrate the immensity of the Grizzly Giant, the largest sequoia in the Mariposa Grove, Carleton Watkins had a group of tourists pose at its base.

linked. He took extreme umbrage when the influential French naturalist Georges-Louis Leclerc, Comte de Buffon, contended that the animals of North America were smaller than those of Europe, implying that the continent's climate somehow produced inferior species—including human beings. Jefferson had devoted part of his only full-length book, *Notes on the State of Virginia,* to refuting such notions, but as minister to France in 1786, he found a more dramatic way to make his point. He asked the governor of New Hampshire to ship to Paris the skin, skeleton, and horns of a moose, and sent it on to the museum where the Comte de Buffon was superintendent. (The Frenchman was duly impressed, Jefferson reported to Daniel Webster, and "promised in his next volume, to set these things right also; but he died directly afterwards.")

As Jefferson's nation had grown, the country's sense of itself and its possibilities had grown as well, not only in the political sphere, but in the arts, literature, and in its citizens' relationship to God. In the early nineteenth century, the Transcendentalist writer Ralph Waldo Emerson began telling Americans that God was more easily found in nature than in the works of man. "At the gates of the forest," he said, "the surprised man of the world is forced to leave his city estimates of great and small, wise and foolish."

> *The knapsack of custom falls off his back with the first step he makes.*
>
> *Here is sanctity which shames our religions, and reality which discredits our heroes. Here we find Nature to be the circumstance which dwarfs every other circumstance, and judges like a god all men that come to her. . . . Here no history, or church, or state is interpolated on the divine sky and the immortal year.*

Emerson's disciple, Henry David Thoreau, had called for "little oases of wildness in the desert of our civilization." If the kings of England had forests to shelter game for sport and food, he asked, "why should not we, who renounced the king's authority, have our national preserves" in which wild animals would not be "civilized off the face of the earth," but protected "for inspiration and our own true recreation." "Or shall we," he added, "like villains, grub

them all up, poaching on our own national domains?"

> *We need the tonic of wildness—to wade sometimes in marshes where the bittern and the meadow-hen lurk . . . to smell the whispering sedge where only some wilder and more solitary fowl builds her nest, and the mink crawls with its belly close to the ground. . . .*
>
> *We can never have enough of Nature. . . . In wildness is the preservation of the world.*

But the notion of America as a new Eden was in danger, as the nation, in the name of Manifest Destiny, marched inexorably across the continent, systematically dispossessing Indian peoples from their homelands and transforming the land to new uses. In 1832 the artist George Catlin, traveling on the vast Great Plains in search of "the grace and beauty of Nature," had come across a teeming herd of buffalo and was suddenly struck with the premonition that they—and the Indians who depended on them—would someday be gone forever. Then he had an epiphany. Much of nature, he realized, was destined "to fall before the deadly axe and desolating hands of cultivating man," and yet the further mankind became separated from "pristine wildness," the "more pleasure does the mind of enlightened man feel in recurring to those scenes."

> *What a splendid contemplation when one imagines them . . . by some great protecting policy of government, preserved . . . in a* magnificent park.
>
> *A* nation's Park, *containing man and beast, in all the wild and freshness of their nature's beauty.*
>
> *I would ask no other monument to my memory, nor any other enrollment of my name amongst the famous dead, than the reputation of having been the founder of such an institution.*

Catlin published his thoughts in a letter to a New York City newspaper the next year, but his idea for a "nation's park" attracted little attention. At the same time, however, more American artists, writers, and thinkers, looking for ways to distinguish themselves and their country from the influences of the Old World, started arguing, as Jefferson had suggested,

EXERCICES DE L'ÉCHELLE PÉRILLEUSE

Exécutés par **M. HANLON**, en Amérique, sous le **Pont** suspendu de la **CATARACTE** du **NIAGARA**.

A French poster pokes fun at the carnival atmosphere and crass commercialization of Niagara Falls. Americans, Alexis de Tocqueville wrote, were more interested in subduing nature than preserving it and "habitually prefer the useful to the beautiful."

that America's greatness could best be measured in the natural wonders it seemed to possess in such abundance. Whatever it might lack in terms of an ancient Parthenon or a grand cathedral or a museum filled with cultural treasures, they asserted, America more than compensated for in its endless forests, stunning canyons, and awe-inspiring waterfalls.

Yet by the 1860s, the nation's most famous natural landmark, Niagara Falls, had already been nearly ruined. Every overlook on the American side was owned by a private landowner charging a fee. Tourists could expect to be badgered—and oftentimes swindled—by the hucksters and self-appointed guides who swarmed the railroad depot and carriage stands. The atmosphere was closer to that of a carnival than a cathedral. Europeans were publicly belittling Americans for allowing such a majestic work of nature to become blighted by commercial overdevelopment. "Hasten to Niagara if you wish to see this place in its grandeur," warned Alexis de Tocquevillle. "If you delay, your Niagara will have been spoiled for you." "In Europe," the Frenchman noted, "people talk a great deal about the wilds of America, but the Americans themselves never think about them."

They are insensible to the wonders of inanimate nature and they may be said not to perceive the mighty forests that surround them till they fall beneath the hatchet.

Their eyes are fixed upon another sight . . . the march across these wilds, draining swamps, turning the course of rivers, peopling solitudes, and subduing nature.

They will habitually prefer the useful to the beautiful, and they will require that the beautiful should be useful.

It was the Comte de Buffon all over again. To Europeans, Niagara Falls was not evidence of America's superiority in terms of nature's gifts; it was proof that the United States was still a backward, uncivilized nation.

America as Eden rediscovered; America as Eden despoiled. Nature as the undiluted connection to God; nature as a commodity to be used and tossed aside. Into that mix of injured nationalism, unbridled commercialism, and idealistic theology came Senator John Conness and his bill to save Yosemite Valley and the Mariposa sequoias:

> *The Mariposa Big Tree Grove is really the wonder of the world. . . . The trees contained in that grove have no parallel. . . . They are subject now to damage and injury, and this bill . . . proposes . . . their preservation, that they may be used and preserved for the benefit of mankind.*
>
> *. . . It is a matter involving no appropriation whatever. The property is of no value to the Government.*

To help ease approval of his Yosemite bill, Conness assured his colleagues a second time that the land was otherwise "worthless"—not suitable for anything other than its scenery—and that no federal money was to be spent. After only a few questions and no objections, the Senate passed Conness's bill and moved on to other business. A month later, the House did the same thing. And on June 30, 1864—a day during which he also signed bills increasing import duties and broadening an income tax in order to continue a war to preserve the Union—President Abraham Lincoln signed a law to preserve forever a beautiful valley and a grove of trees that he had never seen, thousands of miles away in California.

THE PURSUIT OF HAPPINESS

> *It is the will of the Nation as embodied in the act of Congress that this scenery shall never be private property, but that like certain defensive points upon our coast be held solely for public purposes.*
> FREDERICK LAW OLMSTED

On August 9, 1865, a small group of people gathered in Yosemite Valley to hear Frederick Law Olmsted read a report he had written about the future of the new park that had been entrusted to the state of California. As a member of the board of commissioners appointed by the governor to oversee the park, Olmsted had already paid for a boundary survey out of his own pocket and drawn up some ideas on how the park should be managed.

Frederick Law Olmsted

Switzerland, he noted, benefited economically from the tourists who visited the Alps, staying in hotels, buying food from local farmers, supporting the creation of better roads, and contributing greatly to the country's revenues. So, too, Olmsted predicted, would the scenic attractions of Yosemite and the big trees become a financial asset to California and the United States.

But there was another reason for preserving Yosemite, much more important than economics, he said, one that struck at the heart of the very meaning of democracy and the enduring promise of America. From the beginning of time, he argued, the world's aristocracies and wealthiest families had set aside land for their own recreation.

> *The enjoyment of the choicest natural scenes in the country and the means of recreation connected with them is thus a monopoly, in a very peculiar manner, of a very few, very rich people. The great mass of society, including those to whom it would be of the greatest benefit, is excluded from it.*

Unless the government intervened to withhold such places "from the grasp of individuals," Olmsted continued, "the great body of the people" would find itself shut out from the places it needed for "the recreation of the mind and body." This, he said, would be contrary to the founding principles of the United States. To reinforce his argument, he even borrowed from Jefferson's list of "inalienable rights" in the Declaration of Independence.

> *It is the main duty of government, if it is not the sole duty of government, to provide means of protection for all its citizens in the pursuit of happiness against the obstacles, otherwise insurmountable, which the selfishness of individuals or combinations of individuals is liable to interpose to that pursuit.*
>
> *. . . The establishment by government of great public grounds for the free enjoyment of the people under certain circumstances, is thus justified and enforced as a political duty.*

Having invoked one of the nation's sacred texts as a rationale for the creation of public parks, Olmsted got down to specific plans for Yosemite. He recom-

Three tourists admire the view from Mirror Lake in Yosemite.

mended that the state of California immediately start work on an improved road to the valley and grove of sequoias, so that Yosemite did not become, by virtue of its inaccessibility, a "rich man's park." He estimated the road would cost about $25,000 and suggested the state spend an additional $12,000 for better trails, surveys, advertising, and construction of five strategically placed cabins as free resting places for visitors.

At the same time, he urged his fellow commissioners to enact and enforce regulations to protect the landscape from anything that would harm it, and prevent the construction of any buildings that would "obscure, distort or detract from the dignity of the scenery." This, he insisted, was the most important point: to preserve the natural scenery "as exactly as is possible" against the demands of "the convenience, bad taste, playfulness, carelessness, or wanton destructiveness of present visitors," even if their numbers were only in the hundreds at the moment.

Before many years, if proper facilities are offered, these hundreds will become thousands and in a century the whole number of visitors will be counted by millions. An injury to the scenery so slight that it may be unheeded by any visitor now, will be one multiplied by those millions. . . .

[T]herefore, laws to prevent an unjust use by individuals of that which is not individual but public property, must be made and rigidly enforced.

This duty of preservation is the first . . . because the millions who are hereafter to benefit . . . have the largest interest in it, and the largest interest should be first and most strenuously guarded.

In a place as special as Yosemite, Olmsted declared, "the rights of posterity" were more important than the immediate desires of the present.

Olmsted had, in essence, delivered his own combination of a Declaration of Independence and a Constitution for the park idea—a lofty statement of principles coupled with the nuts and bolts of how to put them into action. No one at the campsite disagreed with his far-ranging proposals, and within a matter of weeks Olmsted left California and returned to New York to resume his work on Central Park. He would never visit Yosemite again.

Once Olmsted was gone, however, a small group of Yosemite commissioners secretly convened, decided his recommendations were too expensive and too controversial to bring to the state legislature, and then quietly shelved his report. (His radical document would not be published until 1952.)

The job of protecting the new Yosemite Grant—all sixty square miles of it—now fell to one man: Galen Clark, a restless fifty-two-year-old from Dublin, New Hampshire, who had worked his way across the continent, failing at everything he attempted: farming, the grocery business, house painting, even coffin making, and finally, in California, gold prospecting. In 1857, having been lured to Yosemite by James Hutchings's lavish accounts, Clark had become the first white man to see the collection of giant sequoias that he named the Mariposa Grove of Big Trees, and by 1864 he had built a small cabin there to provide shelter for the increasing number of visitors who came to him for food, lodging, and directions. "Clark," one magazine writer declared, "is one of the best informed men, one of the very best guides I ever met." After California officially accepted the land grant from Congress, he was the natural—and unanimous—choice

Galen Clark became the first guardian of the Yosemite Grant and Mariposa Grove of Big Trees. His job would eventually put him at odds with James Mason Hutchings, whose glowing descriptions had attracted him to the valley in the first place.

to become guardian of the Yosemite Grant and Mariposa Grove.

For $500 a year Clark was expected to maintain bridges and roads, deal with hotel owners and other businesses in the new preserve, and prevent overeager tourists from ruining the sights they had come to enjoy. It was a nearly impossible task, but Clark threw himself into it. He stopped some merchants from putting up advertising signs in his beloved grove of sequoias; packed a disassembled carriage into the valley and put it back together for the use of saddle-sore tourists; and suffered financially when the state legislature refused to appropriate adequate funds for the grant's maintenance, even withholding his promised salary four years in a row.

But Clark's greatest headache came from the man whose words had brought him to Yosemite in the first place: James Mason Hutchings. No one had done more than Hutchings to bring Yosemite and its incomparable wonders to the nation's attention; but now that the nation had moved to protect it in perpetuity by declaring it public, not private, property, no one fought that decision with greater vehemence.

Hutchings was technically a squatter in Yosemite. The valley had never been surveyed by the government or officially opened for settlement, and therefore he did not have legal title to the hotel and land he claimed around it. But he stubbornly refused to recognize Congress's actions and turned down Clark's proposal that he continue his hotel business under a government lease at the minimal sum of one dollar a year.

Meanwhile, in brazen defiance of Clark and the Yosemite commissioners, Hutchings went about expanding his operations in the valley. He built a log cabin so his family could live more comfortably year-round and began making plans for improvements to his hotel. To provide the lumber, he would need a sawmill, he decided, and someone to run it.

Just at that moment, in the fall of 1869, a wandering sheepherder from Scotland would show up to apply for the job. He called himself "an unknown nobody," but in time he would do far more than Hutchings to extol the beauty of Yosemite, and more than Frederick Law Olmsted or Galen Clark to protect it.

NEAR THE HEART OF THE WORLD

I know that I could under ordinary circumstances accumulate wealth and obtain a fair position in society, and I am arrived at an age that requires that I should choose some definite course for life. But I am sure that the mind of no truant schoolboy is more free and disengaged from all the grave plans and purposes and pursuits of ordinary orthodox life than mine.

JOHN MUIR

When he applied for the job at Hutchings's sawmill, John Muir was thirty-one years old, but still seeking his place in the world. Born in Dunbar, Scotland, and raised in Wisconsin, he had suffered a harsh childhood at the hands of a tyrannical father, an itinerant Presbyterian minister who insisted that Muir memorize the Bible—and repeatedly beat him until, by age eleven, he was able to recite three-quarters of the Old Testament and the entire New Testament by heart.

He possessed a natural talent for inventions. As a teenager he had devised an automatic horse feeder, waterwheels and latches, clocks with precise timepieces whittled from wood, and an "early-rising machine," a bed balanced on a fulcrum and connected to one of his clocks that would tip forward and deposit the awakened occupant onto the floor. At the University of Wisconsin, where he studied geology and botany, Muir designed a mechanical "study desk," which, at preset intervals, automatically rotated the textbooks he was reading.

With the outbreak of the Civil War, facing the possibility of being drafted, Muir ultimately decided to do what one of his brothers had already done: he "skedaddled" and went to Canada for two years. Returning at war's end, at a time when new industries were rapidly transforming America, he showed great promise by increasing the productivity of every business that hired him—from a maker of broom handles to a carriage manufacturer.

But he had become worried, he wrote his sister in 1867, "that I am doomed to live in some of these noisy commercial centers." That year, a factory accident temporarily blinded him for several months. When he regained his sight, he set out on a thousand-mile walk to the Gulf of Mexico pursuing his passion for the natural sciences, studying plants and flowers. Intending eventually to continue his solitary botanical journey in South America, Muir made it as far as Florida, where he contracted a fever, probably malaria, that gripped him for three months. When he couldn't find passage to Venezuela or Colombia, he headed instead for California. He had read a brochure about a place called Yosemite and thought he might inspect it before finally settling on a career.

John Muir

Seeking directions in San Francisco, he was asked, "Where do you wish to go?"

Muir answered, "Anywhere that's wild." Once more on foot, he set off for the Sierra Nevada and soon enough, hired on as a sheepherder, he was rambling across the vast mountains he called "the Range of light, surely the brightest and best of all the Lord has built." That June of 1869, he wrote, "seems the greatest of all the months of my life, the most truly, divinely free."

> *We are now in the mountains and they are in us, kindling enthusiasm, making every nerve quiver, filling every pore and cell of us. Our flesh-and-bone tabernacle seems transparent as glass to the beauty about us, neither old nor young, sick nor well, but immortal.*
>
> *I am a captive. I am bound. Love of pure unblemished Nature seems to overmaster and blur out of sight all other objects and considerations.*

Then he left the high country and descended into Yosemite Valley. It was, Muir wrote, "by far the grandest of all the special temples of Nature I was ever permitted to enter . . . the sanctum sanctorum of the Sierra." There, he met James Mason Hutchings and learned of the hotel keeper's job opening. Taking it would allow him to make the "sanctum sanctorum" his home.

He built Hutchings's sawmill on Yosemite Creek and, using only fallen trees recently toppled by a devastating storm, began producing lumber for the many projects Hutchings directed him to undertake—replacing the muslin sheets with wooden partitions in the hotel's sleeping quarters; improving a space called the "Big Tree Room," built around the

trunk of a giant cedar; and erecting two additional cottages to accommodate the increasing number of tourists, now exceeding a thousand a summer.

For himself and a fellow worker, Muir built a one-room cabin near the base of Yosemite Falls, complete with a single window facing the falls, a floor paved with stones spaced far enough apart to allow ferns to continue growing, and a small ditch that brought part of the creek into a corner of the cabin with just enough current, Muir wrote, "to allow it to sing and warble in low, sweet tones, delightful at night while I lay in bed, suspended from the rafters." It cost him a total of three or four dollars, Muir bragged, but he considered it "the handsomest building in the Valley."

Every moment of his free time, Muir devoted to exploring the valley and the mountain ramparts surrounding it—traveling for days with only a few pounds of crackers, oatmeal, and tea for nourishment; clambering up rocky slopes in shoes whose soles he had studded with nails; pondering the geology of the Sierras; closely inspecting everything he encountered; thinking nothing of covering fifty miles in a two-day excursion.

> *I drifted from rock to rock, from stream to stream, from grove to grove. . . . When I discovered a new plant, I sat down beside it for a minute or a day, to make its acquaintance and hear what it had to tell. . . . I asked the boulders I met, whence they came and whither they were going.*

It was all part, Muir said, of his "unconditional surrender to Nature." The winds and cascading creeks seemed to sing "an exulting chorus" audible to anyone willing to listen. He contemplated the life of a raindrop, probed the mosses growing underneath alpine meadows, marveled at the tenacity of plants somehow clinging to life on bare granite, soaked sequoia cones in water and drank the purple liquid "to improve my color," he explained, "and render myself more tree-wise and sequoical."

Everywhere Muir turned, he believed he was witnessing the work and presence of God—not the stern and wrathful God of his father, who placed man above nature, but a God who revealed himself through nature and for whom mankind was merely one part of a great, joyously interconnected web of being. "When we try to pick out anything by itself," he wrote, "we find it hitched to everything else in the universe. . . . The whole wilderness in unity and interrelation is alive and familiar . . . the very stones seem talkative, sympathetic, brotherly."

Muir now felt he had discovered something else: his own destiny.

I will follow my instincts, be myself for good or ill, and see what will be the upshot. As long as I live, I'll hear waterfalls and birds and winds sing. I'll interpret the rocks, learn the language of flood, storm, and the avalanche. I'll acquaint myself with the glaciers and wild gardens, and get as near the heart of the world as I can.

He would devote himself to understanding the wilderness and then teach others the lessons he had learned. If Yosemite was God's temple, he would become its high priest. "Heaven knows," he wrote, "that John [the] Baptist was not more eager to get all his fellow sinners into the Jordan than I to baptize all of mine in the beauty of God's mountains."

In his fervor to discover everything he could about his new temple-home, Muir was willing to try anything. Following Yosemite Creek as it courses from the high country toward its sudden plunge into the valley, he found himself approaching the lip of Upper Yosemite Falls and its 1,430-foot sheer drop. Perhaps he could peek over the edge, he thought. But as he neared the brink, the water was roaring and the polished rock "dangerously smooth and steep." "I therefore concluded not to venture farther," he later remembered, "but did nevertheless." He eased himself toward a narrow shelf—three inches wide by his estimate—and shuffled along it, his body pressed against the rock, until he reached the raging, foaming crest of the falls and "obtained a perfectly free view down into the heart of the snowy, chanting throng of comet-like streamers." From this precarious perch he listened to "the death song of Yosemite Creek."

Another time, at the base of the falls, he wedged himself into a small declivity in the granite wall behind the pounding water—all for a chance to see the full moon through the veil of the falls. A change in the wind's direction began pushing the waterfall in his direction, nearly crushing him. Muir was almost

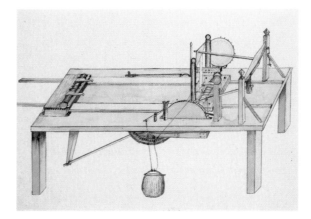

On the inside of the journal he kept during his thousand-mile walk to Florida in 1867, top, Muir inscribed his name and the words "Earth, Planet, Universe." Among his many inventions—from clocks to thermometers to a rotating "study desk"—was this table saw, left, that operated with weights and pulleys.

crushed again one winter when he decided to climb the massive cone of ice—four hundred feet high—that forms at the bottom of the falls in cold weather. The whole cone began to vibrate when a mass of ice broke free and it "sped past me dangerously near," he wrote, "so I beat a hasty retreat, chilled and drenched, and lay down on a sunny rock to dry."

A different winter day, hiking in deep snow to a ridgeline in hopes of witnessing an avalanche, he instead became part of one. Somehow Muir survived being swept several thousand feet down a canyon on a cascade of ice and snow. He described the experience as "the most spiritual and exhilarating of all the modes of motion I have ever experienced. Elijah's flight in a chariot of fire could hardly have been more gloriously exciting."

When a series of earthquakes struck the valley, shaking the ground with such violence that giant Eagle Rock tumbled from the granite walls and broke into thousands of boulders, the tourists were petrified by fear. Not Muir. "Come, cheer up; smile a little and clap your hands," he told the terrified visitors gathered outside Hutchings's hotel, "Mother Earth is trotting us on her knee to amuse us and make us good."

Everything in nature drew him closer to it. Coming across a grizzly bear in a meadow, he impulsively rushed toward it, "that I might study his gait in running." The bear stood its ground. Muir called it "my interview with a bear" and "never afterward forgot the right manners of the wilderness." He made a perilous, solo ascent of Mount Ritter, becoming the first person known to have reached its 13,000-foot summit. He climbed a hundred-foot Douglas fir in a raging storm and clung to its swaying top, "free to take the wind into my pulses," exulting in "the Aeolian music of its topmost needles," and drawing, as he always did, something new from his firsthand embrace of nature.

We all travel the milky way together, trees and men; but it never occurred to me until this storm-day, while swinging in the wind, that trees are travelers, in the ordinary sense. They make many journeys, not extensive ones, it is true; but our own little journeys, away and back again, are only little more than tree-wavings.

The gaunt mountaineer with blazing blue eyes and long whiskers who seemed to talk to flowers and rocks was considered by many people as an eccentric, one more of Yosemite's curiosities. On one excursion into the mountains, he met a total stranger and told him he was rambling across the Sierra Nevada, looking at trees. "Oh, then," the stranger replied, "you must be John Muir."

Not everyone appreciated his growing notoriety. Josiah D. Whitney, California's state geologist, commissioner of the Yosemite Grant, and author of an official guidebook to the region, grew indignant when he heard that Muir was disputing his theory that Yosemite had been created by a cataclysmic col-lapse of the valley floor. Muir instead believed that over thousands of years, glaciers had gouged out the valley and polished smooth the granite domes. Whitney derided Muir as "a mere sheepherder" and "an ignoramus," and scornfully dismissed his conclusions. But Muir persevered—and in 1871 during a solitary hike discovered a "living glacier" in the far recesses of the Sierra, the first of sixty-five he would eventually encounter and study. When he led other leading geologists to his evidence, they, too, supported him over Whitney.

In just a few years, Muir had come to know Yosemite and its mountains better than anyone else. And as his reputation spread, visitors began asking for him—not Hutchings—to be their guide. With the completion of the transcontinental railroad, even more tourists were arriving in the park—writers, artists, scientists, wealthy Easterners who enjoyed listening to Muir excitedly expound on Yosemite's natural wonders as they hiked from one viewpoint to another.

Among them in 1871 came Ralph Waldo Emerson, a personal hero of Muir's. "You are yourself a sequoia," he told the aging philosopher as he guided Emerson through the Mariposa Grove of Big Trees. "Stop and get acquainted with your big brethren." The visit would rank as one of the highlights of Muir's life, he said later, despite his disappointment when Emerson's companions refused to let the old man accept Muir's suggestion that they camp for the night under the trees. Emerson, who enjoyed his time in what he described as Muir's "mountain tabernacle," would later enter Muir's name on a short list of great men he had met. He urged Muir to give up his reclusive life in Yosemite to teach or write.

Others had made similar suggestions. After the initial success of a few newspaper articles, Muir himself now decided they might have a point. "I care to live only to entice people to look at Nature's loveliness," he said, despite realizing it would require him to spend more time in cities, closer to publishers and libraries, and less time in his beloved mountains.

By November of 1873, Muir and Hutchings had already parted ways. Hutchings had grown jealous of Muir's popularity with sophisticated tourists; Muir

O these vast, calm measureless mountain days, inciting at once to work and rest. Days in whose light everything seems equally divine, opening a thousand windows to show us God.

Nevermore, however weary, should one faint by the way who gains the blessings of one mountain day; whatever his fate, long life, short life, stormy or calm, he is rich forever!

JOHN MUIR

Whether meditating on the smallest speck of lichen (top right) or rejoicing in the "fine, savage music" of Yosemite Falls (left), Muir found his soul's home in Yosemite. In 1869, he proudly added to his journal a drawing of the house he had built (right) as close to the falls as possible.

Cabin in Yo. Val. 1869

considered Hutchings shallow and vain. Packing his meager belongings, Muir moved to Oakland, to begin work on a series of reports for the *Overland Monthly* and other magazines.

How little note is taken of the deeds of Nature! What paper publishes her reports? . . . Who publishes the sheet-music of the winds, or the written music of water written in river-lines? Who reports the works and ways of the clouds, those wondrous creations coming into being every day like freshly upheaved mountains?

Who reports the works of the clouds? John Muir would. Writing, he said, was "like the life of a glacier, one eternal grind." But he felt compelled to give it a try.

May 22, 1875. James Hutchings was evicted on Monday . . . by the sheriff.
On Tuesday . . . George Coulter, his wife, and daughter, together with Mr. Murphy, immediately took possession [of Hutchings's hotel] and are now dispensing good cheer.

MARIPOSA GAZETTE

For eight years, James Mason Hutchings had refused to acknowledge that all of Yosemite Valley—including the land he claimed as his own—was public property. His friends in the California legislature had passed a special bill, exempting him from the provisions of the law setting Yosemite aside. When the governor vetoed the bill, the legislature had overridden it. In Washington, the House of Representatives had also gone along on two separate occasions, but both times the Senate held firm. Giving in to Hutchings's claims, one senator said, "would be to give up the idea of the public enjoyment of the valley, and surrender it wholly to the purposes of private speculation."

Undeterred, Hutchings took his case to court, challenging the federal government's right to designate unsold portions of the public domain for any purpose other than settlement. Once again he prevailed at the California level, but the United States Supreme Court ruled against him. Unintentionally,

he had done the park idea a lasting favor, in effect establishing a precedent that national public parks are constitutional. Still, Hutchings refused to budge, even after the state legislature granted him $24,000 to extinguish his claim. In 1875, a sheriff finally evicted him from his hotel.

Out of sympathy for the old promoter, Galen Clark, the Yosemite guardian, agreed to let him store some of his furniture in a vacant building—only to learn that Hutchings had set up business in it running a hotel and had even moved his Wells Fargo office, his telegraph equipment, and the valley's post office to the new location. When Clark asked him to vacate the premises, Hutchings refused once more. "In the classical language of our friend," the *Mariposa Gazette* reported, "he promises to remain in his new abode until hell freezes over, and the devil can take a trip to Yosemite on the ice."

Hutchings managed to hang on until the end of the summer tourist season, when he finally left the valley and moved his family to San Francisco, where he opened up a tourist agency, gave illustrated lectures about Yosemite, and wrote two best-selling books about the park from which he had been unceremoniously banished.

One theory held that Yosemite had been created by a cataclysmic collapse of the valley floor, but Muir contended that glaciers had carved it out of the surrounding granite over thousands of years.
Below: A diagram he drew to support his theory. *At right:* An 1872 photograph taken by Eadweard Muybridge from a perch above the valley.

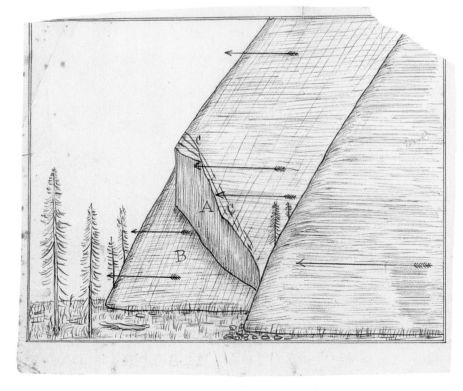

COLTER'S HELL

I had indulged, for several years, a great curiosity to see the wonders of the upper valley of the Yellowstone. The stories told by trappers and mountaineers of the natural phenomena of that region were so strange and marvelous that . . . I [organized] an expedition for the express purpose of exploring it . . . with several gentlemen who expressed like curiosity.

NATHANIEL PITT LANGFORD

In the late summer of 1870, an expedition set out from Helena, Montana, in search of a mysterious place near the headwaters of the Yellowstone River, the longtime home of the Sheepeater band of Shoshone Indians, where, it was rumored, the earth was so hot that mud boiled and steam rose from the ground.

John Colter, a former member of the Lewis and Clark Expedition, had described it first in 1807—and been laughed at by people who began jokingly referring to the region as "Colter's Hell." A generation later, the legendary mountain man Jim Bridger had also told tales of the place. It included a lake, he claimed, where a man could catch a fish in one spot and then swing his line over a few feet to instantly cook his catch in a hot spring; and there was a canyon so deep, he added, that a man could shout down into it at night and be awakened by his echo the next morning.

As recently as 1869, a group of prospectors had ventured into the area they called the "Valley of Death," but upon their return to Helena were reluctant to talk much about it, for fear of being considered liars. When they finally wrote a detailed account of their journey, magazines in the East refused to publish it. "Thank you," one editor responded, "but we do not print fiction."

Now, in 1870, a more highly organized group intended to put an end to the mystery and either confirm or deny the rumors once and for all. Accompanied by a small military escort and led by Henry D. Washburn, the surveyor general of the Montana Territory, their membership included a prominent banker; a son of a United States senator; a struggling

Norris Geyser Basin, Yellowstone National Park

young lawyer and part-time newspaper correspondent named Cornelius Hedges; and Truman C. Everts, at age fifty-four the oldest member of the expedition, a Vermonter who had just lost his patronage job as the territory's assessor of internal revenue and who had come along on a lark.

But the moving force behind them all was Nathaniel Pitt Langford, a well-connected Montana politician who believed the future prosperity of the territory rested with completion of a proposed second transcontinental railway, the Northern Pacific. Earlier in the year, Langford had met privately with Jay Cooke, the financial tycoon underwriting $100 million worth of Northern Pacific bonds, and the two had agreed that any publicity about Montana's attractions would be good for the territory, good for the Northern Pacific's bond sales, and good for Nathaniel P. Langford, who had quietly been put on the railroad's payroll.

"Colter's Hell" might be just the kind of an attraction Langford and the railroad were hoping for—if it really existed. Two weeks into his expedition's journey along the Yellowstone River, Langford found his answer.

Monday, August 29, 1870. We came suddenly upon a basin of boiling sulphur springs . . . boiling like a cauldron, throwing water and fearful volumes of . . . vapor higher than our heads.

The spring lying to the east of this, more diabolical in appearance, filled with a hot brownish substance of the consistency of mucilage, is in constant noisy ebullition, emitting fumes of villainous odor.

They kept moving, past more mudpots that made noises, they said, like the safety valve of a laboring steamboat engine; over ground that sounded hollow under their horses' hooves; near vents that were too hot to touch, even with gloved hands—places to which they would attach names like Hell-Broth Springs, Devil's Den, Brimstone Basin.

Farther on, they came to two waterfalls slicing through a steep and narrow canyon they estimated at half a mile in depth, the one Jim Bridger had once bragged about: the Grand Canyon of the Yellowstone. "We are overwhelmed with astonishment and wonder at what we have seen," Langford wrote.

The rapids and foam from the dizzy summit of the rock overhanging . . . the cañon were so terrible to behold, that none of our company could venture the experiment in any other manner than by lying prone upon the rock, to gaze into its awful depths; depths so amazing that the sound of the rapids in their course over immense boulders, and lashing in fury the base of the rocks on which we were lying, could not be heard.

. . . As I took in this scene, I realized my own littleness, my helplessness . . . my inability to cope with or even comprehend the mighty architecture of nature.

Beyond the falls was Yellowstone Lake, which Langford called "the most beautiful body of water in the world," brimming with fish and punctuated, just as Bridger had said, with thermal springs that bubbled with boiling water. Langford was now convinced that the Yellowstone was an even greater attraction than he and the backers of the Northern Pacific had dreamed, and on the lake's shore he thought he could perceive its future.

It possesses . . . the greatest wonders of Nature the world affords . . . beautified by the grandeur of the most extensive mountain scenery, and not

Nathaniel Pitt Langford (left) explored the headwaters of the Yellowstone on behalf of the Northern Pacific Railroad and then publicized the region's wonders. The hapless Truman C. Everts (above) would become equally famous for getting lost in the wilderness.

many years can elapse before the march of civil improvement will reclaim this delightful solitude, and garnish it with all the attractions of cultivated taste and refinement.

During their exploration around the lake, the nearsighted Truman Everts somehow got separated from the main group and went missing. Over the next several days, search parties were dispatched to find him. They encountered grizzly bears; heard the terrifying, humanlike screams of a mountain lion and the howls of wolves; but found no trace of Everts or his horse.

On September 13, a surprise storm dropped two feet of snow on them. Running low on supplies, the expedition finally had no choice but to turn for home, leaving notes behind for Everts at each campsite, along with what little food they could spare from their dwindling rations. Heading for the Madison River and the mining town of Virginia City, they struggled for days through snow and dense timber, until they emerged onto a large clearing. They had already "seen what we believed to be the greatest wonders on the continent," Langford said, where "Nature had crowded so much of grandeur and majesty with so much of novelty and wonder."

Judge, then, of our astonishment on entering this basin, to see at no great distance before us an immense body of sparkling water, projected suddenly and with terrific force into the air to the height of over one hundred feet.
. . . General Washburn has named [it] "Old Faithful," because of the regularity of its eruptions, the intervals between which being from sixty to sixty-five minutes.

The sight of Old Faithful's eruption, with the atomized water creating myriads of tiny rainbows, was so exhilarating, Washburn remembered, that the entire group "threw up their hats and shouted with ecstasy at the sight." They affixed names to other geysers—the Castle, the Beehive, the Giant and the Giantess—but because of their shortage of food, could not stay long. As they followed the steaming Firehole River, through the greatest concentration of geothermal features on earth, they came across still more basins and still more curiosities—a vast array of

geysers, fumaroles, mudpots, and hot springs of unimaginable strangeness and beauty.

Finally, more than a month after their departure, the expedition reached Virginia City and then Helena. Newspapers proclaimed that Langford was finally confirming what had once been considered wild rumors about a place called Colter's Hell. But people were more fascinated by the news that Truman Everts was still lost there.

On the day that I found myself separated from my company . . . our course had been impeded by the dense growth of the pine forest . . . [and] I strayed out of sight and hearing of my comrades.
. . . As separations like this had frequently occurred, it gave me no alarm, and I rode on . . . in the direction which I supposed had been taken, until darkness overtook me. . . . I selected a spot for comfortable repose, picketed my horse, built a fire, and went to sleep.

TRUMAN C. EVERTS

At first, Everts thought his separation from the expedition would be a momentary inconvenience. But on the second day, his horse ran away, taking with it his guns, blankets, fishing tackle, and matches—everything but the clothes on his back, a small opera glass, and two knives, which he promptly managed to lose in the underbrush.

I realized I was lost. Then came a crushing sense of destitution. No food, no fire; no means to procure either; alone in an unexplored wilderness, one hundred and fifty miles from the nearest human abode, surrounded by wild beasts, and famishing with hunger.

He wandered for days, vainly searching for his friends or any sign of their trail, subsisting almost exclusively on the bitter roots of a plant called the elk thistle—his only food, except for a small bird he caught with his hands, the tip of a seagull's wing he found on the ground, and a few minnows he somehow managed to catch and then ate raw, making him violently sick.

He spent a night in a tree, cowering from a mountain lion prowling underneath; suffered frostbite on his feet from the snowstorm that blanketed the region and saturated his clothes; found refuge for a week huddling day and night against the warm ground of one of the thermal features.

I was enveloped in a perpetual steam bath. At first this was barely preferable to the storm, but I soon became accustomed to it, and before I left, though thoroughly parboiled, actually enjoyed it.

At another hot spring, Everts broke through the thin crust of earth and his hip was severely scalded by hot steam before he could escape. He taught himself to use the magnifying lens of his opera glass to ignite campfires—and then realized that this method meant he either needed to start each fire long before sundown or he had to carry a burning torch with him as he wandered from place to place. One evening, in his sleep, he lurched forward into the fire and burned his hands.

Wasting away from exhaustion and hunger, Everts began hallucinating, seeing apparitions and hearing voices that pointed him back toward the falls of the Yellowstone, where he spent what he called "the most terrible night of my journey," his body seemingly paralyzed from the cold until he dragged himself to the canyon's rim and kindled a big fire once the morning sun came up.

The great falls of the Yellowstone were roaring within three hundred yards, and the awful cañon yawned almost at my feet; but they had lost all charm for me. In fact, I regarded them as enemies which had lured me to destruction, and felt a sullen satisfaction in morbid indifference.

On October 16—thirty-seven days after being separated from the expedition—Everts was found, crawling along a hillside. His starvation diet of thistle roots had reduced him to a mere fifty pounds. The scalded flesh on his thighs was blackened; his bare and frostbitten feet had been worn to the bone; his burnt fingers were said to resemble a bird's claws.

He was incoherent for days, though he slowly recovered, and in time produced a firsthand account of his ordeal, "Thirty-Seven Days of Peril," that *Scribner's Monthly* published for popular consumption.

My narrative is finished. The time is not far distant when the wonders of the Yellowstone will be made accessible to all lovers of sublimity, grandeur, and novelty in natural scenery, and its majestic waters become the abode of civilization and refinement; and when that arrives, I hope, in happier mood and under more auspicious circumstances, to revisit scenes fraught for me with such . . . mingled glories and terrors.

Years later, a 7,831-foot peak in the northwest corner of Wyoming would be named Mount Everts in his memory, although he had never climbed it. But the more lasting legacy of Yellowstone's first tourist misadventure is the thistle whose roots he had eaten for more than a month in order to survive. The plant still thrives there, now known as the Everts thistle.

A PLEASURING GROUND

N. P. Langford delivered a very interesting lecture at the Cooper Institute last evening, entitled, "The Upper Waters of the Yellowstone River." The large hall was filled to its utmost capacity by an appreciative audience, and Gov. Langford's graphic description of the beautiful scenery on the banks of the Yellowstone River frequently elicited warm applause.

THE NEW YORK TIMES
January 22, 1871

Nathaniel Pitt Langford wasted no time in publicizing what he called "The Wonders of the Yellowstone." He wrote glowing magazine articles about the expedition's discoveries, and in early 1871—on a trip underwritten by Jay Cooke and the Northern Pacific—he began touring the East Coast, delivering a series of twenty lectures to packed halls where audiences hung on his every word.

You can see Niagara, comprehend its beauties, and carry from it a memory ever ready to summon before you all its grandeur. You can stand in the valley of the Yosemite, and look up its mile of vertical granite, and distinctly recall its minutest feature; but amid the cañon and falls, the boiling springs and sulphur mountain, and, above all,

On October 28, 1870, the *Helena Daily Herald* announced that Truman Everts, lost for thirty-seven days, had at last been found.

the mud volcano and the geysers of Yellowstone, your memory becomes filled and clogged with objects new in experience, wonderful in extent, and possessing unlimited grandeur and beauty.

It is a new phase in the natural world; a fresh exhibition of the handiwork of the Great Architect; and while you see and wonder, you seem to need an additional sense, fully to comprehend and believe.

Sitting in the audience at one lecture was Ferdinand V. Hayden, head of the Geological and Geographical Survey of the Territories, who decided it was time for professional explorers to take a look. By the summer of 1871, Hayden was there, with a botanist, zoologist, mineralogist, meteorologist, and a team of topographers to collect reams of scientific data about a landscape that only a few years earlier had been the realm of rumors and tall tales.

Perhaps even more important than the work of the scientists was the presence of two men, both accompanying Hayden's expedition at the behest of the Northern Pacific. Thomas Moran was a young English-born artist who had taken up painting in

Philadelphia and landed a job with *Scribner's* reworking some rough sketches submitted with Langford's article into illustrations the magazine could publish. Now he was about to see Yellowstone's wonders with his own eyes. Moran had never ridden a horse before and required a pillow on his saddle when riding over rough ground. William Henry Jackson, a Civil War veteran from upstate New York, was more accustomed to the outdoors. He had gone west in search of adventure, served as a bullwhacker on a wagon train along the Oregon Trail, and finally settled in Omaha, where he opened a photography studio. Most recently, Jackson had used his camera to chronicle the lives of Plains Indians and the building of the first transcontinental railroad. While the other men in Hayden's expedition collected their samples and took their measurements, Moran and Jackson set out to capture Yellowstone on canvas and glass plates, often getting up early to start their work at first light.

In his speeches, Langford had warned his audiences that "you seem to need an additional sense, fully to comprehend and believe" the Yellowstone country. Moran's paintings and Jackson's photographs now provided it, once the expedition

Having already illustrated Langford's magazine article "The Wonders of Yellowstone" without seeing the place itself, Thomas Moran finally got a firsthand look with the Hayden expedition—and he made the most of it. At left, *Castle Geyser with Crested Pool* (top), *Mammoth Terraces* (center), and *The Great Springs of the Firehole River* (bottom), 1871. Above, his famous painting, *The Grand Canyon of the Yellowstone*, 1872, based on Moran's sketches from a perspective now known as Artist Point

I place no value upon literal transcripts from Nature.
My general scope is not realistic; all my tendencies
are toward idealization. . . .

Topography in art is valueless. The motive or incentive of my "Grand Canyon of the Yellowstone" was the
gorgeous display of color that impressed itself upon me.

Probably no scenery in the world presents such a
combination. The forms are extremely wonderful and
pictorial, and, while I desired to tell truly of Nature,
I did not wish to realize the scene literally, but to preserve and to convey its true impression.

THOMAS MORAN

No photographs [of Yellowstone] had as yet been published, and Dr. Hayden was determined that the first ones be good. A series of fine pictures would not only supplement his final report but tell the story to thousands who might never read it. That was where I came in.

WILLIAM HENRY JACKSON

A second photographer, T. J. Hine, was in Yellowstone the same time as the Hayden expedition, but back in Chicago all his negatives were destroyed in the great fire of 1871. So Jackson's pictures became the first to reach the world. Among them: Riverside Geyser (left), Yellowstone Lake (right), and Mammoth Hot Springs (below)

returned from the West—showing Americans for the first time what mere words had previously attempted to describe. Moran's landscapes were so stunning, Congress appropriated $10,000 to buy one. Jackson's pictures were so popular, he soon signed up for a series of other western explorations to collect more material.

In Washington, as Hayden prepared his expedition's report for Congress, he received an intriguing letter from a man named A. B. Nettleton, a Northern Pacific lobbyist, suggesting that he do more than merely catalogue his discoveries. "Let Congress pass a bill reserving the Great Geyser Basin as a public park forever—just as it has reserved that far inferior wonder the Yosemite valley and big trees," Nettleton wrote. "If you approve this, would such a recommendation be appropriate in your official report?" Jay Cooke himself was personally interested in the matter. Looking toward Yellowstone's potential as a tourist attraction, he was not eager to negotiate with a multitude of private landholders. "We can probably deal much better with the government in any improvements we may desire to make for the benefit of our pleasure travel," he wrote an assistant, "than with individuals."

Hayden was happy to oblige. His report took pains to assure Congress that at an elevation of six thousand feet above sea level or higher, the Yellowstone region was totally unsuitable for farming and ranching and that, because of its volcanic origins, no valuable mines were likely to be found there. But, he warned, if Congress did not pass legislation protecting Yellowstone from private development, it would become another Niagara Falls. During his exploration, he noted, he had come across men cutting poles in anticipation of marking off the geyser basins and Mammoth Hot Springs for homestead claims. Prohibiting such settlement, he added, "takes nothing from the value of the public domain, and is no pecuniary loss to the Government, but will be regarded by the entire civilized world as a step of progress and an honor to Congress and the nation."

Meanwhile, the Northern Pacific began working quietly behind the scenes. Railroad lobbyists made sure that every senator and congressman received copies of Langford's glowing magazine articles, while Moran's sketches and Jackson's photographs were prominently displayed in the halls of the Capitol. By late January of 1872, a bill was ready for action in the Senate.

Be it enacted . . . that the tract of land . . . lying near the headwaters of the Yellowstone river . . . is hereby reserved and withdrawn from settlement, occupancy, or sale under the laws of the United States, and dedicated and set apart as a public park or pleasuring ground for the benefit and enjoyment of the people.

Senator Samuel Pomeroy of Kansas, the bill's sponsor, reiterated Hayden's finding that the region was unfit for homesteading and reminded his colleagues of the precedent they had set with Yosemite eight years earlier, noting that the Supreme Court had upheld their right to reserve land for these purposes. A few senators worried that Yellowstone might simply become a hunting preserve, and Pomeroy pointed them to a provision in the bill, directing the Secretary of the Interior to institute regulations prohibiting the "wanton destruction" of wildlife.

In the brief debate over the bill, only one senator voiced any objection to the very idea of setting Yellowstone aside. "I do not see the reason or propriety of setting apart a large tract of land of that kind . . . for a public park," argued California Senator Cornelius Cole.

The natural curiosities there cannot be interfered with by anything that man can do. The geysers will remain, no matter where the ownership of the land may be, and I do not know why settlers could be excluded. . . .

If it cannot be occupied and cultivated, why should we make a public park of it? If it cannot be occupied by man, why protect it from occupation? . . . If nature has excluded men from its occupation, why set it apart and exclude persons from it?

Speaking on behalf of the bill, Senator Lyman Trumbull of Illinois said that, without the legislation, people would inevitably file land claims "right across the only path that leads to these wonders" and charge a fee of five dollars to anyone wanting to see Yellowstone's attractions. Besides, he added, "at some future time, if we desire to do so, we can repeal this law if it is in anybody's way." Other supporters focused on Hayden's assurance that the region's high elevation made farming it impossible. "We are doing no harm to the material interests of the people in endeavoring to preserve," said Vermont Senator George Edmunds. "I hope the bill will pass unanimously."

No recorded vote was taken, but a newspaper reported the Senate approved the bill "almost by unanimous consent" and sent it on to the House, where Congressman Henry L. Dawes of Massachusetts, the other principal sponsor, pointed out that unlike the Yosemite Grant, the Yellowstone park was not being given over to a state. Wyoming was still a territory, under federal jurisdiction, and therefore the proposed park within its borders would be a federal responsibility, too. According to Dawes, no other option existed.

> *This bill reserves the control over the land, and preserves the control over it to the United States, so that at any time when it shall appear that it will be better to devote it to any other purpose it will be perfectly within the control of the United States to do it.*

There was even less debate in the House than in the Senate. Nowhere in either chamber did anyone suggest that they were taking a historic step or setting a far-reaching precedent that future generations might look back upon in gratitude. The House passed it, 115 to 65. And on March 1, 1872, President Ulysses S. Grant signed the bill creating Yellowstone Park. Unlike Yosemite, which was being administered by the state of California, this would be a *national* park—the first national park in the history of the world.

The *New York Herald* saw the new creation as one more reason for national bragging rights. "Why should we go to Switzerland to see mountains, or to Iceland for geysers?" it asked, adding that with Yosemite and Yellowstone, "now we have attractions which diminish Niagara into an ordinary exhibition."

But the *Helena Rocky Mountain Gazette* complained that a "great blow" had been struck against the prosperity of the region. The new park, it said, "will keep the country a wilderness" and prevent economic development. Its crosstown rival, the *Helena Herald,* disagreed. "It will be a park," the paper said, "worthy of the great republic."

"WHERE'S LANGFORD?"

By any standard, the new national park at Yellowstone was huge—more than two million acres of remote, mountainous terrain covering the northwestern corner of Wyoming Territory and spilling into Montana. It was bigger than the states of Delaware and Rhode Island combined, and more than fifty times larger than the Yosemite Grant in California. Yet Congress had seen no reason to appropriate any money to manage or protect it.

The job of superintendent was offered to Truman Everts, Yellowstone's most renowned visitor by virtue of his well-publicized ordeal there. Since the position paid no salary, Everts politely turned it down. Nathaniel P. Langford, however, eagerly accepted. He already had a steady income as the newly appointed federal bank examiner for the western territories, and like Congress assumed that the franchise fees from prospective concessionaires would more than cover the costs of administering the park, once the Northern Pacific built its railroad to Yellowstone and brought in thousands of tourists.

But Jay Cooke's financial empire suddenly collapsed, taking the nation's economy down with it in the Panic of 1873. The Northern Pacific's track building stalled in Bismarck, North Dakota, more than five hundred miles from the park. Yellowstone received a total of only three hundred visitors its first year—and no more than five hundred a year for the next four. Those who came had to endure days of dusty, bone-jolting stagecoach travel just to reach a small, one-story log building with an earth-covered roof at Mammoth Hot Springs, the only accommodation in the entire park: "the last outpost of civilization," one guest called it, "that is, the last place where whiskey is sold."

Horses could be rented out for one dollar a day, or tourists could avail themselves of bathhouses built on the hot springs, whose waters were said to be able to heal a variety of ailments. Each bathhouse, reported visitor John Gibbon, had its own specialty:

A CAMPFIRE TALE

Just as baseball, once it became the national pastime, needed a creation myth to turn its complicated evolution into a memorable, all-American story, the national park idea eventually needed one, too.

For baseball, the "inventor" was Abner Doubleday, a Civil War hero, who as a young man was said to have written down the rules of the game on a summer afternoon in Cooperstown, New York, in 1839. None of it was true, but it was a whale of a story and for decades became the accepted history of America's sport.

Nathaniel Pitt Langford was happy to provide something similar for the national park idea. Not surprisingly, he played a central role in it.

According to Langford, as his exploring party was leaving Yellowstone's land of geysers, they reached the confluence of the Gibbon and Firehole rivers, which unite to form the Madison, and realized it would lead them back to the settlements with word of their remarkable discoveries.

Camped along the riverbank on the night of September 19, 1870, they were still concerned about the fate of their missing companion, Truman Everts, but their thoughts also turned to the fate of the remarkable places they had just seen.

In a book published in 1905, purporting to quote from his original diary, Langford described the campfire discussion in painstaking detail.

The proposition was made by some member that we utilize the result of our exploration by taking up quarter sections of land at the most prominent points of interest. . . .

One member . . . suggested that if there could be secured by pre-emption a good title to two or three quarter sections of land opposite the lower fall of the Yellowstone and extending down the river along the cañon, they would eventually become a source of great profit to the owners.

Another member of the party thought that it would be more desirable to take up a quarter section of land at the Upper Geyser Basin, for the reason that that locality could be more easily reached by tourists and pleasure seekers.

A third suggestion was that each member of the party pre-empt a claim, and in order that no one should have an advantage over the others, the whole should be thrown into a common pool for the benefit of the entire party.

Mr. [Cornelius] Hedges then said that he did not approve of any of these plans—that there ought to be no private ownership of any portion of that region, but that the whole of it ought to be set apart as a great National Park, and that each one of us ought to make an effort to have this accomplished. His suggestion met with an instantaneous and favorable response.

This, according to Langford, was the birth of the national park idea—completely ignoring the quasi-precedent already set at Yosemite and the even longer history leading up to it. In later years, the park itself commemorated the meadow at Madison Junction as the idea's birthplace and held regular ceremonies there to extol Hedges, Langford, and the others for their farsightedness.

But Langford's original diary no longer exists, and none of the other men's diaries and reminiscences—at least seventeen in num-

Nathaniel P. Langford (above) would later claim that his group gave birth to the idea of preserving rather than exploiting wonders like the Lower Falls (below).

ber—mention such a discussion about a national park or support his version, written thirty-five years after the fact. "National Park" Langford, as he sometimes signed his name, seems to have never lost the promoter's penchant for telling people what they want to hear. But historians now lump his Madison Junction tale alongside that of Abner Doubleday and baseball—a good story to tell around a campfire, and about as believable.

Should you require parboiling for the rheumatism, take No. 1; if a less degree of heat will suit your disease, and you do not care to lose all your cuticle, take No. 2. Not being possessed of any chronic disease I chose No. 3, and took one bath—no more.

Others came in their own wagons with their own camping gear, provided for themselves from the park's fish and game, and equally freely helped themselves to the park's curiosities, hacking off pieces of the geyser formations as souvenirs to cart back home. Even more destructive were the market hunters who slaughtered the park's elk—four thousand in one year alone—simply for their hides and tongues, leaving their rotting carcasses littering the landscape. The Yellowstone act had specifically empowered the Secretary of the Interior to institute regulations "against the wanton destruction of the fish and game" within the park. "No attempt has yet been made to enforce the act," one outraged visitor wrote, "and unless some active measures are soon taken looking to the protection of the game there will be none left to protect."

Superintendent Langford, meanwhile, did nothing. He often bragged that his initials—N.P.—stood for "National Park" because he liked to claim credit for the park idea, but during his five years as superintendent, he visited Yellowstone only twice and routinely denied every request from potential concessionaires to build roads, hotels, or stores. Some suspected that the N.P. in Langford's name stood for Northern Pacific, since he seemed to be deliberately delaying development of the park until the railroad arrived and the choicest concessions could be awarded to his friends and former employer.

"Where's Langford?" local newspapers complained. By 1877, the Secretary of the Interior decided to replace him. That same summer, events in Yellowstone would make it even more clear that no one was in charge.

Our first sight of the geysers with columns of steam rising from innumerable vents and the smell of the Inferno in the air from the numerous

sulphur springs, made us simply wild with the eagerness of seeing all things at once. . . . We ran and shouted and called to each other to see this or that. . . .

We had at last reached Wonderland.

MRS. EMMA COWAN

In August of 1877, a group of nine tourists from Radersburg, Montana, traveling with a carriage, supply wagon, and small string of horses, entered the park on their own and leisurely made their way along the Firehole River, taking in the sights. Among them were Emma Carpenter Cowan, twenty-four years old, and her husband, George, planning to celebrate their second wedding anniversary in Yellowstone. They were having a glorious time, Emma remembered.

We seemed to be in a world of our own. Not a soul had we seen save our own party, and neither mail nor news of any sort had reached us since leaving. . . . One can scarcely realize the intense solitude which then pervaded this land, fresh from the Maker's hand.

But on the morning of August 24, their anniversary day, Emma heard voices outside their tent, and when she opened the flap she discovered a group of Indians standing by the campfire, demanding food and supplies. They were members of the Nez Percé tribe, part of a much larger band associated with Chief Joseph, currently being pursued by the U.S. Army because they had refused to move onto a reservation. Only two weeks earlier, nearly ninety Nez Percés had been killed—more than half of them women and children—when their sleeping village had been attacked by a column of troops in the battle of the Big Hole.

The Nez Percé war had been on everyone's lips in the West before the Cowans started their vacation, but they had assumed the new national park would be far from the action. General William Tecumseh Sherman himself, touring Yellowstone a few days earlier, had issued an assurance that Indians were too superstitious about the geysers and hot springs to come anywhere close. (Sherman was perpetuating a stubborn myth. Native Americans had a presence in Yellowstone dating back ten thousand years; the

Sheepeaters considered it their home; and half a dozen other tribes regularly traversed it. Though the Nez Percés lived far to the west, in Oregon, Washington, and Idaho, they were familiar with Yellowstone's terrain.)

Now the Cowans and their group found themselves in the midst of Chief Joseph's exodus—seven hundred people, with a horse herd in the thousands—as the Indians swarmed across the Lower Geyser Basin. Some were friendly to the whites they encountered; others, especially the young warriors, were still incensed about the casualties they had suffered at the Big Hole.

The Cowan party's wagon and carriage were ransacked and destroyed, their horses confiscated, but the tourists were unharmed and sent on their way. Then they met a different group of warriors. George Cowan was shot in the leg. Emma tried to shield her husband from the warriors who quickly surrounded him, but was roughly shoved away.

A pistol shot rang out, my husband's head fell back, and a red stream trickled down his face from beneath his hat. The warm sunshine, the smell of blood, the horror of it all . . . my sister's scream, a sick faint feeling, and all was blank.

In the confusion, another tourist was shot in the face, while three members of the party escaped into the nearby woods. Emma Cowan, her brother, and her thirteen-year-old sister were taken as captives. When he was informed about it, Joseph and the other chiefs ordered that the whites not be harmed. They were released the next day, finally reaching safety at the north end of the park.

Meanwhile, as the Nez Percés hurried across the park in their flight from the army, there were other incidents with unlucky tourists. Several were wounded and two were killed, including Richard Dietrich, a young musician from Helena who was standing idly in the doorway of the hotel at Mammoth Hot Springs when he was shot down. As the army moved through in pursuit a few days behind the Indians, they picked up the survivors. Among them—remarkably—was George Cowan, somehow still alive. Army surgeons probed his head by candlelight and removed the bullet, flattened by his skull.

By the time Cowan was reunited with his wife, the Nez Percé war was ending hundreds of miles away, with Chief Joseph's surrender in northern Montana. Yellowstone's new superintendent soon arranged for the native Sheepeaters, who had not taken part in the conflict, to be evicted from their homeland so he could assure the public that Yellowstone National Park was now free of *all* Indians.

Years later, when the Cowans returned to visit the park, Emma would say she was surprised any of her group had been spared, given the horrible treatment the Indians had suffered before and during their uprising. George, meanwhile, happily recounted the tale of their second anniversary at the Lower Geyser Basin—and then capped his story by showing off his proudest Yellowstone souvenir: the bullet that had been removed from his skull, which he had made into a watch fob.

THE ICE CHIEF

Glaciers, back in their white solitudes, work apart from men, exerting their tremendous energies in silence and darkness. Outspread, spirit-like, brooding above predestined landscapes, they work on unwearied through immeasurable ages, until, in the fullness of time, the mountains and valleys are brought forth, channels furrowed for rivers, basins for lakes and meadows, and . . . soils spread for forests and fields; then they shrink and vanish like summer clouds.

JOHN MUIR

In 1879, John Muir found himself in Alaska Territory, canoeing along its still relatively unknown coastline. Alaska, he wrote, "is Nature's own reservation, and every lover of wildness will rejoice with me that by kindly frost it is so well preserved."

For five years he had tried his best to confine himself to his writing desk in Oakland, California, turning out article after article for the *Overland Monthly, Scribner's,* and *Harper's Magazine* about the majesty of Yosemite and the Sierra Nevada, about the necessity to preserve forests from destruction, and about the joy to be found in quietly observing everything from the Douglas squirrel to a small bird called the water ouzel—all part of his desire, he said, to "preach Nature like an apostle."

But he had soon grown restless to travel again, and when the opportunity came to visit Alaska, a

In his Alaska notebook of 1879, Muir added sketches of the Native Americans, their boats, and totem poles (above). Near Muir Glacier, he and some friends later built a small cabin (top right; Muir is on the left) to ease their explorations. They were overwhelmed when steamships began arriving in Muir Inlet (bottom right) with hundreds of passengers who had come hundreds of miles to see the glacier, but spent more time gawking at the man for whom it had been named.

vast wilderness that had been part of the United States for barely a decade, he had jumped at the chance. At the coastal settlement of Fort Wrangell, hearing talk of a remote and unexplored bay lined with glaciers, he and a new friend, the Reverend S. Hall Young, a Presbyterian missionary, had hired four Tlingit Indians and their big canoe to make the long, eight-hundred-mile journey.

It was Glacier Bay. Here, the glaciers marched right down to the sea and were of an entirely different scale from the remnants Muir had tracked down high in the Sierra Nevada. They confirmed every theory Muir had proclaimed to so much derision years earlier. He reveled in studying them up close—watching glaciers calve, shedding avalanches of ice into the deep waters as seals lounged nearby, seemingly unconcerned by the noise and waves; measuring their incredible advances and retreats, up to fifty feet a day in some instances; and crossing the treacherous crevasses of their ice fields alone to make a camp on their cold surface.

He had arrived in poor health, bothered by a persistent cough. After camping out on a glacier, the cough went away, prompting Muir to observe: "no lowland microbe can survive on a glacier." "Any man who does not believe in God and glaciers," he added, "is the worst kind of unbeliever."

If among the agents that Nature has employed in making these mountains there be one that above all others deserves the name of Destroyer, it is the glacier. But we quickly learn that destruction is creation.

. . . Nature is ever at work building and pulling down, creating and destroying, keeping everything whirling and flowing, allowing no rest but in rhythmical motion, chasing everything in endless song out of one beautiful form into another.

Meanwhile, the conversations he shared around the campfires with his Tlingit companions provided him with his first in-depth exposure to Indian beliefs, prompting him to reassess the stereotypical biases he had developed earlier in the Sierras. "Don't you believe wolves have souls?" one of the Tlingits asked the Reverend Young—and the discussion that followed impressed upon Muir, for whom the natural world was equally alive and sacred, that Native Americans held some beliefs not much different from his own. One Indian in particular, a chief named Toyatte, became a friend. Muir named a glacier in his honor. The Indians, in turn, bestowed their own name on the man who pursued glaciers with such unbounded enthusiasm. They called him the "Ice Chief."

Muir's writings and sketches for the *San Francisco Evening Bulletin,* the first descriptions of Glacier Bay to reach the nation, proved so popular that the newspaper's circulation increased—and copies were reprinted all over the country.

> *From here a new world is opened—a world of ice with new-made mountains standing vast and solemn in the blue distance round about it.*
>
> *In God's wildness lies the hope of the world— the great fresh unblighted, unredeemed wilderness. The galling harness of civilization drops off, and the wounds heal ere we are aware.*

The publicity he created prompted a steamship company to start running tours to Glacier Bay. To attract more customers, promoters had named one of the inlets "Muir Inlet," and its most prominent feature, "Muir Glacier."

Several years later, Muir got a vivid demonstration of his growing fame. He was spending part of a summer there with some friends, building a small hut and going off alone for explorations. One day, a steamer arrived and disgorged 230 passengers who had come to see Muir Glacier, but were even more delighted to find "Nature's high priest" himself as an added attraction. "What a show they made with their ribbons and kodaks!" he exclaimed.

> *All seemed happy and enthusiastic, though it was curious to see how promptly all of them ceased gazing when the dinner-bell rang, and how many turned from the great thundering crystal world of ice to look curiously at the Indians that came alongside to sell trinkets, and how our little camp and kitchen arrangements excited so many to loiter and waste their precious time prying into our poor hut.*

THE PARK GRAB

In 1883, the much delayed Northern Pacific Railroad was finally completed across the continent. Tourists from the East could now reach the entrance to Yellowstone National Park in relative comfort and speed. That first year, attendance increased fivefold. The park was totally unprepared for the influx.

A grand eight-hundred-room hotel was being built at Mammoth Hot Springs, the nearest entrance to the railroad terminal, illuminated by the same electric arc lights used at the opening of the Brooklyn Bridge that year. Patrons complained of the noise and discomfort caused by the ceaseless construction, the disappointing food, and the high prices for everything—"four or five times what you pay in the East," according to one disgruntled guest. The hotel staff routinely disposed of the garbage by simply dumping it into some nearby steam vents and fumaroles, a practice later blamed for an outbreak of diarrhea.

The interior of the park was still accessible only by horse or stagecoach, and a few tent hotels had been erected near the major sites. Conditions were cramped—four beds per tent, two people per bed, towels to be shared—yet the prices seemed fixed at even more outlandish levels. "Traveling in the National Park, like the poverty to which it leads," one visitor wrote, "makes a man acquainted with strange bed-fellows."

Everything—the hotel, the food, the tents, the stages, the guides—was now under the exclusive control of the Yellowstone Park Improvement Company, a politically connected firm with close ties to the Northern Pacific and led by a Wall Street financier named "Uncle" Rufus Hatch, who openly bragged that he could buy a United States senator's vote for a $5,000 retainer fee. Arguing that he could save the government money by privately financing Yellowstone's development, Hatch had quietly arranged for the Secretary of the Interior to grant his company a remarkable monopoly within the park. For a fee of just two dollars an acre, the lease allowed them to cut as much timber as they needed; kill elk, deer, and bison in the park to feed their work crews and guests; plant crops and graze horses and cattle wherever they wished; even mine coal for their furnaces and rechannel some of the hot springs for water supplies. The

Rufus Hatch (above) and his company tried to monopolize the tourist trade in Yellowstone, including renting the tents (bottom) arrayed at Mammoth Hot Springs.

The Northern Pacific's efforts to promote Yellowstone as a "Wonderland" included colorful brochures that linked it to Lewis Carroll's best-selling book, *Alice's Adventures in Wonderland*.

contract further granted the company the right to choose seven different parcels for its own use within the park. Each parcel was to be 640 acres—one square mile.

The prime attractions of what the railroad's advertising brochures were promoting as the "Wonderland" were about to be completely surrounded and exploited by Hatch and his cronies. "By God," one local rancher complained, "they're fixing that thing so that if you want to take a whiff of a park breeze, you will have to pay for the privilege of turning your nose in that direction."

Then someone stepped forward to stop what he called "The Park Grab." As owner and editor of *Forest and Stream*, a sportsman's magazine published in New York City, George Bird Grinnell used its pages to champion his causes. Yellowstone, which he had visited in 1875, was one of them. Outraged at "the monopolists who desire to appropriate for the benefit of their pockets the only National Park possessed by the American people," he decided to take them on publicly.

Forest and Stream, *January 4, 1883.*

The project of the worthy speculators who are after the peoples' pleasure ground appears to be flourishing. Here and there a feeble voice is raised in protest against the steal, but with a powerful lobby to back them, and no opposition from the Interior Department, the grabbers have little to fear.

The time will soon come, even if it is not already here, when the Yellowstone Park will be cheap to this nation at a million dollars a year. The picayune policy of saving a few dollars now, and by that means losing in the future something that it will be then wholly out of our power to regain, cannot be too strongly condemned.

The Park is at present all our own. How would the readers like to see it become a second Niagara—a place where one goes only to be fleeced, where patent medicine advertisements stare one in the face, and the beauties of nature have all been defiled by the greed of man?

Grinnell's fight against the railroad interests was soon joined by an unlikely ally—General Philip Sheridan, a cavalry hero of the Civil War and celebrated Indian fighter, now commander of the U.S. Army for much of the West. In 1882 Sheridan had led an expedition that blazed the trail from Wyoming's Jackson Hole northward into the park. On that trip, he had become disgusted with the indiscriminate slaughter of Yellowstone's wildlife and even more incensed when he learned of the plans of Rufus Hatch and his Improvement Company.

I regretted exceedingly to learn that the national park had been rented out to private parties. . . . The improvements in the park should be national, the control of it in the hands of an officer of the government. . . .

I can keep sufficient troops in the park to accomplish this object, and give a place of refuge and safety for our noble game.

Sheridan offered to station army troops in the park to restrain vandalism and prevent depredations against the wildlife. He also suggested that the park be dramatically expanded by more than three thousand square miles—doubled in size—to provide greater protection for the elk and buffalo by conforming Yellowstone's boundaries to their seasonal migrations. It was a radical idea, immediately opposed by western politicians who believed that Yellowstone was already too big.

With Missouri Senator George Vest, Sheridan persuaded President Chester A. Arthur to join them in a camping trip to Yellowstone, the first presidential visit to the national park. The purpose of the trip was relaxation, not politics—Vest and the president engaged in a fishing contest one day, hauling in a total of 105 pounds—but the senator used several occasions to bend the president's ear about the dangers of a monopoly controlling the park. And Sheridan, who issued strict orders that no game be shot within the park boundaries to feed the group, explained his views on an expanded Yellowstone as a game preserve.

Back in Washington, Grinnell, Sheridan, and Vest moved against Hatch and the railroad lobby directly, calling for an investigation into the park contracts, proposing an expansion of Yellowstone, and trying to write park regulations concerning hunting into law. The debate that followed would be echoed in every debate on national parks for the next century.

I do not understand myself what the necessity is for the Government entering into the show business in the Yellowstone National Park. I should be very glad myself to see [it] surveyed and sold, leaving it to private enterprise.

. . . The best thing that the Government could do with the Yellowstone National Park is to survey it and sell it as other public lands are sold.

Senator John Ingalls, Kansas

The great curse of this age and of the American people is its materialistic tendencies. Money, money . . . is the cry everywhere until our people are held up already to the world as noted for nothing except the acquisition of money. . . .

I am not ashamed to say that I shall vote to perpetuate this Park for the American people. I am not ashamed to say that I think its existence answers a great purpose in our national life.

There should be to a nation that will have a hundred million or a hundred and fifty million people a park like this as a great breathing place for the national lungs.

Senator George Vest, Missouri

The bill to expand Yellowstone failed, but Vest eventually managed to reduce Hatch's 640-acre parcels down to leases of no more than ten acres each, no closer than a quarter of a mile from the geysers or the falls. He persuaded Congress to appropriate $40,000 for the park, including money to pay the superintendent and ten assistants. And at Sheridan's urging, he slipped through an amendment authorizing the Secretary of the Interior to call in troops, if necessary, to administer new regulations against hunting and vandalism.

As the fight continued, a series of politically appointed superintendents proved inept. One removed an entire geyser cone for shipment to the Smithsonian and proposed that the Liberty Cap, a distinctive rock formation near Mammoth Hot Springs, be equipped with plumbing so it could project a reliable column of water to any desired height. His replacement was the brother of a congressman. The next one, a brother of a governor, supported a proposal in Congress that the northern section of Yellowstone be separated from the park and reopened for settlement; he was fired only when it was discovered that he already had filed preliminary

George Bird Grinnell

Top: In 1883, Chester A. Arthur (seated, center) became the first president to visit a national park. During Arthur's tour of Yellowstone, two allies of Grinnell—General Philip Sheridan (seated, second from left) and Senator George Vest (seated, far right)— argued against the railroad's commercial monopoly of the park.

claims at the choicest spots for himself and his friends, in case the bill passed.

Meanwhile, the congressional debate over Yellowstone's fate continued. Proposals were made to shrink the park's boundaries, to place it under Montana's legal jurisdiction, or to follow the Yosemite example and simply turn the park over to Wyoming, once the territory became a state. The powerful railroad lobby—supported by nearby Montana and Wyoming towns—began pushing for the right to run trains through the park, rather than just to its borders.

George Bird Grinnell would have none of it. "Leave the people's park undisturbed," he declared. "The Park has already been overrun by surveyors," he warned his readers, "and if all the railways that have been surveyed there should be built, the delightful quiet of this now peaceful region would be gone forever."

No railroad should ever be allowed to penetrate the Yellowstone Park. . . . The shriek of the engine and the rumble of the train would drive away the game, and the beautiful and wonderful Park would become commonplace and unattractive.

Once again Grinnell, Sheridan, and Senator Vest joined forces to stop each repeated attack on Yellow-

Muir and his wife, Louie, with their daughters Wanda and Helen on the steps of their home in Martinez, California, c. 1888

stone—until August 4, 1886, when Congress simply stripped away any money to pay the superintendent and his assistants and provided nothing in its place. It was, Grinnell raged, "one of the most astoundingly foolish and short-sighted acts of the present incompetent and neglectful House of Representatives." Yellowstone, it seemed, would have to fend for itself.

Coming to the rescue, Lieutenant General Philip Sheridan gladly dispatched Troop M of the 1st United States Cavalry to take control of the world's first national park. They arrived believing—as everyone else did—that military supervision of Yellowstone would be a temporary stopgap. Thirty years later, the cavalry would still be there.

WILDNESS IS A NECESSITY

I am losing precious days. I am degenerating into a machine for making money. I am learning nothing in this trivial world of men. I must break away and get out into the mountains to learn the news.

JOHN MUIR

By 1888, John Muir was restless again. Immediately following his trip to Alaska he had married Louie Wanda Strentzel, the prim and reclusive daughter of a prosperous fruit grower, and settled down on her parents' estate near the town of Martinez in California's Alhambra Valley. Two children quickly followed, and Muir had single-mindedly thrown himself into providing for his family. He took over management of his in-laws' three thousand acres, bringing to bear the same intensity and mechanical inventiveness he had demonstrated as a young man rising through the ranks of industry. He improved the farm's productivity and converted extra land from pasture into cash crops of cherries, tokay grapes, and Bartlett pears, and steadily amassed considerable wealth.

Muir was tender and devoted to his wife and daughters, but his health deteriorated from the ceaseless, dawn-to-dusk farmwork and his isolation from the mountains and forests and glaciers that had always seemed to replenish him. His wife grew concerned, and when he was called away to visit his dying father in Wisconsin, she had insisted that he at least stop briefly at Yellowstone National Park, a place he had never seen, in hopes it would revive his spirits and his health.

A violent illness struck him at Old Faithful, and later he was injured by a fall from his horse, then thoroughly soaked by rain and hail at his campsite. But the national park left a lasting impression on him, and made him think once more of Yosemite: the geysers reminded him of inverted waterfalls, with their columns of water as large as sequoias. "Take a look into . . . the grand geological library of the park," Muir said of Yellowstone, "and see how God writes history."

It is called Wonderland, and . . . may be regarded as laboratories and kitchens, in which . . . we may see Nature at work as chemist or cook, cunningly compounding an infinite variety of mineral messes; cooking whole mountains; boiling and steaming flinty rocks to smooth paste and mush . . . making the most beautiful mud in the world.

Back home, Muir's health worsened again. He lost weight and once more developed a hacking cough. "Nerve-shaken and lean as a crow—loaded with care, work and worry," he wrote his brother.

Louie Muir persuaded her husband to take another outing to the mountains, first to Mount Shasta in northern California, which he quickly urged should also be made into a national park to save it from destruction by the lumbermen, and then on to Mount Rainier in the state of Washington, where he camped at what he called "the most extravagantly beautiful of all the Alpine gardens I ever beheld," with the volcanic cone looming overhead, reflected in a crystalline blue lake.

Captivated by the view, he felt some of his old energy returning, and when the young men camping with him set off to climb the 14,000-foot peak, the fifty-year-old Muir impulsively joined them, despite his weakened condition. The grueling ascent took them seven and a half hours, and one of the climbers would be blinded for two days by the sun's reflection off the snow on the barren ice cap near the summit.

Mount Rainier's 14,000-foot peak catches the day's last light.

Above: Tourists exuberantly wave Old Glory from Over-hanging Rock at Glacier Point in Yosemite, 3,254 feet above the valley floor.

Left: Visitors in the 1880s have set up a genteel camp with Bridalveil Falls as their backdrop.

But Muir often found himself leading the group and encouraging them onward. "This is a good mountain to prove one's mettle," he told them. When they reached the top, theirs became the sixth recorded ascent of Mount Rainier.

"Did not mean to climb it," Muir wrote his wife later, "but got excited, and soon was on top." The climb, he said, had left him with "heart and limb exultant and free."

The mountains are fountains of men as well as of rivers, of glaciers, of fertile soil. The great poets, philosophers, prophets, able men whose thoughts and deeds have moved the world, have come down from the mountains—mountain-dwellers who have grown strong there with the forest trees in Nature's workshops.

Louie Muir, meanwhile, had written her husband a letter that released him just as surely as the thrilling vista from Rainier's mountaintop. They could sell or lease much of their land and still live comfortably, she assured him. The most important thing now was that he must heed the calling of his life's work.

August 9, 1888. My dear John,
A ranch that needs and takes the sacrifice of a noble life, or work, ought to be flung away beyond all reach and power for harm. . . .
The Alaska book and the Yosemite book, dear John, must be written, and you need to be your own self, well and strong, to make them worthy of you.

His first chance to return to the mountains he loved the most came the next year, in 1889, when Robert Underwood Johnson, associate editor of *Century Magazine,* arrived from the East, and asked Muir for a tour of Yosemite. In the last eight years, Muir had managed only one brief visit to the place that had so profoundly changed his life, and he eagerly accepted.

But as they approached Yosemite Valley, he saw disturbing signs. In ignoring Frederick Law Olmsted's advice, the state of California had allowed John Muir's temple to be turned into a tourist trap. Tunnels had been carved through the heart of some of the big trees as gawdy attractions to entice visitors to use one road over another. In the valley itself, he found piles of tin cans and other garbage in plain view, and the meadows had been converted into hayfields and pastures—even a hog pen whose stink, Muir wrote, "has got into the pores of the rocks." He was dismayed to learn of plans to throw colored lights upon the majestic waterfalls, as if that would make them more beautiful. "Perhaps," he said, "we may yet hear of an appropriation to whitewash the face of El Capitan or correct the curves of the Domes."

Glacier Point, 3,254 feet above the valley, had been one of Muir's favorite spots from which to contemplate the place he considered nature's cathedral in deep reverence. Now it was a place where tourists mugged for the camera. James McCauley had built the Mountain House hotel there. On summer nights, his sons would collect donations from tourists for a "firefall"—a dramatic and wildly popular display in which McCauley would build a huge bonfire using wood and gunny sacks soaked in kerosene, and then light sticks of dynamite to send the fire cascading over the sheer cliff. The crowds loved it.

Daytimes, after his guests had amused themselves by dropping rocks tied in a handkerchief from Glacier Point, and watched with binoculars to see if they could detect its impact on the valley floor more than half a mile below, McCauley would show up with a chicken under his arm and then, to everyone's horror, toss it, squawking, over the edge. "With an ear-piercing cackle that gradually grew fainter as it fell," one tourist recalled, "the poor creature shot downward; now beating the air with ineffectual wings, and now frantically clawing at the very wind."

Thus the hapless fowl shot down, down, until it became a mere fluff of feathers no larger than a quail. Then it dwindled to a wren's size, disappeared, then again dotted the sight a moment as a pin's point, and then—it was gone!
After drawing a long breath all around, the women folks pitched into the hen's owner with redoubled zest. But the genial McCauley shook his head knowingly, and replied: "Don't be alarmed about the chicken, ladies. She's used

to it. She goes over that cliff every day during the season."

And sure enough, on our [hike back down], we met the old hen about half way up the trail, calmly picking her way home.

Distressed at everything he saw within Yosemite Valley, Muir fled with Robert Underwood Johnson into the high country, hoping to reexperience the combination of solace and exhilaration he had always found there. But here, too, much had changed. Beyond the boundaries of the Yosemite Grant and therefore unprotected by even the lackluster vigilance of the state, the headwaters of the streams feeding into the valley had been left to the mercy of the lumbermen and sheepherders. Johnson asked why they hadn't seen the mountain meadows Muir had written about, "with flowers growing luxuriantly up to the breast of one's horse."

"No," said Muir, "we do not see any more of those now. Their extinction is due to the hoofed locusts." This was the first time I heard him use this graphic expression for sheep. . . .

Muir told me that they not only nibbled off everything in sight but that they succeeded in digging up the roots of most of the plants, so that nothing but barrenness was left.

That evening around their campfire at Tuolumne Meadows, Muir spoke passionately about what they had seen. "The harm they do goes to the heart," he said of the sheep, and he predicted that if the destruction continued unchecked, without the trees and grasses of the high Sierra to trap and hold the winter snows, the springtime melts would become swifter and more destructive, the clear streams would become muddy with silt, and by summertime the valley and the waterfalls that nourished it would be dry.

Johnson suggested that the high country be set aside as a national park, using Yellowstone's legislation as a model, and urged Muir to become the public voice for the campaign by writing articles again describing not only the region's beauty, but its vulnerability. Muir threw himself into what became a pitched battle to preserve the high country. He was quoted and requoted in newspapers around the country, and public petitions were soon flooding Congress. Frederick Law Olmsted himself wrote a letter of support.

But vested interests and local politicians in California feared that once the surrounding high country was put under federal control, pressure would mount to take Yosemite Valley away from the state and make it a national park, too. They launched a counteroffensive, questioning Muir's motives, publicly impugning his integrity, even lying about his past. "Before he abandoned himself to profitable rhapsody and became a pseudo-naturalist," a state commissioner wrote the *Oakland Tribune,* Muir "figured among the squatters in the Yosemite."

There he cut and logged and sawed the trees of the Valley with as willing a hand as any lumberman in the Sierras.

When the State of California became trustee of the grant, Muir and the mill were expelled . . . and his teeth have been on edge ever since. The State got there, however, in time to save the forests from Mr. Muir's lumbering operations, and to prevent the clogging of the Merced [River] with sawdust.

JOHN P. IRISH

Oakland Tribune, *September 16, 1890.*
To the Editor:
I never cut down a single tree in the Yosemite. . . . Furthermore I never held, or tried to hold any sort of claim in the valley, or sold a foot of lumber there or elsewhere.

Respectfully,
John Muir

Meanwhile, Johnson had won support for the new park from the Southern Pacific Railroad, whose officials had seen how the promotion of Yellowstone improved passenger traffic for the Northern Pacific. They also believed that the future of farming in California's Central Valley—the key to the railroad's profits—depended on protecting the Sierra watersheds. The railroad's help, Johnson's personal contacts, and the public pressure generated by Muir's

Concerned that pristine places like Tuolumne Meadows (right) in Yosemite's high country were being despoiled by sheep and lumbermen, Muir called for their protection as a national park.

Even after a national park was created, the wildlife and plant life within it were not completely protected. In General Grant National Park (now Kings Canyon), the majestic sequoia called the General Noble Tree was cut down (left) at the government's orders, and a thirty-foot section was hollowed out and shipped to Chicago for the 1893 World's Columbian Exposition. There, in one of the pavilions, it became a two-story structure that amazed the visitors. Later, the "house" was reassembled, complete with a gabled roof, on the grounds of the Smithsonian in Washington (below, right), where it stood as a combination exhibit and gardener's shed until the 1930s.

The equally massive Mark Twain Tree was cut down (bottom, left) in 1891 for scientific study and museum displays. The slab sent to New York's American Museum of Natural History was sixteen feet in diameter and weighed nine tons—so heavy that it had to be split into a dozen pieces for shipment and reassembly. Its stump is still a tourist attraction.

articles all combined to move the measure quickly through Congress. On October 1, 1890, President Benjamin Harrison signed into law a bill that set aside more than 900,000 acres—nearly 1,500 square miles—for another national park.

The original Yosemite Grant, encompassing the incomparable Yosemite Valley, was still left under state control, but this new park was thirty times bigger and to Muir's delight included one of his favorite places, the nearby Hetch Hetchy Valley, which he considered "a grand landscape garden, one of Nature's rarest and most precious mountain temples." At the same time as the Yosemite bill, two more groves of big trees on the western flank of the Sierra Nevada had also been preserved as Sequoia National Park and General Grant National Park. There were now four national parks.

Flushed with the success of his first venture into the world of politics, Muir immediately began making new plans. He wanted more parks, bigger parks, and more park supporters to defend them against the enemies he knew would oppose them. He was more convinced than ever that Yosemite Valley still needed better care than the state of California seemed capable of providing.

John Muir was fifty-two years old now. It had been nearly a quarter century since the time when, as a self-described "unknown nobody," he had first entered Yosemite and been transformed by his "unconditional surrender to Nature." He was unknown no longer. He had become a national figure, and through his example and his words had convinced many others to surrender as well:

The tendency nowadays to wander in wilderness is delightful to see. Thousands of tired, nerve-shaken, over-civilized people are beginning to find out that going to the mountains is going home; that wildness is a necessity; and that mountain parks and reservations are useful not only as fountains of timber and irrigating rivers, but as fountains of life.

In 1895, exactly forty years after becoming the first tourist to visit Yosemite Valley, James Mason Hutchings published his last book, *Souvenir of California, Yo Semite Valley and the Big Trees: What to See and How to See It*—a pocket-sized guidebook with many illustrations, which he sold during his lectures all over California and to travelers who signed up for the tours he still led each summer. Like all the other promotional books he had written over the years, this one pointedly failed to mention John Muir, the man who had once worked for Hutchings and then eclipsed him in the public's mind as Yosemite's true spokesman. For that, Hutchings had never forgiven Muir.

At the age of eighty-two, the old man decided to make one more camping trip to the valley that had so impressed him nearly half a century earlier. On the afternoon of October 31, 1902, traveling on the Big Oak Flat Road, Hutchings stopped his carriage so he and his wife, Emily, could have their photograph taken before making their final descent into the valley. Coming down the steep and rocky trail, they rounded a corner and El Capitan loomed into view. Hutchings was awestruck once more. "It is like heaven," he told his wife.

Suddenly, one of the horses was startled and shot off down the road. Both Emily and her husband were thrown from the careening carriage; she escaped without serious injury, but Hutchings landed headfirst on some rocks and died almost immediately.

A few days later, his funeral service was held in the Big Tree Room in the hotel that had once been called the Hutchings House. Then Hutchings was buried in a small cemetery near Yosemite Falls—the waterfall he had first read about in 1855 as being six times higher than Niagara's and found impossible to resist coming to see for himself.

James Mason Hutchings and his wife, Emily, posed for this photograph as they approached Yosemite Valley in 1902, just minutes before the fateful accident that took his life.

AN INTERVIEW WITH GERARD BAKER

HOMELAND

When Gerard Baker was a boy growing up on the Fort Berthold Reservation in North Dakota, he loved listening to the stories his parents and tribal elders told of his Mandan and Hidatsa ancestors. He took that love of history—along with his proud sense of his people's traditions—with him into a career in the National Park Service.

Over the course of more than thirty years with the parks, Baker has done everything from cleaning restrooms in campgrounds to making arrests in the backcountry; from managing a buffalo herd at Theodore Roosevelt National Park to lecturing on the intricacies of Indian-white commercial relationships at Fort Union Trading Post to demonstrating how to tan animal hides at Knife River Indian Villages, where the Hidatsas were living when Lewis and Clark arrived in 1804 on their way west.

His more recent postings have been as superintendent. For four and a half years he was in charge of Little Bighorn Battlefield National Monument in Montana, site of the dramatic battle between George Armstrong Custer's 7th Cavalry and the Lakotas and Cheyennes led by Crazy Horse and Sitting Bull. Next he oversaw the Park Service's three-year commemoration of the Lewis and Clark Expedition's bicentennial, and worked to include the sixty-eight tribes the explorers encountered in their epic journey. Now, as the first American Indian superintendent at Mount Rushmore National Memorial in South Dakota, Baker is trying to ensure that a deeper, more complex, and complete story is told at one of the nation's most hallowed shrines.

What should we remember when we enter a national park?

If you go into a national park, you have stories—about the trees and about the grasses, for example, and about the animals and about the water and about all that. You also have a human story. And the human story did not start when national parks came in. We need to make sure that people who visit those parks understand that there was somebody here before them. That there was somebody here before the national park and this is how they used that land.

When you walk into any natural, national park you're walking into somebody's homeland. You're walking into somebody's house. You're walking into somebody's church. You're walking into somebody's place where they've lived since the time the Creator made it

for them. And so you're not walking into a wilderness area, you're walking into someplace that has been utilized for generations upon generations in every form you could imagine.

When the white men came in and discovered a wilderness, to us that was fascinating. Because it didn't need to be discovered—it was never lost. We have no word for "wilderness." It wasn't wilderness to us, it was the place where we lived. To us it was our backyard, to us it was our home. Every time I hear about someone coming into a national park and discovering something, I can almost see them standing there on top of this mountain saying, "From now on, we'll call this mountain so-and-so, 'cause we're the first ones here." In the meantime, I can see my relatives hiding behind some rocks, looking at them, saying, "Wow, what are these guys doing up here?"

Do American Indians have a different reaction to national parks?

I think their general feeling about national parks is just like everybody else's in America, which is a lot of different emotions. Good feelings, bad feelings, sad feelings. There are memories of a time, of being a free people within that area we now call a national park.

I'm a member of the Mandan-Hidatsa tribe on the west side of North Dakota. The connection to a national park was Theodore Roosevelt National Park. My grandfathers camped there before it

Gerard Baker and his mother, Cora Young Bird Baker, at Fort Union Trading Post National Historic Site, 1982. At right, Theodore Roosevelt National Park in North Dakota, part of the homeland of the Bakers' tribe, the Mandan-Hidatsas.

was a national park, fished there before it was a national park, hunted there before it was a national park. I can remember folks saying, "Yes, we used to hunt there, we used to collect berries there, we used to do our ceremonies there. But now they put us on reservations, and now it's not ours anymore. It is a foreign place to us."

It's a place to remember the past. It's a place to think about the future for them. They want to go in there because it is a sacred area. It is a saved area. They take their children there. They're interested in the programs. But they take it one step farther. Because it is saved, because the environment is still there as in the time of creation, we believe that it is still alive.

Many early white visitors to the parks also described the places in religious terms—called them temples and cathedrals.

Sacred means different things to different people. And to the American Indians sacredness means everything was alive. The trees, the rocks, everything inside where we now have national parks had a spirit. And that was the sacredness. They came there to learn, they came there to pray.

Now you can go in there and you can walk as our ancestors did. You can go in there and you can see what the Creator has made for us. And things are alive. You can feel it, you can feel the spirits.

That sounds a little bit like John Muir when he said "the very stones seem talkative, sympathetic, brotherly."

I believe that John Muir could have been a great medicine man in his day, because he was listening, he was truly listening. He wasn't exploring, he was learning, he was living with the elements out there. John Muir wasn't *discovering*, John Muir was living *with*.

Had he been an American Indian, he would have been one of those elders that kids would have gathered around. They would have sat with him and they would have listened to his stories. I think they also would have watched him as he walked off from the village and went to the areas where he would listen to those trees, where he would talk to the rocks, where he would listen to the waterfalls. And they would have respected that. They would have seen him walk away and they would have seen him come back again with new stories. And I could see him again sitting down with young people and explaining what he experienced, what he saw out there, and advising them how to listen and how to see.

What role did Indians play in the national parks, even as late as the early twentieth century?

In the early days of the national parks, the Indians were brought back not as a people who would tell their story, but as somebody who can dance for the tourists, as somebody who can sing for the tourists.

This was their homeland. This is where they had lived. They got removed from those areas, and what the National Park Service did was bring them back in for the tourists. And of course at that time, the most that people knew about Indians were the northern Plains Indians with the war bonnets and the bells and all the feathers. They were there in their feathers, their markings on their faces, their bells, their drums.

They were expected to be the "Indian." To sing, to dance, and to use the terms that the tourists would be using in those days, for example, "How." That's all they would say. That's what attracted the tourists to come there, not necessarily to learn that much other than to take their pictures and to see them dance. And so that's how they were used.

And now you're the superintendent at Mount Rushmore. That would seem to represent a big change from those earlier times.

I'm the first American Indian to be the superintendent of Mount Rushmore National Memorial, and I was told, "There's not many Indians going to be there, because they have a different feeling about the place." And so the first week I was there, I was out walking around, looking at the visitors and asking them questions, just viewing everything, and I saw an American Indian family. I was so excited, I went up there, shook hands with them, we had a very good discussion—who they were, where they were from—and then they asked me, "What do you do here?"

And I said, "Well, I'm the superintendent." And they all burst out laughing. They didn't believe me at all. They thought I worked in maintenance or they thought I was a groundskeeper or something. And I said, "No, really, I am the superintendent." And they all started laughing again. I actually had to take them back in my office and prove to them that actually, yes, I am an Indian and I am in charge of Mount Rushmore. And they were so proud of that fact.

And it opened their eyes, as well. We started talking about their daughter, who can come into the Park Service and who can be a ranger and who can work her way up and so forth.

What about Mount Rushmore and its unique place in the complicated story of America?

There were two places in my career that I told my family that I would never work. One of them was Little Bighorn and the other was Mount Rushmore. And I've been superintendent at both of them now. Coming to Mount Rushmore—it was very challenging to accept the job, because for Indian people it means the desecration of the sacred Black Hills; it means the losing of the Black Hills; a lot of negative things.

But I'm proud of the fact that I am the first American Indian to be a superintendent there, telling the freedoms that America has to offer and the democracy that we have in America. When I first came, I'd go out in the park and I would watch people. They would look at those four presidents and they'd get teary-eyed. This place

Gerard Baker, superintendent of Mount Rushmore National Memorial

draws emotion. And it should. But we were only telling half the story.

We need to look at *all* the stories, not only talk about those four presidents and what they did as far as freedom is concerned. We also have to start talking about what happened to everybody. Mount Rushmore gives us that opportunity. We're promoting all cultures of America. That's what this place is. For goodness sake, this is Mount Rushmore. It's America.

I'm talking about all of America because that's what we represent. The parks don't belong to me. They don't belong to you. The parks belong to America. And what is America made up of? So in order to tell our story, we need to do a better job of getting the multitude of cultures into our story. We need national parks to have people—especially our kids—understand what America is. America's not sidewalks. America's not stores. America's not video games. America's not restaurants. We need national parks so people can go there and say, "Ah, this is America."

Do you have a favorite moment in a national park?

My favorite memory of working in a national park is from my early years when I was working at our old villages—what we call the five villages, *Awadi-xiue,* which is now Knife River Indian Villages National Historic Site in Stanton, North Dakota. The earth lodges, of course, they're all gone now. There's nothing there but depressions. And it was a brand-new national historic site in 1974 and I was there—walking out there, believe it or not, with the journals of Lewis and Clark, going to a place where a lodge would have been. And in my mind I could see the lodge standing up. I could see people moving around and I went to the front door and cleared my throat to announce myself, because I didn't know whose lodge it was.

And my memory's going in there, sitting down where I thought the men should sit, and reading the journals and trying to go back in time—and actually sitting there and closing my eyes and going back and going back and coming to a point where I really believed that I had a veil left to go. And had I crossed that veil, I would have been there. That's my best memory. And because of that, every place I go, I try to do that in national parks.

Every national park has this place where you can get away, where you can sit down. Nobody around. You hear the wind, you may hear a coyote, you can see the sun go down or the sun come up. That's my favorite place. It is a place where it does have a lot of ties and a lot of memories for family, and they can bring them back over and over and over. And my grandchild, I'm hoping, can see the same thing that my great-grandfather did.

CHAPTER TWO

FOR THE BENEFIT
OF THE PEOPLE

62 THE NATIONAL PARKS: America's Best Idea

IN 1883, a young politician, the eldest son of a prominent New York City family, became alarmed about reports that the vast herds of buffalo that had once blanketed the Great Plains were quickly disappearing. So he hurried west on the Northern Pacific Railroad and got off when he reached the heart of the Badlands in the Dakota Territory.

His name was Theodore Roosevelt. He was twenty-four years old and afraid the buffalo would become extinct before he got the chance to shoot one. He hired a local guide and endured days of rough travel by horseback, until he finally came across a solitary buffalo bull, killed it, and then removed its head for shipment back to New York to be mounted on his wall. He couldn't have been more pleased with himself.

> *The very toil I had been obliged to go through . . . made me feel all the prouder of it when it was at last in my possession.*
>
> *I felt the most exulting pride as I handled and examined him; for I had procured a trophy such as can fall henceforth to few hunters indeed.*

That first trip to the West, Roosevelt said later, was an important turning point for him. Over the next several years, he would return again and again—to take more hunting trips into the mountains, to ranch on the open plains, to build up his health and character by pursuing what he called "the strenuous life," to become, in his own words, "at heart as much a Westerner as I am an Easterner." Roosevelt would never lose his love of hunting, but in time he would learn there were much bigger—and more important—trophies to pursue.

> *The great wilds of our country, once held to be boundless and inexhaustible, are being rapidly invaded and overrun in every direction, and everything destructible in them is being destroyed.*
>
> *How far destruction may go is not easy to guess. Every landscape low and high seems doomed to be trampled and harried.*
>
> JOHN MUIR

Preceding pages: Old Faithful goes off on schedule, Yellowstone National Park. *Left:* A young Theodore Roosevelt, with buckskins and six-shooter, in the Badlands of North Dakota

As the nineteenth century entered its final decade, Americans began to take stock of what they had made of the continent they had been so busily subduing. Only fifty years earlier, the nation's western border had been the spine of the Rocky Mountains. Buffalo numbering in the tens of millions teemed on the Great Plains. Vast forests had never witnessed the sound of an ax. Indian peoples still controlled much of the West.

Now, the nation stretched all the way to the Pacific. Railroads had pushed into every corner of the country. Indians had been driven from their homelands and forced onto reservations. White settlements had sprung up in so many places that the director of the Census of 1890 announced he could no longer find an American "frontier." The bountiful land Thomas Jefferson considered "Nature's Nation" had seemingly been conquered.

In America's four national parks, the army was in charge of their protection, but park wildlife were still routinely killed; cows and sheep still overgrazed park meadows; forests of ancient trees were still endangered. Tourists seemed intent on squandering the treasures a previous generation had bequeathed them. The park idea, not yet a quarter century old, still seemed an uncertain experiment, the issues of what was permissible and proper for people who visited the parks still unresolved.

But as a new century was about to dawn, a handful of Americans began to question the headlong rush that had caused so much devastation to the natural world—and saw in the national parks a seed of hope that at least some pristine places might be saved before it was too late. Among them would be the young assemblyman from New York City, who had gone west on a boyish impulse, but who would mature into a president whose most lasting legacy was rescuing large portions of America from destruction.

THE GRAND TOUR

To-day I am in the Yellowstone Park, and I wish I were dead. . . . The Park is just a howling wilderness of three thousand square miles, full of all imaginable freaks of a fiery nature.

I have been through the . . . Park in a buggy, in the company of an adventurous old lady from Chicago and her husband, who disapproved of the scenery as being "ungodly." I fancy it scared them.

RUDYARD KIPLING

In 1889, Rudyard Kipling, a young Englishman and aspiring writer on his way from India to his homeland, was making his first tour of the United States, financing the trip by writing dispatches for newspapers overseas. Like many foreigners, Kipling could not resist stopping at Yellowstone, a place already known around the world as the "Wonderland."

Most visitors in those days were well-to-do, able to pay the $120 train fare across the continent to the remote northwestern corner of Wyoming, and then $40 more for the five-day stagecoach trip through the park known as the "Grand Tour."

The first stop was the hotel at Mammoth Hot Springs, where everyone unpacked quickly and then rushed to a nearby store to buy souvenirs: spoons dipped in the hot springs and now encrusted with colorful travertine, or postcards and stereopticons made by the park's resident photographer, Frank J. Haynes. Many guests were perfectly content to view the mammoth springs from the comfort of the hotel veranda, but some bought guidebooks and hiked up to the terraces for a closer look, sometimes hiring one of the bellboys, who were always willing to give a personal tour on the promise of a big tip. Kipling went on his own.

Rudyard Kipling

I found a basin which some learned hotel-keeper has christened Cleopatra's pitcher, or Mark Antony's whiskey-jug, or something equally poetical. . . . I do not know the depth of that wonder. The eye looked down . . . into an abyss that communicated directly with the central fires of the earth.

The ground rings hollow as a kerosene-tin, and some day the Mammoth Hotel, guests and all, will sink into the caverns below and be turned into a stalactite.

The next morning, the passengers loaded back into their assigned carriages, and one by one set off toward the park's interior, spaced about every five hundred yards to lessen the effects of dust that clung in the air, Kipling wrote, as "dense as a fog." The drivers were known for their colorful nicknames— Society Red, Cryin' Jack, Geyser Bob—as well as for their even more colorful explanations of Yellowstone's natural wonders. Geyser Bob Edgar, who worked in Yellowstone from 1883 until the day he died in 1913, liked to drop his handkerchief into one geyser and several miles down the trail pretend to pick it out of another thermal feature, telling his amazed patrons it must have traveled underground from one spot to the next.

Kipling found his fellow tourists equally colorful, especially the older woman from Chicago sitting next to him, who chewed gum and talked constantly, pontificating with her husband on everything they encountered, especially once they reached the first geyser area.

> *Regarding the horrors of the fire-holes, [she] could only say, "Good Lord!" at thirty-second intervals. Her husband talked about [the] "dreffel waste of steam-power."*
>
> *"And if," continued the old lady, "if we find a thing so dreffel as all that steam and sul-*

phur allowed on the face of the earth, mustn't we believe that there is something ten-thousand times more terrible below prepared [for] our destruction?"

"There was a potent stench of stale eggs everywhere," Kipling noted, "and that odor mixed with the clean, wholesome aroma of the pines in our nostrils throughout the day."

At noon they stopped at a rustic wooden-framed tent next to the road—the lunch stop called "Larry's," run by Larry Mathews, a friendly and loquacious Irishman known for lavishing special attention on his genteel guests.

> *Larry enveloped us all in the golden glamor of his speech ere we had descended and the tent with the rude trestle table became a palace, the rough fare [became] delicacies of Delmonico's, and we, the abashed recipients of Larry's imperial bounty.*
>
> *It was only later that I discovered that I had paid eight shillings for tinned beef, biscuits, and beer.*

Like the other establishments within the park, Larry's encouraged tourists to believe that *all* the

A brave—or foolhardy— tourist peeks down the throat of the crater of Giantess Geyser in Yellowstone.

THE WYLIE WAY

When William Wallace Wylie, an Iowa school superintendent, was offered the job of running the schools of Bozeman, Montana, in the late 1870s, he jumped at the chance. Bozeman was near Yellowstone National Park, and ever since reading about Nathaniel P. Langford's expedition into the "Wonderland" in *Scribner's Magazine*, Wylie had wanted to see the place for himself.

He would never be the same. By 1882, after only two trips to the park, Wylie had published one of the earliest guidebooks to Yellowstone. By 1883, he and his wife were offering "traveling camps" to tourists seeking a cheaper alternative to the "Grand Tour." Wylie charged $35 for a seven-day trip at a time when the established Yellowstone concessionaire was charging $50 for a six-day tour.

At first, most of Wylie's customers were teachers, but as his business caught on—with camps of distinctive green-and-white-striped tents erected on wooden platforms at eight locations within Yellowstone—his clientele broadened to include more affluent travelers,

not because of the lower price but because seeing Yellowstone "the Wylie Way" was simply more fun. His staff, recruited from colleges and fellow schoolteachers, were young, enthusiastic, and sufficiently well informed to provide accurate answers to visitors' questions about the park's array of attractions. After dinner, many of the employees organized spontaneous songfests around a roaring fire—a precursor of the popular campfire programs eventually

adopted by the National Park Service and its rangers.

Wylie's competitors did their best to undermine his business and were successful enough to prohibit the Interior Department from ever granting him anything longer than a year-to-year lease, which discouraged him from borrowing money to make a bigger investment in his operation. (Congressman John Lacey, one of Wylie's satisfied customers, once had to intervene to make sure the government didn't close him down.) But Wylie carried on—and prospered by providing innovative services and lower prices.

"The professor," as he was called, finally retired to Pasadena, California, in 1905, but a decade later a railroad company hoping to generate tourism in southwestern Utah persuaded him to set up his trademark camps at Zion and the North Rim of the Grand Canyon—and eventually at Bryce Canyon and Cedar Breaks—where "the Wylie Way" helped introduce a new generation of Americans to a new collection of parks and monuments.

Striped tents (below) were the signature feature at Wylie's lower-budget encampments, where the staff (above) were often schoolteachers and college students who led campfire discussions and songfests.

water in Yellowstone was impregnated with sulphur and therefore unfit for drinking. It was untrue, but it boosted sales of mineral water and beer at the inflated price of 50 cents a bottle—and created roadsides littered with empties.

When the parade of stagecoaches reached the Lower Geyser Basin, the tourists encamped for two nights at the Firehole Hotel or, after 1891, the more luxurious Fountain Hotel, built at a cost of $100,000 and capable of handling 350 guests, complete with electric lights, steam heat, and hot baths fed by one of the thermal springs. The next two days of the Grand Tour were devoted exclusively to visiting the spectacular array of geysers and thermal pools and fumaroles—the largest concentration of them in the world. Tourists would peer down the throat of gaping holes in the ground, taking their chances that a geyser was not about to erupt in their face. They marveled at the beauty of translucent pools of emerald water and washed pieces of linen in Handkerchief Pool, which quickly turned the cloth white as snow.

In those early years no one knew, exactly, how to act in a national park. Some tourists took pleasure in "soaping" a geyser: pouring laundry soap down its mouth on the belief, Kipling reported, that the geyser "will presently be forced to lay all before you and for days afterwards will be of an irritated and inconsistent stomach." Kipling refused to try it, out of "sympathy" for the geyser. Then he had second thoughts. "I wish that I had stolen soap and tried to experiment on some lonely little beast of a geyser in the woods. It sounds so probable—and so human."

Other visitors would bring armloads of deadwood, even big logs, to toss into a geyser's opening, hoping to watch it all be catapulted skyward at the next eruption. Kipling noted that these attractions were guarded by soldiers "with loaded six-shooters, in order that the tourist may not bring up fence-rails and sink them in a pool, or chip the fretted tracery of the formations with a geological hammer, or, walking where the crust is too thin, foolishly cook himself."

The old lady from Chicago poked with her parasol at the pools as though they had been alive. On one particularly innocent-looking little puddle

she turned her back for a moment, and there rose behind her a twenty-foot column of water and steam.

Then she shrieked and protested that "she never thought it would ha' done it," and the old man chewed his tobacco steadily, and mourned the steam-power wasted.

No visit to Yellowstone was considered complete without seeing Old Faithful go off on schedule.

At the appointed hour we heard the water flying up and down the mouth with a sob of waves in a cave. Then came the preliminary gouts, then a roar and a rush, and that glittering column of diamonds rose, quivered, stood still for a minute. Then it broke, and the rest was a confused snarl of water not thirty feet high.

All the young ladies—not more than twenty—in the tourist band remarked that it was "elegant," and betook themselves to writing their names in the bottoms of shallow pools.

Nature fixes the insult indelibly, and the after-years will learn that "Hattie," "Sadie," "Mamie," "Sophie," and so forth, have taken out their hairpins and scrawled in the face of Old Faithful.

The final night in the park was spent at the Canyon Hotel, near both the majestic Upper and Lower falls. For many years, a grizzly bear cub was chained to the hotel's back door as an added attraction. But for those seeking something more natural, the view from the lip of the Grand Canyon of the Yellowstone was considered the inspirational grand finale. Even the cynical Rudyard Kipling was impressed.

All I can say is that without warning or preparation I looked into a gulf seventeen hundred feet deep with eagles and fish-hawks circling far below. And the sides of that gulf were one wild welter of colour—crimson, emerald, cobalt, ochre, amber, honey splashed with port-wine, snow-white, vermilion, lemon, and silver-grey, in wide washes.

So far below that no sound of its strife could reach us, the Yellowstone River ran—a finger-wide strip of jade-green.

. . . Now I know what it is to sit enthroned amid the clouds of sunset.

The final day consisted of a stagecoach ride back to the start of the tour; lunch once more at Larry's; shouting out the names of their home states and countries to passing wagons filled with fresh loads of tourists heading into the park; dinner at the hotel at Mammoth Hot Springs; then on to the train waiting at the station to carry them—and their memories—away.

"And to think," Kipling reported the woman from Chicago as exclaiming, "that this show-place has been going on all these days an' none of we ever saw it."

MAKE THE MOUNTAINS GLAD

Americans have a national treasure in the Yellowstone Park, and they should guard it jealously. . . . Let us respect her moods, and let the beasts she nurtures in her bosom live, and when the man from Oshkosh writes his name with a blue pencil on her sacred face, let him spend six months where the scenery is circumscribed and entirely artificial.

Frederic Remington

The U.S. Army had been sent into Yellowstone in 1886 on a stopgap basis, when Congress—frustrated by a series of incompetent and occasionally corrupt civilian superintendents—had simply refused to appropriate any money to oversee it. By the 1890s, the "temporary" arrangement had become permanent. Up to four troops of cavalry were stationed at the newly constructed Fort Yellowstone, near the Mammoth Hot Springs.

They patrolled the sprawling two million acres of park on horseback, doing their best to enforce improvised regulations against poaching, vandalism, and negligence with campfires. But they were hampered by the fact that the federal park existed in something of a legal no-man's-land; usually their only recourse was a warning, or in the most serious cases, expulsion from the park.

The officers in command learned to become creative. Troopers were told to look for fresh graffiti painted or scratched into the soft stone of the geyser formations, check the names against hotel registers, and if it produced a match, the offender would be marched back the next day and forced to scrub the name off.

Slowly, the soldiers and their commanders brought some semblance of order to the park. For the first time, designated campgrounds were established, and it was discovered that publicly expelling one or two tourists who had been careless with campfires went a long way each season in reducing forest fires. Army engineers built and improved the roads and bridges that guided travel within the park to the places tourists wanted to see, while leaving major portions of Yellowstone a roadless wilderness.

The officers enjoyed the responsibility of protecting such a world attraction—as well as the chance to mingle with the seemingly constant stream of famous and influential people who showed up throughout the summer season. Life for the enlisted men was different. Winter in Yellowstone was the hardest duty. With the tourists gone, the cavalrymen found themselves holed up in small cabins scattered around the park, patrolling for poachers on skis in frigid temperatures and lethal snowstorms. Men were lost transporting mail from one isolated outpost to another; others died in avalanches; some may have been killed by poachers, who were often better equipped and more experienced at maneuvering through the backcountry in deep snow. One soldier became so weak from illness while his cabin mates were on patrol that he couldn't keep the stove fed with firewood; they found him frozen to death on

As the first guardians of Yellowstone, soldiers of the U.S. Army dealt with everything from graffiti-writing tourists to deadly poachers. Troops from Minnesota's National Guard (top right) rest in the Upper Geyser Basin, while a soldier and tourist peer into the cone of Giant Geyser (below). Two soldiers on ski patrol (bottom right) have an easier time in the deep snow than the elk they are there to protect.

their return. In another isolated outpost, the sagging morale turned into a deadly case of cabin fever when a sergeant was forced to shoot two of his men who were attempting a mutiny.

The cavalry was also in charge of the nation's three other national parks—Yosemite, General Grant, and Sequoia, all in California. Each spring, troops stationed at the Presidio in San Francisco would make the two-week, 250-mile ride to the Sierras and patrol the three parks during the summer season. Some of

them were African Americans—the celebrated Buffalo Soldiers who had made a name for themselves in the Indian wars.

Their commander was Captain Charles Young, born into slavery in Kentucky, whose father had escaped bondage during the Civil War to enlist in the Union army. Young followed his father's example of military service, becoming the third black man to graduate from West Point—and the first to be put in charge of a national park. (He would later lead one of

During the height of the bicycle craze of the 1890s, the army mounted a group of African American Buffalo Soldiers on the hundred-pound, two-wheeled alternative to the horse. They garnered great attention in their visit to Yellowstone (above) and later during a 1,900-mile ride from Montana to St. Louis, but the experiment was soon abandoned.

Captain Charles Young (above) was put in charge of Sequoia and General Grant national parks, where he served with great distinction. Buffalo Soldiers (right) also patrolled Yosemite, where they dealt with sheepherders illegally grazing their flocks in the high country.

the last horse cavalry charges in the history of the U.S. Army, fighting in Mexico against Pancho Villa.)

As superintendent of Sequoia, Young directed his men to complete the first wagon road into the Giant Forest. They accomplished more in one summer than had been done in the three previous years combined. His troops adored him. "He was a father, brother, teacher and a real true friend at all times under all conditions," one of his men remembered. "I really loved him." They built the first trail to Mount Whitney, the highest peak in the contiguous United States, and erected fences around the big trees to prevent vandalism.

Like their counterparts at Yellowstone, the troops in California had to operate without clear legal authority and therefore invented techniques to protect their parks. They confiscated travelers' rifles upon entry, for return when the tourists left, and the wildlife staged a comeback. Sheepherders defiantly bringing their flocks into the parks' alpine meadows had been openly scornful of the troops, once they

realized that the army had no power of criminal arrest and prosecution—until commanders learned to expel the sheepherder at one side of the park, and then drive the sheep out at the opposite side, many miles away. The illicit grazing slowly came to an end.

No one had been more outraged at the widespread destruction of virgin forests and unspoiled lands taking place in the Sierras—and throughout the West—than John Muir. And no one was more thankful for the army's intervention.

Mere destroyers . . . tree-killers, wool and mutton men, spreading death and confusion in the fairest groves and gardens ever planted—let the government hasten to cast them out and make an end of them.

. . . Any fool can destroy trees. They cannot run away; and if they could, they would still be destroyed—chased and hunted down as long as fun or a dollar could be got out of their bark hides. . . .

The soldiers in Yosemite's high country, he wrote, "found it a desert as far as underbrush grass and flowers were concerned, but in two years the skin of the mountains is healthy again." "Blessings on Uncle Sam's soldiers," he added. "They have done their job well, and every pine tree is waving its arm for joy."

Happy as he was about the work of the army in the three Sierra parks, Muir was still not satisfied. Yosemite's high country was a national park, but the valley itself remained under the control of a California state commission and its political appointees, a group of "blundering, plundering, money-making, vote-sellers," Muir said, who seemed uninterested in preserving it as a place of natural beauty. Barbed wire fences had gone up for stock raising, and one commissioner had proposed seeding the entire valley floor to grow hay for sale as a source of revenue.

To Muir, this was sacrilege—and not at all what Congress had intended when it granted the valley to California in 1864. He wanted it ceded back to the federal government and made part of a larger Yosemite National Park. Only then, he believed, would it be safe from ruin. "As long as the management is in the hands of eight politicians appointed by the ever-changing Governor of California, there is but little hope," he reported to Robert Underwood Johnson after a lengthy visit. The valley floor, he added, "is downtrodden, frowsy, and like an abandoned backwoods pasture."

In 1892, to help promote Yosemite's protection—and the larger cause of convincing the public and its government to cherish, not exploit, the mountains and forests of the Pacific Coast—Muir and a small group of prominent Californians formed a new organization, which they called the Sierra Club. Muir enthusiastically agreed to serve as its president, "hoping," he said, "that we will be able to do something for wildness and make the mountains glad."

During an outing in Yosemite, members of John Muir's Sierra Club (left) pause for a musical rest.

THE DUST OF CENTURIES

To know you are the first to set foot in homes that had been deserted for centuries is a strange feeling. It is as though unseen eyes watched, wondering what aliens were invading their sanctuaries and why.

AL WETHERILL

A few months before Rudyard Kipling visited Yellowstone, some cowboys searching for stray cattle in southwestern Colorado, along the edge of a high plateau known as Mesa Verde, came upon what looked to them like the ruins of an ancient city, with buildings three stories high, tucked into the side of a cliff. Using a tree trunk and their lariats, they improvised a ladder and descended for a closer look. "Things were arranged in the rooms," one of them recalled, "as if people might just have been out visiting somewhere."

> *It was so much like treading "holy ground" to go into those peaceful-looking homes of a vanished people. . . .*
> *The dust of centuries filled the rooms and rose in thick clouds at every movement.*

In quick succession, they soon came across even more such ruins nestled into the remote canyon walls of Mesa Verde and gave names to them all: Cliff Palace, Balcony House, Long House, Spruce Tree House. It was the largest concentration ever found of the cliff dwellings built, occupied, and mysteriously deserted nearly a thousand years earlier by the ancestors of some of the modern Pueblo Indians of the Southwest.

For years, the Four Corners area had been known to include remnants of an ancient civilization, and a number of smaller sites had already been identified, occasionally photographed, and most often stripped of its artifacts by so-called pothunters who vandalized the ruins and then sold off their antiquities piece by piece. At first, it appeared Mesa Verde would suffer the same fate.

The busiest diggers among Mesa Verde's ruins were the cowboys who had chanced upon them in 1889, the five Wetherill brothers. They came from a family of devout Quakers who had moved from

Cliff Palace ruins, Mesa Verde National Park

Kansas eight years earlier to homestead south of Mancos, Colorado. They had quickly made friends with the nearby Ute Indians, who let them range cattle on Ute land around Mesa Verde. Richard, the oldest, had an amateur interest in archaeology. After coming across the incredible collection of cliff dwellings at Mesa Verde, he quickly organized his brothers into spending every free moment among the ruins.

"We knew that if we did not break into that charmed world someone else would, sometime," Al Wetherill remembered, "someone who might not love and respect those emblems of antiquity as we did. We had started in as just ordinary pothunters, but, as work progressed along that sort of questionable business, we developed quite a bit of scientific knowledge by careful work and comparisons." The

Wetherills gathered artifacts as carefully as they could, keeping notes about where each one was found. Once they had a complete collection, they put it on display at Durango, then Pueblo, then Denver—and ultimately sold it to the state historical society to recoup their expenses.

Meanwhile, they wrote to Washington, asking the Smithsonian Institution for funds and official backing to continue their excavations—and proposing greater protection of the ruins they had unearthed by making it a national park. The government turned them down, but news of the Wetherills' discoveries had already started to spread.

One day, a stranger showed up, a young Swedish aristocrat with an interest in archaeology, Gustaf Nordenskiöld. When the Wetherills showed him Mesa Verde's ruins, "his enthusiasm," one of the

brothers remembered, "increased almost beyond his control." Nordenskiöld decided to undertake a major excavation.

For two months, from sunup to sundown, he kept the Wetherill brothers busy, simultaneously teaching them more scientific ways of doing their work. He showed them how to use a mason's trowel instead of a spade, digging slowly and carefully to reveal a relic without damaging it; insisted on labeling and photographing everything; and often saved items that no other archaeologist of the time would have kept: wood ash from firepits, dust and trash from the floors, even dried pieces of human excrement that one day might help determine what the ancestral Puebloans had been eating so long ago.

In all, he amassed six hundred items, including one mummified corpse, for shipment back to Sweden. But when his pack animals, loaded down with artifacts, reached the railway station in Durango, Nordenskiöld said, "I was disagreeably surprised." Local newspapers had accused Nordenskiöld—a foreigner—of looting Mesa Verde, damaging the cliff dwellings, and, worst of all, preparing to ship priceless treasures of America's past out of the country. The Denver and Rio Grande Railroad refused to handle the collection. Nordenskiöld was arrested and forced to post a $1,000 bond. He contacted the Swedish ambassador, who in turn protested to the State Department.

But two weeks later, when Nordenskiöld appeared in court, he found the charges had been dropped. He couldn't have violated the law, authorities decided, because no law existed at the time governing the pro-

Gustaf Nordenskiöld (above) put the Wetherill brothers (top right) to work excavating the cliff dwellings at Mesa Verde and taught them to keep careful notes of everything they uncovered (left). When Nordenskiöld shipped his crates of artifacts home to Sweden, the uproar highlighted the lack of laws protecting the ancient ruins.

tection of antiquities. Nordenskiöld took his shipment home to Scandinavia and published the first scientific study of the cliff dwellers, which brought worldwide attention to the remarkable ruins.

Back in Colorado, struggling to keep their ranch financially afloat and to satisfy their burgeoning interest in archaeology, the Wetherills decided to try something new. "We commenced," Al Wetherill remembered, "into the tourist trade." For five dollars a day, the brothers provided guided tours of Mesa Verde. For two dollars a day, those not willing to make the rugged trip by horseback to the ruins could relax at the family's Alamo Ranch and inspect the collection of ancient and contemporary Indian items—all properly classified and catalogued—the brothers had assembled. Richard went into partnership with a photographer and sold pictures of the cliff dwellings for tourists to take home.

But if the Wetherills tried to be as professional as possible with the ancient ruins, others did not feel the same restraint. Local residents—so-called Sunday diggers—organized picnic outings at the ruins to search for treasure. Sometimes they set off sticks of dynamite simply to frighten away the rattlesnakes. A local banker was rumored to be grubstaking pothunters for a percentage of their profits in the booming trade in artifacts.

Archaeologists became horrified by it all—concerned that, before it could be adequately studied, a precious historical record of an ancient civilization would be lost forever. In their eyes, the Wetherills were as much to blame as anyone else. "We never destroyed, nor permitted destruction of any of those buildings nor their contents, feeling that we were the custodians of a priceless heritage," Al Wetherill complained, but "those who followed us in working the ruins thought of us as vandals. It's been a sore spot with all of us every time we've heard of ourselves referred to in that category."

More than anything, Richard Wetherill wanted to be seen as a respected archaeologist, despite his lack of formal education. Underwritten by two young men who had just inherited a fortune, he formed the Hyde Exploring Expedition and began scouring the Southwest for other significant ruins. In Utah, he located the remains of a culture that predated the Mesa Verde cliff dwellers—a people he called the

Basket Makers—and sent his partners an impressive collection that they donated to the American Museum of Natural History. In Arizona, he discovered Kiet Siel, nearly as large as Mesa Verde's Cliff Palace—and shipped off another collection to the East. Next he set off for New Mexico, hoping, he wrote his partners, "to see if I cannot find some more accessible ruins."

With him went the Palmer family, fellow Quakers from Kansas, talented musicians who spent much of each year traveling the United States, staging concerts in small towns. The father, Sidney Palmer, had recently developed a passion for antiquities, and after touring Mesa Verde with Richard Wetherill, he inquired about a place he had heard of to the south, called Chaco Canyon, rumored to contain more ruins. Wetherill quickly agreed to take the Palmers there.

His eagerness seems to have been more than archaeological. He was equally interested in the Palmers' eldest child, nineteen-year-old Marietta, a high-spirited young woman with a beautiful soprano voice. During the long wagon ride into New Mexico, Wetherill did his best to get to know her better, giving her his undivided attention—until they reached Chaco Canyon and came upon its largest ruin, Pueblo Bonito. With walls of remarkable workmanship, some rising five stories, it included remnants of an enclosed plaza; thirty-five circular kivas; more than two acres honeycombed by 650 rooms connected by small passageways and doors—the religious and cultural hub of the civilization that dominated the Four Corners area between 850 and 1200 A.D.

By itself, Pueblo Bonito was several times bigger than anything at Mesa Verde; surrounding it was an array of nearly a dozen other smaller, though clearly significant, ruins. "We knew Pueblo Bonito was one of the greatest things that we had ever seen outside of Mesa Verde," Marietta Palmer wrote.

Mr. Wetherill disappeared for hours and hours after we first arrived. He just threw the harness off his mules and turned them loose and left.

Next we knew he was up on top of the cliff looking down. . . . He was so delighted he was speechless.

Sidney Palmer and his musical family accompanied Richard Wetherill to Chaco Canyon's ruins in New Mexico in 1895. Along the way, Richard fell in love with Palmer's daughter, Marietta (standing, right).

By the time he left for home a month later, Richard Wetherill had come to a conclusion about his future: he would return to Chaco Canyon, where he intended to study its secrets and make his mark as an archaeologist. And when he returned, Marietta Palmer would be his bride.

THE LAST REFUGE

We have seen . . . the Indian and the game retreat before the white man and the cattle, and beheld the tide of immigration . . . move forward, at first slowly, and then, gathering volume and strength, advance with a constantly accelerated power which threatens before long to leave no portion of our vast territory unbroken by the farmer's plow or untrodden by his flocks.

There is one spot left, a single rock about which this tide will break, and past which it will sweep, leaving it undefiled by the unsightly traces of civilization. Here in this Yellowstone Park the large game of the West may be preserved from extermination . . . in this, their last refuge.

GEORGE BIRD GRINNELL

By the 1890s, few Americans understood as keenly as George Bird Grinnell how fearful the price had been for the nation's relentless expansion across the continent. Raised on the estate of the famous painter and naturalist John James Audubon at the north end of Manhattan, when the city of New York was still a good seven miles away, Grinnell could remember spotting a bald eagle from his bedroom window and watching immense flocks of passenger pigeons darkening the sky from horizon to horizon as they passed overhead.

Educated at Yale in ornithology and paleontology, he had gone west on an expedition to dig for fossils in 1870; accompanied George Armstrong Custer and the 7th Cavalry into the Black Hills in 1874, acting as official zoologist; and a year later served as naturalist for an early government survey of Yellowstone National Park, then only three years old. Traveling across Kansas, he had once encountered a buffalo herd so vast that his train was forced to stop for three hours while the beasts crossed the tracks. He had hunted elk in Nebraska, when elk could still be found on the plains; ridden with the Pawnees in a great buffalo chase as the Indians brought down their prey with bows and arrows.

Now, all that—and so much more—suddenly seemed gone or on the verge of disappearing. Passenger pigeons had been so systematically killed that a bird once numbering in the hundreds of millions had been reduced to a handful; and soon the death of a solitary bird in a Cincinnati zoo would bring an end to the species' existence. The hide hunters had been equally effective with the buffalo. By the mid-1880s, the last of the great free-roaming herds had been slaughtered. Now, the only wild herd left in the country was in Yellowstone National Park—estimated at only a few hundred animals.

"We have cut down our forests, drained our swamps and plowed up our lakebeds," Grinnell wrote.

For four centuries . . . we have been killing and marketing game, destroying it as rapidly and as thoroughly as we knew how, and making no provision toward replacing the supply.

. . . We are just beginning to ask one another how we may preserve the little that remains, for ourselves and our children.

Having sold his father's investment business, Grinnell had taken control of *Forest and Stream* magazine. He regularly used its pages to try to point Americans in a new direction, to make them understand that the nation's bountiful natural resources were not inexhaustible, and to urge them to do something about it. It wasn't that he was against hunting; in fact, he loved to hunt. Grinnell feared that without wise management, there would be nothing left for hunters to shoot.

In 1886, he proposed the creation of an organization aimed at stopping the heedless killing of wild birds. In honor, Grinnell wrote, of the "man who did more to teach Americans about birds of their own land than any other who ever lived," he named the new group the Audubon Society. A year later, when Grinnell published a mildly critical review of Theodore Roosevelt's book chronicling his own western adventures, the young author burst into Grinnell's office to confront him. The two men turned the awkward moment into the beginning of a lasting friendship—and together formed the Boone and Crockett Club, named for the famous frontiersmen Daniel Boone and Davy Crockett.

The club's stated purpose was "to promote manly sport with the rifle," and its membership was restricted to one hundred men, virtually all of them prominent New Yorkers who shared an interest in big game hunting. But Grinnell purposefully directed the group to use its considerable political influence on behalf of his broader conservation causes: outlawing nighttime deer hunting with bright lights to stun the prey; founding the New York Zoological Society to preserve living specimens

An early pledge card for the Audubon Society, signed by its founder, George Bird Grinnell, who inked in his own exception—"scientific purpose"—for killing wild birds

TESTAMENTS TO THE SLAUGHTER: A mountain of bison skulls (above) is heaped at trackside in Detroit, ready to be hauled away to the Michigan Carbon Works, while a line of elk carcasses (right) awaits loading at the train station outside Yellowstone National Park, c. 1880.

Man has been as wasteful of his natural possessions as the sun of its energy. We have not been content with using these resources; we have wasted them as reckless prodigals.

The annihilation of the noblest of all the American mammals is one of the crimes of the nineteenth century. Our children's children would curse us, and they ought to, if we do not prevent this reproach on the American people from being consummated.

. . . Today there are nearly as many millionaires in this city [of New York] as there are buffaloes in the whole world. The natural suggestion is that we are getting long on millionaires and short on buffaloes.

REPRESENTATIVE JOHN F. LACEY

of some rare and endangered animals; suggesting that parts of the West be set aside as game refuges. In an editorial entitled "Spare the Trees," Grinnell had launched a campaign to create the first national forests with a simple equation for his sportsman friends: "No woods, no game," he wrote. "No woods, no water; and no water, no fish."

It is of the utmost importance that [Yellowstone] Park shall be kept in its present form as a great forestry preserve and a National pleasure ground, the like of which is not to be found on any other continent than ours. . . .

So far from having this Park cut down, it should be extended, and legislation adopted which would enable the military authorities . . . to punish in the most vigorous way people who trespass upon it.

The Yellowstone Park is a great park for the people, and the representatives of the people should see that it is molested in no way.

THEODORE ROOSEVELT

As president of the Boone and Crockett Club, Theodore Roosevelt was increasingly drawn into Grinnell's battles, including the long-standing crusade to keep Yellowstone as protected as possible. It was a constant fight. There were regular attempts in Congress to reduce the park's size, open it up to greater commercial exploitation, even do away with it altogether. On the park's twentieth birthday in 1892, complaining that Yellowstone was not a "profitable industry" for the government, Senator James H. Berry of Arkansas had proposed carving it into homesteads of 160 acres each. Then, he said, the nation could "sell it to the highest bidder and place the money in the Treasury."

Roosevelt, a rising political star and now the civil service commissioner for the federal government in Washington, helped defeat them all—drafting petitions on behalf of the Boone and Crockett Club, testifying before committees, organizing informal dinners to influence key legislators.

But despite those successes, to Grinnell's and Roosevelt's dismay there was still no law giving Yellowstone's caretakers clear authority to protect its wildlife, including its dwindling herd of wild buffalo. With bison heads selling for $1,000 in London, Yellowstone's superintendent reported, taxidermists were offering up to $500 for a fresh kill, and "many a hardy frontiersman, who has no sentiment for their preservation and no respect for the law, will take his chances of capture for such a sum."

Edgar Howell was one such "hardy frontiersman." In March of 1894, he quietly slipped into Yellowstone National Park, dragging a toboggan with 180 pounds of supplies across the snow to a secluded camp he had already set up in the Pelican Valley, the wintering ground of the nation's remnant buffalo herd. Then he methodically went about killing as many as he could, planning to haul out their heads for sale to a Montana taxidermist.

On March 13, a soldier and a scout named Felix Burgess, out on patrol, heard two shots in the distance, hurried in that direction, and came across some dead buffalo with a man hunched over one of them, so busily skinning its carcass that he didn't realize the troopers were there until Burgess was beside him with a drawn gun. It was Howell.

As luck would have it, a reporter named Emerson Hough, on assignment for *Forest and Stream*, was in the park, traveling with a guide and a photographer to do a feature story about Yellowstone in winter. Near the Norris Geyser Basin, Hough's group encountered Howell and his captors as they escorted the poacher back to Fort Yellowstone. Hough was horrified at Howell's crime, but even more appalled at the poacher's attitude.

He was very chipper and gay [and] apparently little concerned about his capture, saying . . . that he stood to make $2,000, and could only lose $26.75 [in confiscated equipment].

He knew he could not be punished, and was only anxious lest he should be detained until after the spring sheep shearing in Arizona.

"I'm going to take a little walk up to the Post," [he said], "but I don't think I'll be there long."

Hough realized that he had stumbled onto a great story and quickly telegraphed it to Grinnell in New York City. Grinnell, in turn, knew just what to do with it. He gave Hough's story prominent display, alerted his well-connected friends, and began railing

THE FINAL STRAW: When George Bird Grinnell publicized news of the capture of poacher Edgar Howell in Yellowstone and the fact that he would not suffer any real punishment, public opinion forced Congress to enact tougher laws.
Top right: Howell (right) and his captors
Bottom right: Soldiers display the buffalo heads Howell intended to sell.

against Congress's "criminal negligence," hoping to convince the public that permitting such an outrage was "a disgrace to every American citizen."

Every citizen shares with all the others the owner-ship in the wonders of our National pleasure ground, and when its natural features are

defaced, its forests destroyed, and its game butchered, each one is injured by being robbed of so much that belongs to him.

Within a week, legislation was working its way through Congress, sponsored by Representative John F. Lacey of Iowa. (Lacey was already well acquainted with Yellowstone's lawlessness: on the Fourth of July in 1887, his stagecoach had been stopped inside the park and he had been robbed of $16 and two exotic coins.)

Lacey's bill authorized regulations that protected the park, its wildlife, and its geysers; prohibited all hunting; called for fines up to $1,000 and jail sentences of up to two years for offenders; and provided for U.S. marshals to help enforce the law and a commissioner to hear the cases. Similar bills had gotten nowhere in the past, but because of the Howell affair, the Act to Protect the Birds and Animals in Yellowstone National Park now began moving through both houses. Grinnell kept up the public outcry while Theodore Roosevelt stalked the corridors of the Capitol, lobbying for the bill's passage—though he sent a private message to Yellowstone's superintendent that "you made the greatest mistake of your life in not accidentally having that scoundrel [Howell] killed." On May 7, 1894—less than two months after Howell's capture—President Grover Cleveland signed Lacey's bill into law.

Since his crime had preceded passage of the law, Howell himself had to be released from the Fort Yellowstone stockade. Much as he hated to let Howell go, Captain George Anderson, the acting superintendent, considered the incident "the most fortunate thing that ever happened to the Park, for it was surely the means of securing a law so much needed and so long striven for." Two months later, Anderson felt even better about it all.

On the evening of July 28 I found [Howell] coolly sitting in the barber's chair in the hotel [here in the park]. I instantly arrested him and reconfined him in the guardhouse, had him reported to the U.S. attorney for this district . . . for returning after the expulsion, in violation of . . . Park regulations . . . and on the evening of August 8 he received the first conviction under the law which he was instrumental in having passed.

THE GREATEST GOOD

In 1891, at the urging of George Bird Grinnell, Congress had enacted the Forest Reserve Act, empowering presidents of the United States, without consulting Congress, to set aside parcels of public land as national forest reserves, and providing some measure of protection from the wholesale destruction of woodlands that had already swept across so much of the East and upper Midwest and threatened to leave vast swaths of the West logged off and overgrazed.

By 1896 a succession of chief executives had exercised that authority, creating forest reserves first around Yellowstone National Park, then around Yosemite, and then in a few other corners of the West. But there was no consensus on what should be permitted in the forest preserves and how—or even whether—they were different from national parks.

John Muir considered forests sacred places of contemplation and communion with nature. He wanted them treated as parks: protected by the army, with logging, grazing, and hunting prohibited.

That view wasn't shared by Gifford Pinchot. He wanted forests protected, too, but he believed the best way to do it was to manage their use, not leave them alone.

The first principle of conservation is development, the use of natural resources now existing on this continent for the benefit of the people who live here now. The first duty of the human race is to control the earth it lives upon.

Pinchot was nearly thirty years younger than Muir, and came from a wealthy upbringing instead of a hardscrabble farm. After graduating from Yale, he had studied forestry in Germany and France, and returned as the first American to declare himself a professional forester. He and Muir met while serving on a national forestry commission sent out to survey the western forests. At first they enjoyed each other's company, camping together on the rim of the Grand Canyon. (Muir stopped Pinchot from killing a tarantula, arguing that "it had as much right" there as they did; and then he persuaded Pinchot to join in something Muir liked to do to give himself a new perspective on the natural world: look at it upside down.)

But while the two men agreed that America's forests were being rapaciously destroyed, they ultimately parted company on the solution. Pinchot's favorite saying was "the greatest good for the greatest number." National forests, he said, should be administered by professionally trained foresters, who would supervise selective cutting and grazing. His view of conservation-through-use would come to be known as "utilitarian." Muir, on the other hand, was what came to be called a "preservationist." To him, the great value of forests and wilderness was more spiritual than practical: the ability of unspoiled nature to inspire and to heal. Besides, having personally witnessed so much devastation by sheep and lumber syndicates in the Sierra Nevada, Muir was skeptical of their motives and doubted they could be controlled.

Much is said on questions of this kind about "the greatest good for the greatest number," but the greatest number is too often found to be number one. It is never the greatest number in the common meaning of the term that make the greatest noise and stir on questions mixed with money. . . .

Complaints are made in the name of poor settlers and miners, while the wealthy corporations are kept carefully hidden in the background.

Let right, commendable industry be fostered, but as to these Goths and Vandals of the wilderness, who are spreading black death in the fairest woods God ever made, let the government up and at 'em.

Responding to outcries in western states that too much public land was being set aside, Congress and the administration of President Grover Cleveland sided with Pinchot, who was appointed the nation's chief forester. National forests would become part of the Department of Agriculture, used and managed like a crop, not preserved like a temple.

If Muir could not prevail on the future of all national forests, he and his supporters at least eked out a partial victory by protecting one of them as a national park. It was in western Washington state, within sight of the city of Seattle, the ancient homeland of nearly a dozen Indian tribes, including the Cowlitz, Nisqually, Puyallup, and Yakima, who

Gifford Pinchot

called it *Tahoma,* "the big mountain where the waters begin." Whites called it Mount Rainier.

In 1893, when the Pacific Forest Reserve was created, encompassing the mountain that had played a role in reinvigorating Muir and convincing him to rededicate his life to nature, he had quickly persuaded the newly formed Sierra Club to support a movement to give Rainier the more protected status of national park.

> *Altogether this is the richest subalpine garden I ever found, a perfect floral Elysium. The icy dome needs none of man's care, but unless the reserve is guarded the flower bloom will soon be killed, and nothing of the forests will be left but black stump monuments.*

Other groups joined the cause—the National Geographic Society and scientific associations, who wanted Rainier preserved as a place to study volcanic action and the work of glaciers; commercial leaders in Tacoma and Seattle, who saw the prospect of a national park as good for the region's image and tourist business; and the Northern Pacific Railroad, already instrumental in the creation of Yellowstone National Park, which figured that another such attraction along its main line would increase ridership.

The effort lasted more than five years, included six different attempts to push a bill through Congress, and ultimately required assurances that none of the new park was suitable for farming or mining and that no federal appropriations would be necessary for its management. But on March 2, 1899, Mount Rainier became the nation's fifth national park—and the first ever created from a national forest.

*The Mount Rainier Forest Preserve should
be made a national park and guarded while
yet its bloom is on; for if in the making
of the West Nature had what we call parks
in mind—places for rest, inspiration, and
prayers—this Rainier region must surely be
one of them.*

*Of all the fire-mountains which, like
beacons, once blazed along the Pacific Coast,
Mount Rainier is the noblest in form.*

*Above the forests there is a zone of the
loveliest flowers . . . so closely planted and
luxuriant it seems as if Nature, glad to
make an open space between woods so dense
and ice so deep, were economizing the
precious ground, and trying to see how
many of her darlings she can get together in
one mountain wreath. . . .*

JOHN MUIR

A fog-shrouded Mount Rainier looms over a field of flowers.

Within the past few years, the destruction of our birds has increased at a rate which is alarming. This destruction now takes place on such a large scale as to seriously threaten the existence of a number of our most useful species.

It is carried on chiefly by men and boys who sell the skins or plumage to be used for ornamental purposes—principally for the trimming of women's hats, bonnets and clothing.

GEORGE BIRD GRINNELL
The Audubon Magazine

For centuries, the nation's greatest breeding ground for its most beautiful plumed birds was southern Florida, where the fresh waters of Lake Okeechobee drain slowly toward the Gulf of Mexico through cypress swamps and mangrove forests and the biggest saw grass marsh in the world—the Everglades.

But by 1900, the long plumes of the great white and snowy egrets had become more valuable per ounce than gold, and nearly 95 percent of Florida's shore birds had been killed by plume hunters. More than five million birds a year were perishing to keep up with the latest fashion trend: using bird feathers to decorate women's hats. Strolling the streets of New York for part of an afternoon, one ornithologist counted 542 feathered hats on women's heads, representing forty different species. Some hats included an entire stuffed bird.

The Audubon Society founded by George Bird Grinnell in 1886, now a collection of societies within individual states, had done its best to try to persuade women not to buy such hats, even promoting the sale of featherless hats called "Audubonnets," decorated with ribbons. Nothing seemed to change. Women still preferred feathered hats. "Fashion decrees feathers," Grinnell complained, "and feathers it is."

The millinery industry, based principally in New York City, used its influence in Congress to defeat a series of national laws aimed at stopping the slaughter. Meanwhile, throughout the United States, market hunters were killing game birds—ducks, quail, prairie chickens—by the tens of thousands and selling them by the sackful to restaurants and wholesalers. Entire species were threatened with extinction.

Once again, Representative John F. Lacey stepped forward.

When on the streets I meet young girls and matrons with their kindly faces, and see the aigrettes in their bonnets and hats, I can not help feeling that these daughters of Eve do not know how these feathers were obtained.

These plumes only grow while the bird is rearing its young, and I believe that if most of the women who wear them knew they were obtained by shooting the mother on her nest they would be ashamed to keep them, even in secret, much less to display them on the public streets.

We have a wireless telegraph . . . a thornless cactus, a seedless orange, and a coreless apple. Let us now have a birdless hat.

As the Republican Party began fracturing at the start of the twentieth century into a progressive wing and a group of die-hard conservatives known as "Standpat" Republicans, Lacey, of Oskaloosa, Iowa, counted himself with those opposed to change. So much so, that he proudly called himself "the Standpatter from Standpatville." Whenever issues of maintaining high tariffs or helping the railroads came up, his vote could always be relied upon.

Despite promotional campaigns in magazines like *Frank Leslie's Illustrated Newspaper* (left), entitled "The Cruelties of Fashion," the demand for feathers for women's hats kept climbing— and plumed birds in places like the Everglades (right, top) kept perishing to provide them. Finally, Representative John F. Lacey (right, bottom) pushed through a law to stop the slaughter.

But when it came to defending wildlife or saving America's remaining unspoiled lands, Lacey's definition of "conservative" placed him not only outside his fellow "Standpatters" but in the vanguard of even the most progressive politicians of the day. "Americans," he said, "have been the spendthrifts of the centuries."

The first settlers found this continent a storehouse of energy and national wealth. . . . [But] we have not been content with using these resources; we have wasted them as reckless prodigals.

For more than three hundred years destruction was called "improvement."

Mankind must conserve the resources of nature, or the world will at no distant day become as barren as a sucked orange.

It had been Lacey, working with George Bird Grinnell and Theodore Roosevelt, who pushed through the bill that finally gave government officials the tools they needed to protect Yellowstone National Park, saving America's last wild buffalo herd from extermination. Now, after eight years of ceaseless effort, he won passage of the Lacey Bird and Game Act of 1900, a carefully crafted bill that steadfastly recognized individual states' rights to enact their own game regulations, but invoked the interstate commerce clause of the Constitution and made it a federal crime to transport birds killed in violation of any state law. Soon, government agents were confiscating huge shipments of bird skins and bird feathers, and with the encouragement of their local Audubon societies, more and more states passed their own bird protection bills.

The Lacey Act did not put an end to plume hunting entirely, however, especially in the relatively unpopulated and lawless Everglades. Five years after the bill's passage, a game warden named Guy Bradley—employed by the Audubon Society—was murdered by poachers. Three years later, another warden was gunned down. Some people began thinking that the uniquely abundant array of wildlife in southern Florida would never be safe unless the Everglades was set aside, like Yellowstone, as a national park. John F. Lacey believed perhaps the tide was turning:

The attempt to preserve and restore some of the wild life of America is no longer looked upon as a fad or idle sentiment.

We have given an awful exhibition of slaughter and destruction, which may serve as a warning to all mankind. Let us now give an example of wise conservation of what remains of the gifts of nature.

As America moved into a new century, a new word—"conservation"—had crept into the nation's vocabulary. Now, a new president would turn the word into a movement.

ESSENTIAL DEMOCRACY

Like all Americans, I like big things; big prairies, big forests and mountains, big wheat-fields, railroads, and herds of cattle too; big factories, steamboats, and everything else.

I am, myself, at heart as much a Westerner as an Easterner.

THEODORE ROOSEVELT

In the spring of 1903, Theodore Roosevelt once again boarded a train headed west, and on April 8 he stepped off at the Northern Pacific terminal just outside Yellowstone National Park. He was no longer the scrawny and inexperienced Easterner cowboys had laughed at and called "Four Eyes" twenty years earlier. He was a national hero, the leader of the Rough Riders in the war with Spain; a former governor of New York state; President William McKinley's running mate in 1900; and now, following McKin-

ley's assassination in 1901, the youngest president in United States history.

"The President," remarked the nature writer John Burroughs, "unites in himself powers and qualities that rarely go together."

The qualities of a man of action with those of the scholar and writer . . . the instincts and accomplishments of the best breeding and culture with the broadest democratic sympathies. . . . He loves solitude, and he loves to be in the thick of a fight.

He is doubtless the most vital man on the continent, if not on the planet, to-day. He is many-sided, and every side throbs with his tremendous life and energy.

Not since Thomas Jefferson a century earlier had there been an American president with greater interest in the natural world. Roosevelt had been sickly as a boy, and devoted much of his childhood to studying birds and animals, learning taxidermy and starting his own, well-organized collection of stuffed specimens. At age twelve he donated some of them—a dozen mice, a bat, a turtle, four bird's eggs, and the skull of a red squirrel—to the American Museum of Natural History. Eleven years later, he presented 622 carefully preserved bird skins to the Smithsonian.

Determined to build up his strength as a young man, he had taken up boxing and then, in his trips to the West, became an avid outdoorsman. The trophies hanging on the walls and the hides on the floor in his home at Sagamore Hill on Long Island testified to his success as a big game hunter: grizzly bears, bighorn sheep, Rocky Mountain goats, elk, caribou, and his prized buffalo. With his friend and mentor George Bird Grinnell he had founded the Boone and Crockett Club to promote sportsmanlike hunting versus the wholesale destruction of game animals. The two men had edited a series of influential books about hunting and camping, helped create the National Zoo in Washington, worked for legislation to set aside the Adirondack Forest Preserve in upper New York State, and led the national fight that resulted in Yellowstone's park protection act of 1894.

As New York's governor, Roosevelt had battled the powerful millinery industry in his own state on behalf of the birds being sacrificed to women's fashion—and he even joined the Audubon Society of Florida to try to stem the carnage of plumed birds. "When I hear of the destruction of a species," he said in 1899, "I feel just as if the works of some great writer had perished."

Only a few years into his accidental presidency, after learning that federally owned Pelican Island in

Florida was being overrun by plume hunters, endangering the egrets, ibises, and other colorful birds breeding there, he asked if any law prevented him from simply declaring it a "bird reservation." Told that there wasn't, he created, with a stroke of his pen, the nation's first wildlife refuge—one of fifty-one he would establish while in office.

By 1903, his interest in conservation and love of the outdoors brought Roosevelt to Yellowstone. He was in the midst of a national tour unprecedented in its ambition: 14,000 miles, twenty-five states, 150 towns and cities, more than two hundred speeches in the space of eight weeks, but from the day he left Washington he had been looking forward to some time off in the park. Immediately upon his arrival, he set off on horseback with Major John Pitcher, the army's acting park superintendent as his host, leaving the rest of the presidential entourage behind, including his staff, his Secret Service men, his physician, and all the reporters covering the trip. Only John Burroughs, the aging nature writer and longtime Roosevelt friend, was allowed to come along.

The summer tourist season was still months away, so the president and his small group had Yellowstone essentially to themselves. He delighted in seeing so many animals—herds of mule deer and whitetails and pronghorn antelope, flocks of bighorn sheep. He

THE VIGOROUS LIFE: President Theodore Roosevelt can't hide his enthusiasm to leave his nationwide train trip behind and ride into Yellowstone National Park (top). Nature writer John Burroughs (bottom, with white beard) called his restless camping companion "the most vital man on the continent, if not the planet, to-day."

watched an eagle swoop down to try to capture a yearling elk; saw cougars feasting on the carcasses of their prey; spent four hours one afternoon looking through his field glasses, trying to count all the elk within sight, ultimately estimating them to number three thousand.

On Easter morning he insisted on leaving the campsite entirely on his own. He tramped eighteen miles over rough ground in order to sneak up to within fifty yards of another elk herd, sat down on a rock, and gazed rapturously upon them while he ate his lunch of hardtack and sardines. "He came back looking as fresh as when he started," Burroughs marveled, saying Roosevelt's energy and boundless enthusiasm were reminiscent of an overgrown boy.

Roosevelt was witnessing firsthand the results of the wildlife protection bill he and George Bird Grinnell and Congressman John Lacey had worked so hard to pass back in 1894. The game animals were now much more numerous, he assured Burroughs, than when he had last visited the park twelve years earlier on behalf of the Boone and Crockett Club. Even so, the president was itching to shoot something. At the time, although game hunting was prohibited, park managers were routinely killing predators. Roosevelt hinted that he'd like to go after a mountain lion, since they weren't off limits. His advisers thought killing any animal in a national park would be bad politics, and quietly dissuaded him.

He did, however, manage to capture a mouse he believed might be new to science. While his companions went fishing, Roosevelt skinned and stuffed his discovery "as neatly as a professed taxidermist would have done it," Burroughs reported, carefully adding, "This was the only game the President killed in the Park."

In all, the president spent two weeks in Yellowstone, including several days traveling by horse-drawn sleigh to the park's interior, still covered in places by up to six feet of snow. He saw the Norris Geyser Basin and Old Faithful, and skied to the rim of the Grand Canyon of the Yellowstone. But these "wonders" held only passing interest to him, compared to the park's wildlife. In addition to the larger animals, he recorded sightings of pine squirrels and snowshoe rabbits and scores of different birds,

including a pygmy owl, the first he had ever seen. He responded with boyish glee, Burroughs wrote: "I think the President was as pleased as if we had bagged some big game."

On April 24, at the end of Roosevelt's visit, the entire population of the town of Gardiner, Montana, walked over to the park's north entrance for a special ceremony. A new arch to welcome visitors to Yellowstone was under construction, and the president had agreed to speak at the laying of the arch's cornerstone. For the occasion, Roosevelt reluctantly changed out of his camping clothes, put on a business suit, and rode through town to the awaiting crowd. He watched as the cornerstone was carefully put into place, then climbed to a rough platform on the stonework of the incomplete pillar and began to speak.

My fellow citizens:

The Yellowstone Park is something absolutely unique in the world so far as I know. Nowhere else in any civilized country is there to be found such a tract of veritable wonderland made accessible to all visitors, where at the same time not only the scenery of the wilderness, but the wild creatures of the Park are scrupulously preserved. . . .

The scheme of its preservation is noteworthy in its essential democracy. . . . This Park was created, and is now administered for the benefit and enjoyment of the people. . . .

It is the property of Uncle Sam and therefore of all of us. The only way that the people as a whole can secure to themselves and their children the enjoyment in perpetuity of what the Yellowstone Park has to give, is by assuming ownership in the name of the nation and jealously safeguarding and preserving the scenery, the forests, and the wild creatures.

"I cannot too often repeat that the essential feature" of the principle behind Yellowstone and other national parks, he told them again, "is its essential democracy—it is the preservation of the scenery, of the forests, of the wilderness life and the wilderness game for the people as a whole instead of leaving the enjoyment thereof to be confined to the very rich who can control private preserves."

ESSENTIAL DEMOCRACY: Roosevelt speaks to the citizens of Gardiner, Montana, during ceremonies laying the cornerstone of the arch that now stands at Yellowstone's north entrance.

In his speech, Roosevelt had deliberately quoted from the act of Congress that had made Yellowstone the world's first national park: "for the benefit and enjoyment of the people." Later that year, when the arch was completed and a new railroad terminal had been built near it, that phrase would be permanently carved into the arch's lintel so that everyone who entered Yellowstone would be reminded of why the park was there—and for whom.

After the ceremonies, just before his train left Gardiner, the president wrote a short letter to his old mentor, George Bird Grinnell, saying that his two weeks in Yellowstone, watching the game animals and birds, had been a wonderful break from his presidential duties. But "tomorrow," he wrote, "I go back to the political world, to fight about trusts and the Monroe Doctrine and the Philippines and the Indians and the Tariff."

Two grueling weeks later, Roosevelt's whirlwind tour brought him to Arizona's Grand Canyon for a brief stop on the way from New Mexico to southern California. Roosevelt had never before seen the Grand Canyon and he was overwhelmed by the vista from the South Rim. He longed to spend more time there, but his schedule permitted only this quick visit and a few remarks to the crowd that had gathered to greet him.

I want to ask you to do one thing in connection with it in your own interest and in the interest of the country—. . . keep this great wonder of nature as it now is.

Leave it as it is. You can not improve it. The ages have been at work on it, and man can only mar it. What you can do is to keep it for your children, your children's children, and for all who come after you, as one of the great sights which every American, if he can travel at all, should see.

Then he was gone. And by the next day, he was whistle-stopping his way through California, giving two to three speeches a day, attending banquets and dinners in his honor, presiding at dedications and groundbreakings—setting the frenetic pace that had become his hallmark.

NATURE'S PEACE

Nothing can be done well at a speed of forty miles a day. . . . Far more time should be taken. Walk away quietly in any direction and taste the freedom of the mountaineer. Camp out among the grass and gentians of glacier meadows, in craggy garden nooks full of Nature's darlings.

Climb the mountains and get their good tidings. Nature's peace will flow into you as sunshine flows into trees. The winds will blow their own freshness into you, and the storms their energy, while cares will drop off like autumn leaves.

JOHN MUIR

By 1903, John Muir was sixty-five and more famous than ever. Mountain peaks and canyons, campsites and glaciers now bore his name. Magazine editors besieged him with requests for articles. The Sierra Club he had founded was growing steadily, and the hikes he personally led into the mountains were always the club's most heavily attended. People loved to hear him preach his deeply held gospel that salvation could be found through immersion in the natural world. "He was rapt, entranced," one woman wrote of listening to Muir during a club outing.

He threw up his arms in a grand gesture. "This is the morning of creation," he cried, "the whole thing is beginning now! The mountains are singing together."

He had recently published his second book, entitled *Our National Parks,* in which he sang the praises—as only he could—of Yellowstone, Yosemite, Mount Rainier, and the two smaller California parks, General Grant and Sequoia. In it he had also advocated adding a new national park at the Grand Canyon—where, he told his readers, "for a few moments at least there is silence, and all are in dead earnest, as if awed and hushed by an earthquake."

But his deepest passion was still Yosemite, the place that had transformed his life more than thirty years earlier. For nearly a decade now he had been struggling to have the Yosemite Valley ceded back to the federal government and made part of a larger Yosemite National Park. But nothing he seemed to say or do had proven successful. California's legisla-

President Roosevelt and his wagonload of politicians stop for a photograph at the Wawona Tunnel Tree on their way to Yosemite's Mariposa Grove of sequoias. Somewhere in their midst sits John Muir.

ture was reluctant to give up state control of the valley, even though most people now agreed that the commission in charge was doing a poor job preserving it. Concessionaires and other private interests in and around the valley, accustomed to a cozy relationship with the state commission, resisted the thought of the federal government taking over and dispatching its troops to administer the valley.

Things remained at a standstill in the spring of 1903, as Muir prepared to embark on a trip to Europe and Asia with some friends. Suddenly, he had a change of plans. "An influential man from Washington wants to make a trip into the Sierra with me," he told a friend, "and I might be able to do some forest good in freely talking around the campfire."

It was the president, still working his way up through California, asking Muir to accompany him during a short visit to Yosemite. "I do not want anyone with me but you," Roosevelt had written, "I want to drop politics absolutely . . . and just be out

in the open with you." Muir realized this was the opportunity of a lifetime. He purchased a brand-new woolen suit for the occasion and hurried to join the presidential entourage.

On May 15, they set off from the town of Raymond for the Mariposa Grove of Big Trees in a caravan of wagons. Muir was seated in the president's coach—along with the governor of California, the secretary of the navy, the surgeon general, two college presidents, and Roosevelt's personal secretary. The other wagons carried more staff and dignitaries; a detachment of thirty African American troopers from the 9th Cavalry rode along as escorts.

It was hardly the trip he had been promised, but Muir tried his best to squeeze in words to the president and governor about the issue of making all of Yosemite a national park. As they approached the grove of mighty sequoias, the president's group paused, as all tourists did, for a photograph at the famous Wawona Tunnel Tree. Later they posed for

an official photograph lined up along the base of the Grizzly Giant, the oldest and most famous sequoia in Yosemite; estimated to be 2,700 years old, it boasted a single branch that was six and a half feet in diameter.

Then the troops, the phalanx of reporters and photographers, and virtually all of the official party, headed back to the Wawona Hotel, where a series of receptions and a grand dinner were scheduled in the president's honor that evening. None of them knew that Roosevelt had no intention of attending. Instead he remained behind with only Muir and a few park employees, who started preparing a camp at the base of one of the sequoias. They built a fire and sat around it, eating a simple supper, talking as twilight enveloped them, getting to know one another in the glow of the blaze.

"The night was clear," Roosevelt wrote, and "in the darkening aisles of the great sequoia grove . . . the majestic trunks, beautiful in color and symmetry, rose round us like the pillars of a mightier cathedral than ever was conceived even by the fervor of the Middle Ages. Hermit thrushes sang beautifully in the evening." Roosevelt would later remark that "Muir cared little for birds or bird songs"—a failing the ornithologist-president found noteworthy. Muir, in turn, could not help commenting on the President's well-earned reputation for hunting. "Mr. Roosevelt," he asked, "when are you going to get beyond the boyishness of killing things?"

But it quickly became clear that under the darkening canopy of ancient trees, a deep friendship was being born. "I had a perfectly glorious time," Muir wrote his wife.

> *I never before had a more interesting, hearty, and manly companion. I stuffed him pretty well regarding the timber thieves, the destructive work of the lumbermen, and other spoilers of the forest.*

TWO CHAMPIONS OF THE PARKS: In the midst of what may have been the most extraordinary camping trip in American history, Roosevelt and Muir admire the view of Yosemite Valley from Glacier Point.

Long after sundown, with no tent and only a pile of army blankets for comfort and warmth, the two men finally went to sleep. The next morning at 6:30 they saddled up for the long ride to Yosemite Valley, with the guide under strict orders from the president to avoid at all costs the Wawona Hotel and the delegation of officials he had jilted the night before.

In the high country near Glacier Point, with its spectacular panorama of the valley and its waterfalls arrayed at their feet, they stopped and once more made camp. Then, their guide, Charlie Leidig, reported, they resumed their exchange of opinions and ideas.

> *Around the campfire Roosevelt and Muir talked far into the night regarding Muir's glacial theory of the formation of Yosemite Valley. They also talked a great deal about the protection of forests in general and Yosemite in particular. I heard them discussing the setting aside of other areas in the United States for park purposes.*

"There was some difficulty in their campfire conversation," Leidig added, "because both men wanted to do the talking."

They awoke the next morning covered by a light snow that had fallen in the high country during the night. Rather than feeling inconvenienced, Roosevelt couldn't have been more thrilled. "We slept in a snowstorm last night!" he exclaimed to the crowds that been patiently waiting for him on the valley floor. "This has been the grandest day of my life."

Hundreds of tourists had crowded into the valley's hotels or established campsites in the meadows, all in hopes of seeing the president. The board of commissioners in charge of the Yosemite Grant, already jealous of the way Muir had seemingly monopolized Roosevelt's visit so far, planned to make up for lost time. They had prepared a lavish banquet catered by a French chef borrowed from a swank San Francisco club, to be followed by $400 worth of fireworks, and then a grand illumination of Yosemite Falls by special calcium searchlights. A comfortable bed with a cozy feather mattress was waiting in an artist's studio that had been specially fitted out for the president's private lodging.

Roosevelt would have none of it. He paused long enough to shake some hands and talk for a few minutes with his disappointed hosts, and then mounted up and rode farther down the valley to camp one last night with Muir—this time in the meadows between Bridalveil Falls and the massive granite face of El Capitan. Early the next morning, the wagon train of dignitaries, with its military escort, rushed the president back to the Raymond train station for the resumption of his cross-country tour, while Muir returned home to his writing.

"Camping with the President was a remarkable experience," Muir told a friend. "I fairly fell in love with him." Roosevelt, too, was changed by the experience. "When he reached the Mariposa Grove of Big Trees [last] Friday evening the President was a tired, worried man," the *San Francisco Call* reported. "This evening he is bright, alert—the Roosevelt of old."

And when the president spoke at the state capitol in Sacramento a day later, Roosevelt's words sounded as if they could have come from the lips of John Muir.

Lying out at night under those Sequoias was lying in a temple built by no hand of man, a temple grander than any human architect could by any possibility build, and I hope for the preservation of the groves of giant trees simply because it would be a shame to our civilization to let them disappear.

They are monuments in themselves. . . . I want them preserved.

I am impressed by the immensely greater greatness that lies in the future, and I ask that your marvelous natural resources be handed on unimpaired to your posterity.

We are not building this country of ours for a day. It is to last through the ages.

Within three years, the California legislature and United States Congress approved the transfer of the Yosemite Valley and Mariposa Grove back to the federal government. Yosemite National Park now encompassed almost everything Muir had been fighting for. "Sound the timbrel," he wrote a friend, "and let every Yosemite tree and stream rejoice!"

I am now an experienced lobbyist; my political education is complete. Have attended Legislature, made speeches, explained, exhorted, persuaded every mother's son of the legislators, newspaper reporters, and everybody else who would listen to me.

And now that the fight is finished and my education as a politician and lobbyist is finished, I am almost finished myself.

A WOMAN'S PARK

By 1903, no one had done more to advertise the cliff dwellings of Mesa Verde than Virginia Donaghe McClurg, a well-known writer, poet, and lecturer with a seemingly boundless determination to leave her mark on the world, and a flair for self-promotion to make sure it happened.

McClurg had first visited Mesa Verde in the 1880s and, after writing a series of flowery newspaper accounts about its marvels, went on a nationwide lecture tour with her husband, in which she illustrated her talks with glass slides, shown with a gas lantern projector.

In 1897 she had persuaded the Colorado State Federation of Women to authorize a special committee, with McClurg as chairwoman, to press for greater protection of the area; three years later, in a meeting held in her home in Colorado Springs, her committee had reorganized itself as a separate group: the Colorado Cliff Dwellings Association, whose emblem carried the Latin words *Dux Feminina Facti*—"the women lead the way." McClurg assumed the title of regent general and now threw herself into the work with redoubled zeal.

We shall live to see Mesa Verde Park the [principal attraction] of the nation; unique, unrivalled. We shall hear those who scoffed admit that not in her mines, scenery, agriculture, or health values lie Colorado's greatest interest and wealth—but in her Cliff Dwelling Park.

. . . We must not fail, for much is expected of us.

McClurg organized petitions, wrote personal letters to the president, and encouraged other women's groups across the nation to do the same. Part of her own home was converted into what she called her "Indian room," where she hosted afternoon teas for prominent women and wealthy tourists stopping by on their way to Mesa Verde.

She built up the association's ranks and treasury with a two dollar initiation fee and one dollar annual membership; for a hundred dollars a woman received a lifetime membership that could be passed down to her daughter. Association projects—building a road up to the mesa and developing a spring to provide

Virginia Donaghe McClurg

McClurg's efforts to save Cliff Palace (right) and other ruins in Mesa Verde relied on the activism of women's clubs in Colorado and across the nation.

water for weary travelers at Spruce Tree House—were financed by a call for 10 cent contributions from the public, and a rummage sale that McClurg called "an undertaking which demands more heroism than a Boston tea party, and more endurance than an anthracite coal strike."

She returned to the lecture tour, even promoting Mesa Verde in Paris with a speech in French. And when the National Irrigation Congress offered a $50 prize for the best ode to irrigation, she wrote a poem that called the ancient Puebloans the nation's first irrigators—and claimed first place. Later, it was set to music and sung in Madison Square Garden by the Mormon Tabernacle Choir.

Everywhere she went and in everything she wrote, McClurg emphasized the dangers of inaction with colorful, if slightly exaggerated examples.

Because of [their] abundant relics; because of the fame of the Cliff dwellings, the treasures of Mesa Verde . . . fell an early prey to the destroyers whom hitherto our Government has suffered, unchecked.

Farmers carted away ancient stone walls piece meal with which to line irrigating ditches; cowboys dug out coiled ware jars, set them in rows and beguiled Sunday afternoon leisure by peppering at them in lieu of tin cans; the relic hunter . . . separated relics from their environment (thus rendering them valueless to science) and bartered them for groceries or tobacco.

Her efforts began to pay off, as support for protecting Mesa Verde became a national cause. But just when Congress seemed ready to act and create a new national park, it became clear that McClurg had developed a different vision of how Mesa Verde should be preserved. "Let this be a woman's park," she said, with her and her association in charge of it.

McClurg listed a variety of reasons. The area was too small for a national park, she argued; the Secretary of the Interior might allow too many institutions to excavate in the ruins; Coloradoans would be giving up control of their "birthright." She pushed a last-minute alternative that would give the park to the state, which would turn it over to her association.

I do not see . . . why this small and compact tract . . . in the proposed park (which can be made self-supporting) should not be under the protective care of a body of 125 women, with hereditary membership, who know more about the matter and care more about the matter than anyone else.

Twice, McClurg even negotiated leases between her group and the Ute Indians—only to have the federal government remind her that private citizens couldn't make treaties. The uproar she created threatened to derail the bill in Congress at the very moment it seemed headed for passage. Even some of her closest allies now suspected that Virginia McClurg had lost sight of the real goal.

Lucy Peabody of Denver, the association's vice regent, had done much of the group's quiet organizational work over the years, preferring to get results

*I saw a little city of stone, asleep . . .
pale little houses of stone nestling
close to one another, perched on
top of each other, with flat roofs,
narrow windows, straight walls. . . .*

*Such silence and stillness and
repose—immortal with the
calmness of eternity. . . . It was
more like sculpture than anything
else. I knew at once that I had
come upon the city of some extinct
civilization, hidden away in this
inaccessible mesa for centuries,
preserved in the dry air and almost
perpetual sunlight like a fly in
amber.*

WILLA CATHER

Square Tower House ruins, Mesa Verde National Park

rather than grab headlines. But she wholeheartedly believed that only as a national park could Mesa Verde be properly saved for future generations.

It must come to be understood that we as a nation should be proud of these prehistoric ruins which offer as great a field to the archaeologist as the famed Egyptian ruins.

Let us leave to posterity as a result of the club movement the restoration and preservation of the cliff dwellings of our state which will in time be famous both historically and artistically and we may feel assured that our energy will not have been spent in vain.

McClurg called an emergency meeting at her home in Colorado Springs and engineered a vote—21 to 14—placing the Cliff Dwellings Association officially against the national park idea. Peabody felt compelled to resign from the association; and with her went many other members, including some of the group's most nationally prominent women. McClurg, once the darling of the press, found herself disparaged in newspaper editorials, which now overwhelmingly supported Peabody's position. The bill in Congress passed, and on June 29, 1906, President Roosevelt signed the law creating Mesa Verde National Park.

Virginia McClurg, who had wanted it to be "a woman's park," never recovered from the setback. She tried to get her husband appointed as the park's first superintendent; someone else got the job. When she gave her name and support to a tourist attraction called Manitou Springs—a faked re-creation of Mesa Verde's cliff dwellings—even more members of the association she had founded resigned in disgust. Later she wrote, directed, and starred in a pageant called "The Marriage of the Dawn and the Moon," allegedly based on a Hopi Indian legend and staged in the park's Spruce Tree House in hopes that a film version of it would publicize Colorado's great prehistoric treasures. It flopped.

Lucy Peabody, on the other hand, who had never sought the spotlight, would receive honors and accolades for the work she had done. "The whole nation," one newspaper wrote, "owes her a debt of gratitude." Another predicted she would always be

MISS COLORADO: "THEY'LL BE SAFER IN YOUR CARE, UNCLE!"

remembered as "the Mother of Mesa Verde National Park." With her success, the park idea had broadened. Mesa Verde was the first national park of its kind, meant to celebrate not majestic scenery, but a prehistoric culture and its people.

ANASAZI

If destruction of the cliff-houses of New Mexico, Colorado, and Arizona goes on at the same rate in the next fifty years that it has in the past, these unique dwellings will be practically destroyed, and unless laws are enacted . . . for their protection, at the close of the twentieth century many of the most interesting monuments of the prehistoric peoples of our Southwest will be little more than mounds of debris at the bases of cliffs.

. . . It would be wise legislation to prevent this vandalism as much as possible and good science to put all excavation of ruins in trained hands.

DR. JESSE WALTER FEWKES
American Anthropological Association

When Mesa Verde finally became a national park (top), rather than a state park managed by a women's club, the credit belonged to Lucy Peabody (above), who had broken with her friend Virginia McClurg over the issue.

Mesa Verde had been saved, but there were many other important prehistoric ruins scattered throughout the Southwest—with no law to protect them from the intensifying search for evidence of what was called America's "lost civilization."

Settlement was growing across the region, and with it the number of local residents moonlighting as pothunters. Wealthy private collectors added to the demand. And every museum and prestigious university now wanted its own collection of relics from a site excavated and studied by its own professionals in the young fields of anthropology and archaeology, who eyed each other with fierce jealousy.

In the midst of it all stood Richard Wetherill, the cowboy who had first brought Mesa Verde to the nation's attention and then uncovered a string of important ancient sites in three other states. Now he was at Chaco Canyon in New Mexico, living with his new wife, Marietta Palmer, who seemed to love the

massive ruin of Pueblo Bonito as much as her husband did. "I don't think I'll ever be happy anywhere else," she had told him.

Supervising the extensive excavations he had started on behalf of the Hyde Exploring Expedition, Wetherill employed up to one hundred Navajos in the work. He learned their language and started a trading post that soon began purchasing their handiwork—especially the distinctive Navajo blankets—for sale in stores back East. Because of his interest in the ruins, they all called him "Anasazi," the name the Navajos used for the ancestral Puebloans. (Roughly translated, it means "enemy ancestors" and for many years was the accepted term for the people who had built the magnificent structures.)

It had been immediately clear to Wetherill that Chaco was as important a site as Mesa Verde, and despite his lack of formal training, he tried to carry on his work as carefully as possible. "The work we do

Marietta Palmer Wetherill (center, standing by stove) set up temporary housekeeping next to Chaco Canyon's Pueblo Bonito until her husband, Richard, could build them a home with a roof.

must stand the most rigid inspection," he wrote to his partners, "and we do not want to do it in such a manner that anyone in the future can pick flaws with it."

But professional archaeologists still considered him a pothunter. Now, as the relics he was unearthing at Chaco Canyon reached his partners in the East—fifty thousand pieces of turquoise, ten thousand pieces of pottery, five thousand stone implements, and much more, gleaned from the excavation of 190 rooms at Pueblo Bonito—the professional community called him a vandal. And when they learned that he had filed for a homestead among the ruins at Chaco Canyon, they grew even more indignant and insisted on a government investigation.

Two separate inspectors, however, concluded that Wetherill was doing his work under the general directions of Dr. Frederic Ward Putnam of the American Museum of Natural History, and all of the recovered items were being turned over to the museum, with none of them sold individually. As for his homestead claim, Wetherill submitted affidavits swearing he considered it the only way to protect the ruins from other people intent on vandalizing them. He said he would gladly turn over any portions of the land with ruins on them, if the federal government wanted them.

Having spent many years of [my] life in exploring ruins of the Southwest [I have] only a desire to see the work carried on in a scientific manner and it is entirely proper that it should be under Government supervision.

[Chaco Canyon] should be owned and protected by the Government of the United States under some appropriate reservation or park.

But the drumbeat against Wetherill in the East was too strong. The General Land Office used a technicality to notify him his homestead application was suspended, while the Interior Department was pressured to order the Hyde Exploring Expedition to cease all operations at Pueblo Bonito.

Ironically, the furor over Wetherill's excavations at Chaco Canyon prodded Congress into doing exactly what he had proposed. Since the turn of the century, Representative John Lacey had been pushing unsuccessfully for some kind of legal protections for ancient ruins; now he seized the moment to pass the Act for the Preservation of American Antiquities, making any unauthorized disturbance of a prehistoric ruin a federal crime. More than that, in order to allow the government to respond quickly to potential threats against any particular site, the Antiquities Act granted the president an extraordinary power: the exclusive authority—without any congressional approval—to preserve places that would be called, not national parks, but national monuments.

Included in Lacey's final bill were two seemingly minor changes in language that no one at the time conceived would one day make it perhaps the most important conservation law in American history. In addition to the "historic landmarks and historic and prehistoric structures" that could be set aside as national monuments, the bill provided protection for "other objects of historic or scientific interest." This loosely worded phrase was thrown in at the last minute, and an earlier restriction confining the size of national monuments to no more than 640 acres was reworded to say, "the smallest area compatible with proper care and management of the objects to be protected."

The Antiquities Act moved through Congress at roughly the same time as the bill creating Mesa Verde National Park. President Roosevelt signed it on June 8, 1906. Three months later he proclaimed the first national monument: a unique mass of grooved rock called Devils Tower, sacred to several Indian tribes, rising nearly nine hundred feet above the plains of eastern Wyoming. Then he named El Morro National Monument in New Mexico—a rock abutment bearing prehistoric Indian petroglyphs, as well as the inscriptions of early Spanish expeditions that had come north from Mexico three hundred years earlier and founded a colony fifteen years before the Pilgrims landed at Plymouth Rock. And on March 11, 1907, he did exactly what Richard Wetherill had wanted by creating Chaco Canyon National Monument.

Before he was done, Roosevelt would use the Antiquities Act to proclaim eighteen national monuments, including several, like California's Lassen Peak and Washington state's Mount Olympus, that would one day become national parks. North of San Francisco, he also set aside an endangered grove of

Devils Tower in northeastern Wyoming (top) was Roosevelt's and the nation's first national monument, in 1906; the old Spanish mission at Tumacácori in southern Arizona (bottom) was saved by Roosevelt in 1908.

coastal redwoods, purchased and saved from destruction by California Congressman William Kent, given to the United States under another provision of the Antiquities Act, and named in honor of the man who had first introduced Roosevelt to the giant trees: Muir Woods National Monument.

Meanwhile, just as he had promised, Richard Wetherill readily relinquished any claims to the ruins at Chaco Canyon, once it was protected as a national monument. The government lifted its suspension of his homestead filing and encouraged him to continue improving those acres for final ownership. But bureaucratic delays occurred, and the patent on his

Also among the eighteen national monuments Roosevelt unilaterally preserved using the Antiquities Act were Muir Woods (left) outside San Francisco, and Natural Bridges (below) in southern Utah.

land would not arrive until 1912, by which time Wetherill could not receive it. Two years earlier, a new Indian agent among the Navajos became jealous of Wetherill's close ties with the Chaco Canyon Indians and told them that with Wetherill back in the cattle business, his cows would soon push their sheep off all the available grass. One of them believed it enough to kill the man they all called "Anasazi."

Less than a year after Mr. Wetherill died I moved from Pueblo Bonito . . . [and] I was a gypsy the rest of my life. . . . [But] Chaco Canyon still haunted me.

I want . . . the world [to] give Mr. Wetherill credit for what he did . . . and the sort of person he was.

I will tell you this: if we could put the time back and I was a girl again, there is no man I would want to marry but Mr. Wetherill.

MARIETTA PALMER WETHERILL

OUR CHILDREN'S CHILDREN

There is nothing more practical than the preservation of beauty, than the preservation of anything that appeals to the higher emotions of mankind.

I believe we are past the stage of national existence when we could look on complacently at the individual who skinned the land and was content for the sake of three years' profit for himself to leave a desert for the children of those who were to inherit the soil.

THEODORE ROOSEVELT

For Theodore Roosevelt, conservation became one of the defining causes of his presidency. He was the first American president to use the word "conservation" in an annual message to Congress; the first to convene a White House conference on preserving America's natural heritage, where he delivered a speech entitled "Conservation as a National Duty"; the first to use the Antiquities Act.

Before his presidency was over, he would create fifty-one federal bird sanctuaries, four national game refuges, eighteen national monuments, and, often in the face of fierce congressional opposition, 100 million acres' worth of national forests. Under his leadership, more than 280,000 square miles of federal land—an area larger than the state of Texas—would be placed under one kind of conservation protection or another.

Roosevelt also added five new national parks, including Mesa Verde and Oregon's Crater Lake. Two others—Platt National Park in Oklahoma and Sullys Hill National Park in North Dakota, pushed through Congress by local promoters, despite their small size and lack of distinctive features—would be redesignated by later Congresses as a recreation area and a game preserve, respectively.

Roosevelt's fifth national park was in South Dakota, at a place where the Lakotas say human beings and the buffalo first emerged from the subterranean depths of the sacred Black Hills. In 1881 two white men heard a strange whistling sound that drew them to a hole in the ground. The wind coming out of it reportedly blew one man's hat off his head and then later sucked the hat out of his hands. It turned out to be an entrance to a cave—a labyrinth of natural tunnels and passageways extending more than a hundred miles through thick beds of limestone, the fourth longest cave in the world. Changes in barometric pressure pushed and pulled the air inside as if the cave were breathing. White settlers called it Wind Cave.

After making a visit there, Representative Lacey proclaimed it "substantially what the Yellowstone country would be if the geysers should die." "This tract of land ought to be reserved to the American people," he told his fellow congressmen, and he would not quit until they agreed with him by creating Wind Cave National Park, the world's first underground park.

Early visitors, candles in hand, gather around the Stars and Stripes in Wind Cave's Grand Army of the Republic Hall.

THIS WONDERFUL LAKE

William Gladstone Steel (insert) and the "sunken lake" (above) he worked tirelessly to protect. *Overleaf:* Crater Lake National Park in winter

Back in 1870, a fifteen-year-old boy in Kansas was idly skimming through the newspaper that had been used to wrap his lunch when he came across an article about a mysterious "sunken lake" in Oregon. He vowed to visit it some day. Fifteen years later, in 1885, William Gladstone Steel finally got there.

Imagine a vast mountain six by seven miles through, at an elevation of eight thousand feet, with the top removed and the inside hollowed out, then filled with the clearest water in the world, to within two thousand feet of the top . . . and you have a perfect representation of Crater Lake.

When a volcanic eruption, witnessed by the ancestors of the Klamath Indians, blew the top off a mountain peak in the Cascades 7,700 years ago, the hole that was left began slowly filling with each year's rainfall and snowmelt. The result was Crater Lake, which reaches a depth of nearly 1,943 feet, making it the deepest lake in America. Because of the lack of sediment suspended in its waters, the lake is also the world's clearest—an eight-inch disk lowered into its sky blue waters is still visible 142 feet beneath the surface.

William Steel resolved that it should be protected forever, just like Yellowstone and the other parks. That quest took him another seventeen years of tireless promotion and

lobbying before he finally succeeded in 1902, when Crater Lake became the nation's sixth national park. Steel was ecstatic.

My heart bounds with joy and gladness, for I realize that I have been the cause of opening up this wonderful lake for the pleasure of mankind, millions of whom will come and enjoy and unborn genera- tions will profit by its glories.

Later, Steel was named superintendent of the park and would be involved in its affairs until his death in 1934, sixty-four years after the accidental lunchtime reading that had changed his life—and park history—forever.

In 1905, John Muir's life had been beset by sorrow. His devoted wife, Louie, died of lung cancer, and he buried her next to her parents near an orchard on their farm in Martinez, California. President Roosevelt, who had lost a wife himself as a young man and found solace in the open spaces of the West, sent his personal condolences. "Get out among the mountains and trees, friend," he wrote. "They will do more for you than either man or woman could."

But the aging mountaineer could not retreat to his beloved Sierras. His daughter Helen was suffering from repeated bouts of pneumonia, and her doctor insisted that her only chance of recovering was a year in the desert. Muir and both daughters took up residence in a rambling hotel at Adamana, Arizona, a lonely coal and water stop on the Atchison, Topeka, and Santa Fe Railway. Helen slept each night in a tent in the hotel's backyard, while her worried father grieved.

To pass the time, Muir began exploring the surrounding area and discovered that in fact he was once again in a majestic forest—only *this* one was more than 200 million years old, and all of the trees had long ago fossilized into solid rock. It was the Petrified Forest.

Soon, Muir was himself again, leading his daughters—and sometimes total strangers—on long walks through the tumbled and broken stone.

The man of science, the naturalist, too often loses sight of the essential one-ness of all living beings in seeking to classify them in kingdoms, orders . . . species . . . etc. . . . while the eye of the Poet, the Seer, never closes on the kinship of all God's creatures, and his heart ever beats in sympathy with great and small alike as "earth-born compan-ions and fellow mortals" equally depen-dent on Heaven's eternal love.

By 1906, in what he now called "these enchanted carboniferous forests," he loved nothing more than to sit near the trunk of a petrified tree and inspect it minutely with a magnifying glass.

But even this forest was endangered. Scavengers used dynamite to blow up large logs in hopes of finding amethyst crystals inside

At Petrified Forest in Arizona, John Muir (above) became fascinated with trees that were more than 200 million years old and were now solid rock (below).
Preceding pages: Stone logs lie strewn across the landscape at Petrified Forest National Park.

them. Boxcar-loads of petrified wood were being shipped east to be made into tabletops and mantelpieces. At Adamana, an enormous stone crusher was being constructed to pulver-ize the logs for use as industrial abrasives.

Muir's old fervor for preservation was reignited. For years, John Lacey had been trying to protect the area by making it a national park. Congress would not go along. But Muir knew somebody who now could save his enchanted forest with a stroke of his pen.

On December 8, 1906, President Roosevelt invoked the Antiquities Act again, and Petrified Forest National Monument was created. Fifty-six years later, it would become a national park.

A region which should be set aside as a national park without delay is the Grand Canyon of the Colorado. It is true that the puny efforts of man cannot do much to injure such stupendous natural works as have here been wrought. Nevertheless the Grand Canyon ought to be under the control of the Government and properly protected by it.

President Roosevelt has more than once expressed an earnest desire that [it] should be made a National Park, but he recognizes, as every one must, that the demand for such legislation must come from the people of the regions where these areas are situated.

GEORGE BIRD GRINNELL

National parks, Roosevelt said, "represent one of the best bits of National achievement which our people have to their credit of recent years . . . where bits of the old wilderness scenery and the old wilderness

"Leave it as it is," President Roosevelt (below, second from left) said of the Grand Canyon during his first visit in 1903. He wanted the canyon preserved as a national park, but local opposition kept Congress from acting. Once more, Roosevelt turned to the Antiquities Act.

life are to be kept unspoiled for the benefit of our children's children." He wanted one more park added to his list: the Grand Canyon. Because of local opposition, however, Congress refused.

Despite Roosevelt's admonition during his visit in 1903 to keep the canyon's rim pristine and clear of any buildings, a hotel and other structures had been built there. A local politician announced plans to operate a railroad with its tracks so close to the edge of the canyon that passengers could do some sightseeing without leaving their seats. Miners were filing claims and ranchers were grazing cattle all along the rim.

Roosevelt looked for some way to prevent the Grand Canyon from becoming another overdeveloped and overcommercialized Niagara Falls. He found his solution in the loose phrases of the Antiquities Act. It allowed protection of places of "scientific interest," and although it had originally been aimed at only small-sized parcels—most of the previous national monuments Roosevelt had created so far ranged in size from 160 to five thousand acres—the act did not absolutely restrict the number of acres a president could set aside.

And so, on January 11, 1908, declaring the Grand Canyon "an object of unusual scientific interest, being the greatest eroded canyon within the United States," Roosevelt declared 806,400 acres, an area larger than Rhode Island, a national monument. It would not enjoy the same protections as a national park, but it was a step in the right direction—and the beginning of a larger fight that would last more than a decade.

Politicians in Arizona were outraged and threatened to challenge the president in court. Members of Congress grumbled that the president had overstepped his authority. Roosevelt ignored them all.

Surely our people do not understand even yet the rich heritage that is theirs. There can be nothing in the world more beautiful than the Yosemite, the groves of giant sequoias and redwoods, the Canyon of the Colorado, the Canyon of the Yellowstone, the Three Tetons; and our people should see to it that they are preserved for their children and their children's children forever, with their majestic beauty all unmarred.

THE CROWN OF THE CONTINENT

Forest reserves are good and useful, but their purpose is wholly utilitarian. Their game may be hunted; cattle may be grazed on them; settlers may take up claims on non-forested areas within their borders; prospectors may run over them, sinking holes for minerals, or washing the gravel bars and running the mud into their streams.

In the few National Parks which we possess, on the other hand, these utilitarian pursuits are forbidden. Like the parks in our great cities, they are set aside as breathing places for the people, pleasure grounds which every one may visit and enjoy with the utmost freedom, so long as he does not encroach on the rights of his fellows.

GEORGE BIRD GRINNELL

By 1909, George Bird Grinnell was sixty years old and had devoted most of his adult life to the emerging conservation movement. But now his energies were focused on the northern reach of the Rockies, on the border of Montana and Canada—remote, rugged, and haunting, where glaciers could still be found sculpting and polishing mountains that rise to elevations of ten thousand feet above sea level; alpine cascades feed into more than 650 crystalline lakes; a home to grizzly bears, bighorn sheep, and mountain goats.

It had become Grinnell's favorite spot in the entire nation, and he treasured it almost as if it were his own. It was, he wrote, "the Crown of the Continent . . . one of the most beautiful mountain regions in the world."

How often, in dreams of the night or day, have I revisited these scenes during the years that have past. . . . How often, in fancy, have I seated myself on some rock . . . and gazed over the beautiful scene!

Few people know these wonderful mountains, yet no one who goes there but comes away filled with enthusiasm for their wild and singular beauty.

Grinnell Glacier feeds into Grinnell Lake, c. 1910.

No white man knew the region more intimately than Grinnell, who had been visiting it almost yearly since 1885. Combing through its jumble of mountain peaks and valleys, living off the game he and his companions shot for food, he had drawn and published some of its earliest maps and given names to many of its features—Singleshot and Going-to-the-Sun mountains, Cataract and Swiftcurrent creeks. A young army lieutenant along on one trip had attached Grinnell's name to a lake and a glacier, in honor of his explorations. As early as 1891, Grinnell had written in his journal that this should be a national park.

Na'pi, the Old Man, came down from his home in the sun to help his people, the Blackfeet. When his work was done, he went up into the mountains, where he came to two lakes. There, he said to himself, "I believe I will go up on that highest mountain and change myself into stone."

In the crevice in the mountain he lay down, with just his face peeking out, and turned himself into a rock. He is still there . . . watching for people to come looking for him.

For centuries, the Blackfeet Indians had claimed the land as their own. They lived on the plains just east of the solitary peak they called Chief Mountain, where they could hunt the buffalo they depended upon for survival. For them, the mountains provided other game as well as a sacred place for vision quests and spiritual nourishment.

Grinnell had become their good friend, just as he had to the Pawnees and the Cheyennes years earlier. He studied their beliefs and their way of life, treated them with respect, intervened on their behalf when he learned a corrupt Indian agent had withheld government rations and allowed white ranchers to graze on reservation lands. In gratitude, the Blackfeet made him an honorary member of the tribe and gave him the name "Fisher Hat."

Then a mining boom erupted in the northern Rockies and hundreds of prospectors began openly trespassing into the mountain portion of the Blackfeet reservation. Rather than enforcing the Indians' treaty rights, the government decided the easiest solution would be to buy the land from the Black-

feet. Grinnell was asked to help negotiate a new treaty.

At first he declined. "The only motive that can influence me in this matter is the good of the Indians," he said. But he eventually changed his mind, figuring that if a boundary change was inevitable, perhaps he could at least help arrange a more favorable price for the Blackfeet. Once the negotiations began, however, Grinnell found his loyalties divided. His zeal for a park turned out to be greater than his concern for the Blackfeet's bargaining position. He used his standing with the tribe to persuade them to sign the new treaty for a price they had originally turned down. "The mountains have been my last refuge," a chief named White Calf said. "Chief Mountain is my head. Now my head is cut off."

Two years later, in 1897, Grinnell parlayed his national reputation and political connections into persuading Washington to set the area aside as the Lewis and Clark Forest Preserve. Then he immediately set about trying to convince Congress to take the extra step of turning it into a national park. This time white residents in the area stood in his way. They wanted to continue filing settlement claims around the scenic lakes, to hunt in the mountains,

George Bird Grinnell and his friend Two Moon. Few white men of the time were as genuinely interested in the lives of Native Americans, or as sympathetic to their plight, but Grinnell's zeal for a new park on Blackfeet land was even stronger.

and to have lumber companies cut timber on the land—all of which were permitted in Gifford Pinchot's national forests, but prohibited in national parks. "There may be some local people who favor the park plan," the Kalispell *Inter Lake* reported, "but we have observed only two." Years passed, but as different bills were proposed and then died in Congress, Grinnell kept at it, until he finally succeeded with the creation of Glacier National Park in 1910.

With that behind him, he sold *Forest and Stream* and focused his writings instead on compiling the stories of the Blackfeet and Cheyenne and Pawnee, turning out books—still considered classics—about their culture and history from the Indians' point of view. He advocated game preserves to be carved out of national forests. He suggested that a national park be established somewhere in the Appalachians, and he pushed for the national monuments at the Grand Canyon and Olympic Peninsula to be turned into national parks.

All the while, he kept returning to Glacier—the place, he admitted in a letter, he had once considered his "private estate." He would complain about hotel prices, argue with a park employee who refused to let him take a horse into the backcountry without a hired guide, and laugh when a tourist he met on a

train described the park in enthusiastic detail and suggested Grinnell ought to go see it.

When he learned that a trail was being made to the glacier that bears his name, Grinnell was pleased at first. But as he conducted a firsthand inspection and climbed to the river of ice, which had been slowly but steadily retreating back up the mountain since he had first discovered it a quarter of a century earlier, he grew wistful about the whole experience.

I knew that if this was made a National Park that fact would mean my practical expulsion from the region. . . . [Although Yellowstone and Glacier have been] ruined by the tourists . . . if we had not succeeded in getting these regions set apart as National Parks, by this time they would have been . . . cut bare of timber, dotted with irrigation reservoirs, the game would have all been killed off, the country would have been burned over.

"The scenery was as beautiful as ever," Grinnell told a friend after one visit, "but the crowds there were larger than usual and I became rather weary of the place after a time.

"But after all," he added, "that is what the Park is for—the benefit of the people."

In 1910, Grinnell's dream was realized with the creation of Glacier National Park, although the influx of tourists (below) made him yearn sometimes for the days when just he and the Blackfeet had the place to themselves.

If we treat these natural things solely as commercial assets and turn them into dollars and cents, we expend and destroy them. Their use is ended. They leave nothing behind them.

If we preserve them, they reproduce themselves, retain their value for recreation, and will yield to us and to our children a never ending income in health, strength and pleasure.

Preserved, they are everlasting; consumed and destroyed, their value is gone for all time.

GEORGE BIRD GRINNELL

Sunset over St. Mary Lake and Wild Goose Island,
Glacier National Park

THE DEVIL AND HIS RELATIONS

The very first reservation that ever was made in this world . . . contained only one tree—the smallest reservation that ever was made. Yet, no sooner was it made than it was attacked by everybody in the world—the devil, one woman and one man.

This has been the history of every reservation that has been made since that time; that is, as soon as a reservation is once created then the thieves and the devil and his relations come forward to attack it.

JOHN MUIR

Since the start of the twentieth century, the city of San Francisco had been looking for a better supply of water to fuel its growth. And it had set its sights on the Tuolumne River and the Hetch Hetchy Valley as the perfect place for a dam and reservoir—a narrow valley with a flat bottom and high granite walls on both sides, and remote enough to ensure that the waters trapped from the yearly Sierra runoff would stay pure.

The fact that it was within the boundaries of Yosemite National Park only added to its attractiveness to city planners: no competing claims to water rights existed, and the only "landowner" to deal with was the federal government. Damming and flooding Hetch Hetchy would be cheaper and easier than finding alternative sites.

But to John Muir, allowing a dam in any national park would betray the parks' very purpose and set a dangerous precedent for the future.

That any one would try to destroy such a place seems incredible; but sad experience shows that there are people good enough and bad enough for anything. . . .

Their arguments are curiously like those of the devil, devised for the destruction of the first garden. . . . Few of their statements are even partly true, and all are misleading.

Even worse in Muir's eyes, Hetch Hetchy was among his favorite places in Yosemite. With its own majestic waterfalls and massive granite faces, it had all the beauty of the more famous Yosemite Valley

twenty miles to the south, he said, without the clutter of tourist hotels. When he had helped draw the boundary lines for the national park back in 1890, he had deliberately included Hetch Hetchy as one of the principal features. He called it "a grand landscape garden . . . one of Nature's rarest and most precious mountain temples." Now it was imperiled.

These temple destroyers, devotees of ravaging commercialism, seem to have a perfect contempt for Nature, and, instead of lifting their eyes to the God of the mountains, lift them to the Almighty Dollar.

Dam Hetch Hetchy! As well dam for water-tanks the people's cathedrals and churches, for no holier temple has ever been consecrated by the heart of man.

At first, Muir's view had prevailed. Theodore Roosevelt's Secretary of the Interior, Ethan Allen Hitchcock, turned down San Francisco's application three different times, on the grounds that the project would violate the intent of creating the park, in the first place, and that other sites should be investigated for a city reservoir.

Then, on April 18, 1906, a tremendous earthquake had shaken San Francisco, bringing down hundreds of buildings and igniting fires that consumed most of the city, killing thousands. With San Francisco reduced to ashes, politicians had redoubled their efforts for a reservoir at Hetch Hetchy, claiming—erroneously—that its water supply could have prevented the destruction. In a referendum, San Franciscans voted 7 to 1 in favor of the dam. The city's mayor, James D. Phelan, launched a campaign impugning Muir's motives for trying to obstruct the project. "John Muir loves the Sierras and roams at large, and is hypersensitive on the subject of the invasion of *his* territory," the mayor said. "The 400,000 people of San Francisco are suffering from bad water and ask Mr. Muir to cease his aesthetic quibbling."

Muir's own Sierra Club had split over the issue, with some prominent members advocating the dam. But the Appalachian Mountain Club joined his cause; so did George Bird Grinnell, the old champion of Yellowstone and Glacier national parks. "If this scheme can be carried through," Grinnell warned, "it is evident that no one of our national

John Muir (fourth from left) often enthralled audiences such as this one, on a Sierra Club outing in Yosemite National Park.

parks is safe. . . . If the Hetch-Hetchy Valley is to be destroyed we may look after a while to see power houses built in the Grand Canyon of the Yellowstone."

Meanwhile, an old nemesis of Muir's stepped forward on the city's behalf. As the nation's top forester and President Roosevelt's trusted adviser, Gifford Pinchot had become one of the most powerful men in Washington. At his urging, Roosevelt had reserved millions of acres of western land as national forests despite fierce congressional opposition. Pinchot steadfastly believed that conservation meant wise use of nature, not preserving it for its own sake, and he had never been a wholehearted supporter of national parks, let alone John Muir's unbending vision of protecting and expanding them. He believed that if San Francisco needed a new water supply, Yosemite National Park was a good place to get it. "I will stand ready to render any assistance which lies in my power," he promised officials in San Francisco. When a new Interior Department secretary, James Garfield, joined the administration, Pinchot began lobbying him for the dam and encouraged the city to apply once more.

In response, Muir took his case to the man with whom he had shared three magical nights in the park

Tourists admire the Hetch Hetchy Valley as they—and John Muir—wanted it to remain. Wapama Falls is visible in the background.

back in 1903, the outdoorsman he considered a friend and kindred spirit.

April 21, 1908. Dear Mr. President:

The few promoters of the present scheme . . . all show forth the proud set of confidence that comes of a good, sound, substantial, irrefragable ignorance.

Hetch-Hetchy . . . is . . . one of the most sublime and beautiful and important features of the Park, and to dam and submerge it would be hardly less destructive and deplorable . . . than would be the damming of Yosemite itself.

Faithfully and devotedly yours,
John Muir

My dear Mr. Muir:

Garfield and Pinchot are rather favorable to the Hetch Hetchy plan. . . . I have sent them your letter with a request for a report on it. I will do everything in my power to protect not only the Yosemite, which we have already protected, but other similar great natural beauties of this country; but you must remember that it is out of the question permanently to protect them unless we have a certain degree of friendliness toward them on the part of the people of the State in which they are situated. . . .

[S]o far everyone . . . has been for it and I have been in the disagreeable position of seeming to interfere with the development of the State for the sake of keeping a valley, which apparently hardly anyone wanted to have kept, under national control.

How I do wish I were again with you camping out under those great sequoias or in the snow under the silver firs!

Theodore Roosevelt

Pinchot was in Washington, and Muir was in California: in the end, Pinchot's view prevailed. Pending congressional approval, Secretary Garfield granted San Francisco's application, calling it "the greatest benefit to the greatest number" of people. President Roosevelt did nothing to stop it.

But the fight was not over. A year later, with Roosevelt out of the White House, the new president, William Howard Taft, came to California on his own tour of Yosemite, and to the dismay of San Francisco's politicians chose Muir as his guide. Before the visit ended, Taft decided to oppose the dam.

By 1913, however, yet another president had taken office—Woodrow Wilson—who chose as his Secretary of the Interior Franklin K. Lane, the former city attorney for San Francisco. Lane wasted no time getting the project back on track. Supporters of the dam passed out photographs, heavily retouched in the darkroom, purporting to show how a reservoir would make the valley more beautiful and create a tourist attraction for families to visit and enjoy. California newspapers clamored for the dam to be built and castigated Muir as a selfish contrarian for opposing it.

Muir was now seventy-five, and the long battle over Hetch Hetchy had taken its toll. Ten years earlier he had anticipated completing twenty books in his old age; because of what he called "this everlasting Hetch Hetchy business," he had managed to finish only two. "I wonder," he wrote his daughter, "if leaves feel lonely when they see their neighbors falling."

Still, he soldiered on—giving speeches, writing articles, urging anyone who would listen not to flood the exquisite valley. "I still think we can win," Muir told his daughter Helen in November of 1913, adding, "Anyhow I'll be relieved when it's settled, for it's killing me."

Three weeks later, the bill approving the dam cleared its final hurdle in Congress. President Wilson quickly signed it into law.

It was sorrowful indeed to see [Muir] sitting in his cobwebbed study in his lonely house . . . with the full force of his defeat upon him, after the struggle of a lifetime in the service of Hetch Hetchy. . . .

I could not but think that if Congress, the President, and even the San Francisco contingent, could have seen him, they would certainly have been willing to have delayed any action until the old man had gone away—and I fear that is going to be very soon, as he appeared to me to be breaking very fast.

Robert Marshall

A VALLEY ENTOMBED: The view of Hetch Hetchy Valley (left) once the dam was built. Wapama Falls still flows, but the part of Yosemite National Park that John Muir (right) considered "one of Nature's rarest and most precious mountain temples" is now buried under hundreds of feet of water. Losing the battle broke Muir's heart, but Hetch Hetchy would become a rallying point for future conservationists.

Exhausted and frail, a widower since his wife's death in 1905, Muir forced himself to finish a book on his travels in Alaska. He built new bookcases in the big and empty house he had once shared with Louie and their two children. He even had electricity installed for the first time. He tried to look to the future.

The battle for conservation will go on endlessly. It is part of the universal warfare between right and wrong.

Fortunately wrong cannot last, soon or late it must fall back home to Hades, while some compensating good must surely follow.

They will see what I meant in time. There must be places for human beings to satisfy their souls. Food and drink is not all. There is the spiritual. In some it is only a germ, of course, but the germ will grow!

But in December of 1914, he came down with pneumonia, which quickly progressed into double pneumonia. He died on Christmas Eve.

Theodore Roosevelt, the man who had become his friend and ally in the cause of conservation—and then broken Muir's heart over Hetch Hetchy—remembered him as "a dauntless soul . . . brimming over with friendliness and kindness."

Ordinarily, the man who loves the woods and the mountains, the trees, the flowers, and the wild things, has in him some indefinable quality of charm which appeals even to those sons of civilization who care for little outside of paved streets and brick walls. John Muir was a fine illustration of this rule.

Four years after Muir's death, the dam he had opposed with all his strength was completed, and the Hetch Hetchy Valley, whose tranquil meadows he had compared to a "landscape garden" and a "mountain temple," would slowly be entombed under hundreds of feet of water.

But Muir's fight had struck a chord in many Americans, who now wondered, if a lovely valley in Yosemite National Park could be turned into a water reservoir, were any national parks safe from being despoiled?

Meanwhile, a proposal that Muir had supported now began gaining greater ground across the nation: to create an agency within the federal government whose sole job would be to promote, administer, and protect the national parks—and make sure they fulfilled their lofty promise and endured for countless generations.

This grand show is eternal. It is always sunrise somewhere; the dew is never all dried at once; a shower is forever falling; vapor is ever rising. Eternal sunrise, eternal sunset, eternal dawn and gloaming, on sea and continents and islands, each in its turn, as the round earth rolls.

JOHN MUIR

TRANSCENDENCE

As a kid in an inner-city neighborhood in northwest Detroit, Shelton Johnson grew up about as far from the natural world as an American can get. When he entered a Master of Fine Arts program at the University of Michigan, his focus was creative writing, not history or nature. But on a whim he filled out an application for a summer job in Yellowstone, hoping to earn some money washing dishes at the Old Faithful Inn and thinking the park might be a quiet place for him to work on a manuscript. His life changed the moment he got off the bus at the park's north entrance gate.

Johnson has been working in national parks ever since—as a ranger in Yellowstone, Great Basin, National Capital Parks–East in Washington, D.C., and now Yosemite, where he shares the story of the African American Buffalo Soldiers, the park's first protectors. His Web site, Shadows in the Range of Light, *has helped him reach people beyond the park's borders, and his work has won him a regional Freeman Tilden Award, the highest honor given by the National Park Service for interpretation.*

What was the first experience in a national park like for you?

When I was a child in Detroit, national parks really didn't exist. There were no family trips to national parks. They really didn't exist for me and for my friends. We didn't sit around talking about, "Boy, I can't wait to get to the Grand Canyon." That didn't come up as a topic of conversation in Detroit for me as a child.

But always out there somewhere inside me there was this desire to see Yellowstone. There was a desire to see the Grand Canyon. That's a part of America that I didn't know and I wanted to become familiar with it.

Yellowstone was my first experience of a national park. It basically reconfigured my universe. I got off a bus in Gardiner, Montana, right outside the north entrance where there's that wonderful stone arch that says, "For the Benefit and Enjoyment of the People." And it doesn't say "For the Benefit and Enjoyment of *Some* of the People" or "a *Few* of the People." It means "*All* of the People." For me, that meant democracy; and for me, that meant I was welcome.

And as I was stepping down onto the ground, there was a bison—a two-thousand-pound animal—walking by. There was no one else around, and the bison was just strolling by. I looked up at the driver and I said, "Does this happen all the time?"

And he looked at me and said, "All the time." And I said to myself, "I've arrived." And to be honest with you, once I stepped off that bus, I never got back on.

What's the source of that transformational power?

National parks, for me, provide a doorway into a transcendent experience. A sense of something that's greater than yourself, a way of being that's greater than yourself. And often all you have to do is pay an entrance fee. You pay that fee and you pass over that threshold into that national park, and it's a place that's bigger than the name. It's a place, it's an experience that's beyond words.

So whenever someone enters a national park, it's like going to another world. It is going to a wonderland. And I think that people feel that transition. They feel that sense that they've gone to someplace better than what they've left behind. But the irony is that where they've gone is the place where they've always been. It's just now they understand it. Now they see it. Now they feel it. Because parks are like going home.

You're describing a feeling of transcendence.

Yes, it's transcendent, just as walking into a cathedral is transcendent. But what could be more cathedral in feel than the Grand

A young Shelton Johnson with his parents in Detroit (above) and portraying a Buffalo Soldier in Yosemite (right)

Canyon or Yosemite Valley? John Muir, I think he thought it was somewhat ironic that there's a chapel in Yosemite Valley because you're building a church in the greatest cathedral in America. And I think that when people go into these spaces they find if they have enough spirit that they can fill the space and they can be filled by those spaces.

When I think of Sequoia National Park, I think of a cathedral or a mosque or a church, a place where you're not necessarily worshipping the name of something, but the presence of something else. When you're in a grove of giant sequoia, there's no need for someone to remind you that there is something in this world that is larger than you are, because you can see it. There's no need to stand on airs and think that you're better than this person or not as good as that person, because we're all diminished and at the same time amplified by being in their presence.

I remember one day I was walking in the Cook's Meadow in the central part of Yosemite Valley. There was a woman there, and she was just looking up and around her, and she just kept saying, "Oh, oh my, oh my." And I went up to her and I said, "Ma'am, are you all right?" And she said, "Yes, I'm just fine. I just . . . oh, oh my."

I didn't have to talk to her about the transcendent experience. She was having one. And it wasn't a transcendent experience because it was a national park; it was transcendent because it was Yosemite Valley. But because it had become a national park, she could have that transcendent experience.

You had a different kind of experience at Yosemite when you came across an old photograph of some Buffalo Soldiers patrolling the park.

It was like stumbling into your own family while traveling in a foreign country. Most people see soldiers, they see the uniform, they see the emblem of rank. But when I think of Buffalo Soldiers, I'm drawn to people. I'm drawn to men. I'm drawn to African Americans, whose experiences were such that that was a pathway out of poverty, a pathway out of a sense of worthlessness, which wasn't internalized, but was external in terms of a force put upon them.

The early parks—Yellowstone, Sequoia, and Yosemite—you had to have park protectors because otherwise people would be going into those areas doing what they've always done: cutting trees down for firewood or shooting the game to feed their family. How do you tell someone who's just trying to keep their children fed that it's illegal now to shoot the game in Yosemite or in Sequoia National Park? How do you tell a husband or a wife that their children are going to be cold because you can't cut those trees down for firewood anymore? And that'd be a difficult proposition if you were a white soldier. But when you add the overlay of race, which is no

overlay at all, and you have an African American, a colored man, giving orders to people who are not used to taking orders from anyone who looks like me, then you have the beginning of a very interesting day.

And they were led by a remarkable officer, Captain Charles Young.

If there's a person in history that I would love to have met, love to have sat down and had a conversation with, it would have been Charles Young. I can just imagine him with my eyes closed riding by on his horse. And I can just see him sitting just straight up in the saddle, and his feet down, and his toes up, and he just looks the model of a soldier. And I think that that's the kind of person that he was, that he was always a soldier.

Charles Young was a model to every single colored man who served in the military in his day. By the time of his death, he was

the highest-ranking African American in the United States military. So, if you're an enlisted man, and you're used to a white second lieutenant or captain telling you day in and day out what you could do, what you cannot do, how to spend your life, and then you see an African American officer, an *officer,* that stays in your mind and it also sparks a fire in your own sense of self-worth, your own sense of what is possible in this world.

So national parks are not just about transcendent experiences in the natural world, they're a connection to history?

When we look at parks and we look at the United States and we examine the whole idea of democracy—which can be distilled into one word, which is freedom—I think that the park experience is an exploration of the idea of freedom. Where do I come from? Where am I going? How did I get here? How did we as a people get here? And so the parks become a mirror of who we are, of our own identity, not just as Americans, our identity as human beings, as how we fit into everything else around us.

I think that when people go to a national park, they're provided a compass to history. They're given a barometer to see how the pressures of social change have affected their own experience and their family's experience. They're getting grounded in the reality in which they've found themselves.

I'm part Cherokee and Seminole, so that means when I go to the Great Smoky Mountains, that's a homecoming. I go to the Everglades, that's also a homecoming. That's part of the ancestry that I share. But I think it's more complex than that. I think it's not just our relationship with the land. I think another part of that is family. If your parents take you to national parks, you're going to go to national parks. If it's part of your own personal history, it'll be part of your history that you pass on to your children.

As your own history shows, family trips to national parks haven't necessarily been traditions for all segments of our society. In the early years especially, the parks were often seen as refuges for white upper- and middle-class Americans.

Everyone needs beauty. And African Americans, Hispanic Americans, Asian Americans—whatever group that you happen to be referring to—they all need beauty. Everyone needs to have something that constitutes the beautiful in their life.

Most barriers are imagined, or maybe not imagined, but they're psychological barriers. I think that for African Americans, it's the psychological barriers that have the most profound influence in

Left: Yosemite Falls is reflected in a seasonal pond on the valley floor, Yosemite National Park.

keeping them out of the park experience. If you're forced, and your parents and your grandparents and your great-grandparents and your great-great-grandparents are forced to work the land from which the bounty of that land is not for them, they're going to have a particular relationship with that land. And how do you move from that forced servitude to love of the land? And I think that there is a continuum of this relationship between African Americans and their own country and we're still on that continuum.

You can now meet African Americans who travel all over the world. They go to Venice, Italy. They go to Spain. They go to China. They go all these different places. But they've never been to the Grand Canyon. Or they've never been to Yosemite. I have run into them, but it's still few and far between. But when I see them there, it's the same look of excitement. It's the same look of exhilaration, and it's the same look of transcendence. "What a beautiful place this is. How lucky I am to be here."

It's been a long journey for someone who personally didn't grow up with family trips to national parks. Looking back, is there a favorite memory?

One of the last jobs I had in Yellowstone was delivering the mail on snowmobile. There I was, in the world's first national park, and I was by myself with just snow and just mountains. I remember going down into Hayden Valley. There were bison crossing over the road. And it was so cold—about 60 below zero.

The bison, as they breathed, their exhalation would seem to crystallize in the air around them. And there were these sheets, these ropy strands of crystals, kind of flowing down from their breath. And they just moved their heads and were looking at me.

I remember thinking that if I had not been on that machine, I would have thought I had been thrust fully back into the Pleistocene, back into the Ice Age. And I remember turning the snowmobile off, because the only way you could hear is to turn that thing off, and I would listen.

I felt like this was the first day, and this morning was the first time the sun had ever come up, and the shadows that are being cast right now is the first time those shadows have ever been cast on the earth. And I was all alone, but I felt I was in the presence of everything around me, and I was never alone.

It was one of those moments when you get pulled outside of yourself into the environment around you. I felt like I was just with the breath of the bison as they were exhaling and as I was exhaling, and they were inhaling, it was all kind of flowing together.

And I forgot completely about the mail. All I was thinking of was that a single moment in a place as wild as Yellowstone—or most of the national parks—can last forever.

THE JOHN MUIR OF THE ROCKIES

By 1914, the area around Longs Peak in Colorado, in the heart of the Rocky Mountains, was already well known as a tourist destination.

Years earlier, a European nobleman, the Fourth Earl of Dunraven, had tried to buy up the surrounding land and turn it into a private hunting preserve for himself and his wealthy friends. Then the multimillionaire Freelan O. Stanley—one of the inventors of the Stanley Steamer automobile—had purchased Dunraven's estate and built a luxurious resort catering to upper-class clients, who were picked up at the railhead thirty miles away and chauffeured to Stanley's hotel in one of Stanley's specially made eleven-passenger cars, traveling over Stanley's roads.

Farther up into the mountains, however, was another, less lavish hotel, the Longs Peak Inn, owned and operated by an aspiring nature writer named Enos Mills. Mills had first come to the Rockies from Kansas at age fourteen on doctor's orders that without clean, alpine air, he would not live to adulthood. Thirty years later, he was still there—and healthy enough to spend his winters traipsing alone from one Colorado mountain peak to another, measuring the depth of the snowpack as the state's official "Snow Observer."

Mills had equally high expectations for his summer guests. Drinking, dancing, and card playing were strictly prohibited, in favor of strenuous hikes and the serious study of nature. Three times a week Mills himself would deliver lectures, drawn from the articles he was constantly writing for national magazines, extolling the beauty of the Rockies and, for the last five years, crusading to have the Longs Peak region preserved not for royalty or the rich, but for everyone. He wanted it made into a national park.

Enos Mills inspects the top of a pine tree (left), lectures his guests while posing for photographs at his Longs Peak Inn (below), and, with his daughter Enda on his back (opposite), admires the view of the place he helped save as a national park.

[This] is a natural [park]—a mingling of meadows, headlands, groves, winding streams deeply set in high mountains whose forested steeps and snowy, broken tops stand high and bold above in romantic loveliness.

It is a marvelous grouping of gentleness and grandeur; an eloquent, wordless hymn, that is sung in silent, poetic pictures. . . .

As a National Park it would become a scenic resource of enormous and exhaustless richness.

For his inspiration, Mills credited John Muir. "I owe everything to Muir," Mills said. "If it hadn't been for him I would have been a mere gypsy." It was Muir's writings—and a chance encounter with the famous man himself on a beach near San Francisco in 1889—that had given Mills's life new purpose and direction.

As he prepared once more to push for a national park in the Colorado Rockies, Mills sent a letter to his hero and role model.

I shall leave for Washington in a few days to help set things moving for the conservation of scenery. . . . It is the work that you have done that has encouraged me . . . in the big work I am planning to do.

"I [will] glory in your success," an aging Muir had written Mills. "Strange," he added, "that the government is so slow to learn the value of parks." But as congressional hearings began in December of 1914, word arrived that John Muir had died. Calling him the "Father of National Parks," one person testified, "it will be a great courtesy to the memory of that grand old man if you gentlemen unanimously recommend creation of this park."

The bill now moved quickly through Congress, and in less than a month, Enos Mills's dream came true. Rocky Mountain National Park was finally established. And for the rest of his life, Mills would be called "the John Muir of the Rockies."

A National Park is a fountain of life. . . . It holds within its magic realm benefits that are health-giving, educational, economic; that . . . are inspirational.

To save ourselves, to prevent our perishing, to enable us to live at our best and happiest, parks are necessary.

ENOS MILLS

CHAPTER THREE

EMPIRE OF GRANDEUR

The present situation in regard to the national parks is very bad.

They have been created one at a time by acts of Congress which have not defined at all clearly the purposes for which the lands were to be set apart, nor provided any orderly or efficient means of safeguarding the parks.

FREDERICK LAW OLMSTED JR.

BY 1914, the national park idea had grown far beyond Yellowstone and Yosemite, where the notion of setting aside special places for all Americans had first taken root half a century earlier.

Parks could now be found surrounding snow-capped Mount Rainier in the Pacific Northwest, at the ancient cliff dwellings of Mesa Verde in the southwestern deserts, within the dark caverns of South Dakota's Wind Cave, in the reflection of the deep blue waters of Crater Lake in Oregon, and half a dozen other locations the nation had decided to preserve, usually at the urging of individual Americans willing to turn their passion for a particular landscape into a crusade for government action.

The departments of Agriculture, Interior, and War each claimed some responsibility for the parks, but in truth no one was in charge. Nothing proved it more than the fact that the city of San Francisco had been given permission to construct a dam in Yosemite National Park's lovely Hetch Hetchy Valley and bury a scenic wonder under a water reservoir. The national park idea was nearly half a century old, but some of the nation's most spectacular landscapes were still unprotected, vulnerable to the acquisitive and extractive energies that twentieth-century America possessed in such abundance.

The battle over Hetch Hetchy had been the last for John Muir, the park idea's most articulate spokesman for nearly fifty years. Now, an unlikely alliance would carry on in his name or in his spirit. Railroad barons saw in the parks a chance to increase their profits, while some of the nation's wealthiest men, at a time when the disparity between rich and poor was growing as never before, would use their

Preceding pages: View from the Rock Cut area on Trail Ridge Road, Rocky Mountain National Park
Right: Dedication ceremonies of Rocky Mountain National Park, September 4, 1915

fortunes to advance the public good. From their ranks, a new leader would step forward, an impulsive and seemingly self-confident businessman, who would promote the parks as never before, and then struggle to bring them under a single management. Where Muir had changed things with his words, he would do it with his wealth and connections. Where Muir had emphasized the ecstatic, he would emphasize the economic and patriotic. But even more than John Muir, he would have his own, intensely personal reason that drew him to the parks.

AN INCANDESCENT ENTHUSIASM

In the summer of 1914, during a visit to Sequoia and Yosemite National Parks in California, a vacationing businessman named Stephen Mather became disgusted at what he was seeing. Hiking trails in the Sierra Nevada were in poor condition. Cattle could be found grazing where park rules prohibited it. Misusing provisions of the federal Swamp Land Act, speculators had managed to file private claims on choice parcels of the majestic big trees, planning to log the sequoias that Mather believed should be protected forever.

In anger, he dashed off a letter of complaint to an old college classmate, Franklin Lane, the Secretary of the Interior, whose standing among conservationists was already low, since Lane had personally approved construction of the dam in Yosemite's Hetch Hetchy Valley. Lane was aware of Mather's reputation as a self-made millionaire and sent back a terse reply. "Dear Steve," Lane wrote, "If you don't like the way the national parks are being run, why don't you come down to Washington and run them yourself." Soon enough, Mather showed up in Lane's office and accepted the offer.

A nationwide search could not have found a better man for the job. Tall and athletic, with prematurely white hair, Stephen Tyng Mather possessed what reporters called "incandescent enthusiasm" and "an eight-cylinder 60 mile-per-hour sort of personality." A reporter from *Woman's Magazine* gushed that "to describe Mr. Mather, one must roll all the matinee idols and Gibson models into one, and then put the red blood of a real man into him; he has the kindest of blue eyes, as clear and frank as a child's,

but the mouth and chin of a man who had fought his way in life."

Born in California to a family with deep, patrician roots in New England, Mather had graduated from the University of California at Berkeley, taken a job as a reporter for the New York *Sun,* and then moved on as sales manager for the Pacific Coast Borax Company, where his special genius for promotion found a national outlet.

He produced a flood of publicity by glamorizing the company's beginnings in California's Death Valley and branding its product as 20 Mule Team Borax; wrote letters to women's magazines, posing as a contented housewife whose life had been miraculously improved by using the product; even published a book of borax recipes and distributed 100,000 copies in a single month. Sales skyrocketed. Mather quickly realized he could make more money working for himself. He helped start a competing borax company and soon became rich beyond belief. But by 1914, at age forty-seven, he was restless for a new challenge.

Years earlier, during a climb up Mount Rainier, he had discovered that time in the great outdoors seemed to calm his nerves and revive his prodigious

A born salesman, Stephen Mather (left) made a fortune in the borax business through innovative public relations campaigns. One of his pamphlets (above) was filled with glowing borax testimonials and recipes, which he had encouraged housewives to submit to their local newspapers; he paid them a dollar for each one published. Horace Albright (right), as poor as Mather was rich, became the older man's most trusted assistant in the campaign for a National Park Service.

energies. He joined John Muir's Sierra Club, took part in the group's yearly outings, and counted as one of the highlights of his life meeting the legendary Muir himself on a hike in Sequoia National Park in 1912, where he listened for hours as the old man denounced the dam at Hetch Hetchy and described the other threats to wilderness from commercial interests and an uncaring government. Now Mather was being offered the chance to promote and protect the parks Muir had taught him to love. He told Secretary Lane he would take on the job, but only for one year.

To help him with the task, Mather was assigned a legal assistant in Lane's office, a fellow Californian and Berkeley graduate named Horace M. Albright, an earnest and ambitious twenty-four-year-old who had arrived in Washington a year earlier, so poor he wore a borrowed suit and took a room at the local YMCA. Like Mather, Albright had become enthusiastic about national parks because of a personal encounter with John Muir, but much of his time so far in the Department of the Interior had been spent responding to angry letters protesting the decision to flood the Hetch Hetchy Valley. "I hated this job," Albright remembered, "for I was in sympathy with the protests." He had been intending to quit and return to California to practice law, when Mather entered his life and persuaded him to stay for one more year.

Each man, Albright wrote, brought different but complementary skills to the job.

He . . . created instant rapport with strangers, had a personality that radiated poise, friendliness, and charm, could talk easily with anyone he met, confidently instilling perfect strangers with enthusiasm.

I was knowledgeable about Washington, the Interior Department, and the Congress, was quite good at detail and administrative work, which he obviously hated . . . and, above all, was loyal and conscientious.

"He was old enough to be my father," Albright added, but "I instantly felt a strong kinship with him. . . . His was a lightning fast brain with an electric nervous energy to go with it. I so admired him

that I found that I was imitating him right from the beginning."

After being sworn in as assistant to the Secretary of the Interior on January 21, 1915, at a salary of $2,750 a year, Mather's first action was to more than double Horace Albright's yearly pay—with $2,400 from his own pocket. Next he hired Robert Sterling Yard, a gifted editor of the *New York Herald,* to begin churning out a flurry of publicity for the parks, luring Yard to Washington with the promise of $5,000 a year and a personal secretary—all of it paid by Mather, not the government.

Then Mather and his small team set out to generate greater public interest in national parks and build support for a single government bureau devoted exclusively to their interest. Mather wined and dined congressmen and senators, newspaper and magazine publishers; pushed through legislation that would allow private individuals to make gifts of land and money to the parks; and began making plans for a whirlwind inspection tour of the national treasures now entrusted to his care. "With ideas popping from Mather's head every minute," Albright said, "he simply couldn't sit still at a desk and handle details."

"Talking over" an idea meant listening, while he restlessly paced around the room, gesturing to make his points, his words barely keeping up with his mile-a-minute brain.

I thanked my stars I was young, strong, and healthy. His energy would have killed someone who wasn't.

Before 1915 ended, Mather and Albright's tour would cover nearly 35,000 miles. In Colorado they joined a crowd of three hundred for the dedication of Rocky Mountain National Park, the nation's newest. Mather spoke briefly, calling the new park a "glorious" place and promising to do everything he could to attract more tourists to it. A brief visit to the Grand Canyon—still a national monument and still under the control of the Forest Service—convinced Mather that it needed greater protection. He thought he knew the best way to do it. "Make this unbelievable wonder your next national park," he proclaimed to anyone who would listen. At Mount Rainier in Washington state, he decided the superin-

tendent was an ineffectual political hack and fired him on the spot.

And at Glacier National Park in Montana, he and Albright rode horseback for three days through the rugged mountains to get from one side of the park to the other, pausing from time to time to rest—and to contemplate the region's endless array of breathtaking sights. Albright never forgot the moment.

It seemed impossible that every new national park appeared more spectacular than the last—or at least more unusual. . . .

As I stood gaping at the awesome beauty, Mather joined me. Neither of us spoke for some time. Then I heard him say, "Horace, what God-given opportunity has come our way to preserve wonders like these before us? We must never forget or abandon our gift."

When he arrived at Glacier's park headquarters, Mather decided the building and its location were totally inadequate. He scouted around, found a parcel of land that was up for sale, wrote out a check for $8,000 to buy it, and then donated it as an addition to the park.

In California's Yosemite National Park, he learned that the fifty-six-mile-long Tioga Road, the only east–west road through the park, was still in private hands and in terrible disrepair. Mather got out his checkbook again—putting up half of the $15,500 price tag and raising an equal amount from wealthy acquaintances. Then he just as quickly gave it away to become part of the park forever.

For too long, he told Albright, Congress had been willing to create parks but not to provide them with the money they needed to survive. "He felt he had to get people to use the parks before he could get legis-

Mather (left, with plate and cup) and Albright (far right) take part in Rocky Mountain's dedication, along with Robert Sterling Yard (next to Mather), the writer Mather paid with his own funds to churn out publicity about the parks.

lation and appropriations," Albright said. "Too few people knew about them."

He believed the Congress had the cart before the horse, that it wouldn't appropriate money until proof was furnished that the parks were being used.

Our quandary was: if we can't get anybody in because of no roads, no development, no accommodations, how can we get any money [from Congress]? And vice versa.

More tourists meant that more appropriations could be squeezed from Congress for better roads and perhaps even an enlargement of the boundaries. That meant more tourists. A perfect circle.

Mather concluded that a well-coordinated public crusade for the parks was needed. To launch it, he invited a select list of influential Americans—editors, publishers, politicians, leading businessmen and railroad builders—to join him for two weeks in the Sierra Nevada of California. He called it his "Mather Mountain Party."

They would travel by horse and mule from Sequoia National Park across the crest of the Sierra Nevada, a rugged trip over daunting terrain, though Mather made sure that no expense was spared to ease the way. And he paid for it all: from the newfangled air mattresses placed under their sleeping bags to a Chinese cook named Ty Sing, who brought along a sheet metal cook stove to prepare gourmet dinners. Breakfasts included fresh fruit, steaks, eggs, sausages, and hot, freshly baked rolls; suppers were capped off

The influential men invited to join the "Mather Mountain Party" of 1915 in the Sierra Nevada were treated to exquisite meals cooked by Ty Sing (top right) and then roaring campfires (bottom right), where their host preached to his captive audience about supporting the parks.

Mather's group surveys Mineral King Valley (left), which he wanted added to Sequoia National Park. After putting up his own money—and getting additional donations from his friends and the Sierra Club—Mather purchased the Tioga Road, a privately owned toll road in Yosemite National Park's high country, then donated it to the nation (above) in a dedication ceremony on July 28, 1915.

Mather wanted the group to appreciate the magnificent Sierra scenery, but he also wanted them to learn something of the issues needing attention: private holdings within national parks that did not belong there and should be removed, and some public domain land that ought to be brought into national park status.

The trip . . . convinced most of the writers and politicians of the need for getting a national park service act through Congress. They agreed to support the expansion of General Grant National Park to include the Kings Canyon area.

HORACE ALBRIGHT

by English plum pudding and brandy sauce for dessert—all of it served on white linen tablecloths with fine silverware and china, carefully packed and transported by mule to the next campsite.

At every opportunity, Mather preached to his guests about his vision for the national parks: better protection and fewer private inholdings, improved services for tourists, more parks and expansions of existing parks, all brought together in a unified system under a single government agency. Coming across cattle grazing in the park, Mather lectured about the damage cows and sheep could do to pristine areas. At a campsite littered with tin cans and paper, he got his wealthy guests to help pick up the mess, leaving a note that said: "We have cleaned your camp. Keep it clean."

They spent a night at Redwood Meadow, just outside the boundary of Sequoia National Park, amidst a privately owned stand of majestic trees Mather could not bear to think might be cut down. He bought the grove and donated it to the nation. Others became enthused by Mather's example. Gilbert Grosvenor, president of the National Geographic Society and editor of its magazine, who was making his first trip to the West, was appalled to learn of all the private inholdings within the park's Giant Forest—and pledged $20,000 from the society to help buy them out.

Slowly, the group worked its way up the western flank of the Sierra, fishing, hiking, swimming in cold mountain streams, passing through national forest land Mather fervently believed should be incorporated into a much enlarged Sequoia National Park, an old dream of John Muir's. Then the hardiest of the bunch ascended Mount Whitney, at 14,494 feet the tallest peak in the contiguous forty-eight states, from which they could survey the vast wilderness Muir had wanted preserved. Mather felt the same way, and urged his friends to join him: "Each member of the party will sing of the 'Greater Sequoia' until all the world shall have heard them, and will unite to preserve this wonderful region for the benefit and enjoyment of the whole people for all time."

By the end of their two weeks in the outdoors, Albright said, "everyone in the party looked like a caveman." But his boss had converted them all into

disciples for his cause, and when they gathered for their last meal together he sent them on their way with an exhortation:

Now I want you to know that our job is not over. It is just beginning.

Think of Sequoia as incomplete until the Kings Canyon area is added, until Mt. Whitney [is] under the care of a national park, until the magnificent Giant Forest is out of private hands. And Yosemite—virgin timber and toll roads in private hands, lovely flatlands still owned by early squatters. And never forget Hetch Hetchy! These must be restored to our country.

Those are just two parks. We have many others and they all need protection. We must acquire and care for vast areas not under our control at this time.

But most of all, none of this will mean anything unless we have a safe haven for these wilderness places. We must have a National Park Service. Everyone of us must pull our oar!

. . . Remember that God has given us these beautiful lands. Try to save them for, and share them with, future generations.

Go out and spread the gospel!

That night, Ty Sing had prepared a special farewell dessert: a delicious pastry into which he slipped a message written in both English and Chinese for each member of the party. On Mather's was written, "The sound of your laughter will fill the mountains when you are in the sky." Albright's fortune was, "You are the spirit and soul of your leader."

Back in Washington at the end of 1915, Mather told his young assistant that the year he had promised to the parks was now over. It had been well spent, he said, but Congress still had not created a new agency to oversee the parks. He was willing to remain for six more months or a little longer to get that done, if Albright would agree to stay on as well.

Albright had to think about the request for a while. It would interfere with his plans to move back to California, get married, and start a legal career. But in the end, like everyone else, he couldn't say no to Stephen Mather.

THE NATION'S HEALTH SANITARIUM

In late 1915, Stephen Mather and Horace Albright finished their ambitious inspection tour at a place unlike any of the national parks they had been visiting: Hot Springs, Arkansas. There, forty-seven thermal springs bubble from the flanks of the Zig Zag Mountains on the eastern edge of the Ouachita Range—the result of rainwater that has taken four thousand years to seep thousands of feet down through the bedrock until it is superheated and forced back up through the sandstone fissures to reemerge at the surface at a temperature of 143 degrees: pure, flavorless, and odorless.

Native tribes were already well familiar with the hot springs when conquistadors under the command of Hernando de Soto came through and supposedly bathed in them in 1541. The Dunbar-Hunter Expedition—dispatched into the newly acquired Louisiana Territory by President Jefferson—camped there for a month in 1804, taking scientific measurements and reporting back that the springs were "a great curiosity." In 1832, to protect the principal sources of the springs and exert some control over their commercial development, President Andrew Jackson set aside four sections of land as Hot Springs Reservation.

By the time of Mather and Albright's visit, the town of Hot Springs surrounded the reserva-tion, and a string of luxury spas and ornate hotels along Bathhouse Row were doing a brisk business with the health seekers flocking to "The Nation's Health Sanitarium." A handout signed by the surgeon general of the U.S. Army made extravagant claims for the water's curative powers:

> Relief may be reasonably expected at the Hot Springs in the following conditions: In various forms of gout and rheumatism; neuralgia, especially when depending on gout; metallic or malarial poisoning, paralysis not of organic origin, the earlier stages of locomotor ataxia, chronic Bright's disease . . . functional diseases of the liver, gastric dyspepsia . . . chronic diarrhea, catarrhal affections of the digestive and respiratory tracts [and] chronic skin diseases, especially the squamous varieties.

"Mather and I felt we were not only going to see the wonders of the bath house but experi-ence a fountain of youth," Albright remembered. At the resplendent Fordyce, with its pink marble staircases and an art nouveau dome depicting Neptune's daughters, they got the full treat-ment—a Turkish hot room, sun-ray cabinets,

workouts on the "Zander-gymnastic" equip-ment, the "vapor experience," tumblers of mineral water to drink, immersions into deep hot tubs, and much more, culminating in what Albright considered "the highlight of our visit—a long remarkable rubdown and, for me at least, a short catnap."

During their five-day inspection, whenever his boss turned up missing from department business, Albright always located him at one of the bathhouses. "Mather," he said, "almost became addicted to them."

Mather's enthusiasm never abated. He returned again and again (including one time as recuperation from a breakdown), ordered construction of a new Government Free Bath-house so that people who could not afford the more expensive spas might still partake of the experience, and in 1921 convinced Congress to change the reservation's designation to Hot Springs National Park (at 4,837 acres, the nation's smallest).

"Somehow it never seemed like a national park," Albright admitted years later, but he always had fond memories of his time there. For Christmas 1915, he sent Mather a framed copy of the last page of the Fordyce brochure.

Like many others who took the treatment at Hot Springs, Arkansas (below), Stephen Mather swore by the curative powers of the thermal waters seeping from underground fissures (above right).

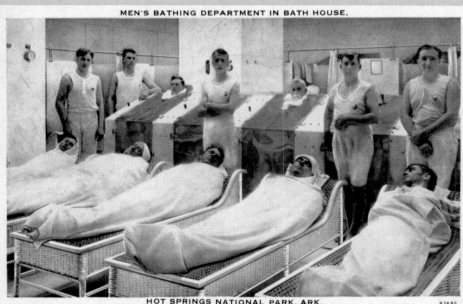

MEN'S BATHING DEPARTMENT IN BATH HOUSE.

HOT SPRINGS NATIONAL PARK, ARK.   93695

SEE AMERICA FIRST

Now it's Glacier National Park. Established as America's Vacation Paradise, discovered by thousands of American tourists, who, deprived of the Old World, found a still greater wonderland at home. They came last year to Glacier National Park, Uncle Sam's greatest playground, twenty thousand strong... answering again the call irresistible of the "land of shining mountains."

GREAT NORTHERN RAILWAY

From the very beginnings of the park movement, long before Stephen Mather burst upon the scene, railroad companies had been busily promoting America's national parks—if for no other reason than the hardheaded belief that more tourists riding the rails would help their bottom line.

The Northern Pacific's considerable political influence with Congress had been instrumental in the creation of Yellowstone National Park back in 1872, as well as that of Mount Rainier National Park in 1899. The Southern Pacific had worked behind the scenes on behalf of Yosemite, General Grant, Sequoia, and Crater Lake national parks.

And on the border of Montana and Canada, amidst the spectacular mountains George Bird Grinnell had called "the crown of the continent," Glacier National Park owed its existence in part to the tireless efforts of Louis Hill and his Great Northern Railway. When Congress failed to appropriate adequate funds for the park's development, Hill felt free to treat it as his own little mountain kingdom, since he was spending more than $2.3 million to improve it himself.

Hill envisioned Glacier as "America's Switzerland," with Swiss-style chalets, connected by a network of hiking and riding trails so his guests could get from one chalet to the next in a day's time, in the same way travelers did in the Alps. At each stop, chalet employees adorned in Swiss costumes stood ready to serve the travelers. Two luxury hotels were also constructed as the main hubs of activity. At one, the imposing Glacier Park Hotel, located at the Great Northern's railway station, Blackfeet Indians were paid to greet arriving passengers in full regalia and set up an array of tepees for those who wanted an "authentic" western experience by renting a bed

inside of one for 50 cents a night. The hotel's majestic lobby, meanwhile, was festooned with Japanese lanterns and cherry blossoms, and a Japanese couple served tea every day—all as reminders that the Great Northern's premier train, the *Oriental Limited*, and its steamship company were America's main links to Asia. Louis Hill, one reporter wrote, was "a Christopher Columbus. He... discovered altitudinous America.... He want[s] to make it possible for every man, woman, and child, with or without a capable pair of legs, to stand in Gunsight Pass and saturate his soul."

On every Great Northern Railway brochure and timetable, on every company press release and billboard, Hill insisted that three words be attached: "See America First." Western boosters had been using the slogan for more than a decade, part of a sporadic promotional campaign aimed at a very specific audience: upper-middle-class Americans, predominantly eastern and overwhelmingly white, who were spending an estimated $500 million each year vacationing in Europe. For years, railroad men like Hill had been trying to lure some of that business

Louis Hill (above) of the Great Northern Railway was a tireless promoter of Glacier National Park. To attract tourists who might otherwise vacation in Europe, he called the park "America's Switzerland" and urged them to "See America First" (below left); he also employed Blackfeet Indians to dress in full regalia (right) and mingle with people arriving on his trains.

back to the States. When World War I broke out in Europe in 1914, closing off overseas travel to American tourists, the railroads saw their chance to promote "See America First" as never before.

As a publicity stunt, Hill and the Great Northern dispatched a group of Blackfeet Indians to tour the East. They camped in tepees on the roof of New York City's McAlpin Hotel; rode the subway and visited the Brooklyn Bridge; attracted huge crowds when they performed war dances at the annual Travel and Vacation Show. Everywhere they went, the press referred to them not as the Blackfeet but as "the Indians of Glacier National Park."

Meanwhile, well-known writers were invited to the park at the Great Northern's expense in hopes that they would turn out favorable articles. Mary Roberts Rinehart, a best-selling mystery novelist who had become a national celebrity as the first female war correspondent to report from the battle lines of Europe, took several guided horseback trips through Glacier, and then wrote about them in a series of "See America First" articles, which in turn became two popular books. Hill liked them so much, he used Rinehart's words in his advertisements.

> *I have traveled a great deal of Europe. The Alps have never held this lure for me. Perhaps it is because these mountains are my own—in my own country. . . . There is no voice in all the world so insistent to me as the wordless call of these mountains.*

No one was more enthusiastic about the campaign to "See America First" than the new assistant to the Secretary of the Interior, Stephen Mather.

> *A hundred thousand people used the national parks last year. A million Americans should play in them every summer. Our national parks are practically lying fallow, and only await proper development to bring them into their own.*
>
> *The move to "see America first" is a step in the right direction, and should be commended by the American public to the extent that they will make it their duty as well as their pleasure to assist in this patriotic movement.*

Some park purists worried that the railroads already wielded too much influence within park boundaries and were suspicious of the companies' motives. Mather saw them as partners. He particularly admired the grand hotels the railroads were responsible for constructing in some parks' most scenic locations.

Yellowstone already had three of them, including the Old Faithful Inn, a massive structure advertised as being "as famous as the geyser." Initial government

regulations stipulating that no structures in a national park be closer to a natural feature than a quarter of a mile had been relaxed—and cut in half—so that guests at the Old Faithful Inn could be that much nearer the sights they had traveled so far to see. Mather could foresee golf courses and tennis courts added to the attractions, "and the park should be extensively advertised as a place to spend the summer instead of five or six days of hurried sight-seeing under the constant pressure to keep moving."

In his quickly evolving vision for the national parks, Mather saw them marketed and promoted as resorts, with a grand hotel in every one, built and operated by concessionaires willing to make the considerable investment of private capital and be regu-

lated by the federal government in exchange for being granted a monopoly within the park.

Under his prodding, luxurious hotels went up in Paradise Valley at Mount Rainier; on the lip of the ancient volcanic cone at Crater Lake; and in Yosemite Valley, where Mather even invested some of his own money in the venture, despite Horace Albright's concerns that it might prove to be an embarrassing conflict of interest. Mather wasn't worried; his focus was on providing the best possible lodgings for his park visitors. "Scenery is a splendid thing when it is viewed by a man who is in a contented frame of mind," Mather said, but "give him a poor breakfast after he has had a bad night's sleep, and he will not care how fine your scenery is."

In Louis Hill's hotels and chalets, the main decorative motif was Swiss—except in the lobby of the Glacier Park Hotel, where Japanese lanterns were hung as a reminder that the Great Northern's steamship company was available for passage to Asia.

Stephen Mather thought each national park should have a premier hotel, similar to Yellowstone's majestic Old Faithful Inn (below right). And although he hoped people would hike or ride horses in the parks' backcountry to commune with nature, he was also interested in providing resort-style amenities such as tennis courts, golf courses, and swimming pools, like the one above in Yosemite.

A silversword plant (above) grows on the rim of Haleakala's ancient crater (right). *Below right:* Molten lava from Kilauea forms three different patterns as it flows toward the sea.

It is the most wonderful feature of the National Park Service, surpassing the geysers of the Yellowstone, the waterfalls of the Yosemite, and even the big trees of Sequoia National Park.

It is the most awe-inspiring thing that I have ever observed, and I have no hesitation predicting that when once the people of the United States realize what a remarkable thing this volcano is, it will become the objective of thousands of visitors.

HORACE ALBRIGHT

THE SUBLIMEST SPECTACLE

By 1916, Americans had been aware of the fiery displays on Hawaii's volcanic islands for half a century, thanks in great part to the reporting in 1866 of a young newspaperman, Samuel Clemens, writing under the pen name Mark Twain. Twain had been among the first tourists to stay at the new Volcano House on the rim of Kilauea, an active volcano on Hawaii's Big Island—the home, according to native Hawaiians, of Pele, the goddess of destruction and creation.

Twain's vivid descriptions helped launch his career.

I turned my eyes upon the volcano again. . . . For a mile and a half in front of us and half a mile on either side, the floor of the abyss was magnificently illuminated . . . like the campfires of a great army far away.

. . . It looked like a colossal railroad map of the State of Massachusetts done in chain lightning on a midnight sky. Imagine it—imagine a coal-black sky shivered into a tangled network of angry fire!

Here and there were gleaming holes twenty feet in diameter, broken in the dark crust, and in them the melted lava . . . was boiling and surging furiously; and from these holes branched numberless bright torrents in many directions. . . .

Through the opera glasses we could see that they ran down small, steep hills and were genuine cataracts of fire. . . . Every now and then masses of the dark crust broke away and floated slowly down these streams like rafts down a river.

A colossal column . . . towered to a great height in the air immediately above the crater. . . . It glowed like a muffled torch and stretched upward to a dizzy height toward the zenith. I thought it possible that its like had not been seen since the children of Israel wandered on their long march through the desert . . . over a path illuminated by the mysterious "pillar of fire." And I was sure that I now had a vivid conception of what the majestic "pillar of fire" was like, which almost amounted to a revelation.

The smell of sulphur is strong, but not unpleasant to a sinner.

Compared to the huge caldera of Kilauea, with its lakes of fire, Twain wrote, Italy's more famous Mount Vesuvius was "a mere toy, a child's volcano, a soup kettle." The nearby Mauna Loa, also an active volcano, was even bigger—rising 56,000 feet from the bottom of the Pacific, 13,679 of them above sea level, it was the most massive mountain on earth.

And on the island of Maui was the dormant volcano called Haleakala, the "House of the Sun." Twain climbed to its ten-thousand-foot summit, peered into its vast and desolate crater (large enough, he wrote, to "make a fine site for a city like London"), and with his companions spent an afternoon idly pushing boulders off the edge, simply to watch them tumble thousands of feet to the crater's floor. "It was magnificent sport," he admitted. "We wore ourselves out at it."

After camping on the crater's edge, they awoke early the next morning with a blanket of clouds far below their feet, stretching endlessly across the Pacific toward the rising sun.

I felt like the Last Man, neglected of the Judgment, and left pinnacled in mid-heaven, a forgotten relic of a vanished world.

A growing warmth suffused the horizon, and soon the sun emerged and looked out over the

The Volcano House (below) as it looked when Mark Twain visited Kilauea in 1866. Fifty years later, the hotel had been remodeled a number of times, but tourists (right) were treated to the same view of steaming vents and lakes of fire in the volcano's crater.

KILAUEA CRATER
3 MILES LONG. - 2 MILES WIDE
550 FT. DEEP   2650 ACRES

*cloud-waste, flinging bars of ruddy light across it,
staining the folds and billow-caps with blushes,
purpling the shaded troughs between. . . .*

*It was the sublimest spectacle I ever witnessed,
and I think the memory of it will remain with
me always.*

Fifty years after Twain's visit, the Volcano House
had been remodeled several times. Tourists were now
coming in greater numbers to gawk at Kilauea's
pyrotechnics. As proof that they had been there,
some would break off stalactites in the lava caves or
singe their postcards by extending them into the
furnace-hot fissures. At Haleakala, the only place in
the world where the distinctive silversword plant
grows, taking half a century to mature, so many visi-

tors had gotten into the habit of carting one off as a
souvenir that the species was threatened with extinction.

For more than a decade, a coalition of naturalists
and scientists hoping to protect the volcanoes and
their unique environments, as well as businessmen
and boosters intent on promoting Hawaii tourism,
had been pushing for a national park on the islands.
Stephen Mather was enthusiastic about the idea, as
well. On August 1, 1916, they finally succeeded, with
the establishment of Hawaii National Park. (Fifty
years later, it would be divided into two parks:
Haleakala and Hawai'i Volcanoes.)

A week after Hawaii National Park's creation, a
volcano on the mainland was also set aside. Lassen
Peak in California, the southernmost volcano of the

Photographer B. F. Loomis chronicled many of Lassen Peak's eruptions with his camera (above), making the volcano a national sensation. In some places, the ash created a lunar landscape (left), where trees nonetheless carry on their lives.

The eruption came on gradually at first, getting larger and larger until finally it broke out in a roar like thunder. The smoke cloud was hurled with tremendous velocity many miles high, and the rocks thrown from the crater were seen to fly way below the timberline before they were followed by a comet-like tail of smoke which enabled us to tell definitely the path of their flight.

For a short time the smoke cloud ran down the mountain side, melting the snow very fast, and the water could be seen running down the mountain side in a rush twenty feet wide. But soon after the cloud lifted going straight up so the amount of water running down our direction was slight.

B. F. LOOMIS

Cascade Range on the Pacific Coast, had awakened from nearly two hundred years of slumber, and was in the midst of a seven-year cycle of dramatic eruptions—some that deposited their ash as far as three hundred miles away. To preserve this living laboratory of the primal forces that had shaped the earth, Lassen Volcanic National Park was created on August 9, 1916.

Congress, however, declined to appropriate any significant money for the development and protection of the new parks, on the belief, one senator explained, that "it should not cost anything to run a volcano."

That same year, nearly half a world away from Hawaii, another island would also be considered for national protection, a large island on the Atlantic seaboard, whose tall peaks rise so close to the sea that they catch the nation's first rays of sunlight each morning.

For centuries it had been the home of the Micmac and the Abenaki—"the people of the dawn." Then, in 1604, sailing off the coast of what would one day become the state of Maine, the French explorer Samuel de Champlain had made special note of it.

It is very high, with notches here and there, appearing from the sea like seven or eight mountains ranged near each other. The summits of . . . these are bare of trees, because they are nothing but rock. . . . I named it l'isle des Monts-deserts, the Island of Desert Mountains.

For 150 years after Champlain, the French claimed it as part of their North American possessions—calling it Acadia—before it passed to British, and then American hands. Known as Mount Desert Island, it was a lightly populated and little known collection of fishing villages until 1844, when the renowned landscape artist Thomas Cole arrived in search of new scenery for his palette. Because of Cole's influence, the island quickly became the favorite summer locale for other painters, all of them drawing inspiration from the rugged shorelines, crystalline lakes, and tranquil forests.

CHAIN REACTION: Thomas Cole's *View Across French-man's Bay from Mt. Desert Island, After a Squall*, 1845 (below) attracted more artists to the island on Maine's coast; their paintings then prompted wealthy Easterners to visit— and eventually build summer "cottages" (right) in Bar Harbor and other parts of the island.

The future at all our leading seashore places, in truth, belongs to the Cottager, and it is really useless to resist him. . . . [He] moves on all the "choice sites" . . . with calm and remorselessness. . . . His march along the American coast is nearly as resistless as that of the hordes who . . . [overthrew] the Roman Empire.

The flurry of paintings, in turn, touched off a tourism boom on the island. Calling themselves "rusticators," wealthy Easterners began showing up, hoping to spend the summer at the place the nation's top artists had made so fashionable. Soon, instead of renting rooms from locals, they began buying up land on the island and building their own summer homes: places with room enough to properly entertain—and impress—their socially prominent friends.

"A few years ago, before Bar Harbor's fame as a summer resort was world-wide," the local newspaper reported, "those who dwelt here in the summer were content with a simple home, but since fashion and wealth have adopted her for their own, they try to outbid each other. There are hundreds of thousands of dollars spent yearly in additions and alterations and the trend seems to be to build more costly places each year."

The proud owners had a special name for their new summer dwellings. They called them "cottages." Edwin Lawrence Godkin, editor of the *New York Evening Post,* predicted that they would inevitably monopolize the entire seaboard.

One "cottager," however, worried that too much of Mount Desert was being locked up. As a boy, Charles Eliot had spent many happy summers vacationing there, and in college had formed the Champlain Society to undertake expeditions to study the island in greater detail. He had even persuaded his father to buy some property and build a summer home in Northeast Harbor.

After joining the landscape architecture firm of Frederic Law Olmsted in Boston, Eliot had been inspired by the great public spaces Olmsted had helped create or preserve, including New York's Central Park and Yosemite Valley. Eliot decided something similar was needed at Mount Desert Island.

The finest parts of the coast are already controlled by land companies and speculators, while the natives' minds are inflamed by the high prices which the once worthless shore lands are now supposed to command. . . .

Can nothing be done to preserve for the use and enjoyment of the great, unorganized body of the common people some fine parts, at least, of this seaside wilderness of Maine?

But before he could put any of his ideas to work, Eliot contracted cerebro-meningitis and died suddenly at age thirty-eight. Going through his son's papers to prepare a loving biography, Eliot's grief-stricken father, Charles W. Eliot, came across his namesake's idealistic dreams for Mount Desert.

As president of Harvard University and one of the most prestigious members of the island's summer community, the elder Eliot was in a position to do everything possible to make his son's dream come true. In the late summer of 1901, he summoned the island's most influential leaders to his home and reminded them that many of their favorite places to hike and picnic and enjoy a scenic vista were now off

Inspired by his late son, Charles W. Eliot (top right) persuaded George Dorr (top left) and other "cottagers" to buy scenic spots like Jordan Pond (left) and preserve them for public use.

limits because of new owners. He also urged them to heed a higher calling.

> *One of the greatest satisfactions in doing any sound work for an institution, a town, or a city, or for the Nation is that good work done for the public lasts, endures through generations; and the little bit of work that any individual of the passing generation is enabled to do gains through association with such collective activities an immortality of its own.*

They established the Hancock County Trustees of Public Reservations, to acquire, by gift or purchase from the island's residents, land deemed important for its scenic or historic value—and then hold on to it and manage it for public use. Eliot was elected president and for the succeeding years would continue to guide the group's efforts to protect Mount Desert Island. But the day-to-day work soon fell to another "cottager" who gladly took up the cause.

George Bucknam Dorr was nearly fifty years old in 1901 and had never needed to work for a living, thanks to a generous inheritance from his parents, whose investments in the textile industry had placed them among New England's social elite. As a young man Dorr had suffered from poor eyesight, an embarrassing stutter, and a nervous breakdown, though he had graduated from Harvard and briefly considered joining his brother's New York law firm, before giving up the idea of a career when his brother died from typhus.

Now he lived alone in his family's grand house, called Oldfarm, in Bar Harbor, where he carried on the family tradition of entertaining prominent guests, dabbled in horticulture, and insisted on taking a swim in the frigid waters of the Atlantic every morning. What Dorr loved best was putting a few crackers in his pocket and taking long, rigorous hikes over Mount Desert's peaks and valleys; many of the island's trails had been blazed by him. The idea of preserving much of the island, he said, struck a deep chord within him.

When President Eliot brought out his plan for the protection and saving of our Mount Desert landscape, it made a strong appeal [to me] . . .

I had seen . . . the wreckage of the great natural landscape by the hotel builder and the private owner.

Dorr quickly became the new organization's most dedicated worker. He scouted out properties for the trustees to buy, researching complicated land titles that stretched back to the time of the French, negotiating purchases and soliciting donations of property or money. He oversaw boundary surveys, which he often paid for with his own funds. Slowly he accumulated important, scenic parts of the island: the Bowl and the Beehive; the watersheds surrounding Eagle Lake and Jordan Pond; the bare summit of Cadillac Mountain, the island's most prominent feature; and a lovely freshwater spring, which Dorr improved to provide cool drinking water for hikers and named Sieur de Monts Spring, in honor of the nobleman who had been granted the first colony by the king of France.

Not everyone in Maine appreciated the trustees' land acquisitions—or the special tax-exempt charter they had been granted by the state—and Dorr found himself making constant trips to the state legislature to fend off attacks of one kind or another. In 1913, he

made a decision that would change the fate of Mount Desert forever.

I thought it over as I lay awake and decided that the only course to follow to make safe what we had secured would be to get the Federal Government to accept our lands for a National Park. . . .

I went . . . to see President Eliot and tell him. . . .

He thought a while, then said:

". . . When will you go on to Washington?"

In Washington, Dorr learned that creating a new park was not going to be easy. At the time there were no national parks east of the Mississippi. Moreover, his plan to create one from donated land was the first proposal of its kind.

Horace Albright advised Dorr that Congress could be bypassed, if President Woodrow Wilson could be persuaded to use the Antiquities Act and issue an executive order setting aside a portion of the island as a national monument. Dorr made the offer official in a letter to the Secretary of the Interior:

On behalf of the Hancock County Trustees of Public Reservations, State of Maine, I have the honor to offer in free gift to the United States a unique and noble tract of land upon our eastern seacoast. . . .

The tract offered is rich in historic association, in scientific interest and in landscape beauty [and contains] the only heights that immediately front the open sea with mountainous character upon our eastern shore.

Yet even giving the land away proved difficult. For three years Dorr persevered—frantically clearing up any loose ends regarding the trustees' legal title to the land, and using his considerable social connections to meet with the president, the president's wife, the president's daughter and son-in-law, and anyone else with influence in the administration to argue his case. On July 8, 1916, President Wilson signed a proclamation creating the Sieur de Monts National Monument from five thousand acres of Mount Desert Island donated to the people of the United States by Charles Eliot, George Dorr, and their friends.

But Dorr was still not satisfied. If a president could unilaterally create a national monument, Dorr feared, he could just as easily take it away. His own inheritance was becoming dangerously depleted (and taking the job as the new monument's caretaker for one dollar a month would not help matters), but he vowed to acquire even more land. He wouldn't rest until the national monument became a congressionally authorized, full-fledged, permanent national park.

THE PARADOX

We have, as yet, no national park system. The parks have just happened. . . . Nowhere in official Washington can an inquirer find an office of the national parks, or a desk devoted solely to their management.

This is no one's fault. Uncle Sam has simply not waked up about his precious parks.

J. HORACE MCFARLAND

Robert Sterling Yard

Since 1900, when Congressman John Lacey had first proposed it, park supporters had been arguing that the haphazard collection of national parks needed to be brought together under a single federal agency. And yet bill after bill to create one had died in Congress, the victim of quiet but effective lobbying by powerful commercial interests hoping to exploit park lands and by John Muir's old nemesis in the battle over Hetch Hetchy. "We couldn't openly state it," Horace Albright remembered, "but we felt that the perpetual defeat of a park service was due to the unrelenting pressure of Gifford Pinchot . . . [who] always believed the Forest Service should take over the national park areas."

Then, in 1916, Stephen Mather entered the debate and added an economic argument on behalf of parks and a new park service. His hero, John Muir, had complained that "nothing dollarable is safe" when it came to America's havens of natural beauty; Mather's solution was to make those places "dollarable." Only under a single government agency, he said, could the parks be properly promoted, creatively packaged together into something much more valuable to the nation than a loose collection of far-flung, individual parks. Mather envisioned a national park *system*.

This Nation is richer in natural scenery of the first order than any other nation, but it does not know it.

It possesses an empire of grandeur and beauty which it scarcely has heard of. It owns the most inspiring playgrounds and the best equipped nature schools in the world and is serenely ignorant of the fact.

In its national parks it has neglected, because it has quite overlooked, an economic asset of incalculable value.

The Nation must awake, and it now becomes our happy duty to waken it to so pleasing and profitable a reality.

Mather's crusade for the parks now shifted into high gear. The same promotional skills that had made 20 Mule Team Borax a household word were put to use on behalf of creating a national park service. Washington had never seen anything quite like it.

All over the country, newspapers and magazines ran glowing feature stories about the parks—the result of Mather's constant cultivation of publishers and writers. Mather's mouthpiece, Robert Sterling Yard, wrote many of them himself.

What has the United States been doing with [the national parks]? Conserving them. Just conserving them. . . . But another day has dawned. . . . The closing of Europe turned the eyes of this people upon its own land. . . . The cry of "See America First" focused the national gaze. American scenery was discovered.

What this people wants its Congress grants, and we want our national parks developed. We want roads and trails like Switzerland's. We want hotels of all prices from lowest to highest. We want comfortable public camps in sufficient abundance to meet all demands. . . . We want . . . convenient transportation at reasonable rates. . . . We want good fishing. We want our animal life conserved and developed. . . .

We have the biggest and finest stock of scenery in the world and there is an enormous market for it. We can sell it at a profit. . . . It is a business proposition.

Schoolchildren were encouraged to write essays about the parks for cash prizes; magazines and newspapers were persuaded to editorialize in favor of a new park service. Gilbert Grosvenor, who had been part of the Mather Mountain Party in the Sierras a year earlier, devoted an entire issue of *National Geographic* to the scenic wonders of America. Mather made sure a copy was placed on every congressman's desk. Then he directed Yard to produce something even better.

The *National Parks Portfolio* was a hardbound book of several hundred pages, filled with glossy photographs of every national park and every national monument in the country—"the first really representative presentation of American scenery of grandeur ever published," Mather boasted. Publishing the *Portfolio* cost $48,000—exactly $48,000 more than Mather had in his government budget. He put up the first $5,000 with his own money and persuaded the western railroads to contribute the rest.

Some 275,000 copies were printed, with special leather-bound editions going to Congress. The rest were mailed to likely park supporters culled from the membership lists of professional societies, chambers of commerce, and social registers by a team of volunteers recruited from the General Federation of Women's Clubs. The book was such a hit, Mather ordered a smaller paperback version to be created and offered for sale in bookstores and in parks; 2.7 million copies were sold in the first year.

With Mather's publicity machine operating at a fever pitch, a small group began convening to draft a bill establishing a separate parks bureau within the Interior Department and to plot strategy on how to move it through Congress. Mather himself attended only sporadically, preferring to leave such detail work to Horace Albright, Robert Sterling Yard, and others.

Two of them, who would prove to be perhaps the most influential participants, had already been fighting for similar legislation for nearly a decade. J. Horace McFarland was the nation's best-known horticulturalist, an expert on roses, successful publisher of seed catalogues, and author of "Beautiful America," a regular column in *Ladies' Home Journal*. As president of the American Civic Association, he had led a successful campaign to prevent hydroelec-

tric companies from ruining Niagara Falls by siphoning off its water; and alongside John Muir he had battled—and lost—against Gifford Pinchot in the Hetch Hetchy fight. Now, nothing was more important to McFarland than creating a new government agency to make sure that Pinchot's view of conservation was not applied to the national parks.

The primary function of the nation's forests is to supply lumber. The primary function of the national parks is to maintain [the well-being] of the people who must use that lumber.

The forests are the nation's reserve wood-lots. The parks are the nation's reserve for the maintenance of individual patriotism and federal solidarity.

McFarland, in turn, brought with him Frederick Law Olmsted Jr., whose very name was synonymous with American parks. Olmsted's famous father had designed New York City's Central Park and, as one of Yosemite's original commissioners in the 1860s, had played a crucial role in the birth of the national park idea. The younger Olmsted had been groomed to follow in the same footsteps. At age thirty-one, he had been chosen by then-President Theodore Roosevelt to help design plans that transformed the District of Columbia into a model of civic parks.

J. Horace McFarland (top), and Frederick Law Olmsted Jr.

As the group drafted the nuts-and-bolts language of the bill creating a new federal agency, they turned to Olmsted to add what one of them called "the essential thing . . . the reason it is worthwhile"—a statement of purpose meant to stand the test of time and guide park policy into the unseen future. It would also enshrine in words the seeming contradiction that has always been a part of the story of the national parks.

The "fundamental purpose" of the new agency, Olmsted wrote, was to "conserve the scenery and the natural and historic objects and the wild life" of the parks, and "provide for the enjoyment of the same in such manner . . . as will leave them unimpaired for the enjoyment of future generations." The parks were for the enjoyment of the people, but not just for the current generation; they were to be available for public use, but only in a way that left them "unimpaired" for future Americans.

Stephen Mather (seated) meets with a delegation of Blackfeet Indians asking that the names of some of Glacier National Park's features be restored to tribal names. Most often, Mather was on the road and left office chores to Horace Albright (standing in the background).

Albright and everyone else in the working group understood the tension inherent in those two impulses.

We were aware of and discussed the paradox of use and enjoyment of the parks by the people versus their preservation "unimpaired." Of course we knew there was this paradox. . . .

We had finally come to the belief that, with rational, careful, and loving thought, it could be done.

Mather himself noted what he called a "dual mandate" in the legislation's statement of purpose, but he was less concerned about it than simply getting a park service bill enacted. And he grew impatient as the bill slowly worked its way through the labyrinth of House and Senate committees. "He was like a wound spring," Albright remembered. "He simply couldn't sit still in the office."

On August 25, 1916, he was deep in the high Sierras, leading a second Mather Mountain Party, when President Woodrow Wilson signed into law an act creating the National Park Service to oversee 5.5 million acres of some of the most beautiful scenery on earth. Stephen Mather was named the new agency's first director; Horace Albright agreed to stay on as his second in command.

Five months later, Mather convened a five-day conference in Washington, D.C., a gathering of every park supporter from across the country, meant to showcase the park movement and the new federal agency it had finally produced. There were speakers on every conceivable topic—fishing, hiking, and winter sports in the parks; the role of authors, painters, and women; a minister describing the "spiritual uplift" parks could provide.

Mather also unveiled an art exhibit at the National Museum—forty-five paintings by twenty-seven renowned artists, exclusively devoted to depicting different scenes from America's national parks and brought together in one place for the first time. Highlighting the show were works by the late Albert

In his old age, Thomas Moran (above, with his daughters) became more famous for his paintings of the Grand Canyon than for his earlier work that helped make Yellowstone a national park. *Right:* Grand Canyon from Hermit Rim Road, 1912

It has often occurred to me as a curious and anomalous fact, that American artists are prone to seek the subjects for their art in foreign lands, to the almost entire exclusion of their own. . . .

That there is a nationalism in art needs no proof. It is bred from a knowledge of and sympathy with [one's own] surroundings and no foreigner can imbue himself with a spirit of a country not his own. Therefore he should paint his own land.

THOMAS MORAN

Bierstadt, who had done so much to show the world the scenic beauties of Yosemite back in the 1860s; and by Thomas Moran, who had accompanied the first government expedition into Yellowstone in 1871 and whose stunning paintings had been instrumental in convincing Congress a year later to set the region aside as the world's first national park. Moran, now in his eighties, was still working and spending much of his time painting scenes of the Grand Canyon. Mather had become a friend and patron of the aging artist and had persuaded Moran to personally loan a few works to the exhibit.

The birth of the new National Park Service, Mather proclaimed in his opening remarks, was "like the bursting of the chrysalis." But as the conference went on, Albright found himself having to locate people to fill in as presiding officer, because his boss was mysteriously absent from the proceedings. The night after the conference ended, Albright was summoned to the Cosmos Club and ushered into a private room, where he found Mather, surrounded by a few of his closest friends.

> *He was rocking back and forth, alternately crying, moaning, and hoarsely trying to get something said. I couldn't understand a thing. He was incoherent.*
>
> *Suddenly he broke out of my hold, rushed for the door, and, with an anguished cry, proclaimed he couldn't live any longer feeling the way he did. We all understood what he said that time.*
>
> *He felt . . . that he had accomplished little or nothing. . . . He was a failure. He would leave the Park Service. There really was nothing more in life for him.*

They contacted Mather's wife, who asked them to bring him to a family doctor in Pennsylvania. She confided that her husband had suffered a similar breakdown in 1903. Three subsequent episodes had been prevented from spiraling out of control, she added, only by his retreating into the wilderness solitudes of the West—the trips that had originally inspired his passion for the parks.

After accompanying Mather to the doctor, Albright returned to Washington, where he and Interior Secretary Lane agreed to keep Mather's condi-

tion secret until more could be learned about his chances of recovery. In his absence, Albright would serve as acting director.

Mather, meanwhile, was sent to a sanitarium outside Philadelphia. His condition worsened at first; twice he attempted to kill himself. But his wife believed he would pull through, as long as he could be convinced he had something to look forward to. On the wall of his hospital room, she permitted only two decorations. Both of them were framed pictures of Yosemite National Park.

ATOMIC INSIGNIFICANCE

> *I have often wondered . . . in listening to descriptions of emotions evoked by the scenery of our national parks . . . why it was that animals are not more mentioned. . . .*
>
> *Does not . . . like the spire in the civilized landscape, a wild animal . . . so adorn it that we feel that it is complete?*
>
> CHARLES SHELDON

Among the speakers at the national parks conference was Charles Sheldon, a Vermont native and Yale graduate who had made a fortune in the railroad and mining business, allowing him to retire at age thirty-five and devote his energies to his personal passion: the study of wild mountain sheep.

Like his friend Stephen Mather, Sheldon did not do anything halfway. As an avid hunter and skilled but amateur naturalist, he embarked on field trips to observe North American sheep that took him from the mountains of Mexico all the way up the Rockies, through Canada, to the territory of Alaska and the tallest mountain on the continent: Mount McKinley, 20,320 feet above sea level. Sheldon never forgot his initial glimpse of it.

> *When I first . . . saw this tremendous upheaval of mountains, this range before me with McKinley rising in the center, and the stupendous grandeur of it, my impressions were exactly the same as those given me by looking down into the Grand Canyon. One was nature carved down into the surface of the earth, and the other was the most magnificent upheaval of nature above it.*

Stephen Mather's wife, Jane, and their daughter Bertha

Some adventurers, such as those in the expedition from 1910 (top), came to Mount McKinley to try to conquer the highest peak in North America; Charles Sheldon (above) arrived to study its animals.

At such times man feels his atomic insignificance in this universe.

The local Athabaskan Indians reverently called the perpetually icebound and snow-covered mountain *Denali*, "The High One." But in 1896, when the region was still marked as "unexplored" on official maps, a failed businessman-turned-prospector who had been arguing politics with his companions named it Mount McKinley, in honor of the presidential candidate, who, like them, supported the gold standard. The new name stuck.

By 1903, the allure of being first to scale the continent's tallest summit had begun to attract a handful of adventurers. One of them, Frederick Cook, president of the prestigious Explorers Club, announced that he had made it to the top in a wild dash of two weeks, and produced a photo to support his claim. But a later expedition established that Cook had been lying, replicating his photo at one of the mountain's lower peaks as proof of his deceit.

A few years later, four prospectors in a Fairbanks bar decided they would claim the honor of being the first to conquer Mount McKinley. Before setting off on their dogsleds in December of 1909, they promised to place an American flag on the summit, where their friends might see it through telescopes. It took them four months, most of it spent simply getting to

the mountain and establishing a base camp from which to make a determined push to the summit. In March of 1910, two of them, wearing overalls and unlined parkas, with a bag of doughnuts and a thermos of hot chocolate as provisions, made a dash to the top and planted their flag in an outcropping on the summit of McKinley's North Peak. Many people refused to believe their story. Others pointed out that the North Peak is 850 feet lower than the mountain's South Peak.

Finally, in 1913, a team led by Hudson Stuck, Alaska's Episcopal archdeacon; Harry Karstens, an experienced local outdoorsman; and Walter Harper, the half-Indian son of a fur trapper, made it all the way to the top of South Peak. Stuck blacked out several times during the final ascent, and at the summit his fingers were so numbed by the cold that he double-exposed the photograph of their triumph. But the experience changed him forever.

There was no pride of conquest, no trace of that exultation of victory some enjoy upon the first ascent of a lofty peak, no gloating over good fortune that had hoisted us a few hundred feet higher than others who had struggled and been discomfited.

Rather was the feeling that a privileged communion with the high places of the earth had

been granted . . . and to cast our eyes down from them, seeing all things as they spread out from the windows of heaven itself.

As awe-inspiring as the mountain might have been, what made the region unique for the naturalist Charles Sheldon was the abundance of wildlife teeming all around it: grizzly bears roaming unconcerned about the presence of any other animal, including humans; moose, which Sheldon described as "looking more like prehistoric beasts than any animal we have"; caribou, he said, that "surrounded me like cattle on a cattle ranch"; and the species that had drawn him north in the first place, the distinctive Dall sheep, nearly pure-white animals that he counted by the thousands on the mountainsides.

With Harry Karstens as his guide, Sheldon made two visits to the wilderness around Mount McKin-

ley—one for an entire year—to observe the sheep, study their habits, and collect specimens for the American Museum of Natural History. During a long and lonely winter, when the sun barely rose above the horizon and the temperature rarely rose above zero, Karstens remembered, Sheldon "was continually talking of the beauties of the country and of the variety of the game and wouldn't it make an ideal park. . . . We would [even] talk over the possible boundaries."

Back in New York City, Sheldon made the most of his elite connections and began promoting his idea of making McKinley a park among his fellow members of the Boone and Crockett Club, including the founders, George Bird Grinnell and ex-President Theodore Roosevelt. Nearly twenty years earlier, they had led the effort for laws that saved the buffalo in Yellowstone National Park from being hunted to

TWO TYPES OF SCENERY: Without disputing the majesty of Mount McKinley (above), Sheldon argued that protecting the region's unique Dall sheep (right) and other wild animals was the real reason for creating a national park.

extinction. With a new railroad being built from Anchorage to Fairbanks, Sheldon warned them, the sheep and caribou and other large animals near Mount McKinley faced an equally dire threat from market hunters dispatched to keep the railroad crews fed.

The Boone and Crockett Club swung into action again. In December of 1915, Sheldon had written Stephen Mather, inviting him to become an associate member of the club and asking him to endorse the club's proposal of creating a national park and game refuge around Mount McKinley. Mather had quickly and enthusiastically agreed—and in turn had asked Sheldon to give a speech at his national parks conference. In it, Sheldon argued that a national park was justified for more reasons than spectacular geological formations.

It has been said that the mountains would remain there. . . . Why make it a national park now?

The principal reason for doing it immediately, is to save the magnificent herds of game which . . . are now threatened. . . .

They exist there as a link connecting this life with the life of the past ages just as the records in the rocks show the records of the past ages there before you.

Sheldon kept pushing. He moved to Washington full-time to work on the bill, prowling the halls of the Capitol to push it through. On February 26, 1917, he personally delivered it to President Wilson for signing. His only disappointment was that Congress, in creating Mount McKinley National Park, had ignored his repeated pleas to return the mountain—and its new park—to its original name.

Denali, The High One . . . more sublime perhaps than any other mountain in the world. The Indians who have lived for countless generations in the presence of these colossal mountains have given them names that are both euphonious and appropriate. . . .

Can it be too late to make an exception to current geographic rules and restore these beautiful names—names so expressive of the mountains themselves, and so symbolic of the Indians who bestowed them?

UNKNOWN TERRITORY

With his mentor, Stephen Mather, hospitalized, the task of organizing the brand-new National Park Service fell to Horace Albright. At twenty-seven, he was the youngest person in the fledgling organization—two years younger, even, than the Interior Department's messenger boy.

There was much to be done: testifying before Congress for the funds they had neglected to appropriate when the agency was created, embarking on a ten-thousand-mile inspection of the western parks, fending off questions about his boss's whereabouts, and drafting a lengthy document for the Interior Secretary to issue regarding park policies. "The devil of the thing is the conflicting principles in our organic act," he wrote a friend.

How can we interpret the unrestricted use of the parks for the public and still retain them totally intact for the future?

I think of myself as an explorer in unknown territory. Each idea I have must be tested, each fork of the trail must be examined. Or maybe it's like constructing a house. I'm at the stage where I am laying the foundations. I have no blueprints and no architect. Only the ideal and principles

CRATER LAKE
National Park
OREGON

HAWAII
National Park
HAWAIIAN ISLANDS

ZION
National Monument
UTAH

MT. RAINIER
National Park
WASHINGTON

UNITED STATES RAILROAD ADMINISTRATION
NATIONAL PARK SERIES

UNITED STATES RAILROAD ADMINISTRATION
NATIONAL PARK SERIES

for which the Park Service was created—to preserve, intact, the heritage we were bequeathed.

So it comes down to when I make a decision, I lay another brick for the foundation but must always be concerned that it does not impair the construction of the building as it rises.

Albright's task became even more challenging in April of 1917, when the United States entered the Great War, which had been raging in Europe for almost three years. Almost immediately, western lumber and livestock interests saw the war mobilization as an opportunity to exploit the national parks.

President Wilson was persuaded to reduce the size of Mount Olympus National Monument by one half, in order to open up virgin stands of forest for timber cutting. Ranchers eager to graze their sheep and cattle in the parks encouraged friendly newspapers to editorialize that "soldiers need meat to eat, not wildflowers," and they rewrote a famous Civil War song to become "The Battle Cry of Feed 'Em," which was sung at rallies around the West. There were even proposals that Yellowstone National Park's elk and buffalo herds be slaughtered for canned meat to send to the troops overseas.

Albright did the best he could to protect the parks from it all. When Interior Secretary Lane ordered him to let fifty thousand sheep graze in Yosemite Valley and turn more loose in other parks, Albright reminded him that Muir had called sheep "hoofed locusts" because of the destruction they could cause. Lane persisted. Albright threatened to resign. Ultimately, they compromised: there would be no sheep, but Albright was to permit cattle grazing in some park locations. He quietly arranged to grant the leases to a few sympathetic Sierra Club members, who agreed to graze a minimum number of cattle— and only in areas where they would do the least amount of damage.

As part of the war effort, the government placed the railroads under the control of the United States Railroad Administration and imposed travel restrictions. Arguing that time spent in a national park would be helpful relaxation for soldiers and citizens alike, Albright got park travel exempted from the regulation, even convincing the Railroad Administration to act as a national promotion bureau.

During World War I, the United States Railroad Administration took control of the rail lines. Horace Albright not only got the parks exempted from national travel restrictions, he persuaded the Railroad Administration to promote visitation with colorful brochures.

Despite his efforts, in 1918 the parks experienced their first drop in visitation.

His time as acting director of the Park Service, however, wasn't all headaches. Albright accepted an invitation to visit southern Utah, where the Virgin River carves its way through a beautiful canyon of sandstone cliffs. It had been set aside as a national monument in 1909—named Mukuntuweap, from a Paiute word for "canyon"—but had been virtually ignored by the federal government ever since. Albright was the first senior official from the Interior Department to actually see it.

I was surprised, excited, and thrilled. More than that, I was just plain stunned. I had no concept of the staggering beauty I beheld. Local Utah people said that Yosemite was a [Mukuntuweap] without color. But this didn't faintly prepare me for the reality of the towering rock walls, splashed with brilliant hues of tans and reds interspersed with whites.

The great towers, temples, spires, and peaks appeared unearthly as they encircled the narrow, lush gorge cut by the sparkling Virgin River.

It was love at first sight for me. I was so impressed . . . that I determined we should expand Mukuntuweap and have it made a national park.

Albright's enthusiasm was enough to convince President Wilson to expand the national monument and to change its name from Mukuntuweap—which Albright believed was too hard to pronounce, spell, and remember—to the name the local Mormons had always used for the canyon: Zion, the New Jerusalem, set aside by God for the "pure at heart." Within a year, Congress would set it aside as a national park.

But throughout it all, Albright had to do everything without any guidance from the man he looked up to as a father figure.

[Mr. Mather's doctor] recommended that I be the one and only visitor other than Mrs. Mather for a while. "His life depends upon national parks . . ." [the doctor] said. "I think I can bring him back through the parks, but without them I don't know what may happen."

A lonely pine clings to a sculpted outcropping (above) while trees sprout from the roof of Double Arch Alcove, Zion National Park.

I was so impressed by the red cliffs and wilderness surroundings of Zion Canyon that I determined we should . . . have it made a national park.

In some ways, it was like a smaller but more colorful Yosemite. It had been described as "Yosemite painted in oils."

Horace Albright

The doctor said I could discuss national park affairs, but . . . when a troublesome problem was touched on, I was to treat it in the lightest vein and give cheerful news that things were clearing up nicely.

"Feed him some good news," the doctor advised, "and I think we may be able to bring him out of this thing."

In his regular visits with Mather, Albright always brought along things to cheer up his boss: a copy of the bill creating Mount McKinley National Park and a stack of photos from Alaska; pictures from the 1915 Mather Mountain Party, which Mather insisted on reviewing over and over again as they recounted anecdotes from the adventure. "He loved jokes," Albright wrote, so Albright told him one about a woman tourist at Mesa Verde who had listened to a guide describe the marvels of the ancient Puebloans who built the astonishing cliff dwellings.

Suddenly she inquired, "Well if these people were so marvelous, why did they build their towns so far from the railroad?"

Mather loved it, slapped his knee, and roared with laughter. I left on this high note, promising to come back very soon.

In the fall of 1918, eighteen months after his initial collapse, just as World War I came to an end, Stephen Mather returned to his job—and once again threw himself into his work. It was as if he had never been away. The national parks, he wrote in a popular magazine, seemed "destined" to play a role in "satisfying the longings of the people in times of great nervous tension through the calming and inspiring influence of nature."

The parks will have a constantly enlarging, revivifying influence on our national life, for which there is no other public agency. . . . They are our antidote for national restlessness. . . . They are national character and health builders. . . . They are giving a new impetus to sane living in this country.

Shortly after his return, Mather toured Zion and immediately agreed that his young assistant had been absolutely right about its unique beauty. Then he decided to make a side trip to visit an even lesser known and almost never visited scenic attraction in southern Utah, and at the urging of his guide closed his eyes as they approached. When he was told to open them, he was at the brink of a magnificent natural amphitheater carved by erosion from the side of a mountain ridge, filled with eerie rock spires and minarets called hoodoos.

"He chortled with glee, saying 'marvelous; exquisite; nothing like it anywhere,' " one of his hosts remembered. It was Bryce Canyon, named in honor of an early settler, Ebenezer Bryce, who had long since left the area, after reportedly saying of the canyon that now bore his name: "It's a Hell of a place to lose a cow." Mather saw it instead as a perfect place for a national park and immediately launched a grandiose campaign that eventually brought Bryce Canyon into the fold.

Reinvigorated by his time in the parks, and enthusiastic about the park possibilities of the southwestern deserts, Mather pushed for the creation of Arches National Monument (later a national park) in southeastern Utah, the world's largest collection of exquisite red sandstone architecture, sculpted over the eons by wind, rain, and ice. He also lobbied for a national monument around Lehman Caves in Nevada, in what eventually became a much expanded Great Basin National Park, home of the tough and gnarled bristlecone pines—the oldest living trees on earth, some growing for nearly five thousand years. To accomplish it all, he enlisted the help of the Union Pacific Railroad, persuading them to develop and promote what was called the "celestial circuit" that shuttled tourists from one southwestern treasure to the next.

But now, Mather set his sights on the biggest treasure of them all.

To people of other lands, to whom the Grand Canyon has been known for many years as the greatest scenic wonder in the world, our failure to make it a national park after so many years of appeal to Congress is a matter of astonishment.

Mather (left) and Albright (right) admire the view from the rim of Bryce Canyon. *Overleaf:* Sunset light illuminates the vast array of hoodoos in Bryce Amphitheater.

Wheeler Peak (above) and Lehman Caves (right) in Nevada's Great Basin National Park. Delicate Arch (left), the most widely recognized of the two thousand natural sandstone arches in Arches National Park, also appears on Utah's license plates.

In many of the foreign estimates of the great natural spectacles of America the Grand Canyon stands at the top. Its absence from the list of our national parks, therefore, seems to belittle, in foreign eyes, our entire national-park system. What can the system amount to, they ask, if it doesn't even include the Grand Canyon?

Mather was asking himself the same question. Nothing was more important to him than filling what he considered an inexplicable, inexcusable hole in the system he was building.

THE HEART OF THE WORLD LAID BARE

There is of course no sense at all in trying to describe the Grand Canyon. Those who have not seen it will not believe any possible description. Those who have seen it know that it cannot be described. . . .

It is not a show place, a beauty spot, but a revelation. The Colorado River made it; but you feel when you are there that God gave the Colorado River its instructions. The thing is Beethoven's Ninth Symphony in stone and magic light.

I hear rumors of visitors who were disappointed. The same people will be disappointed at the Day of Judgment.

J. B. PRIESTLY
Harper's Magazine

It is 277 miles long. Ten miles wide. A mile deep—and getting a foot deeper every thousand years, as the Colorado River patiently cuts its way through layer upon layer of geological time. John Muir called it a "grand geological library, a collection of stone books covering . . . tier on tier conveniently arranged for the student," from limestone and sandstone and shale all the way down to some of the oldest exposed rock on earth, Precambrian Vishnu schist, formed 1.7 billion years ago.

Over thousands of years, it has been the home of the ancestral Puebloans and the Hopi, the Hualapai and Havasupai, the Paiute and the Navajo. In 1540, it first entered recorded history when Spanish conquistadors under the command of Coronado, referring

to it only as a *barranca*, or large canyon, peered into its depths and were awed and staggered by its immensity, just as every visitor who followed them would be.

Three hundred years later, in 1857, an American explorer named Joseph Christmas Ives wrecked his boat trying to ascend the river, but brought back the first sketches of what he called the "Big Canyon of the Colorado," as well as a dire prediction of its future. "The region is, of course, altogether valueless," Ives wrote.

After entering it there is nothing to do but leave. Ours has been the first, and will doubtless be the last, party of whites to visit this profitless locality.

It seems intended by nature that the Colorado river, along the greater portion of its lonely and

Lava Falls rapids on the Colorado River as photographed on John Wesley Powell's second expedition through the Grand Canyon in 1872

Celebrity salesman Buffalo Bill Cody (second from right) makes his pitch to potential landowners on the Grand Canyon's rim in 1892.

majestic way, shall be forever unvisited and undisturbed.

But in 1869 a one-armed Civil War veteran and college geology professor named John Wesley Powell, hoping to fill in the biggest remaining gap of unknown territory in the maps of the United States, set off down the Colorado to ride the wild, uncharted river and make the first detailed study of the massive architecture of stone that encloses it. Danger, Powell wrote, lay around every bend.

Down in these grand, gloomy depths we glide, ever listening, for the mad waters keep up their roar; ever watching, ever peering ahead, for the narrow canyon is winding, and the river is closed in so that we can see but a few hundred yards, and what there may be ahead we know not; but we listen for falls, and watch for rocks, or stop now and then, in the bay of a recess, to admire the gigantic scenery.

It was a costly, deadly trip—he began with nine men in four wooden boats and emerged with five men and two boats—but Powell's expedition was a huge success, the first known navigation of the Colorado. His subsequent explorations in the 1870s, especially his published report, with illustrations by Thomas Moran, established forever that the place would be known as the *Grand* Canyon.

Other explorers—accompanied by other artists—soon followed. The canyon began attracting more and more attention. By the 1890s, Buffalo Bill Cody was taking time off from his Wild West Show and bringing wealthy Englishmen to Arizona on behalf of a land and cattle company that hoped the world-famous showman could persuade them to invest in expensive hunting lodges along the North Rim. Solitary prospectors were combing the desolate side canyons of the greater gorge, chasing rumors that the old Mormon outlaw, John D. Lee, had once discovered gold in a now secret location.

Near the South Rim, a failed miner named "Captain" John Hance had built a log cabin and was entertaining the occasional tourist with colorful tales of his exploits—like the time, he claimed, that the canyon had been so filled with clouds that he had started walking from rim to rim on snowshoes, only to find himself marooned on one of the solitary pinnacles when a fresh wind swept the clouds away. Hance improved an Indian trail to the canyon's bottom, expanded his cabin into the area's first hotel, and became the canyon rim's first postmaster in 1897 at a post office he named Tourist, Arizona.

John Muir had been one of the early visitors. "No matter how far you have wandered," he said, "or how many famous gorges and valleys you have seen, this one . . . will seem as novel to you, as unearthly in the color and grandeur and quantity of its architecture, as if you had found it after death, on some other star."

It seems a gigantic statement for even nature to make, all in one mighty stone word, apprehended at once like a burst of light . . . coming in glory to mind and heart as to a home prepared for it from the very beginning.

Wildness so godful, cosmic, primeval, bestows a new sense of earth's beauty and size. Not even from high mountains does the world seem so wide, so like a star in glory of light on its way through the heavens.

. . . Here, for a few moments at least, there is silence, and all are in dead earnest, as if awed and hushed by an earthquake.

"Nature has a few big places beyond man's power to spoil," Muir added, "the ocean, the two icy ends of the globe, and the Grand Canyon." Nevertheless, he and others urged that it be protected as a national park.

Proposals to make it a national park dated back to the 1880s, shortly after Yellowstone had been established. Senator Benjamin Harrison introduced bills in 1882, 1883, and 1886; had any of them passed, the Grand Canyon would have become the world's second national park. But they all had failed in Congress because of fierce opposition from local ranchers, miners, and settlers who did not want the federal government imposing restrictions on what they could and could not do. In 1893, Harrison was president and offered at least a modicum of preservation by using his executive powers to create the Grand Canyon Forest Reserve.

Fifteen years later, when Congress again refused to make it a national park, President Theodore Roosevelt had stretched the limits of the newly passed Antiquities Act, and with a stroke of his pen established the Grand Canyon National Monument. The canyon, Roosevelt said, represented "the most impressive piece of scenery I have ever looked at . . . the one great sight which every American should see." "Leave it as it is," he had advised the people of Arizona. "I hope you will not have a building of any kind, not a summer cottage, a hotel, or anything else to mar the wonderful grandeur, the sublimity, the great loneliness and beauty of the canyon." No one had listened to him.

A few rustic hotels were already perched on the canyon precipice when the Atchison, Topeka and Santa Fe Railway extended its tracks to the South Rim. The company quickly began construction of even more buildings—the Lookout, Hermit's Rest, Hopi House, and the massive hundred-room, three-and-a-half-story El Tovar hotel, built for a quarter of a million dollars in the same grand style as its counterparts in Yellowstone, Glacier, and other national parks. The Santa Fe railroad and its partner, the Fred Harvey Company, did everything they could to promote the canyon as a tourist destination, or at least as a quick "must stop" for passengers on their way to and from the West Coast. They advertised heavily in leading magazines, produced thousands of glossy brochures to create a mystique about the natural wonder, and provided lodging, food, and studio space to some of the nation's best-known artists—including Thomas Moran, who returned every season for more than a quarter century and became such an attraction himself the Santa Fe used him in their advertising.

Yearly visitation rose into the tens of thousands. Among them was an itinerant piano player and aspiring composer from Los Angeles named Ferde Grofé, who was so overwhelmed by the experience that years later the memory of it would inspire his masterpiece, *The Grand Canyon Suite*.

An early-twentieth-century tourist on the South Rim admires what Muir called a "grand geological library . . . tier on tier conveniently arranged for the student."

Equally impressed was a humorist from Paducah, Kentucky, named Irvin S. Cobb.

I think my preconceived conception of the Canyon was the same conception most people have before they come to see it for themselves—a straight up-and-down slit in the earth, fabulously steep and fabulously deep; nevertheless merely a slit. It is no such thing!

Imagine . . . the very heart of the world . . . laid bare before our eyes!

. . . There is nothing between you and the undertaker except six thousand feet, more or less, of dazzling Arizona climate.

Most tourists, Cobb observed, arrived by train in the morning, "take a hurried look at the Canyon, mail a few postal cards, buy a Navajo blanket or two and are out again that night." Among them, he added, was a bored young man he encountered on the hotel veranda who asked, "in the patronizing voice of an experienced traveler, 'is there anything interesting to see round here?' "

Unlike those content to limit their experience to the view from the South Rim, Cobb decided to take the long mule ride to the Colorado River, a mile below, on the Bright Angel Trail. He and his companions descended the steep and twisting trail, he said, "as nervous as cats and some holding to their saddle-pommels with death grips."

All at once you notice that the person immediately ahead of you has apparently ridden right over the wall of the canyon. A moment ago his arched back loomed before you; now he is utterly gone. It is at this point that some tourists tender their resignations—to take effect immediately. . . . Nearly always there is some man who

remembers where he left his umbrella or something, and he goes back after it and forgets to return.

. . . You reflect that thousands of persons have already done this thing; that thousands of others . . . are going to do it, and that no serious accident has yet occurred—which is some comfort, but not much. . . .

The natives will tell you the tale of a man who made the trip by crawling round the more sensational corners upon his hands and knees.

Deeper into the canyon, Cobb wrote, "you realize that this canyon is even more beautiful when viewed from within than it is when viewed from without."

Also, you begin to notice now that it is most extensively autographed.

Apparently about every other person who came this way remarked to himself that this canyon was practically completed and only needed his signature as collaborator to round it out—so then he signed it and it was a finished job.

Above: Helping a mule up the Bright Angel Trail, c. 1910
Left: Dawn at Yavapai Point, when, Muir wrote, "every rock temple then becomes a temple of music . . . shouting color hallelujahs."

Back at the rim, the travelers could purchase photographs taken at the start of the trip, "so you can see for yourself," Cobb explained, "just how pale and haggard and wall-eyed and like a typhoid patient you looked." The photographs were the work of two brothers from Pennsylvania, Ellsworth and Emery Kolb, perhaps the most hardworking of all the entrepreneurs who descended upon the Grand Canyon in the early twentieth century, hoping to earn a living off its scenery. In 1902 they had purchased a photographic studio in Williams, Arizona, more than fifty miles from the canyon, and had its contents moved all the way to the South Rim, where they opened up for business, at first in a canvas tent near one of the hotels, and then in a wooden structure they built at the head of Bright Angel Trail.

Every morning, as the muleback caravans began their descent, Emery Kolb would take their photograph at a prearranged spot near the trailhead with his 5-by-7-inch view camera and enter information about them in his logbook. Then he would take off down the trail himself, carrying his glass plate negatives as he ran. With water at such a premium on the rim (it had to be shipped in by rail from a source a long distance away), the Kolbs had constructed a makeshift darkroom near a small spring halfway between the rim and the river. Kolb would develop his pictures, then scurry back up the trail in time to offer the photos for sale when the mule trains returned from the bottom. Each trip to the darkroom was four and a half miles and three thousand vertical feet down; four and a half miles and three thousand vertical feet back up.

During slow seasons, the Kolb brothers set off to explore parts of the canyon tourists never experienced, always lugging their bulky camera equipment and often taking great risks to find the perfect vantage point. They brought back some of the most stunning photographs of the Grand Canyon the world had ever seen, offered them for sale, and had trouble keeping up with the demand for copies.

In 1911 they decided to retrace John Wesley Powell's historic boat trip down the Colorado—and record it, not only with still photographs, but with a motion picture camera. The trip took three rough months and included a number of close calls on the

CANYON CHRONICLERS: No one knew the Grand Canyon better than the enterprising Kolb brothers, who perched their photographic studio (below) at the head of the Bright Angel Trail. To collect dramatic pictures (at right) from unusual vantage points, they were willing to take dangerous risks. At left, Emery lowers Ellsworth, holding his camera, down a vertical chasm.

turbulent river, including one in which Emery insisted on filming his brother's precarious situation before tossing him a life preserver. But the Kolbs emerged with the first moving pictures of the raging Colorado and the majestic canyon it had carved and took their finished product on a lecture tour to packed theaters all around the East Coast. Then they built an addition to their studio on the canyon's rim to house a small auditorium, where every day Emery Kolb would personally narrate the film for tourists who had come thousands of miles to see the Grand

Canyon, but preferred that at least part of their experience be confined to a movie screen.

By 1919 the Grand Canyon was attracting far more tourists than well-established national parks like Glacier or Mesa Verde—and nearly as many as Yellowstone or Yosemite. But it was still a national monument, and still administered by the Forest Service. Grazing was permitted; cattle herds roamed freely right up to both rims; and while settlers were prohibited from filing for homesteads, mining claims were still allowed wherever a prospector thought a valuable mineral might be found. Stephen Mather wanted all that changed by making it a national park. "Mather desperately wanted this park," Horace Albright remembered, adding, "I felt it would be a tremendous boost to his health and well-being, so I put in an enormous amount of time and energy in the project."

But Mather and Albright found themselves blocked at every turn by a man who considered the canyon his own private domain—and was unafraid to take on the federal government, the Santa Fe railroad, or anyone else who got in his way.

I did not go into the Grand Canyon for the purpose of exploring it for a tourist proposition. I went there to seek a fortune, which all prospectors expect to make. . . . I was exploring the Grand Canyon and pioneering in the West, preaching to the world its possibilities before [other] men . . . ever knew there was a Grand Canyon.

I have always said that I would make more money out of the Grand Canyon than any other man.

RALPH HENRY CAMERON

Ralph Henry Cameron's ambitions—and opinion of himself—were as grand as the canyon he planned to exploit. He had left his native New England and come west in 1883, and when he reached the Grand Canyon, everywhere he looked he saw an opportunity. According to his own account, he had blazed the first wagon road from Flagstaff to the South Rim, started the first stage line to travel over it, opened the first successful mining operations within the canyon, and spent nearly half a million dollars to improve the first trails down to the river.

Some of his claims may even have been partially true. Certainly no one in the region ever displayed more talent at persuading faraway Easterners to invest in his grandiose projects, and no one ever used the mining laws so creatively in getting what he wanted. A few of Cameron's mines actually yielded some valuable ore, but the vast majority of his claims seemed conveniently located on the most scenic spots along the South Rim—and he never seemed to do much mining on them.

At one claim, near the head of the Bright Angel Trail (which he preferred to call the "Cameron Trail"), he built a log cabin, named it Cameron's Hotel, and dispatched employees to hound tourists getting off the train to patronize it. The Santa Fe railroad moved its terminal several hundred feet, so its passengers would disembark farther from Cameron's establishment and closer to its own. Cameron responded by filing more questionable mining claims surrounding El Tovar and other railroad properties, tying up the Santa Fe's plans for further improvements in a tangle of legal suits, until they bought him off with a $40,000 settlement.

Based on his prior claims, Cameron controlled access to the Bright Angel Trail and erected a gate at the rim, where his brother collected a toll of a dollar a person. When Coconino County was declared the trail's proper owner, Cameron used his influence as a county commissioner to be awarded the franchise to continue operating it and collecting the tolls.

Halfway down the trail, at a small oasis called Indian Garden where Cameron had filed yet another mining claim, he operated a ramshackle tent camp. There he charged passing travelers outrageous prices for water, then charged again for the only outhouses between the rim and the river. The so-called comfort stations were in such deplorable condition that many people wouldn't use them. "Women in whom modesty has restrained obedience to the demands of nature have suffered permanent and serious injury," one person complained. When the Fred Harvey Company and Santa Fe railroad offered to build better comfort stations—free of charge—at the trail's end, Cameron took them to court on grounds their construction crews would be illegally crossing his claims to get there. Friendly local judges sided with Cameron.

Stephen Mather's introduction to the boss of the Grand Canyon had come in 1915, when his seemingly simple effort to erect a memorial plaque on the South Rim honoring John Wesley Powell's historic exploration turned into a nightmare that lasted for years. Cameron claimed the proposed location for the memorial as his own, so the plaque had to be stored at the El Tovar hotel. "This just made Mather more angry," Albright said, "and determined to safe-

Ralph Henry Cameron (left) tried to monopolize the Grand Canyon's most strategic spots by filing often bogus mining claims. He demanded a dollar toll for use of the Bright Angel Trail, and halfway down, at his Indian Garden rest stop (above), he charged travelers high prices for water—and then charged them again for the use of the only outhouses between the rim and river.

guard this great chasm by creating it a national park."

Meanwhile, as Mather steadily built support in Congress for his park proposal, federal investigators ruled virtually all of Cameron's claims invalid, because of their lack of mineral value. The Secretary of the Interior ordered him to abandon them.

Cameron ignored it all—and instead filed fifty-five new claims, bringing his total to 13,000 strategically placed acres. In a lawsuit working its way toward the Supreme Court, his lawyers were even arguing that Theodore Roosevelt's executive order creating the Grand Canyon National Monument had been an illegal application of the Antiquities Act. "I shall fight it in the courts as long as I live," Cameron warned. "The people of Arizona are behind me. The people of Coconino County are behind me. The people of the United States, when I get through, will say that I have done well."

In 1919, Congress at last passed a bill creating Grand Canyon National Park. A year later, when the Supreme Court finally and unequivocally ruled against Cameron's challenge to the Antiquities Act, Mather and Albright figured that their troubles with him were over at last.

They couldn't have been more wrong. In the election of 1920, Arizona had sent him to Washington as a United States senator. "I feel like getting even," Cameron had written a friend, "and if I live, I certainly will."

AN EYE FOR NATURE

I remember as a boy loving sunsets from my bedroom window. . . . I remember the fairy forms of the trees when they shed their leaves. I remember what the sycamore trees looked like, and the maple trees.

I never had any doubt about the existence of a Divine being. To see a tree coming out in the spring was enough to impress me with the fact that God existed.

I think perhaps I have always had an eye for nature.

JOHN D. ROCKEFELLER JR.

John D. Rockefeller Jr. was the only son of the richest—and some said, most hated—man in America: John D. Rockefeller Sr., the founder of the vast Standard Oil trust, which at the time refined more than 90 percent of the oil sold in America. John D. Jr. had been raised in accordance with his father's strict Baptist creed: to work hard, to watch every penny, and remember to give to charity. As a quiet and serious-minded young boy, he also grew to appreciate the peaceful solitude that could be found in contemplating a beautiful, natural scene.

In 1908, he had come to Mount Desert Island with his wife, Abby, a New Englander who instilled in him an abiding love of the Maine coast. Two years later he purchased an estate near Seal Harbor, on the quiet side of the island, where his growing family could spend their summers in relative privacy and enjoy what he called "one of the greatest views in the world."

That same year, at age thirty-six, Rockefeller had made a momentous decision. He would step away from the pursuit of even greater wealth and the management of his father's extensive business interests, and, partly to reverse the despised public image of the Rockefeller family, devote himself instead to a single goal—"the social purposes," he said, "to which a great fortune could be dedicated."

Then Charles W. Eliot introduced him to George Dorr— "an impulsive, enthusiastic, eager person," Eliot wrote, "who works at high tension, neglects his meals, sits up too late at night, and rushes about from one pressing thing to another; but he is very diligent, as well as highly inventive."

When Dorr approached him, desperately seeking funds to acquire more land to turn the new national monument on Mount Desert Island into a national park, Rockefeller was at first reluctant to help. He was wary of turning over prime coastal real estate to the common man. "Do you not feel that the establishment of this monument will bring an undesirable class of tourists to Bar Harbor in their automobiles who, if automobiles are admitted to the south side of the Island, will be a real nuisance to the residents there?" he had written Eliot. Dorr and Eliot persisted, and Rockefeller relented. He gave $17,500—and then, as Dorr pressed forward with new energy, quickly became the effort's principal benefactor.

While he quietly began buying up more land and giving it to Dorr's organization, Rockefeller poured even more money and personal energy into building the most ambitious network of wilderness carriage roads New England had ever seen, not only paying for it all, but overseeing every detail: insisting on the highest-quality materials and the most sensitive consideration of the scenery, personally establishing the line of each new road before surveyors were dispatched and road crews began their work.

Be sure your men cut trees for too narrow a roadway rather than too wide a one. . . . I want to spare every tree possible, without spoiling the line of the road.

All stumps shall be pulled or grubbed out. . . . Particular care must be taken in the burning of all brush and stumps so as not to scorch or injure growing trees.

. . . I am particularly delighted with the careful and thorough way, slow and tedious though it has been, in which you have cleaned up the ledges over which blasted rock had been thrown. This has immensely reduced the visibility of the road scar.

Meant for the aesthetic enjoyment of people riding in open carriages, on horseback, or on a bicycle, the paths were painstakingly located to present a series of scenic vistas displaying Mount Desert at its best. Mountaintops were avoided, for fear that the roads would spoil their view. Each bridge, made of local granite so it would blend into its setting, was individually designed, including one that was given a graceful curve to save two trees from being destroyed, and oriented so that a nearby waterfall was in the same line of sight as the bridge's arch.

During his frequent inspections, Rockefeller grew to know each workman by name and shared in their satisfaction of creating something of such lasting beauty. If he showed up at a work site in his carriage, dressed in fancy clothes, they called him "Mr. Rockefeller." If he was in work boots and tweeds, they considered him "Mr. Junior" and knew they could approach him with their own suggestions on improving the final product.

By the time he was through, Rockefeller had built fifty-seven miles of carriage roads weaving through Mount Desert Island, donated thousands of acres, and spent $3.5 million for the potential park.

Our idea as to the park has been to develop it for . . . people who would be responsive to the beauty and inspiration of its scenery, and can get away for a brief or longer holiday. . . .

What we want to provide for specially is the need of people of moderate or narrow means who would appreciate what it has to give.

GEORGE DORR

By 1918, George Dorr's single-minded drive to enlarge Sieur de Monts National Monument and turn it into a national park was picking up momentum. Some 15,000 acres of Mount Desert Island—triple the original gift—was now being offered.

Stephen Mather was enthusiastic about the proposed park. Having a national park in the East, closer to the nation's major population centers, could help build public support for the larger park system he was hoping to create. It would also be a different kind of park—smaller, more intimate, and set aside, not from federal land, but as a gift from some of the country's wealthiest citizens.

Eventually, the only stumbling block was what name the proposed park would have. Dorr preferred continuing the name used for the national monument, Sieur de Monts, but "found it difficult of pronunciation for Americans not versed in French." So he proposed Mount Desert National Park, only to run into more confusion and difficulties when he testified in Congress.

Someone asked what the name meant. Was it really a desert?

And I had to explain that in the old French meaning of the word, in Champlain's time, the word "desert" meant uninhabited by man, wild but not devoid of life.

Then another asked, "Where is it?"

And then I realized I had counted too much on the knowledge of our coast and island the country over.

Still hoping to preserve some connection to the island's heritage, Dorr switched the proposed name to Lafayette National Park, in honor of the French general who had befriended the American Revolution. With that, the bill passed and was signed on February 26, 1919, the same day the Grand Canyon became a national park. (Ten years later, the name would be changed again—to Acadia, the French word for "heaven on earth.")

At last, Dorr felt his beloved island was in the proper hands.

The present generation will pass as my own has done, but the mountains and the woods, the coasts and streams that have now passed through the agency of the Park to the National Government will continue as a national possession, a public possession, henceforth for all time to come. It never will be given up to private ownership again.

John D. Rockefeller Jr. and his wife and children outside their summer home on Mount Desert Island (above, left). In addition to buying land to donate toward a new national park, Rockefeller paid for and personally supervised construction of fifty-seven miles of carriage roads (above) with graceful stone bridges (below, right) meant to blend in with the scenery. *Overleaf:* Sunset at Acadia National Park

The men in control will change, the Government itself will change, but its possession by the people will remain.

George Dorr was now sixty-five. Despite his age, he was immediately named the first superintendent of the first national park east of the Mississippi and the first to be created out of private land. He would remain in that position for the next twenty-five years. He would continue badgering his summertime neighbors to donate their property and would so thoroughly sacrifice what remained of his inheritance to the cause that when he died in 1944, his estate had money for his funeral only because its trustee had secretly put $2,000 aside to prevent Dorr from giving it away. Even Oldfarm, his parents' beloved "cottage," had been bequeathed to the park Dorr had devoted half his life to creating and nurturing.

Circling over a part of the island he had especially loved, friends scattered his ashes from a plane. Two wealthy matrons enjoying lunch on the terrace of their summer "cottage" looked up as some of the plane's wafting cargo drifted into their teacups.

"Oh dear," one of them exclaimed. "It's Mr. Dorr."

Left: Bass Harbor lighthouse by moonlight, Acadia National Park
Below: Stephen Mather doing what he loved to do: speak to a crowd at the dedication of a new national park, in this instance Zion in Utah

Who has ever thrilled with pride of country and the desire to fight for it by the sight of factories and closely packed humanity in the towns and cities alone? Our most inspiring patriotic songs speak of the love of the land that is spread about us. . . .

Anyone who has been so fortunate as to witness [the national parks] and spend quiet hours in the inspiring contemplation of their beauties will surely return home with a burning determination to love and work for, and if necessary fight and die for, the glorious land which is his.

STEPHEN MATHER

National parks could now be found in the territories of Hawaii and Alaska, from the coast of Maine to the canyons of Utah and Arizona, and there was a new agency trying to figure out how to care for them all. Stephen Mather could easily claim victory for setting it in motion, and step down. But he was feeling strong again and bursting with more ideas. He wanted more national parks; he wanted them within reach of everyone; and he wanted them promoted to the American people as one cohesive system.

With the world war over and people ready to see America again, Mather believed it more important than ever to promote the national parks as the focus of their travels.

The Yosemite, the Yellowstone, the Grand Canyon are national properties in which every citizen has a vested interest; they belong as much to the man of Massachusetts, of Michigan, of Florida, as they do to the people of California, of Wyoming, and of Arizona.

They are a great national heritage. . . . There is much that can be done in making them better known . . . if they are going to be the true playgrounds of the people that we want them to be.

Meanwhile, in his single-minded quest to build public support for the parks, Mather had begun to ally himself with the machine that was already rapidly transforming American life—while others worried that he was making a devil's bargain.

AN INTERVIEW WITH NEVADA BARR
STORIES OF DISCOVERY

Nevada Barr was in the middle of a career in the theater when a desire to be involved with nature prompted her to take seasonal jobs with the National Park Service—first at Isle Royale National Park, then Guadalupe Mountains, then Mesa Verde, and then Mississippi's Natchez Trace.

Those experiences, in turn, inspired her to begin a series of novels—now numbering fifteen—whose protagonist is Anna Pigeon, a spirited female park ranger who always seems to be working in a different national park when a mysterious murder needs solving. Intertwined with the sleuthing and Anna's personal travails are descriptions of the parks themselves—and a behind-the-scenes look into the lives of park employees.

Why do we need national parks?

I think we require national parks for our psychic stability and sanity. We need national parks because we psychologically need to have a place to go when we can't be "here" anymore. That we physically have a place we can go to that is beautiful, and it's the same when we go back, is a miracle unto itself.

I want to be able to say, "Go see the falls," and the falls will still be there. The parks are always where I can go home again. I go back to my hometown, and there is a Safeway where I used to play with Silvia Gonzales, and they have turned my old school into a junk shop. But the parks don't do that. So these are places we can always go home—and paradoxically, where we can always see into the future and hope for the better things.

How did you like being a park ranger?

The satisfaction of working in the Park Service is amazing. On Isle Royale, I lived in a cabin where little red foxes and their kits cavorted on my lawn, and moose walked by my house. In Mesa Verde, great black bears came up and knocked over my garbage can. I got to go into the ruins at night. In Guadalupe, I spent days up in the wilderness tracking mountain lions.

Isle Royale was the first park that I had worked in, and as a brand-new ranger, I wanted to tell people all about the park, and I realized the first day I was there in the visitor center, they had to tell me about the park. That's when it transferred from me, as the hotshot new ranger who knew everything, to the people. Because my job was to hear them tell their story about their park.

What stories did they tell you?

I think the thing that unites the stories that you hear over and over—and they're all the same but they're all different—is that they discovered something in that park. It doesn't matter what it was. Maybe it was that they could go longer without water, or that they were stronger than they thought, or that they got frightened and they'd never been frightened, or that they found a flower that they are absolutely sure nobody else has ever seen. It's almost always their tales of discovery.

We're a visual people, and when we can go someplace and we can see what God—or whoever you choose to place this on—what nature can do, we are put in awe. And to be put in awe is a sense of freedom, it is a sense of selflessness. When you go into nature and you are overawed by something, it sets you free.

People love the vistas, but mostly we've always gone to the mountaintop to find ourselves. This is in our history, it's in our lit-

Writer and former park ranger Nevada Barr
Above right: Rocky Scoville Point on Isle Royale National Park

erature, it's in our collective conscious that we do this. And people will go to the park, and even being away from civilization for five hours, or a night, people discover something about themselves.

But all of the stories and questions surely can't be that profound.

Park rangers have collections of stupid questions, because we so enjoy them. Wind Cave has one of my favorites. The rangers there occasionally get asked what the cave weighs. "Uh, nothing. It's a hole in the ground." And we get, "What time do the moose come out for pictures?" at Isle Royale. You can't even count the number of silly questions you get.

And of course, when I go to the parks as a citizen, as opposed to a ranger, I ask those questions. Because I'm there to be amazed. I'm not there to read the sign that says "Restroom." So I'll walk right under it and say, "Where's the restroom?"

It's been said that the national parks are a pact between generations. Did you feel that?

One of the Park Service's main statutes, which they drum into you, is to conserve the natural and cultural beauty for future generations. I would see this in people who, they would come in and the grandfathers would tell stories. I'd usually see it at the evening pro-

grams. You'd do your thing and then some old lady or some old guy would say, "I used to come up here with Momma in the 1930s."

And they would have their forty-year-old daughter with them, and there'd be a little kid running around, chasing mosquitoes, or doing whatever, and you know that kid's going to come back, and he's going to say, "You know, I used to come up here with Momma in the 1990s. And back then . . ."

It is a place that, your story goes there and it's different, but the place itself is the same. So you can tie right back into Grandma, and Momma, and your grandson and his grandson. Because it's a through line for you.

Any other ranger stories you want to pass on?

The story is, a man came up to Yosemite and the ranger was sitting at the front gate and the man said, "I've only got an hour to see Yosemite. If you only had an hour to see Yosemite, what would you do?" And the ranger said, "Well, I'd go right over there, and I'd sit on that rock, and I'd cry."

That story is famous in the Park Service. And I think that if we couldn't spend time in the national parks as a people, we would just go sit on our rock and we would cry.

CHAPTER FOUR

GOING HOME

I N LATE 1915, on the train ride back to their home in Lincoln, Nebraska, after visiting the Panama Pacific International Exposition in San Francisco, Margaret and Edward Gehrke decided to take the one-day side excursion to the Grand Canyon offered by the Atchison, Topeka and Santa Fe Railway. Margaret had never seen anything like it before in her life. "A few things in this beautiful old world are too big to talk about," she wrote of the experience. "One can only weep before so supreme a spectacle of glory and of majesty!"

Margaret was thirty-two, a lover of books and poetry who had read and admired John Muir. After studying the classics at the University of Nebraska, she had taught school until shortly after she married Edward, a plumber who had gone into the house-building business. His passion was dogs and fishing—and photographing everything he saw. Hers was dreaming about the yearly excursions the childless couple began taking once Edward's business started to flourish.

Over the course of nearly thirty years, Edward would bring along his Kodak camera, snapping pictures Margaret would later place in photo albums to commemorate their adventures. Margaret would record the start of every trip as "the day of days" in her journal and then set down her impressions at every stop.

> *All day the Canyon grew on us. This afternoon we did some climbing down and regretted that we had not made the trail trip. Sunset came—a gorgeous Arizona sunset and lit the Canyon with a riot of a million colors. It was wonderful!*
>
> *We have had another wonderful day together. Let those who will, buy lands and hoard money; we will have our memories, glad memories of golden experiences together.*

The brief visit to the Grand Canyon had provided Margaret's travel planning with a new focus. In 1917, the Gehrkes took the Chicago, Burlington and Quincy line to Yellowstone, where they settled into one of the Wylie company's tent houses nestled in

Overleaf: Wotan's Throne seen from Cape Royal, Grand Canyon National Park. *Right:* Admiring the view near Mojave Point, Grand Canyon National Park

Following a wooded trail around Lake McDonald.

Writing of these things.

the woods and were thrilled when one of the park's black bears paid a call on their campsite.

Two years later, the Great Northern Railway's *Oriental Limited* took them to Glacier National Park. For a week they hiked and rode horseback from one of the Great Northern's hotels and chalets to another. "We have seen much in a short time," Margaret wrote, "but still I have not found the peace I seek. I have found five hotels filled with crowds, I have seen beautiful scenery, but not the deep silence of the hills."

Then a boat ferried them to a quiet spot on the far shore of Lake McDonald.

We have a wonderful location: camped in a forest of tall pines, over looking the Lake. At last I have found the "spirit of the woods." . . . I shall like it here very much.

They lingered there for eleven more days, alternating between relaxation—for Edward, fishing; for Margaret, writing—and periodic, strenuous forays high into the mountains, including one nineteen-mile hike to Avalanche Lake and then a twenty-mile climb to Sperry Glacier. "It was a good day's work," Margaret told her diary. "Back in the prairies of Nebraska we will remember this."

Then the train delivered them back to Lincoln. "To come home on Edward's birthday was nice," Margaret wrote, "if returning home can ever be said

to be pleasant." Within days, her diary recorded that "the house-keeping wheels begin. I swept and dusted, thoroughly cleaned the front rooms."

But Margaret was already dreaming of more national parks beckoning her and Edward. And although the railroads had introduced them to the parks, in the future the Gehrkes would travel a different way. Outside their house in Lincoln sat a new Buick—one of seventeen Edward would own in the next twenty years.

OPEN SESAME

The national parks themselves . . . are old as we count age in America. But until Stephen T. Mather conceived them all combined as a system . . . they had existed unnoticed.

Once pointed out, however, the imagination of the nation seized the conception with immense zest. . . . From ocean to ocean the plain people hailed this new proof of our national idealism, and massed themselves behind the system's splendid development. . . .

Suddenly our national parks became our most wonderful possession . . . the shining badge of the nation's glory, sharing somewhat even of the sacredness of the flag.

ROBERT STERLING YARD

For Stephen Mather, being the first director of the National Park Service was more than a civil service job—it was a calling to a noble cause, something so compelling it had drawn him away from private industry, where his business skills and genius for promotion had made him a millionaire several times over.

He could be a whirlwind of action, and his intense energy and outgoing personality had earned him the nickname "the eternal freshman." But Mather was also prone to crippling spells of depression, mental collapses that required hospitalization. He always found the solace and rejuvenation he needed so badly in the parks.

Now Mather wanted all Americans to experience that healing power. But he realized that until more people started showing up, Congress would never create more parks, or even support the existing ones.

AN ALBUM OF MEMORIES: Margaret and Edward Gehrke (below, center and right) compiled a remarkable record of their trips to national parks. Edward snapped thousands of photographs, which Margaret placed in a series of scrapbooks, with handwritten notes as captions (left). In addition, she kept her own extensive diary of their adventures.

LODGMENT IN EDEN

I heard the other day that a question has been raised as to whether automobiles should be admitted in the Yosemite Valley. May a word be permitted on that subject?

If Adam had known what harm the serpent was going to work, he would have tried to prevent him from finding lodgment in Eden; and if you stop to realize what the result of the automobile will be in that wonderful, that incomparable valley, you will keep it out.

. . . Do not let the serpent enter Eden at all.

LORD JAMES BRYCE

On the afternoon of June 23, 1900, noises never heard before in Yosemite Valley began reverberating off the granite walls: the rattle and hiss of a brand-new, two-cylinder, ten-horsepower Locomobile, the first car ever to enter the valley.

Its driver was Oliver Lippincott, who at three hundred pounds weighed half as much as the vehicle he was driving. Lippincott's dreams were equally expansive. Pictures of his ground-breaking adventure, he hoped, would generate priceless publicity for himself and for the Locomobile Company, which soon featured them in its advertising.

For several weeks, Lippincott motored around the scenic valley—spooking the horses of passing carriages, turning the heads of hikers, surprising everyone he overtook. He even took his contraption up to Glacier Point, 3,254 feet above the valley floor—though once there, Lippincott thought it more prudent to let someone else stand in his place when the car was posed for the most dramatic shot. Lippincott, meanwhile, pondered his achievement.

As we sat out on that cliff . . . I had a realizing sense of what a very small thing man is, but my respect for my race grew as I reflected upon the wonders it can accomplish, scaling such heights without visible effort and merely by the aid of a little gasoline, some steam and inventive genius.

But would not modern ideas and modern inventions, intruding into the heart of primeval nature, rob it of much of its charm?

Yet there is only one Yosemite, I reasoned, now inaccessible to the majority of people, and if modern invention can bring it closer to the people the result must be beneficial.

Two years later, in January of 1902, Lippincott made history once more by becoming the first person to drive a car to the rim of the Grand Canyon.

That same year, Yellowstone National Park witnessed its first automobile, a Winton driven by a man named Henry Merry—but the car caused such a disturbance that the driver was quickly arrested and ordered to leave.

At the time, the U.S. Cavalry was still responsible for patrolling the national parks, and the officers in charge soon decided that if horses and automobiles couldn't get along, they were on the horses' side. For a decade more, while the rest of the nation switched to the horseless carriage with greater and greater enthusiasm, in the national parks at least, automobiles were banned.

Oliver Lippincott drives his Locomobile, the first automobile to enter Yosemite, through the Wawona Tunnel Tree (below left) in 1900. When he got to Glacier Point (below right), he let someone else pose in his place on the precipice.

Stephen Mather and Horace Albright (top) open a gate made of elk antlers in ceremonies officially starting the season at Yellowstone, 1920s. One of many presidents to visit Yellowstone, Warren G. Harding, escorting his wife (bottom), strolls through a geyser basin with Albright as his guide.

"There never could be too many tourists for Stephen Mather," Horace Albright remembered.

He wanted as many as possible to enjoy his "treasures" . . . no matter how they got to the parks.

He was at heart a public-relations man and wanted the country to be aware of the national parks.

Personally, both Mather and Albright liked nothing better than taking long hikes or horseback camping trips deep into the backcountry of a national park. But they understood that most visitors had neither the time, nor the inclination, to experience a park that way. "American tourist travel is of a swift tempo," Albright noted. "People want to keep moving [and] are satisfied with brief stops here and there."

"This is exactly what we don't want in the national parks," Mather told a friend during a visit to Coney Island. People might enjoy the carnival atmosphere, he admitted, but "our job in the Park Service is to keep the national parks as close to what God made them as possible and as far as we can from a horror like this."

Yet he and Albright were willing to try almost anything to lure more visitors. They approved golf courses, zoos, even a summer racetrack at different parks and proposed Yosemite as an ideal setting to host the Winter Olympics. Albright proposed stringing a cable across the Grand Canyon, so trams could carry tourists from the South Rim to the North Rim and back; at the last minute, Mather rejected the idea when he realized it would ruin the view of the great chasm.

Still, Mather was intent on making sure that national parks attracted the public's attention—and if anything, he knew how to do it. When a new hotel was to be built at Glacier Point in Yosemite, he arranged for the first charge of dynamite to be detonated via remote control by the Secretary of the Interior, sitting at his desk in Washington, a continent away. Adding to the pageantry, as the blast went off a descendant of Chief Tenaya, the last Indian chief to live in the valley, released a covey of white pigeons.

Individual superintendents tried to follow Mather's lead in creative public relations. In Yellowstone, Horace Albright arranged for a "Buffalo Plains Week" in which cowboys and Crow Indians stampeded the park's bison herd for tourists arriving by buckboard. It would be, he promised, "a colorful pageant [that] will give every patron of the exhibition a thrill that will be long remembered." He also allowed a movie crew to film the buffalo stampede for a Hollywood western called *The Thundering Herd.*

When Warren Harding became the first president since Theodore Roosevelt to visit Yellowstone, Albright did everything possible to make sure the president not only enjoyed himself, but that his time in Yellowstone generated the maximum amount of publicity. A geyser, recently named for the president in honor of his visit, did not erupt on schedule; but Harding enjoyed watching Congress Geyser, newspapers reported, because it was always spouting off.

THE ALL-YEAR NATIONAL PARK

Above: Mather, Interior Secretary Albert Fall, and Albright. *Below:* White Sands National Monument

As avid as he was for expanding the number of national parks, Stephen Mather often ended up opposing specific proposals for new ones. Some he rejected because too many private parcels already existed within the proposed boundaries; some because they seemed mere copies of existing parks; and some because he believed they simply were substandard and would diminish the system he was building.

On the whole, Mather's opposition was enough to prevent any proposed park from being approved by Congress. (One exception was Lassen Volcanic National Park. When he finally visited it after the fact and saw its unique beauty, Mather freely admitted he was happy his original objections had been ignored.) But the proposal that gave him the most grief was the one put forward by Mather's boss, the Secretary of the Interior.

Albert Fall, a former U.S. Senator from New Mexico, had come in with the administration of President Warren Harding after the election of 1920. Before his first year as Interior Secretary was complete, Fall began pestering Mather with plans for an "All-Year National Park" in his home state, which had the enthusiastic backing of area business groups and politicians. In 1922, Mather agreed to come to New Mexico with Fall for a personal tour.

Everything he saw troubled him. The proposed park was to be comprised of a group of totally disconnected parcels. One area was the Malpais, some ancient lava beds in south-central New Mexico. Another was the White Sands, glistening dunes of gypsum sand, forty miles to the south. Another was more than fifty miles to the west, the area surrounding the Elephant Butte Dam and reservoir on the Rio Grande. Yet another was to the east—and included land that was part of the Mescalero Apache Indian Reservation. Conveniently located more or less in the middle of it all was Secretary Fall's private ranch.

Complicating matters further, Fall and his supporters saw the "All-Year National Park" as a different kind of park. Within its disjointed parcels would be permitted hunting, grazing, timber cutting, and mining, not to mention the irrigation and hydropower coming from the dam—everything, in other words, that Mather had been fighting against. Albright later summarized the Park Service director's predicament:

> The proposal put Mather in a very difficult position, for it was exactly what he did not want national parks to be. He had been working to establish higher—not lower—standards. In addition to the bad precedents that were involved, there would surely be criticism of Fall for trying to establish a national park surrounding his own ranch.

Fall didn't want to hear any objections to the plan; he expected Mather to draft a letter to Congress supporting it. Mather tried at first, according to Albright, but "the more he wrote the more disgusted he had become." At the same time, submitting a negative report would be considered gross insubordination.

The strain of the situation—compounded by the suicide of a congressman who was a close friend of Mather's—became unbearable. "Evidently seeing himself heading into another breakdown," Albright wrote, "he [went] to a sanitarium in Stamford, Connecticut, and remained out of action for six months."

Fall persisted, and when Albright said his duties at Yellowstone prevented him from making his own inspection and submitting a report, the Interior Secretary pushed ahead anyway. His former colleagues in the Senate—unconcerned about the curious absence of any official comment from the National Park Service, by report or testimony—unanimously passed the proposal.

But in the Park Service's absence, others took up the fight in the House. Robert Sterling Yard testified against it on behalf of the National Parks Association; J. Horace McFarland did the same for the American Civic Association. Even George Bird Grinnell, now in his seventies, showed up and registered the opposition of the Boone and Crockett Club. It was enough to tie things up in committee and prevent a vote in the House.

Then fate stepped in. In early 1923, Secretary Fall suddenly resigned because of his complicity in the granting of oil leases on public lands that became known as the Teapot Dome scandal. Fall was later convicted and imprisoned on bribery charges—ironically, for accepting "loans" from the oilmen to sustain his New Mexico ranch.

White Sands would eventually become a national monument; part of the Malpais would become a national recreation area; a state park would be created at Elephant Butte reservoir; the Mescalero Apaches would open a resort in their reservation's mountains. But no one would ever again propose that they be combined into an "All-Year National Park."

In Mesa Verde, Deric Nusbaum, the twelve-year-old son of the superintendent, was encouraged to write a book aimed at young readers, describing his adventures growing up among the cliff dwellings. Mather himself gladly provided the book's foreword and posed for a photo with its young author.

In Colorado, Agnes Lowe, a twenty-year-old college girl dressed in a leopard's skin, was heralded as a "modern Eve" as she set off barefoot to try to survive for a week in Rocky Mountain National Park. Newspapers breathlessly covered it all: cryptic messages found written with charcoal on tree trunks—"Nearly froze last night" or "Have fire now. Feeling Fine"—and periodic reports by tourists that they had stumbled upon her frolicking naked in the woods, where she quickly put her leopard skin back on and told them of her encounter with a brown bear. By the time she reemerged at park headquarters to pose once more for the cameras, her story had gained such national fame that a mailbag containing sixty-four marriage proposals was waiting for her. This, the superintendent said, "will result in very valuable publicity and undoubtedly [bring] hundreds of people to this park."

Instead, it got him in hot water with Mather, who found it all in bad taste. He was even more displeased to learn that the whole thing had been a hoax. "Eve" had actually spent her time comfortably ensconced in a nearby lodge, while the *Denver Post*, which had dreamed up the stunt as a way to put the national park on the map, fueled the media event each day with fictional accounts of her travails.

But of all the judgments Mather made in the early years, none would have a greater impact on the number of people visiting national parks—and on how they, in turn, impacted the parks—than his decision to wholeheartedly embrace the emerging national fascination with the automobile. "Motorists will find within the parks a warm welcome," he promised, "good roads, good hotels and public camps, and smiling nature in her most gorgeous dress."

Mather's hero, John Muir, had harbored mixed feelings about the horseless carriage—"blunt-nosed mechanical beetles," he called them, that might "mingle their gas-breath" with the fresh air of pines and waterfalls—though Muir also admitted they might help create new allies for the parks if they were allowed in under certain restrictions.

Stephen Mather had no such qualms. Even before he and the Park Service replaced the army, automobiles had been slowly permitted into most national parks. On August 1, 1915, showing his typical flair for promotion, Mather had opened up the last holdout, Yellowstone, with a caravan of vehicles. Robert Sterling Yard, the Park Service publicist paid out of Mather's personal funds, was riding in one of them to make sure the event got the most attention possible. The automobile age in the national parks had officially begun.

By 1917, horse-drawn carriages in Yellowstone had been totally removed, as concessionaires controlled by the railroads switched to open-seated touring cars for transporting tourists from one scenic point to another. By 1918, tourists arriving in Yosemite by automobile outnumbered those coming by train seven to one. And by the end of 1920, in his annual report, Mather proudly announced that, in the two years since the end of World War I, the number of people visiting the parks had more than doubled—and for the first time in history now exceeded one million a year.

The automobile, Mather said, "has been the open sesame."

The first idea of national parks seems to have been that they were stupendous natural spectacles,

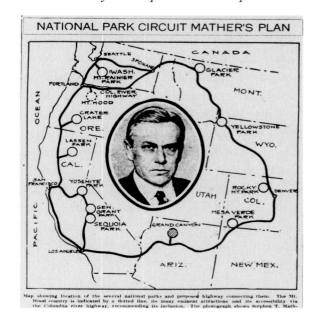

NATIONAL PARK CIRCUIT MATHER'S PLAN

Map showing location of the several national parks and proposed highway connecting them. The Mt. Hood country is indicated by a dotted line, its many eminent attractions and its accessibility via the Columbia river highway, recommending its inclusion. The photograph shows Stephen T. Math-

The *Oregon Sunday Journal* placed Mather's portrait in the middle of a map of his proposed park-to-park highway.

to be seen . . . in a short time, as one might view an art exhibit or a pageant.

Then came the great out-of-doors movement and, especially since the advent of the automobile, people turned to the national parks as places to live during their vacations and to "get next to Nature."

Lastly comes the realization that our parks are not only show places and vacation lands but also vast school-rooms of Americanism where people are studying, enjoying, and learning to love more deeply this land in which they live.

Our people have turned to the national parks for health, happiness, and a saner view of life. . . . This travel has now reached a proportion where it must be seriously considered as an economic factor in the national life.

Mather joined forces with automobile clubs, chambers of commerce, good-roads associations, local governments, and car manufacturers to lobby for a national park-to-park highway—a six-thousand-mile loop of improved roads linking all the western parks. It would be, he predicted in 1921, the "greatest scenic highway in the world," one that would unleash what he called "the great flow of tourist gold" into every community along its route.

Meanwhile, with the number of Americans owning automobiles skyrocketing in the 1920s, a new craze swept the country. It went by a variety of names: "sagebrushing," "gypsying," "autocamping." Even President Harding got caught up in the fad—joining Thomas Edison, Henry Ford, and Harvey Firestone on one of the well-publicized autocamping trips the three millionaires took each summer.

Mather saw the trend as yet another opportunity to get people to the national parks. "I believe we should have comfortable camps all over the country," he said, "so that the motorist could camp each night in a good scenic spot . . . on some kind of public land." He called together representatives from every state and urged them to build their own network of parks under the slogan "A State Park Every Hundred Miles."

Cars park wherever they can find a spot in Sequoia National Park's Giant Forest, 1920s.

In 1925, he told his park superintendents he wanted to see them all at Mesa Verde. To get there, however, they were explicitly instructed not to take the train; they were to form car caravans and travel together on the park-to-park highway—and make as much news about it as possible along the way.

It was a classic Mather publicity stunt, and a huge success. That year, visitation at national parks topped two million for the first time.

In the national parks there is one thing that the motorists are doing, and that is making them a great melting pot for the American people. . . .

This will go far in developing a love and pride in our own country and a realization of what a wonderful place it is.

There is no way to bring it home to them in a better way than by going from park to park, through the medium of an automobile, and camping out in the open. . . .

It is just by trips of that kind that people learn what America is.

STEPHEN MATHER

ASK A RANGER

While trying everything possible to bring more people to the parks, Mather took on another critical task: putting together a group of competent people to run them.

In the past, political patronage had determined who got the jobs. A well-connected employee at Glacier National Park was so inept, his patrols were restricted to following the railroad tracks to keep him from getting lost. The son-in-law of an early Mesa Verde superintendent turned out to be responsible for the looting of precious artifacts from the ancient cliff dwellings. To institute changes, Mather quickly began handpicking new superintendents.

Roger Toll, an engineering graduate of Columbia University, charter member of the Colorado Mountain Club, and former army major in the recent war, was dispatched to Mount Rainier, then to Rocky Mountain National Park.

Jesse Nusbaum, a professional archaeologist, was put in charge of Mesa Verde and its ancient treasures.

John White was an English-born adventurer who had scoured the Klondike for gold and fought in three wars, rising to the rank of colonel during the peace negotiations that ended World War I. But he had gladly taken a low-paying job just to be at the Grand Canyon, until Mather and Albright recognized his leadership skills could be put to better use as superintendent of Sequoia National Park, where White would serve for more than twenty-five years.

At Mount McKinley in Alaska, Mather chose Harry Karstens, already something of a living legend in Alaska by virtue of having led the first successful ascent of the continent's highest peak in 1913. "You will have a difficult job on your hands for some time to convince the public of the necessity of our regulations," Mather wrote his new superintendent, after outlining the rules against hunting and homesteading. "It is my purpose to support you in every way possible," he added, but "the rest is up to you."

The most prestigious post, superintendent of Yellowstone, was entrusted to Horace Albright (who doubled as assistant to the director for field operations in the park's off-season). "I felt so desperately young," Albright later remembered of his important new assignment. "I just prayed to be 30 years old."

A CADRE OF PROFESSIONALS: Mather (on the ladder, above) with his handpicked park superintendents and their wives at Mesa Verde, 1925. Among his favorites were Roger Toll (right, with bobcat) at Mount Rainier and Rocky Mountain; Albright at Yellowstone; and John White (far right, pointing) at Sequoia and General Grant.

To appear more mature, he took to wearing eyeglasses in public.

Below the superintendents, Mather wanted a cadre of equally professional park rangers—"men between the ages of 21 and 40," according to Albright, "of good character, sound physique, and tactful in handling people." They needed to be able to ride and take care of horses, build trails, fight forest fires, handle a rifle and pistol, have practical experience in surviving every extreme of weather in the out-of-doors, and be willing to work long hours with no provision for overtime pay.

The salary was $1,000 a year. From that, rangers were expected to buy their own food, provide their own bedding, and pay $45 for the symbol of the job they had chosen: a specially designed uniform topped by a distinctive flat-brimmed hat.

At Yellowstone, so many men began inquiring about ranger positions that Albright printed out a form letter response to weed out all but the most dedicated:

A ranger's job is no place for a nervous, quick-tempered man, nor for the laggard, nor for one who is unaccustomed to hard work. If you cannot work hard ten or twelve hours a day, and always with patience and a smile on your face, don't fill out the attached blank.

If you want to come for pleasure you will be disappointed. . . . The ranger's job is especially hard. . . . Apply if you are qualified. Otherwise please plan to visit the Yellowstone National Park as a tourist.

"I think a ranger should enter the service with the desire of making it his life's work," Mather said. And the man every ranger looked up to was Stephen Mather. He gave one ranger travel money to make a cross-country trip to visit his parents; occasionally treated rangers and their wives to meals at fancy restaurants; and in Yosemite, spent $25,000 from his own pocket to build the Rangers' Club House, a place where the rangers could relax in private. Mather himself took to staying there, instead of in one of Yosemite's hotels, whenever he visited the park.

"Mather had a special vision of what the rangers should be," Albright said. "He felt they must bring

to the Service not only knowledge and skill, but an ability to relate to the public and a considerable measure of dedication."

Mather had a number of ideas for the national park ranger mystique that he wanted to create. . . . He called it esprit de corps *and he used every means at his disposal to build it.*

Impressed by an educational nature program run by two college professors at a private resort at Lake Tahoe, Mather paid to have the whole thing transferred to Yosemite National Park. Soon, guided nature walks and evening campfire lectures by what he called "ranger-naturalists" began in every national park. They quickly became one of the Park Service's most popular programs and did more than anything else to burnish the image of friendly professionalism Mather was trying to create.

Most of the rangers were men, but a few were women. At the age of fourteen, Claire Marie Hodges

Harry Karstens (above left) was put in charge of Mount McKinley National Park. At Yosemite, Claire Marie Hodges (left) became the Park Service's first female ranger. Isabel Bassett Wasson (above) was Yellowstone's first woman ranger-naturalist.

had ridden horseback for four days to visit Yosemite with her family. Four years later, in 1918, she knew the park's trails as well as anyone, and when World War I made finding male rangers difficult, she applied for the job and was quickly accepted, becoming the Park Service's first woman ranger. She wore a blouse and divided skirt instead of the standard uniform, but donned the same hat as every other ranger.

At Yellowstone, Isabel Bassett Wasson, a Brooklyn native with a master's degree in geology from Columbia University, became the first woman ranger-naturalist. "I didn't 'range,' I talked," she explained, giving lectures at three different locations in the park each day, with each talk on a different topic because crowds tended to follow her wherever she went.

To augment the educational programs—and initially supported almost entirely with private money, principally from the family of John D. Rockefeller Jr.—small museums were started with exhibits explaining the wildlife, plants, geology, and history to the increasing number of tourists arriving at each park.

TELLING THE STORY: Mather's most enduring innovation was instituting nature walks (left, at Mount Rainier) and campfire talks (below, at Yosemite) led by rangers wearing their distinctive flat-brimmed hats—a symbol he deliberately cultivated to represent both authority and approachability.

Mather loved seeing it all in person. He always insisted on wearing a ranger's uniform, too, whenever he visited one of his parks. He gallantly offered people rides in the big touring car he traveled in, with the special license plate USNPS 1; and he especially reveled in showing off the wildlife to passing tourists who would stop their cars to watch.

To further heighten the park rangers' public image, he encouraged Albright to turn a collection of humorous anecdotes about life in the national parks into a book entitled *Oh, Ranger!* It went through thirteen printings.

> *To me no picture of the national parks is complete unless it includes the rangers. . . . Though small in number, their influence is large. . . .*
>
> *If a trail is to be blazed, it is "send a ranger." If an animal is floundering in the snow, a ranger is sent to pull him out; if a bear is in the hotel, if a fire threatens a forest, if someone is to be saved, it is "send a ranger." If a Dude wants to know the why of Nature's ways, if a Sagebrusher is puzzled about a road, his first thought is, "ask a ranger."*
>
> STEPHEN MATHER

The Crater Camp.

En route: "The Rim Road", thirty-five miles around Crater Lake.

HERE I GIVE THANKS

In July of 1921, Margaret and Edward Gehrke set off on their most adventurous trip ever—a three-month journey covering more than seven thousand miles, adding more national parks to their growing list.

July 13, 1921. Again it is "the Day of Days." . . . I see thru these white unwritten pages only our long, long, motor trip.

. . . We enjoyed the morning: the long, dusty road, the summer fields. But I discovered myself sitting "tense" with clenched hands, "trying to let go." . . .

Experienced our first puncture shortly before dinner by the road side. . . .

July 15. This is Colorado! . . . Ahead the snow covered peaks and cool pines, and the long Trail into the Unknown!

ON THE ROAD AGAIN: Traveling by car instead of by train in 1921, Margaret and Edward Gehrke took their Buick over the stone-littered Fall River Road at Rocky Mountain National Park in Colorado (below, top), around the newly built Rim Road at Crater Lake in Oregon (left), and to Mount Rainier in Washington (bottom).

About 20 miles out of Ft. Morgan we made camp . . . at a school house, where mosquitoes made supper and sleep an interesting undertaking. Mosquitoes won.

This time, instead of taking the train the Gehrkes traveled in Edward's new Buick—autocamping across the West, picking each day's itinerary themselves and stopping for the night wherever the mood hit them: schoolyards, municipal parks, or simply on the side of the road. To keep them company, they brought along their pet dog, an Airedale named Barney. Across eastern Colorado, Margaret noted, they made seventy-five miles "over splendidly graveled roads":

The ecstasy one feels when he is going into the mountains that lie ahead . . . the steady purr of a speeding car that bears one on past unfamiliar fields . . . the freedom! The joy!

These, all these good things of God, are ours this wonderful day . . . as we begin our Mountain Trip.

At Rocky Mountain National Park, they drove over the Continental Divide on the Fall River Road, which the Park Service had completed only a year earlier. "We shall long remember going over this new Pass," Margaret wrote, "a ride of forty miles of indescribable scenery and some stretches of inconceivable roads! . . . Altitude 11,000 plus."

From Rocky Mountain they pushed westward across Utah and Nevada to northern California, where they learned that the visit Margaret had planned to Lassen Volcanic National Park would now be impossible, because the mountain roads were in such bad shape. "It would be sensible not to go," Margaret confided to her journal. "To be sensible is to be commonplace. To be commonplace is unpardonable. I shall regret this decision."

They had better luck in Oregon, at Crater Lake National Park. They circled the lake on the newly completed, thirty-five-mile Rim Road, "one of the great scenic highways of the West," Margaret wrote, and motored on to Astoria, Oregon, reaching the Pacific Ocean near the same spot where the Lewis and Clark Expedition had spent the winter of 1805–1806 after becoming the first American citizens to cross the continent. "We have achieved," Margaret bragged in her diary. "We have motored to the Pacific Coast. . . . Can we remember it all?"

Five days later, they reached yet another national park.

Sept. 14. Eighty miles of motoring to-day brought us here to Paradise Valley at the foot of Mount Rainier. . . .

In camping tonight here at the foot of Mount Rainier, its great summit covered with immaculate snow, its outline in sharp contrast against the sky—the clear bright stars above—the icy chill of thin air—a secret dream of my heart has been realized and here I give thanks.

They turned for home—through Washington state, Idaho, western Montana—but in Livingston realized that, although it wasn't on their itinerary, Yellowstone National Park was only fifty-five miles away. While the park's regular tourist season was over, they couldn't resist detouring up the long stony road into the mountains and the park.

It was even better than their first visit in 1917: "A golden October day," Margaret wrote, "blue skies, warm sunshine, and the glories of the Yellowstone all ours. It is like being at a great play and we the only spectators!"

The Gehrkes' autocamping adventure had only whetted their appetite for more trips over the coming years—in Edward's revolving parade of new Buicks, sometimes with different dogs as companions, always with new parks as their destination.

Sept. 25, 1922. Mount Desert Island, off the Coast of Maine.

We have arrived! The tall pines about remind me a little of Glacier: the lake with its low range about, a trifle of Grand Lake [at Rocky Mountain]. So we sleep to-night . . . and rejoice in spite of a cold wind impossible to keep out.

July 30, 1923. "Wind Cave National Park" . . . adding one more national park to our list. . . . We took the medium length trail devoting four hours to the tour. . . . We emerged from the cave to find

Windshield stickers (above) started out simply as a way park rangers marked automobiles whose owners had paid their entry fee. But they soon became something more: emblems that the proud owner (left) was well traveled.

Margaret Gehrke at Mesa Verde, her twelfth national park

some lively other tourists gathered about an open fire, listened to a [park ranger] lecture on this ancient civilization of a prehistoric people.

On Margaret's personal list of national parks, Mesa Verde meant that twelve had been checked off. As the growing number of stickers on their windshield attested, the Gehrkes were now "collecting" parks, just like many other Americans. And there were still more parks to go.

THE BACK OF BEYOND

The mountains have a character all their own. . . . From almost any summit . . . one looks out upon a sea of flowing curves and dome-shaped eminences undulating . . . unto the horizon.

The dreamy blue haze . . . that ever hovers over the mountains . . . softens all outlines, lends a mirage-like effect of great distance to objects that are but a few miles off, while those farther removed grow more and more intangible until finally the sky-line blends with the sky itself.

There are seven peaks of 6,000 feet altitude that have no name. . . . Could anything better prove the astonishing isolation of this majestic region, though set, as it is, in the very midst of American civilization?

HORACE KEPHART

When Horace Kephart had first come to the Smoky Mountains of North Carolina and Tennessee in 1904, he was a broken man, physically and spiritually. Precociously brilliant, he had entered college at age thirteen; enrolled as a graduate student at Cornell when he turned seventeen; took a prestigious job in Yale University's library and got married before he was twenty-five. As head of the St. Louis Mercantile Library, the oldest library west of the Mississippi, he had gone on to make a name for himself as an expert on early western explorations.

But his marriage proved unhappy, Kephart turned to heavy drinking, and when he lost his job and his wife left him, taking their six children with her, he had suffered a collapse requiring hospitalization.

At age forty-two he decided to start over in a place where he could lose himself in the wilderness and

a "sticker" on our car: we have visited our eighth national park.

Hot Springs National Park in the Ozarks of Arkansas was their ninth national park; Platt National Park in Oklahoma was their tenth. In North Dakota, they added their eleventh.

Aug. 7, 1924. Sully[s] Hill National Park.

How anxious I was not to miss Sully Hill—not that there was anything special to see—for it will be fine to have our tour of national parks complete.

Sully is a wooded game preserve covering 800 acres, pleasant picnic grounds [and] a new government road along the shore of Devil's Lake under construction, but there is really nothing to see at Sully's Hill.

Aug. 24, 1925. We are off into Mesa Verde National Park! We again rejoice in the thrill that comes where one is about to see a new national park!

For 31 miles we wound and wound, round and round, up and up: first the switch back Road with its sharp grade curves, then the Knife Edge Highway . . . and Mesa Verde!!! Here it was: a high mesa, scrubby little piñon trees, canyons, and Spruce Tree House over there in full sight—altogether different than we expected.

We made camp at "Spruce Tree Camp" on the edge of a canyon, and it began to rain again. After supper we went up to the Hotel, and with

regain his strength and a purpose for his life. He chose the Smoky Mountains, which seemed, he wrote, like "an Eden still unpeopled and unspoiled."

When I went south into the mountains I was seeking a Back of Beyond. . . . I yearned for a strange land and a people that had the charm of originality. . . . I wanted to enjoy a free life in the open air, the thrill of exploring new ground.

Here, in the wildwood, I have found peace, cleanliness, health of body and mind. Here I can live the natural life, unfettered and unindebted.

The Smokies are the tallest mountains in the Appalachian chain, hosting the world's greatest diversity of plant, animal, and insect life of any region in a temperate climate zone—including more than one hundred species of native trees: spruce and hemlock, giant tulip poplars and chestnut oaks; a greater variety of trees than in all of Europe. Walking among them in the autumn of 1898, John Muir had felt a bronchial cough suddenly replaced by new vigor. "The air has healed me," he wrote. "I think I could walk ten miles and not be tired."

For centuries the mountains had been the home of the Cherokees, until most of them were forced

Horace Kephart
Right: Dawn from Clingmans Dome, Great Smoky Mountains National Park

from their land and sent to Oklahoma on what came to be known as the Trail of Tears. In their place an equally distinctive people had settled in the remote mountaintops and hollows: isolated farmers, moonshiners, Confederate deserters and Union sympathizers hiding out during the Civil War, Cherokees who had evaded removal, and a collection of other people on the run, for one reason or another, from civilization. Kephart fit right in.

Seldom during [my] forest exile did I feel lonesome in the daytime; but when supper would be over, and black night closed in on my hermitage, and the owls began calling all the blue devils of the woods, one needed some indoor occupation to keep him in good cheer: and that is how I came to write my first little book.

Kephart's book, *Camping and Woodcraft: A Guidebook for Those Who Travel in the Wilderness,* became a national hit, known as a "camper's Bible." He quickly published another book, *Our Southern Highlanders,* about the people living around him in the place he now considered home. And he proposed that the Smoky Mountains be made into a national

park. Otherwise, he feared, the great woods would suffer the same fate as all the other eastern forests.

Giant lumber companies were buying up large parcels of land at cheap prices, hiring local workers at equally cheap wages, and beginning to systematically strip the mountains of their forest canopy. This was logging on a new, industrial scale. Railroads were extended into every conceivable valley, bringing steam-powered skidders and log loaders to handle

A logger and his wife (above) outside one of the portable cabins lumber companies transported from one "string-town" to the next. Once a mountainside was cleared (left), everyone—including their housing—moved on.

the steep terrain and the massive trees of the previously untouched woodlands. Cornfields were transformed into sawmills and towns sprang up around them.

Farther up toward the mountain peaks, portable housing called "stringtowns" were hauled to the hillsides to keep the workers close to their jobs. When one section was cleared, they moved everything still farther up and began again. Kephart was appalled at the devastation.

I am not a very religious man; but often when standing alone before my Maker in this house not made with hands I bowed my head with reverence and thanked God for His gift of the great forest to one who loved it.

Not long ago I went to that same place again. It was wrecked, ruined, desecrated, turned into a thousand rubbish heaps, utterly vile and mean.

Did anyone ever thank God for a lumberman's slashing?

By the mid-1920s, more than 300,000 acres had been clear-cut. Much of the Smokies, one resident said, looked as if it had been "skinned." But 100,000 acres of virgin forest still remained. Kephart—and others like him in Tennessee and North Carolina—wanted those trees spared. "I owe my life to these mountains," he said.

Why should this last stand of splendid, irreplaceable trees be sacrificed to the greedy maw of the sawmill? Why should future generations be

The restless journey across America of George Masa (above) eventually brought him to the Smoky Mountains, where he started out in the laundry room of Asheville's Grove Park Inn, but soon became a gifted photographer whose pictures were sometimes made into postcards (below).

Grove Park Inn, the Finest Resort Hotel in the World, Asheville, N. C.—1
"Where life is worth while."

Plateau Studio.

robbed of all chance to see with their own eyes what a real forest, a real wildwood, a real unimproved work of God, is like?

. . . The question, the only question, is: Shall the Smoky Mountains be made a national park or a desert?

Among those joining the cause for a national park, Kephart soon found an unexpected ally, another man whose solitary wanderings had somehow brought him to the Smokies. Masahara Iizuka, born in Osaka, Japan, in 1881, had come to the United States to study mining, though by 1915 his university days were over and he had permanently severed ties with his family in Japan. He was roaming the country in search of a job—Colorado, St. Louis, New Orleans—when his travels brought him to Asheville, North Carolina. In his pocket journal, written in Japanese, he recorded his immediate impressions.

This is a mountainous area, it will be cool enough to require a blanket in the autumn. No mosquitoes! An excellent place to live. Nothing can be better, now if only I make a lot of money.

He changed his name to George Masa, set about to learn better English, and took a position in the laundry room at Asheville's exclusive Grove Park Inn. He was soon promoted to the valet desk, where his intelligence and gentle friendliness made him a favorite of the hotel's elite clientele.

To make a little extra money, Masa began processing the film and printing photographs from the guests' cameras, a skill that quickly blossomed into a new job with a professional photographer, and then a business of his own. Though barely five feet tall and weighing just over a hundred pounds, he lugged his heavy camera equipment everywhere, searching the Smokies for a new vantage point, then waiting for hours for the perfect light to take a picture. The local chamber of commerce bought his photos to promote the region in their brochures. Newspapers and magazines used them, too. Masa turned some into color postcards for sale to tourists.

His love of the mountains inevitably brought him into contact with someone who had been trying to do with words what Masa was doing with photographs. Horace Kephart quickly became Masa's closest friend and easily recruited him into the crusade to save the Smokies.

I have been out with George on several of his trips . . . exploring the wildest and most rugged parts . . . scaling precipitous mountain sides, delving rocky defiles, where no sign has been left by man.

Others were joining, as well. Community leaders in Knoxville, Tennessee, and Asheville, North Carolina, got on the bandwagon—some out of a love of the mountains, some on the belief that tourism would bolster the local economy, some on the hope that a national park would result in better roads for the region. A New York publicity firm, brought in by the Knoxville Automobile Club, suggested that the group call itself the *Great* Smoky Mountain Conservation Association. Soon, the mountains themselves were referred to as the Great Smokies.

On the North Carolina side, boosters published a promotional booklet with five photographs by George Masa and text by Horace Kephart.

We have eighteen national parks in the West. They comprise an area of over 11,000 square miles. East of the Mississippi River there is but one, far up on the Maine coast, and it covers only eight square miles.

Three-fourths of the American people live east of the Mississippi. Most of them cannot afford the time or the money that must be spent to visit the western parks.

Here are the highest and most massive mountains in eastern America. Here stands today, in the Great Smoky Mountains, the last hundred square miles of uncut primeval forest . . . just as it stood, save for added growth, when Columbus discovered America.

It will all be destroyed in ten or fifteen years if the Government does not take it over and preserve it.

With Acadia the only national park in the East, Stephen Mather was eager to add more, closer to the nation's population centers, to help him build broader public support for parks. He particularly

Having lugged his big camera and tripod to an outcropping on Greybeard Mountain, George Masa waits with a friend for just the right moment to take a photograph.

thought that one in the South would help him with some important southern senators, who were otherwise indifferent to the park system he was building. In 1926, Congress authorized the creation of three new southern parks—in Virginia and Kentucky, as well as in the Smoky Mountains—but only if the money to buy the land for them came from the states or private donations. The federal government would not put in a penny.

In Tennessee and North Carolina, the fundraising goal was set at $10 million, which seemed an impossibly lofty figure for one of the poorer sections of the country. But people from all walks of life rallied to the cause.

Local ministers held special "Smoky Mountain Sunday" services to encourage their congregations to contribute. Bellboys at the Farragut Hotel in Knoxville donated a dollar each. Students in the city's high school pledged $2,490—including the entire proceeds from the junior class play. Asheville's newspaper reported that, in addition to major con-

THE GOOSE WITH THE GOLDEN EGGS

By BILLY BORNE

tributions of $1,000 and higher from prominent businesses and families, donations had come in from every grade school—white and African American—in the city's segregated school district, as children raided their piggy banks for pennies and nickels.

The logging industry fought back with full-page advertisements in local newspapers, arguing that a national park would ruin their business and the jobs that went with it; that the possibility of hydroelectricity from damming some of the valleys would be lost forever; and that promises calling tourism a "goose that lays golden eggs" were fairy tales. A rally to solicit park donations in the hometown of one of the timber companies was taken over by angry employees who had been told that "forces of evil" were trying to end their way of life. Undeterred, the park campaign came back the next week and received $10,000 in pledges.

Still, even with more than $3 million promised in bond issues from the legislatures of Tennessee and North Carolina, by the spring of 1927 the fund drive to save the Great Smokies had reached only $5 million in cash and pledges—half of what was needed.

Meanwhile, some of the lumber companies were frantically cutting the old-growth forests within the proposed park boundaries—sixty acres a day, according to one estimate—hoping to extract everything they could before the land was closed to them. Kephart, Masa, and other park supporters were now caught in a race against time and the logger's saw. And time was running out.

ON THE STAFF OF THE
GRAND CANYON

Even to remember that the Grand Canyon is still there lifts up the heart. If I were an American, I should make my remembrance of it the final test of men, art, and policies.

I should ask myself: Is this good enough to exist in the same country as the Canyon? How would I feel about this man, this kind of art, these political measures, if I were near that Rim?

Every member or officer of the Federal Government ought to remind himself, with triumphant pride, that he is on the staff of the Grand Canyon.

J. B. PRIESTLY

For more than 16 years I have been exploring and working in the Grand Canyon of Arizona on power sites. I now have the financial backing to build two huge hydroelectric plants in the Grand Canyon . . . [to electrify] every railroad, mine, city, town and hamlet in Arizona.

As a Senator, I can more readily and quickly secure the concessions, rights of way, etc., so necessary for the perfect development of these great enterprises.

SENATOR RALPH HENRY CAMERON

Since before the turn of the century, Ralph Henry Cameron had considered the Grand Canyon his own private fiefdom. In 1919 he had lost a prolonged fight to keep the canyon from becoming a national park, and a series of court rulings had ordered him to abandon many of the questionable mining claims he had used to gain effective control of some particularly scenic spots.

But after being elected in 1920 to represent Arizona in the U.S. Senate, Cameron carried on as if nothing had changed. Despite repeated court injunctions, he simply refused to remove his buildings and employees from inside the park boundaries, and through his tight grip on the political machine of northern Arizona (all the federal appointees owed their jobs to Cameron) prevented any action from being taken to make him comply. Park rangers opposed to him resorted to having their mail sent in code, because they suspected that the canyon's post-

master, Cameron's brother-in-law, was monitoring their official correspondence.

Now, on behalf of some campaign contributors, Cameron proposed two giant hydroelectric dams and the development of a huge platinum mine within the park. Stephen Mather decided the Senator had gone too far and set out to stop him—or anyone else who wanted to put a dam in a national park. The recently enacted Federal Water Power Act, with the Secretary of the Interior's blessings, specifically allowed it. Dams were being proposed at Sequoia and Glacier national parks; and in Yellowstone alone, four different plans were being advanced. Mather determined to battle them all. In his mind, the flooding of Yosemite's Hetch Hetchy Valley to provide water for San Francisco had been the greatest travesty of national park ideals, and he was not going to let it happen again.

Once a small dam is authorized for irrigation or other purposes, other dams will follow. Once a small lake is raised and a small amount of timber is destroyed . . . once start the national parks toward national forest–status, and it will be logically impossible to stop short. One misstep is fatal.

Can we not preserve a few of our magnificent lakes, a few of the priceless waterfalls, without encountering the grasping, calloused hand of commercialism extended to deprive our children of their heritage?

With their boss, the Secretary of the Interior, squarely on the side of the dam builders, Mather and Horace Albright nonetheless did everything they could to get the parks exempted from the Federal Water Power Act. But the memos they wrote informing Congress of their objections never got passed along; the Interior Secretary had instead torn them into pieces.

Albright was particularly worried about the Bechler River basin, a remote wilderness in the southwest section of Yellowstone. When surveyors for the Bureau of Reclamation announced they would be showing up to look the basin over for a series of dams, Albright turned to bureaucratic sabotage. The first year, he ordered the wooden trail bridges taken up, so the surveyors found the rivers impassable. The

ARIZONA AND PROSPERITY

RALPH H. CAMERON
REPUBLICAN CANDIDATE FOR
UNITED STATES SENATOR

As the United States Senator from Arizona, Ralph Henry Cameron (above) proposed two dams in the Grand Canyon in the 1920s. At the same time, four dams were proposed in Yellowstone, including one on the Bechler River (right), and in Sequoia and Glacier national parks as well.

next year, the bridges were intact but the horses the surveyors had planned on using somehow couldn't be found.

Mather did what he always did best: galvanizing support through a public relations campaign—though this time he had to be careful to do it behind the scenes. He arranged to make Robert Sterling Yard, his chief publicist, the head of the National Parks Association, a new organization Mather had recently helped set up with his own money, meant to bolster the park movement without regard to the political constraints of a federal agency. Yard and the association took the lead in opposing the dams.

Soon, newspaper editorials, women's clubs, and other conservation groups rallied to the cause and lobbied Congress to keep dams out of any existing national park. No one wanted another Hetch Hetchy. The proposed dams, including all of

Cameron's projects in the Grand Canyon, were stopped.

For his part, Ralph Cameron tended to take any opposition to his plans personally. "My life has been practically given over to the development of one of the greatest scenic wonders in the world," he said. "It was my money, my energy and my perseverance." Now he lashed out. He managed to have the entire appropriation for Grand Canyon National Park removed from the Senate budget. He denounced Mather on the Senate floor, saying the Park Service director was "squandering the people's money" and sending it down a "sink hole." And he instigated a congressional investigation that traveled from park to park, trying to embarrass both Mather and Albright by stirring up spurious claims against their integrity.

But it all backfired. Newspapers began their own investigations into Cameron, highlighting how he had used his Senate position to further his private interests; park supporters in Congress took the unusual step of openly criticizing a fellow member for his vendetta; and in 1926, the voters of Arizona refused to reelect him.

Out of power, Cameron could no longer protect his Grand Canyon empire. His fraudulent mining claims finally had to be abandoned. Indian Garden, the dilapidated rest stop on the trail down to the river where Cameron's caretakers brazenly operated a whiskey still and contaminated the only freshwater with their unsanitary facilities, had to be turned over to the park. And at Bright Angel Trail, the toll gate was removed, so the people who actually owned the park could freely use it.

For Mather, the victory was proof that his strategy of aggressively promoting more and more visitors was the best way to save the national parks.

The public is one of the best allies of the Service in many of its practical problems of "preserving the park[s] absolutely unimpaired."

As a result of their visits, the people have learned to love these national areas as their very own; national assets in which every individual of every State in the Union has an inalienable right of possession.

THE HONEYMOONERS

Some ships
Sail from port to port,
Following contentedly the same old way.

While others
Who through restlessness,
Watch new seas at each break of day.

We
Of the night,
Will know
Many things
Of which
You sleepers
Have never dreamed.

BESSIE HYDE

As the sentimental poetry she loved to write made clear, Bessie Haley Hyde always yearned for a life of romantic adventure. By 1928, when she was twenty-two years old, she had already picked up and moved half a dozen times, studied art and design among the bohemians of San Francisco, and in the space of less than two years got married, got a quickie divorce in Nevada, and then got married again.

Her second husband, Glen Hyde, age twenty-nine, was an Idaho potato farmer with his own thirst for the unusual. He had become an experienced river runner in the Northwest, having built and guided a boat called a sweep scow down Idaho's treacherous Salmon River, the fabled "River of No Return."

Few of their friends were surprised, therefore, when Glen and Bessie announced that they would celebrate their honeymoon by attempting something that fewer than fifty people had ever accomplished— take a boat through the Grand Canyon on the turbulent Colorado River. Bessie Hyde would be the first woman ever to try it.

They started out on October 20, 1928, from Green River, Utah, in a two-ton scow Glen had built for $50 and then loaded with supplies: bags of Idaho potatoes and home-canned vegetables, a rifle for shooting deer and ducks along the way, and a set of bed springs so they could sleep in comfort on the boat. Like other Northwest boatmen, Glen had never worn life preservers running rivers, and he saw no need for them on the Colorado.

After two weeks on the river they reached the start of the Grand Canyon at Lees Ferry, where locals advised the couple against proceeding any farther. They considered Glen's boat ill-suited for the huge rapids downstream and thought it folly to be entering the big canyon without companions in a second boat. Glen would hear none of it. They were two days ahead of schedule and the Colorado seemed no harder to master than the Salmon. "We . . . are enjoying it immensely," he wrote his father. They pushed on. Bessie provided more details:

The wind is blowing so much that everything is just about covered with sand, including Glen and I. We should be nearly to Grand Canyon [Village], but of course it is hard to tell.

The scenery . . . is really more majestic.

We've had lots and lots of riffles, large and small, and have been gliding along at a great rate.

We've had all kinds of camps—from beach to rock shelves.

Moving downstream, with the stone walls towering above them, they were seeing the Grand Canyon from a perspective few people had experienced: Dramatic vistas revealing even higher walls reaching to the rim a mile above them—and alternately crowding in on them, "like a prison," as the explorer John Wesley Powell had described. Smaller side canyons of almost unimaginable beauty around every bend of the river. Waterfalls pouring out of sheer stone to feed the Colorado as it coursed by. Stretches of smooth, flat water reflecting the colors and light like a mirror. And always the rapids, where the river's power in its battle with anything in its way was on full display.

Farther into the canyon, the rapids got bigger and more treacherous. Bessie, a tiny woman weighing less than a hundred pounds, had already been tossed into the water like a matchstick by the big sweep oar. Now Glen was knocked from the boat. Bessie somehow managed to throw him a rope and get him back in, but she was badly shaken by the near calamity. "I was ready to climb the canyon wall right then and there," she wrote, "but Glen laughed at me."

At the bottom of Bright Angel Trail, they beached the scow and hiked up to the South Rim, where they enjoyed a big meal at the fancy El Tovar hotel and spent a cozy night in a tent cabin at Grand Canyon Village. The next morning, after buying supplies and arranging to have them hauled by mule down to the boat, the couple paid a visit to Emery Kolb, the photographer who, with his brother, had made a legendary descent of the Colorado in 1911. Emery took the Hydes' photograph and gave them a signed copy of his brother's book about the 1911 trip.

Glen and Bessie's dream was to follow the Kolbs' example: make a name for themselves with their own daring adventure, write a best-selling book about it, and then go on the lecture circuit. The Hydes were certain they would soon be famous when they ran into a reporter from the *Denver Post*, who saw the potential in their story and eagerly hung on their every word. "I have had the thrills of my life," Bessie told him. "I've been thoroughly drenched a

Bessie and Glen Hyde (below) in the homemade scow Glen had built for $50 to take them through the Grand Canyon in 1928. Bessie wrote that the scenery was "majestic," but most of the experience was dominated by raging rapids (bottom, left) and campsites huddled on sand bars (bottom, right) next to the towering cliffs.

they were in the Arctic regions, or the interior of an unexplored continent." Another questioned the wisdom of their attempt to master the Colorado.

Mr. and Mrs. Glen Hyde, now lost in the canyon, certainly could not have been advised of the perils of such a honeymoon voyage. An anxious country watching the search with hope that they will be found and rescued also hopes that the advertisement they have given of the desperate character of this adventure will deter others.

President Calvin Coolidge finally ordered the Army Air Corps to aid in the search by flying over the canyon. At last the scow was sighted, but there was no sign of life. Emery and Ellsworth Kolb grabbed their cameras, repaired a leaky, abandoned boat on the river's shore, and hurried to the site, which they finally reached on Christmas Day.

The scow was floating in the still waters of an eddy, its bowline caught in the rocks thirty feet underwater. Everything seemed untouched on deck: a baked ham, a sack of flour, and other food; hiking boots and warm clothes; the bed springs and blankets; the Hydes' money and the book Emery Kolb had given them; Glen's rifle; Bessie's camera, with six rolls of film—and a small journal in which Bessie had been keeping notes for the book she intended to write. The last entry, from November 30, simply stated: "Ran 16 rapids today."

Bessie and Glen Hyde had found the adventure—and the celebrity—they had been seeking. But neither of them was ever seen again.

dozen times; but I'm enjoying every minute of the adventure."

Others who saw the Hydes that day told a different story—that Bessie had already had enough of the Colorado and was reluctant to continue the journey. When she said goodbye to his family, Emery Kolb remembered, Bessie looked at his daughter's shoes and said, "I wonder if I shall ever wear pretty shoes again."

At the small tourist camp at the bottom of Bright Angel Trail, the Hydes signed the guest book, "Going down the river . . . in a flat bottomed boat," agreed to let a wealthy vacationer ride along with them for one day, and set off once more on November 17. The next day they dropped their passenger off at a place called Hermit Camp, just upstream from the ten biggest cascades in the canyon. He asked to take their photograph and they complied.

Then Glen and Bessie Hyde got back in their boat, and disappeared. By mid-December, news that the two honeymooners had not been heard from in a month was captivating the nation. "The couple could not be more isolated," one reporter wrote, "if

Left: The last photograph taken of Bessie and Glen Hyde, Hermit Camp, November 18, 1929
Below: The Hydes' empty scow, as it was when the Kolb brothers discovered it; the Kolbs' boat is in the foreground. They took both photographs and moving pictures of their highly publicized rescue effort.

Mount Moran (above) looms over the Snake River, Grand Teton National Park. *Overleaf:* An old barn on Mormon Row in Jackson Hole, with the Tetons in the background

THE DREAM

If you have ever stood at Jenny Lake and looked across to Cascade Canyon weaving its sinuous way toward the summit of the Tetons, you will know the joy of being in a sacred place, designed by God to be protected forever.

HORACE ALBRIGHT

On one of their first inspection trips of the parks, Horace Albright and Stephen Mather had been in Yellowstone when they took a day trip to check on a new road being built from the park's southern entrance toward the valley just beyond, called Jackson Hole, in Wyoming. There, they saw something neither of them would ever forget: a stunning series of granite spires rising into the sky from a flat, sagebrush plain, adorned with a necklace of sparkling lakes and the shimmering Snake River. It was the Tetons. "Mather and I were both flabbergasted," Albright wrote. "I had never beheld such scenery."

As far back as 1882, General Philip Sheridan had argued that the Yellowstone park needed to be made even bigger, to encompass the natural grazing range of the world's largest surviving elk herd. The Tetons and surrounding lowlands were an essential part of the elks' migratory home.

Eventually, much of the area had been declared a national forest, but any move to incorporate it into Yellowstone—and afford it the extra protections that would come from being a national park—had been easily defeated in Congress. Ranchers worried about grazing rights, farmers hoped for the chance to build more dams for irrigation, and sportsmen wanted to hunt the elk and other big game that migrated each year into the valley. The U.S. Forest Service, always jealous about giving up land under its control to the upstart Park Service, also opposed the idea and did everything possible to undermine it.

But some conservationists still clung to the hope for what they called "Greater Yellowstone." Meanwhile, a small group of dude ranch owners in Jackson Hole, concerned that the valley was becoming too developed, suggested that some private holdings be purchased and then combined with the public lands. Once he became the Yellowstone's superintendent in 1919, Albright made the cause his own.

This may sound juvenile and presumptuous, but . . . I took it personally.

I really felt I had a mission to preserve the Grand Tetons in the only way I knew, through the National Park Service.

Year after year, every dignitary Albright escorted around Yellowstone would eventually find himself being led to a vantage point offering a view south of the park's borders toward the Tetons, while Albright passionately explained the reasons why they needed to be added to his park. Congressmen, influential journalists, and two different presidents got the treatment.

One day in 1924, Albright learned that a private citizen, traveling incognito under the name of "Mr. Davison," was about to visit Yellowstone. His real identity was John D. Rockefeller Jr., already an important benefactor of national parks. He had put up the money to purchase land on Mount Desert Island in Maine and donated it to the federal government to create Acadia National Park; more recently, his generosity had made it possible to establish a museum at Mesa Verde.

Albright was thrilled to learn that the great philanthropist was now coming to Yellowstone. But

before he arrived, Albright heard from Mather, instructing him to respect Rockefeller's privacy. Albright followed orders, making sure the Rockefeller family enjoyed Yellowstone, but not broaching the topic of the Tetons. (Rockefeller nonetheless approached Albright about unsightly messes along Yellowstone's roads and made a quiet $50,000 donation to clean them up, initiating a pilot project that prompted Congress to underwrite similar clean-ups throughout the system.)

Then, in 1926, the Rockefellers returned, and for some reason—a simple oversight or perhaps a deliberate decision—Mather did not send out the same prohibition about raising the issue of the Tetons. Albright leaped on the first opportunity to drive the couple to Jackson Hole.

Rockefeller soon began to see things he didn't like.

"Why are those telephone lines on the west side of the road, where they mar the view of the mountains?" he asked. . . .

"Why is that ramshackle old building allowed to stand over there where it blocks the view?" I explained that it was on private land. . . .

Mrs. Rockefeller seemed increasingly upset as we passed a woebegone-looking old dance hall,

Horace Albright (seated in auto, top) brought many people to Jackson Hole in Wyoming to explain his dream of including it and the Tetons in a national park; none turned out to be as consequential as the man traveling incognito as a "Mr. Davison" (above), who in fact was John D. Rockefeller Jr.

some dilapidated cabins, a burned-out gasoline station, a few big billboards. . . .

The Rockefellers expressed great concern that this spectacular country was rapidly going to the way of development and destruction.

Near the end of the tour, as the shadows lengthened, they stopped to watch the sunset. This was the opportunity Albright had been waiting for.

As we sat on logs . . . I began to unfold . . . my dream for the area, and how I had been trying for years to save the Tetons and the whole valley north of Jackson.

Mr. and Mrs. Rockefeller listened quietly as I unfolded the story. When I finished, they remained silent as we watched the sun disappear behind the jagged peaks, casting long, sharp shadows across the valley.

I felt a little let down. Here I had laid out my fondest dream, and there was no word of comment.

But four months later, Albright was invited to Rockefeller's New York office to discuss the Tetons again. This time he showed Rockefeller detailed maps and cost estimates for a modest plan to purchase some of the land near Jackson Lake. Rockefeller cut him short. This wasn't a plan he was at all interested in considering, he said. Albright's heart stopped still for a moment.

"I remember you used the word 'dream,' " Rockefeller told him, recounting in detail the grand panorama they had surveyed while watching the sunset. "*That's* the area for which I want . . . cost estimates." "The family," he added, "is only interested in an ideal project."

Albright went back to work and soon presented a much grander proposal: the purchase of more than thirty thousand acres from nearly four hundred individual landowners in the area at a cost that would exceed $1 million, and possibly much more, if word got out that Rockefeller money was behind the purchases and land prices skyrocketed. "I think if it could be consummated," Albright told his new patron, "it would go down in history as the greatest conservation project of its kind ever undertaken."

Rockefeller agreed to it all. "I am prepared to embark on this project of the acquisition of the entire Jackson Hole country," he wrote to Albright, "having in mind its ultimate addition to the Yellowstone Park." To conceal his participation, he formed the Snake River Land Company of Salt Lake City, ostensibly a cattle business, which began buying up properties through a local banker in Jackson, a man who not only did not know the true purpose of the purchases but even opposed the idea of a "Greater Yellowstone."

When Congress finally redesignated some national forest land to create a small Grand Teton National Park two years later, both Albright and Rockefeller were disappointed that the boundaries included only the eastern front of the mountains themselves and none of the surrounding valley. Undeterred, Rockefeller continued secretly buying up land, giving Albright hope that his dream might one day be realized. Rockefeller was becoming, Albright wrote, "one of the best friends the national parks ever had."

JUST AMERICANS

Already the national parks are beneficently affecting the national mind. . . . Nowhere else do people from all the states mingle in quite the same spirit as they do in their national parks.

One sits at dinner, say, between a Missouri farmer and an Idaho miner, and at supper between a New York artist and an Oregon shopkeeper. One . . . climbs mountains with a chance crowd from Vermont, Louisiana and Texas, and sits around the evening camp fire with a California grape grower, a locomotive engineer from Massachusetts, and a banker from Michigan.

Here, the social differences so insisted on at home just don't exist. Perhaps for the first time, one realizes the common America—and loves it. . . . It is the enforced democracy and the sense of common ownership in these parks that works this magic. . . .

In the national parks, all are just Americans.

ROBERT STERLING YARD

In 1928, yearly visitation at the national parks topped three million for the first time—due in part to Stephen Mather's ceaseless promotion, but also because of the steady increase of Americans taking to the road to see their country.

"The parks," Mather proudly proclaimed, "do not belong to one state or to one section. They have become democratized." In many ways he was right. No longer did park visitors come exclusively from the upper classes. They now represented the new, expanding but predominantly white middle class—Americans with their own cars, more money in their pockets, and more time to spend it.

Congress, too, seemed more willing to support the park system. It doubled—and then redoubled—the annual appropriations, though the bulk of the money was for improving roads to accommodate the car-driving tourists pouring into the parks.

The automobile's impact was being felt in every aspect of visitation. Tourists had once been transported from point to point in controlled groups (either in carriages or motor buses), guided by concessionaires usually associated with the railroad companies. Most often, the visitors stayed in the expensive grand hotels or tent cabins owned by the same companies. Now they could travel through the park on their own schedule and stop wherever they wanted; they were more likely to camp; and they were arriving in unprecedented numbers. They parked and camped in open meadows, clogged the roads, overwhelmed facilities that had been designed for an entirely different tourist pattern. Park managers had to respond with organized campgrounds, parking lots, restrooms, and better roads.

Mather believed that for every mile of new road in a park, there should be ten miles of backcountry trails, and he was against what he called "gridironing" any park with paved motor routes. But he embarked on an ambitious plan in which each park was to have one major road that would open up that park's scenic wonders to the motoring public.

In Rocky Mountain National Park, the Fall River Road across the Continental Divide was replaced by the even more challenging Trail Ridge Road. With more than ten miles of it above elevation 11,000 feet, it was one of the highest roads in the country.

At Glacier National Park, the so-called Crown of the Continent, a road was proposed to ascend through the jagged mountains over Logan Pass, in the heart of the park. It would be the missing link in Mather's dream of a park-to-park highway, and he envisioned it as more than a motor route between one side of the park and the other; he wanted it to be a tourist attraction in its own right and took a personal interest in its design. But during an on-site inspection of the plans, Mather was told by Thomas Vint, a landscape architect accompanying him, that the multiple switchbacks proposed by highway engineers would make the scenic vista "look like miners had been in there." Horrified by the prospect, Mather decided to support Vint's suggestion for a radically different design, a straighter road that would have to be carved into the face of the Garden Wall. It would be longer, much more difficult to construct, and much more expensive—but it would not mar the majestic panorama. The result was the Going-to-the-Sun Road, considered one of the most awe-inspiring drives in America.

Now, at Mather's insistence, landscape architects were employed to oversee every detail of all national park roads. In Zion, a mile-long tunnel was blasted through the sandstone to provide not only a better road connection with Bryce Canyon National Park, but also new vistas of Zion Canyon from far above its valley floor. And in Yosemite, where the new Wawona Road would replace an old wagon trail as the park's southern entrance, America's most renowned landscape architect, Frederick Law Olmsted Jr., proposed that the debris from excavating a tunnel near Inspiration Point be turned into a man-made embankment, where drivers exiting the tunnel could pull off and park to enjoy a breathtaking first view of the valley.

Throughout the system, the entire park experience was being redesigned—scenic turnouts, rest stops, new maps and guidebooks—with people traveling in private automobiles foremost in mind.

Not everyone agreed with Mather's aggressive road policy. Even Robert Sterling Yard—who had worked for Mather for years to promote more and more visitation, and who had personally arranged the publicity trumpeting the entry of cars into Yel-

AUTOS ASCENDANT: Mather's embrace of the automobile to bring more Americans to their parks prompted some amazing feats of engineering and road design. Rocky Mountain's Trail Ridge Road (top right) included more than ten miles above elevation 11,000 feet—and required heroic efforts of snowplowing to open in the summer. A long tunnel at Zion (bottom right) included occasional arched openings to provide stunning views of the canyon.

lowstone—now worried publicly that the original park ideals he and Mather had once espoused were being "sacrificed on the altar of Gasoline."

The ultimate usefulness of our National Parks System is not showing people "sights," still less furnishing them recreation, but offering inspiration . . . elevation of the spirit and education.

So rapid is the increase of travel to the parks that it is none too early to anticipate the time when their popularity shall threaten their primary purpose. . . .

While we are fighting for the protection of the national parks system from its enemies, we may also have to protect it from its friends.

As head of the National Parks Association, the group Mather had helped create, Yard also found himself opposing his former benefactor on the creation of more national parks east of the Mississippi.

Shenandoah National Park in Virginia was proposed for a narrow slice of the Blue Ridge Mountains, with the possibility of a "Skyline Drive" running a hundred miles along the mountains' crest

Construction of the Going-to-the-Sun Road through the heart of Glacier (above) proved the greatest challenge, but its dedication on July 15, 1933 (right), drew a huge crowd to Logan Pass.

Even though Mather himself preferred to see the parks on foot or horseback, he felt each park should have one good highway—but no more than one—that would allow people to get deep enough, or through, the park so they could have at least a taste of wilderness.

There never could be too many tourists for Stephen Mather. He wanted as many as possible to enjoy his "treasures."

HORACE ALBRIGHT

Crystal Lake, seen from the shaft above it, Mammoth Cave National Park. Over its history, the cave has been mined for gypsum by Native Americans thousands of years ago; plumbed by slaves for saltpeter (an ingredient used in gunpowder) during the Civil War; and later used to house tuberculosis patients. At more than 350 miles in length, the Mammoth Cave system is three times longer than any other discovered cave in the world. Some estimates put its total length at 600 miles.

to offer motorists commanding vistas of the valleys on both sides. Mather loved the idea. Yard thought it did not meet what he called "national park standards" because of its small size and lack of "primitive" forests; and he complained that it was being promoted principally for political reasons. Congress sided with Mather.

And when the Kentucky delegation began pushing through a bill authorizing a national park at Mammoth Cave, Mather was supportive, even though he had never been there himself and no one in the Park Service had examined its worthiness. It, too, passed easily, much to Yard's mortification.

> *Our National Parks are much more than recreational resorts and museums of unaltered nature. They are also the Exposition of the Scenic Supremacy of the United States.*
>
> *No other trade-mark has cost so much to establish and pays such dividends of business, national prestige, and patriotism.*
>
> *When Zion National Park was created . . . the whole world knew from the simple announcement of the fact that another stupendous scenic wonderland had been discovered. But when pleasant wooded summits, limestone caves, pretty local ravines, local mountains and gaps between mountains become National Parks, the name "Zion National Park" will mean nothing. . . .*
>
> *If one Congressional District secures its own National Park, why not every other Congressional District?*
>
> *. . . A National Park Pork Barrel would be the final degradation.*

Mather was not happy to have his old friend and former employee questioning his judgment, especially when it came to a pet project of his in California, where he hoped to fulfill John Muir's dream of dramatically enlarging Sequoia and General Grant national parks.

William Mulholland, the city engineer for Los Angeles, wanted to dam the Kings River as a water supply for his growing city. Instead of expanding the parks, Mulholland suggested, the government should hire Hollywood producers to take the best moving pictures possible of every canyon and every waterfall in the Sierras. Once that was done, he said,

"I'd stop the goddam waste" and turn them all into reservoirs.

Mather expected hostility to Sequoia's enlargement from people like Mulholland. But when Yard and the National Parks Association also came out against it (on the grounds that it included too many compromises and might set a bad precedent), Mather was bitterly surprised. A much more modest expansion was finally approved—and Mather, whose money had been instrumental in founding Yard's group, withheld his yearly $1,000 contribution.

Meanwhile, Mather could always count on Horace Albright. No one admired Mather more than Albright did; and no one in the Park Service was more privy to the director's occasionally wild mood swings. At least two more times in the 1920s, Mather was incapacitated by depression, while Albright quietly filled in. On other occasions, his young protégé remembered, Mather was just the opposite: "wired as though tied to a battery."

> *He . . . exhibited a frenzied euphoria and extreme aggressiveness, considering himself infallible. He was apparently riding the crest of a wave. He was just as big as all outdoors, the mightiest man in the world.*

Once he impulsively ordered Albright to seize control of all the Yellowstone concessions; when Albright refused, Mather fired him. Albright ignored that order, as well. Another time, reports came into the superintendent's office that a ranger was creating a traffic jam by stopping cars and lecturing the drivers about the most minor infractions. Albright hurried to the scene. The "ranger" was Mather, whom Albright had to sternly, yet diplomatically, reprimand for causing such a scene.

During a visit to Glacier, Mather became agitated that a sawmill used by the Great Northern Railway in building a hotel ten years earlier had not been dismantled when construction was complete. Mather considered it an eyesore, so he ordered some park maintenance men to place thirteen charges of dynamite in it, and then, ignoring the protests of the hotel manager, personally lit the first fuse to blow up the sawmill.

He enjoyed nothing better than traveling from park to park in his big touring car, wearing his park

ranger's uniform, and keeping a frenetic pace that became legendary. "We wore ourselves out trying to stay with him for sixteen hours a day," one traveling companion recalled, "and then [we] had to sit up half the night listening to him talk it over."

He would talk for hours . . . reviewing his plans for the national parks. "They belong to everybody," he used to say. "We've got to do what we can to see that nobody stays away because he can't afford it."

"I hear lots of complaints about the tin-canners," I told him. "They dirty up the parks. Strew cans and papers all over."

"What if they do?" he would say. "They own as much of the parks as anybody else. We can pick up the tin cans. It's a cheap way to make better citizens."

In the spring of 1927, on his way back from inspecting Hawaii National Park, Mather suffered a heart attack. But a month later he was in Yosemite, where he hiked to Glacier Point to prove to his doctor that he was back at full strength and capable of resuming his busy schedule.

He went to Mount Rainier to go over plans for a new road in the park; attended the opening of a majestic lodge on the North Rim of the Grand Canyon; took part in the official dedication of Bryce Canyon National Park, a place he had first seen a decade earlier and declared on the spot that it would someday be part of the system he was building. At

ACTIVE TO THE END:
"He traveled constantly," Albright said of Mather. "He simply couldn't sit still in the office. He felt he had to run the parks out in the field." At left, Mather goes over plans for Mount Rainier National Park; above, he inspects Glacier by horseback.

"Cascade Mountains in Washington?"

His eyes crinkled in a smile. That was it! He wanted to know about the new highway across the northeastern corner of Mount Rainier that the state of Washington was planning to name after him. . . .

I told him that signs were now going up along the highway, designating it "Mather Parkway." A relaxed, satisfied look came over his face, but he didn't try to do any talking.

On January 12, 1929, with Mather incapacitated, Albright was sworn in as the second director of the National Park Service—fourteen years to the day since Mather had first arrived in Washington and agreed to a one-year assignment to promote the parks and push for a federal agency to protect them.

A year later, on January 22, 1930, Stephen Mather died. In his memory, a mountain just east of Mount McKinley would be named Mount Mather; an overlook at the Grand Canyon would be called Mather Point; a scenic stretch of the Potomac River would be named Mather Gorge; a nationwide tree-planting campaign in his honor would also result in Mather Forest near Lake George.

And in every national park, the agency he had created and molded to his vision would erect a bronze plaque with his likeness and these words: "There will never come an end to the good that he has done."

Zion he showed up to check on the progress of the new mile-long tunnel. The tunnel was considered an engineering marvel, and Mather became so excited about it, he stayed for several more days so he could become the first person to walk through it.

On July 4, 1928, he celebrated his sixty-first birthday in his favorite park, Yosemite, and took a long horseback ride up out of the valley to the Tuolumne Meadows in the high country. He had persuaded some newspapers to report on the logging being done on a grove of giant sugar pines located in a privately owned parcel within the park boundaries, and was pleased to learn that their stories had prompted John D. Rockefeller Jr. to put up $1.7 million to help buy the land, make it part of Yosemite, and protect the trees forever.

Then, on November 5, 1928, he suffered a serious stroke. Albright rushed to his side at the hospital in Chicago.

> *[He] had been trying to say something but could not make himself understood. The only word they had been able to get was "cascades."*
>
> *"Cascades in Yosemite?" I asked . . . but that was not it.*
>
> *"Cascade corner in Yellowstone?" . . . but that was not it either.*

TO DREAM AND DO

May 28, 1929. The Grand Canyon.

We arrived this morning after a pleasant run thru national forest over paved highway. We made camp and had dinner before we set out to look at the Canyon. There it was: beautiful, majestic, sublime—but some how I missed the thrill of that first look 14 years ago. (Great moments in our lives do not return.)

There are many improvements on the grounds.
MARGARET GEHRKE

Among the millions of Americans who had felt Stephen Mather's impact on the national parks and the country's vacation habits were Margaret and Edward Gehrke.

Edward Gehrke (far left) pauses for a rest after hiking from the Colorado River to the South Rim during the Gehrkes' return to the Grand Canyon, 1929. That same year, they added more parks to their list, including Yosemite, where Margaret (left) posed at Glacier Point, with Half Dome as her backdrop.
Right: Bypassing Lassen Volcanic National Park in 1921 had always bothered Margaret. In 1929, despite wet snows in June, she and Edward finally checked it off, even if it meant going some of the distance on horses.

In 1915, when they had first visited the Grand Canyon, Mather was just beginning his crusade to promote and develop the parks into a unified system; the Grand Canyon was still a national monument; tourists like the Gehrkes relied on railroads, not only for transportation but for much of their information and services at national parks; parks were watched over by the army; and the number of park visitors—nationwide—was just over 300,000.

By 1929, when the Gehrkes reached the Grand Canyon as part of another park-to-park journey, that number would be ten times bigger: 3,250,000 visitors to a well-publicized string of parks and monuments, administered by the National Park Service and stretching from Maine to California, from Hawaii to Alaska.

By now the Gehrkes were veteran autocampers who had already been to twelve of the twenty-one existing national parks, some of them more than once. For them, driving to different parks each year had become a reason to hit the road and see their country. It was also something of a ritual, with its own sense of comfortable repetition and renewal, mixed with a restless requirement of seeing something new.

May 29. For us the Canyon needs an added experience. . . . While taking the River Road Drive this morning we decided to hike to the bottom, stay over night, and return to-morrow. . . . We are off for the Great Thrill.

May 30. Well, it was a Great Hike! Seven miles to the Bottom and a hundred and seven to the Top. We are stiff and lame but satisfied.
. . . What is life but to dream and do?

Traveling in a Buick they called "Red Peter," with a dog named Pride as their companion, the Gehrkes kept on the move, intent on adding more parks to their list. Improved roads made getting from one park to another easier and quicker.

June 9. A day in Sequoia National Park. We will not forget our visit to the "Big Trees," but to write of it one feels his own littleness. . . . [A]s John Muir has so beautifully said: ". . . Before these forest monarchs one stands awed." Stately, glorious, living masterpieces!

June 10. Up early and off over rain-washed roads to visit more big trees. . . . Although only four square miles in area, [General] Grant [National Park] contains a magnificent grove. . . .

June 11. Yosemite! the incomparable Yosemite of our dreams!!! We followed magic roads into Yosemite: shining pavement, winding thru dense forest, following the tumbling waters of the Merced River. . . .

[Edward] tried so hard to capture it all with his cameras, while I wondered a bit if I could ever get it all down in my diary! ———

I write from our camp looking out over the meadow-like floor of the valley to the majesty of these gray granite walls, the sun dipping behind the precipice.

In these few days Yosemite Valley must in some sense become "ours" and we will feel in part what John Muir felt.

Soon they were on the move again. Back in 1921, impassable roads had prevented them from reaching Lassen Volcanic National Park in northern California. Not this time.

June 16. "Mt. Lassen Volcanic National Park."

All morning we followed wet roads thru the forest, persistent rain turning to snow as we gained higher altitude, the grade more steep and narrow as we went on. After almost 60 miles of hard going we arrived in this wet snow. Landscapes are shut out. We sit inside our tent.

What if we do not get a glimpse of Mt. Lassen! We have come so far to see it, too.

June 17. We see "Mt. Lassen." For many years we will recall to-day's experience with delight. . . . We climbed Mt. Lassen, the second couple on the trail this season.

They turned back east, across Nevada and into southern Utah, to pick off two more parks: Zion, which Margaret noted is "sometimes called a Yosemite done in oils," and Bryce Canyon, which meant that the Gehrkes had now been to eighteen national parks—all but one of the parks in existence at that time in the Lower 48. In honor of the achievement, they named a stray lamb they had temporarily adopted Bryce.

Edward took more photographs, though Margaret thought the moment was better captured in a different way. "It can only live in the walls of memory," she wrote. "And how fine a thought that these walls are never filled. . . . There is always room for more!" But like Edward trying to record everything on film, in the end Margaret could not resist attempting to summarize their experiences with a list in her diary:

How generous is Nature:
Wonderful Yellowstone!
Sublime Grand Canyon!
Lovely Yosemite!
Beautiful Crater!
Romantic Glacier!
Magnificent Zion!
Gorgeous Bryce!
To miss such distinction is to lack keenness of perception; to attempt comparison is to belittle the incomparable; to see each in its own identity, with singleness of eye, is the supreme enjoyment of Nature.

MARGARET GEHRKE

MY BUDDY

George [Masa] and I put in a lot of work on . . . the Park area—George especially; for while I only interviewed old residents throughout the territory . . . he . . . labored long and earnestly on his maps.

It is astonishing that a Jap (not even naturalized, so far as I know) should have done all this exploring and photographing and mapping, on his own hook, without compensation but at much expense to himself, out of sheer loyalty to the park idea. . . . He deserves a monument.

HORACE KEPHART

Nothing was more important to Horace Kephart and his friend George Masa than seeing the Smoky Mountains set aside as America's newest national park. Kephart, with his writing, and Masa, with his photographs, had already done much to bring attention to the mountains. Now they were working together to properly map the region. In addition to carrying his heavy camera equipment, Masa usually pushed along a bicycle wheel attached to an odometer, taking precise measurements of the distances and recording them in a pocket notebook.

But what was needed most of all was money, as the $5 million pledged by the people of Tennessee and North Carolina was only half the $10 million price tag for the land. Park boosters and the Park Service had been desperately looking for other sources to make up the difference. The search ended—once again—at John D. Rockefeller Jr. After being shown some of Masa's photographs of the region, making his own visit and being told about the impending destruction of the old-growth forests, Rockefeller at first pledged $1.5 million. Then he reconsidered and instead offered the entire $5 million from a fund named for his mother, on the sole condition that a plaque be made and placed there saying: "This park is given, one-half by the peoples and commonwealths of the States of North Carolina and Tennessee, one-half in memory of Laura Spelman Rockefeller."

Hikers at the pinnacle of Chimney Tops in the Great Smoky Mountains

But the timber companies had not given up the fight. As owners of 85 percent of the land in the proposed park, they held out for exorbitant prices and kept cutting trees, sometimes even after signing agreements to transfer ownership. "Boys, we sold it," one company supervisor told his employees. "Log her." "When we got done [with] that poor little ridge," one worker remembered, "there wasn't a toothpick left on it."

Finally, the cutting stopped and the lumbermen left. More than 5,500 people—mostly whites and Cherokees—lived within the borders of the proposed park. They, too, would have to leave, willingly or not. Some happily sold their land. Others refused, fought and lost in court, and eventually had to sell under condemnation proceedings. Many were offered leases for up to two years as the park took shape, becoming tenants on the land they had once owned.

As the isolated cabins and the small communities emptied one by one—Webbs Creek, Ravensford, Smokemont, Cataloochee, and Cades Cove—Horace Albright assured them that the Park Service

During a visit to the Smokies, philanthropist John D. Rockefeller Jr. (above) posed for a Masa photograph at the Grove Park Inn. *At left:* A map drawn by Masa and/or Horace Kephart of the Appalachian Trail winding through the proposed park

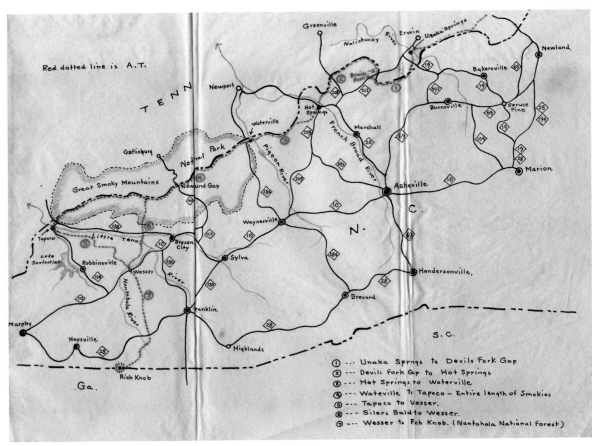

would always allow them to maintain the cemeteries near their now vacant churches. It provided small comfort against the bitterness of the removal. "Their hearts were broken," one resident remembered, and "most of them left crying."

Having lived among them for so long, Horace Kephart understood the emotional cost involved in dispossessing the people who called the Smokies home. And as someone for whom the sight of litter at abandoned campsites was always the cause of a fulminating rage, the notion that his beloved mountains might soon be crawling with tourists was sometimes a troubling thought. But he was convinced that only as a national park would the forests be preserved, and he was confident that in the long run the local people he had chronicled in his books would benefit more from the park than they had from the timber industry.

George Masa hikes a trail with his walking stick, named "Kep" in honor of his departed friend.

The long and difficult task of surveying . . . the Smoky Mt. Nat'l Park lands is finished. . . . It was a big undertaking, and beset with discouragements of all sorts, but we've won! . . .

Within two years we will have good roads into the Smokies, and then—well, then I'll get out.

This will probably ruin the old country for me.

He and George Masa now threw themselves into the effort to create an Appalachian Trail, a hiking route that would start in the Smokies and extend all the way to Maine. And they began plans to go into business together, operating their own campsite and guide service.

But on April 2, 1931, Kephart was killed in a car crash on a mountain road. George Masa, the first to arrive and last to leave Kephart's funeral, served as pallbearer and took a photograph of a memorial service at his friend's gravesite. Masa was despondent.

I don't know what I say about the death of our Kephart. It shocked me to pieces. . . .
God knows, but I don't, fate of life.

When I [am] on trail, I always cry in my heart "wish Kep with me."

I have a walking cane which Kep carried with him . . . so when I gone to Smokies I carried his cane, I call it KEP.

I miss him so much, because he was my buddy.

The stock market crash of 1929, followed by bank failures in 1930, had stripped Masa of his savings. Nevertheless, he now seemed to devote himself even more to the mountain projects he had shared with Kephart. "Money doesn't mean anything for this," he told concerned friends.

He redoubled his work on the Appalachian Trail, founded a hiking club named for Kephart, and when Horace Albright came to inspect the still uncompleted park, Masa served as one of his guides. In early 1933, Masa published a *Guide to the Great Smoky Mountains National Park*, with an introduction from Albright saying "those fortunate enough to have gone into the woods with him know that any guidebook he may issue will be invaluable."

But Masa's finances—and then his health—deteriorated even more. After organizing a hike to commemorate the second anniversary of Kephart's death, he became sick. With no money for his own doctor, he ended up in the county hospital, where he died on June 21, penniless and with no known relatives to notify. His hiking club put together a funeral service in Asheville, but did not have the money to bury him next to Kephart in the mountains, as had been his wish.

A year later, the dream he and Kephart had shared was finally realized when Great Smoky Mountains National Park was officially designated. The Great Depression was devastating the country, and the people of Tennessee and North Carolina, despite their best intentions, were unable to fulfill many of the pledges they had made to create the park. But the new president, Franklin Delano Roosevelt, inspired by all the pennies and nickels that had been collected from everyday people, decided to intervene. To make up the shortfall, he allocated $1.5 million in scarce federal funds to complete the land purchases—the first time in history that the United States government had spent its own money to buy land for a national park.

Within that park, on the main divide of the Smoky Mountains that had offered them so much solace and for which they, in turn, devoted so much of their lives, is a 6,217-foot peak that now bears the official name of Mount Kephart. On its broad shoulder is another, somewhat shorter peak, now called Masa Knob.

THE ZEPHYR

A Motorist's Creed: I believe that travel, familiarity with the sights and scenes of other parts of the country, first hand knowledge of how my fellowmen live, is of inestimable value to me and will do more to make me patriotic and public spirited than daily intimacy with the Declaration of Independence.

AMERICAN MOTORIST MAGAZINE

The thing that is choking out the wilderness is not true economics at all, but rather that Frankenstein which our boosters have [created], the "Good Roads Movement." . . .

The Motor Tourist . . . rules us with the insolence characteristic of a new god. We offer our groves and our greenswards for him to camp upon, and he litters them with cans and with rubbish. We hand him our wild life and our wild flowers [until] there are none left to hand. But of all the foolish offerings, roads are to him the most pleasing sacrifice. . . .

And of all the foolish roads, the most pleasing is the one that "opens up" some last vestige of virgin wilderness. With the unholy zeal of fanatics we hunt them out and pile them upon his altar, while from the throats of a thousand luncheon clubs and Chambers of Commerce and Greater Gopher Prairie Associations rises the solemn chant "There is No God but Gasoline and Motor is His Prophet."

ALDO LEOPOLD

As the new Great Smoky Mountains National Park was being developed, politicians and business leaders from Tennessee and North Carolina began clamoring for something more than better access roads into

and out of the park. They wanted a scenic drive that would follow the crest line of the Smokies—in much the same way that the new Skyline Drive was being built in Shenandoah National Park in Virginia's Blue Ridge Mountains. Such a road, they argued, would make the Smokies an even greater magnet for tourists. Horace Albright and the National Park Service agreed.

But for Robert Sterling Yard this was the last straw—the ultimate violation of everything he believed national parks were supposed to represent; "a crime," he wrote, "against the United States."

To fight the road—and others like it—Yard proposed "a new nation-wide movement . . . and organization to preserve the primitive . . . inside or outside the National Parks." In 1935 he joined with Bob Marshall, an idealistic young forester; Aldo Leopold, the proponent of what was called "the conservation ethic"; and a handful of other like-minded people to form a new group. They called it the Wilderness Society—and quickly won their first victory by persuading Secretary of the Interior Harold Ickes not to permit a skyline drive in the Great Smokies. To those who complained, Yard was unapologetic.

We who defend the National Parks System were [once] charged with opposing the onward march of prosperity. It wasn't true. Now the new enthusiasts charge us with opposing the forward rush of outdoor recreation. It isn't true.

What is true is this—that before the National Parks System can be completed, and turned to its highest usefulness, it must be saved, not only from those who would dump it into the channels of business, but from those, who, out of mistaken conceptions of plans and purpose, would reduce it to the general level of the country's playgrounds.

The national parks movement—and the Park Service it had spawned—had entered a new era. From now on, it would face opposition not only from its enemies who thought it was attempting to protect too much, but also from its friends who thought it was protecting too little.

June 18, 1934. "The Day of days." [Driving] to a little camp over the Colorado state line all in a day! Nearly 400 miles. . . .

We came over good highway all day, and somewhat unfamiliar for the miles and miles of new pavement and shiny new bridges. . . .

We went to bed early and I fell asleep wondering if I'd experience the old thrill over the mountains . . . will eyes that are wide open still see Nature with all their old-time naive wonder—and joy?

MARGARET GEHRKE

In the summer of 1934, Margaret and Edward Gehrke drove from their home in Lincoln, Nebraska, to Colorado's Rocky Mountain National Park for a short vacation. It was their fourth visit to what had become Margaret's favorite national park—a place now filled with memories stretching back to the couple's earliest trips together. They had a different dog with them now, and a new car, in which Edward had installed the latest innovation in motoring: a radio to listen to while the miles rolled beneath their wheels.

June 19. So much new pavement has changed the appearance of the country. We see the mountains! . . . Before you could say "Jack Robinson" we were lugging things up the steep steps into the little cabin [called "Rose-Den"] we have loved so many years. . . .

Edward Gehrke and his homemade "house car," named the Bungie Weck, in the midst of its construction (top) and after its completion (above)
Right: Margaret Gehrke on her way to her favorite place in her favorite park, Rose-Den in Rocky Mountain (bottom) in 1934. It would be the last time she and Edward visited there together.

*The old familiar mountain side with its cab-
ins, the snowy peaks beyond, the rush of water.
All the same, only I am—different.*

Margaret and Edward were both in their fifties
now, and on this visit they tended to do more driving
than hiking from place to place in the park. Margaret
noted more litter on the roadside than ever before.
Edward fished, as always.

*June 24. Sunday at Rose-Den. The twilight hour
is here: I look out to dark clouds on the mountain
sides. . . . Towards evening we have gotten our
things together for quick packing in the morning.*

*Our stay here in Rose-Den comes to an end.
Will we come back again? I wonder.*

In the mid-1930s, Edward would build them a
"house car" (a homemade precursor of the modern
RV) and they would take it on some trial runs to the
Minnesota lakes, but before they could embark with
it on another extended tour of national parks, he
took ill in 1939 and died.

Margaret would accept a job working for the University of Nebraska and no longer spend her winters
dreaming of new adventures—or her summers taking them. But in 1948, she used a two-week vacation
to return to Rocky Mountain National Park and
"Rose Den."

*July 3. I took a five mile walk to the village of
Estes and back . . . found tourists everywhere
buying things and things! But the walk was good.*

*This evening . . . a great storm raging on
Long's Peak and when [I] beheld this majesty [I]
felt equal to the contemplations of Divinity. Perhaps the walk cleared [my] vision.*

On this trip, without Edward to do the driving,
Margaret went out and back the way the couple had
traveled together so many years earlier. She went by
train.

July 13. 5:00 P.M. En route. The Zephyr.

*Here I am this mid-July afternoon going
home. And glad to be going home. Surely I care
little about home and never have. Back to
Nebraska to the hateful heat of summer, to work
day after day, to monotony most would say. But
glad!*

*This long silver train makes swift passage. It is
streaking across the flat Colorado country as I sit
here alone. (Why should I be so near to tears?)
The whole trip to Colorado like a dream now.
The whole thing drops from my shoulders now
like a jeweled coat, and I lay it aside feeling I've
never worn it at all.*

REDEFINING BEAUTY

Paul Schullery went to work as a seasonal ranger in Yellowstone in 1972. Since then, during a long career with the Park Service, he has spent about half of his time living and working in the world's first national park. He is a historian by training, but Schullery is a naturalist by avocation, an avid hiker, fly fisherman, and wildlife watcher.

He is the author or editor of more than thirty books on nature, conservation, and the national parks—including ten about Yellowstone. In 1998, the University of Colorado's Center of the American West presented Schullery with its prestigious Wallace Stegner Award, calling him "America's foremost citizen of the National Parks."

Wallace Stegner called national parks "the best idea we ever had." What's your opinion?

I'm not sure that the Americanness of the national park idea is something that springs from the beginning. I think it springs from what we made of it. The original act creating Yellowstone Park says practically nothing. They had no idea where they were going and thank God they didn't, because they left so much unsaid. We've been creating the national park idea ever since.

They left it up to us, and the parks had to grow if they were going to make it. They had to grow and fit in a rapidly changing American culture. And it was that process that made it so thoroughly American.

It's a truly creative process. It's very improvisational. It's a lot of guesswork, a lot of trial and error. And when a society does that, what they come up with is going to be a terrific reflection of that society, for better or worse. We're always going to get about the quality of national parks that we deserve.

In that evolution, certain people stand out, sometimes almost counterintuitively. George Bird Grinnell and "the Park Grab" at Yellowstone comes to mind.

In the 1880s and 1890s there was very little that was really democratic about the first national parks. It was very expensive to get there, and the railroads would take you there in style, and once they got their better hotels built, you could stay there in style. George Bird Grinnell was himself from the upper crust. He most

often represented that upper crust, but by referring to Yellowstone as "the people's park," he revealed a much broader and more forward-looking vision.

The railroads were rushing into a vacuum—a decision-making vacuum, a philosophical vacuum. Everything was up for grabs. Grinnell happened to come along and we're very lucky he did. He knew that Yellowstone could belong to everybody eventually, and he knew that what the railroad wanted to do would take it in just the opposite direction.

Grinnell was also an avid hunter—like the man he seems to have influenced so profoundly, Theodore Roosevelt. How important were these hunters in the evolution of national parks, where hunting was, after all, prohibited?

Roosevelt will always baffle people who don't hunt because he both loved animals and loved hunting them. When Grinnell and Roosevelt founded the Boone and Crockett Club, there was a society of concerned sportsmen who were ripe to become conservationists. They just needed some place to exercise that energy and that interest, and Yellowstone became the foremost focus for them.

Grinnell and Roosevelt and the other defenders of Yellowstone were thinking in ecosystem terms before anybody was using the term. They saw places like Yellowstone as reservoirs. They actually used the term "reservoir" metaphorically, to describe the park. It was a reservoir for water that drained down into agricultural lands outside the park. It was a reservoir for wildlife.

There were animals moving in and out of the park on their annual migrations, and when they were in the park they were wildlife; when they left the park they became game. The Grinnells and Roosevelts have been criticized—"Well, you only saved those animals so that you could shoot them"—and that's absurd. They saved them for a bunch of reasons. They understood that animals had their own constituencies who could be very good friends of the park.

Another evolution was in how "wild" national parks should be.

The national parks have always been managed pretty much by the values of their time. And in the 1920s and 1930s—the Mather and Albright era—most people still thought predators were a bad

Historian and naturalist Paul Schullery

Some people thought humans could make all decisions about how a park should look and how its natural features should behave, and others thought it was a lot more beautiful if you let nature make the decisions. And gradually nature was given more freedom to do what nature does.

But even in the early 1900s, it was still spectacle. It was still the simplest version of prettiness. Wild beauty was defined on superficial levels that had very little to do with wildness and how wildness actually works. It was the scientists who helped us see past those superficialities. It's the scientists who had the most to do with redefining beauty. When they discovered the underlying sense of wild landscapes—predation, and fire, and all the dramatic forces that shaped the landscape in the first place—they exposed us to far deeper and more challenging beauties than most people even imagined when we started creating parks.

How do you judge Stephen Mather and Horace Albright on this scale?

We look back now at Mather and Albright, and we can condescend and say, well, they didn't get it. They didn't understand ecological process and all those other things, but they were unfailing heroes when it came down to the really tough fights of their day, when all manner of incursions were proposed for Yellowstone, including to create a set of dams and reservoirs on some of Yellowstone's beautiful rivers. Mather and Albright stood up on their hind feet and fought that off. We can easily find things they may have done wrong, and feel smug that we know better now. But what really matters about them is that they saw the big threats and they fought them off.

Albright was the one who agreed to let George Melendez Wright at least conduct his studies of wildlife and plant life in the parks.

In Horace Albright's day, national park superintendents didn't mind a little science, but they didn't necessarily see why it mattered. An awful lot of them still figured they had a pretty good grip on how things should be in the park. The effect of George Wright and his colleagues—this group of ecological thinkers and students—was, in an institution that's always evolving anyway, like a perpetual revolution. The things that they were suggesting were such a reversal of the way society saw nature that I don't think it's an overstatement to call it a revolution.

When Wright said that the rare predators shall be protected in the national parks in proportion that they are persecuted everywhere else, that was unimaginable to a lot of people. It was a sea change.

thing. Most people still thought it didn't matter what kind of fish, native or nonnative, I could catch just so long as there were lots of fish to catch. All people would have regarded forest fires as invariably bad.

But there was a whole separate element of the conservation community, mostly the people who understood how natural systems really work, beginning to lobby for something very different.

After Wright's tragic death, his cause finally found a new champion in Adolph Murie.

I think Adolph Murie may be the best early example of someone who proved how correct Wright was. He did beautifully focused studies on elements of natural communities and demonstrated that they worked in ways people didn't understand at all.

I'm hard-pressed to say what parts of Adolph Murie's work meant the most. When he produced his study of the coyotes in Yellowstone and demonstrated that they weren't this scourge on the landscape, and how they *actually* functioned compared to how people *thought* they functioned—that they weren't turning Yellowstone into a reservoir of evil that produced countless coyotes that went out and killed off ranchers' livestock—it took a long time for that lesson to soak in, but eventually it did. But a study like that doesn't stop with one park; it made people think about many other places and issues. It still should.

Did the same, slow lesson have to be learned about Yellowstone's bears?

Bear feeding began at dumps in Yellowstone in the late 1880s, sort of casually, accidentally. And after traffic increased enough so that you had enough cars and buses by the 1920s, there were a lot of roadside black bears—these are black bears, not grizzly bears—being fed by tourists. They had their "stations," as everyone called them; they'd come back year after year. And on one level it was a charming thing. People got to see these wild animals and get close, kind of get to know them. If they were repeat visitors, they could come back and feed the same bears next year.

At the same time there were hundreds of people who suffered minor injuries, and between 1930 and 1970, an average of twenty-four black bears a year were killed in the park to keep that roadside bear show going. That was the price the bear population paid for our entertainment. Some bears were hit by cars. Some ingested too much junk. A lot of them had to be shot by rangers because finally they'd been abused by too many tourists or thought they were defending a cub or for some other reason became aggressive and hurt somebody. So it was a pretty expensive process in terms of what it cost the bears.

But the professional scientific community and the conservation groups objected to bear feeding for other reasons. They took it on because they saw it as beneath the dignity of a national park. They thought a national park should have a higher goal than this sort of roadside zoo experience and that people should be experiencing the whole setting in a more natural way.

Left: A bison, an elk, and a grizzly bear roam undisturbed in Yellowstone, the park George Bird Grinnell called "the last refuge."

It was a battle of value systems, and sorting it out has never been a simple process. Here's an example. In the 1940s, it became inappropriate in a national park for people to watch grizzly bears eat garbage at a garbage dump, but it wasn't until 1970 that it became inappropriate for grizzly bears to eat garbage at a garbage dump. The dumps were still there. They just weren't part of the visitor experience anymore.

What attracts you to Yellowstone—or any national park?

The excitement I feel when I enter a national park isn't just about the landscape. It's not just about what I'm going to see here. It's about knowing that I've entered this different kind of American institution that stands for a lot of things. It's like going to Yankee Stadium. You walk into this special place that is wonderful for itself, but it's also wonderful for all the cultural richness that it's given us and that we remember.

Very quickly, memory becomes an important part of a park experience. Parks enrich themselves through the accumulated experiences of generations of visitors. There's this terrifically complicated aggregation of memory in a national park that makes it so much more than what it was originally imagined to be.

What role do the national parks play in our nation—in our past and in our future?

I'm not quite sure why it works this way, but we seem to put our highest ideals in our national parks. They're homes for our finest dreams. And therefore they function like consciences. We've set ourselves up with this whole system of places that send us messages—these places that are full of lofty ideas and ideals and goals where we celebrate our finest moments and also remind ourselves of some of our worst moments. The parks remember our dreams, which means that sometimes they have to drag us along, whether we're up to it or not.

National parks have worked for us for so long because they're so flexible, because it's an elastic institution that we keep redefining. It keeps evolving. We keep discovering new things each park can do for us. And as long as we give them the freedom to do that, and as long as they can keep flexing and changing and growing, we're probably okay.

Whenever we want to do something to a national park, whenever we want to change direction, whenever we want to try something new, the most important question we have to ask ourselves is, "Will this action reduce the number of choices the next generation has?" And if it does, then we shouldn't do it.

CHAPTER FIVE

GREAT NATURE

I N JULY OF 1929, a ninety-year-old woman returned to the Yosemite Valley in California. She was called Maria Lebrado, but seventy-eight years earlier, as a young girl, she had been known by her real name, Totuya, the granddaughter of Chief Tenaya, leader of the Ahwahneechees, an Indian tribe who for centuries had called the valley their home—until, in 1851, a battalion of white men had invaded the valley and driven them out at bayonet point. Totuya was the sole remaining survivor of that sad moment. This was her first time back.

Half a generation after the Ahwahneechees' expulsion, the federal government had stepped in to prohibit private development within the beautiful valley and eventually preserved it permanently as a national park. Still, everywhere she looked, Totuya was reminded of how many years had passed and how much things had changed.

Her people's baskets were now exhibited as relics in the park museum; some living Indians were even on display for tourists. In a broken mixture of English, Spanish, and her own ancient language, Totuya told her escorts the valley floor was now more wooded and brushy than in her day; her people had regularly set grass fires to keep the meadows open and the trees and shrubs at bay. The names of all the valley's familiar features—the great stone monoliths and waterfalls—had been changed, too, but she recognized them, one witness recounted, as if she had never gone away.

She saluted Tu-tock-ah-nu-lah, *now known as El Capitan. Her own Indian village had stood in full view of* Loya, *now Sentinel Rock. It seemed very dear to her. A momentary silence, then in quiet supplication she said, "Loya, Loya; long time 'go."*

The waterfalls drawing their substance from the eternal source of rain and snow spoke to her as they had spoken in her childhood. Looking at Yosemite Falls, she cried, "Chorlock! Chorlock no gone!"

Preceding pages: A misty sunrise at Everglades National Park
Right: "Autocampers" fill Stoneman Meadow, Yosemite National Park, 1927

Then, turning toward Half Dome, the cleft rock she knew as *Tis-sa-ack,* she stretched out her arms and raised her voice in a strong, clear, high-pitched call that echoed off the granite walls. It was, she explained, the call her grandfather Tenaya had once used to summon his people together. Until that moment, she had been the last one to hear it.

Possessions, both material and spiritual, are appreciated most when we find ourselves in peril of losing them. The national forests were established just in time to prevent unimaginable disaster. Through the farseeing efforts of men such as John Muir and Stephen Mather the concept of the national parks was solidified and vast areas set aside in perpetuity against the ravages of . . . exploitation.

. . . The national parks represent those intangible values which should not be turned directly to profit or material advantage, and it requires integrity of vision and purpose to consider such impalpable qualities on the same effective level as material resources.

. . . The wilderness is pushed back; man is everywhere. Solitude, so vital to the individual . . . is almost nowhere. Certain values are realized; others destroyed. The dragons of demand have been kept at snarling distance by the St. Georges of conservation, but the menace remains.

ANSEL ADAMS

As the 1920s ended, the United States was about to enter two of the darkest and most frightening decades of the twentieth century—first an economic cataclysm that threatened the foundation of American society, followed by a war that threatened the existence of freedom throughout the world. For a time during those dark years, the national parks would thrive as never before. In the 1930s and 1940s, hundreds of thousands of American boys would go to the parks in pursuit of a paycheck—and discover a new sense of dignity. Then hundreds of thousands more, under different circumstances, would enjoy in the parks a moment of peace in a world at war.

The nation that emerged from that era would be radically different from the one that had entered it. The national park idea was about to change, as well. With the death of Stephen Mather, the parks had lost a powerful and charismatic champion. Now a new president and his progressive administration would vastly expand the number of parks—and then even more dramatically expand the very notion of what a national park could be.

In a time when the future of the country was most in doubt, the symbols of her complicated past would be set aside and cherished—and Americans from every walk of life and every possible background would find in the parks a deeper connection to their land, their nation, and themselves.

GOOD HYGIENE FOR CIVILIZATION

I would only make myself ridiculous if I tried to be another Steve Mather. My job as I see it, will be to consolidate our gains, finish up the rounding out of the Park system . . . guarantee the future of the system on a sound permanent basis . . . [and] go rather heavily into the historical park field.

HORACE ALBRIGHT

When Horace Albright had taken over the reins of the National Park Service in 1929, his first priority

George Melendez Wright interviews Totuya (above, left) in Yosemite, 1929. At right, Papoose Room in Carlsbad Caverns National Park

was carrying on the policies he and Stephen Mather had instituted to make national parks publicly popular and professionally run. Just like Mather, Albright also pushed to secure even more places under Park Service protection. Congress added Carlsbad Caverns in New Mexico as a national park—an underground wonderland of massive stalagmites and stalactites in a series of ninety-four limestone caves, including the deepest cave in the nation. Each evening at dusk, swarms of bats—at the rate of five thousand a minute—pour out of the main cave's entrance, on their way to their nightly feedings, and then return before sunrise.

But Albright persuaded President Herbert Hoover, who had once served as head of the National Parks Association, to do more, by using his unique authority under the Antiquities Act to declare a number of national monuments:

- California's Death Valley, a vast desert in southeastern California, where the Amargosa River sinks into oblivion at Badwater Basin, the hottest, driest, and lowest spot in North America, 282 feet below sea level.

- Colorado's Black Canyon of the Gunnison River, half a mile deep and, at its narrowest, only a thousand feet wide, with sheer cliffs exposing rocks nearly two billion years old.

- Saguaro National Monument in Arizona, home to the distinctively statuesque giant saguaro cactus, which requires 150 years to reach maturity—with a height of nearly fifty feet and a weight of eight tons.

- The Badlands of South Dakota, where the prairies have eroded into an eerie jumble of rock formations holding fossils of creatures dating back millions of years, to the beginnings of the age of mammals.

- The Great Sand Dunes, covering fifty-five square miles and rising to heights of nearly seven hundred feet, the tallest dunes in the Continent; a landscape seemingly transported from the Arabian desert to the foothills of the Sangre de Cristo Mountains of southern Colorado.

Badlands National Park in South Dakota

Left: The Narrows of Black Canyon of the Gunnison National Park, Colorado
Right: Saguaro cactus by moonlight, Saguaro National Park, Arizona
Below: Cracked earth at Death Valley National Park, California
Overleaf: Dunes and the Sangre de Cristo Mountains, Great Sand Dunes National Park, Colorado

In later years, Congress would turn all five national monuments into full-fledged national parks. But Albright had even more expansive plans for the agency he had inherited from Mather:

I had a dream I wanted to make real. For years I had wanted to get the many national military parks, battlefields, and monuments transferred out of the War Department and Department of Agriculture into the National Park Service so we could give proper protection and interpretation to these great historic and cultural treasures.

It had become something close to a crusade for me. . . . I was motivated by a fascination with history that I had felt from early childhood.

In April of 1933, Albright got his chance. Franklin Delano Roosevelt, newly sworn in as president, decided to visit the cabin in Virginia's Blue Ridge Mountains, near Shenandoah National Park, that President Hoover had used for weekend getaways from Washington's heat and political pressures. Albright, recently reappointed as Park Service director by the new administration, was asked to join the entourage accompanying President and Mrs. Roosevelt for the inspection.

Roosevelt enjoyed the spring weather and the view of the Rapidan River from the cabin's front porch, but quickly decided it would not work for him as a presidential retreat. The walkway was too uneven for his weakened legs, ravaged by polio. Albright and two others had to carry him the final distance.

For the long drive back, the president unexpectedly invited Albright to ride with him.

The President got in the front seat, where there was more room, and they took the braces off of his legs. He put a cigarette in his long cigarette holder, sat back, and relaxed. I sat behind him on the jump seat, just a few inches from his ear.

At first, as they traveled the partially finished Skyline Drive along the crest of the mountains, Albright answered Roosevelt's questions about the founding of the National Park Service and issues concerning new parks in the East.

As we approached the Rappahannock River I began thinking—if I'm going to talk to the President about getting the military parks, I had better get to it. Now was the time.

Albright began pointing out sites important to the Second Battle of Bull Run in the Civil War, then broadened the discussion to the myriad other Civil War battlefields and historic sites in the area. "Then I took a deep breath," he later recalled, and told the president why the National Park Service should be in charge of them all. Roosevelt listened intently.

"I knew before we got to Washington that night," Albright remembered, "that I had my foot not only in the door for historic preservation, but I had it

ICONS OF HISTORY: President Franklin Delano Roosevelt (above, center) expanded the national park idea to include battlefields and historic sites such as the Statue of Liberty and Antietam (right), site of the bloodiest day in the Civil War.

in the White House." Roosevelt told Albright to put his proposals in writing—and soon, the president signed two executive orders instituting a sweeping reorganization that overnight transformed the Park Service.

From the War Department, the agency was given responsibility for more than twenty military parks and historic battlefields and monuments—from Castillo de San Marcos, an ancient Spanish fort in St. Augustine, Florida, preserving one of the oldest vestiges of Europe's presence in the New World, to Yorktown, Virginia, where the decisive victory of the American Revolution had been won; from Gettysburg, Antietam, Shiloh, and Vicksburg, where some of the most important battles in the Civil War were fought, to Appomattox Court House, where it ended.

There was much more. Under the reorganization, the Park Service was now expected to protect and interpret more than a dozen nonmilitary historic sites as well:

- The Statue of Liberty in New York's harbor, originally a gift from the people of France, and now the symbol of freedom to millions of immigrants who had sailed past it to reach American shores.
- Mount Rushmore in South Dakota, where the busts of four American presidents—Washington, Jefferson, Theodore Roosevelt, and Lincoln—were being sculpted on a monumental scale into the granite of the Black Hills.
- And many of the District of Columbia's most hallowed places—including the National Mall, the Washington Monument, and the Lincoln Memorial, the shrine to the president who in 1864 had given the national park idea its first, tentative expression.

National parks now preserved more than unique landscapes, they embraced the idea of America itself. And Horace Albright had created a system far bigger than he and Stephen Mather had ever hoped to dream.

THE BOSS

About the only thing that I ever did that was really smart was to go out into the desert and pick a darned good ruin, and sit down by it for 30-odd years.

FRANK PINKLEY

No one better personified the National Park Service spirit that Stephen Mather and Horace Albright had tried to engender than Frank Pinkley, the custodian at Casa Grande Ruins National Monument in Arizona, a four-story adobe ruin of the ancient Hohokam civilization, which had flowered in the Southwest a thousand years earlier.

In 1900, at age nineteen, Pinkley had arrived from Missouri on doctor's orders to find a dry climate because he was susceptible to tuberculosis. A year later, for lack of other applicants, he found himself in charge of the ancient ruin and its 480 acres. Pinkley lived in a tent he pitched nearby, dug his own well, and began carrying out his duties, which consisted primarily of preventing vandals from looting the artifacts and keeping stray cattle out of the site.

A few years later, he married his wife, Edna, and built a shelter over his tent for them to live in. After the birth of their two children, he used his own money and any materials he could scrounge to construct a ramshackle adobe house, earning his family the nickname "the ruined Pinkleys."

Money for improvements seldom arrived, except for a barnlike roof to keep rain off the ruins, but Pinkley didn't complain. He stabilized the old walls to keep them from collapsing, happily wrote his own brochures publicizing Casa Grande, and loved nothing better than providing personal guided tours to the few visitors who showed up. "Did you build this ruin?" one visitor playfully asked Pinkley's young son. "No sir, I didn't," the boy answered, "but my father did."

When Horace Albright stopped by, he was more struck by Pinkley's attitude than the ruins themselves.

There really was not much left of the Hohokam enclave. But you would think you were gazing on one of the Seven Wonders of the World to see the affection and pride Pinkley had in his moldering ruins. It was beyond belief.

He pointed out every spot that had been restored, every plan he had to

complete his dream. To him it appeared a true casa grande, *a magnificent house of the noble Hohokam rising toward the sun, not a melting mound of clay as we saw it.*

Albright and Mather had been so impressed by Pinkley's dedication and drive that when the Grand Canyon became a national park in 1919 they considered him for the plum appointment of superintendent. But he told Albright he preferred staying with national monuments, so he was chosen to oversee all of them in the Southwest.

Each year, he loaded his family into an old Model T and embarked on an inspection tour covering Arizona, New Mexico, and parts of Colorado and Utah. The car, Albright said, was "the most rattletrap auto I'd ever seen. It looked like a decrepit boiler with wheels, with rickety posts to hold the top on." Pinkley called the car "Baby."

In it, he would travel to an increasing number of monuments under his supervision—fourteen at first, then more than twenty-five—checking in with each one's custodian, oftentimes a lonely volunteer being paid just one dollar a month; offering friendly advice on how to do their work more professionally; trying his best to convince them that the lack of federal money did not mean national monuments were second-class places to national parks, even though he suspected many people in the Park Service saw it that way; and always boosting their morale with his folksy encouragement.

About the only satisfaction we can dig out of this situation is that when it came to making real savings . . . to making one dollar do the work of two or three; to doing without necessities; they certainly came to the right outfit when they came to us!

. . . We have always had more job than we had funds to run it, so there's nothing novel about that part of the situation.

. . . We are going to ask [you] to keep all this inside the family; to yowl neither to the high heavens nor into the ear of the visitor. . . . But the gods of the Southwest love a good loser, and so,

Frank Pinkley, "The Boss," in 1934

Casa Grande National Monument in 1903 (right, top) after Pinkley constructed a roof to protect the Hohokam ruins. So devoted was Pinkley to the national monument he had supervised for nearly forty years, that his funeral service was conducted on its grounds (right, below, with an improved steel roof added in 1932).

incidentally, do the visitors, so we won't bother either of them with protestations.

In 1927, as part of his yearly plea for more funds, he pointed out that his collection of monuments was now drawing more visitors than Yellowstone, but received only half as much money from the government. It didn't help. To stretch his budget, Pinkley often paid for his own travel or went without a salary near the end of a fiscal year.

In deference to his leadership, the men under his supervision called him "The Boss," a name he accepted proudly and attached to the newsletter, *Ruminations,* he sent to them each month.

The badge can symbolize the Service and identify the wearer to the park visitor, but the uniform can do more than that: it can build morale and prestige, morale in the man who wears it and prestige in the eyes of the public—when it is worn by the right men.

THE BOSS

Pinkley's wife, Edna—like the wives of the men at all the other underfunded monuments—often ended up typing his reports, leading tours of Casa Grande in his absence, or doing other chores on his behalf. Pinkley thanked the wives as often as possible in *Ruminations* and gave them all a title—"Honorary Custodians Without Pay."

When Edna died in 1929, Pinkley soldiered on in her absence with their two children. Struck by a heart attack eight years later, he kept on working despite his diminished health. National monuments, he told his custodians, were held together with "binding twine and baling wire." So was "The Boss."

In 1940, after more than thirty-five years on the job, Pinkley finally convinced his superiors to fund a training conference for his employees, similar to the yearly meetings the Park Service hosted for its park superintendents. Even though the budget Washington approved was only $25 per person, Pinkley was ecstatic. He gathered his men together at Casa Grande, under strict orders that they wear their uniform, and on the opening morning delivered a speech he had wanted to give them in person for many years.

I think you will all understand that this is one of the red letter days in my life. It was in December 1901 that I started down the lonesome trail which has finally led to today and this room and these co-workers.

. . . The idea behind our organization has been that 27 individual areas, each struggling along in its own individual way, each using its own plan . . . can be welded into one compact group where every man will have benefit of the experience of every other man . . . and the same mistake need not be made 27 different times.

He called the group "Our Outfit," and said he understood the challenges each one of them faced, but also how together they could over-come any obstacle and preserve what he told them were "the 27 finest National Monuments in the United States."

[They are] ours to make or ruin. . . . Let us try hard to make ourselves worthy of these obligations which have been placed upon us.

May we leave this meeting three days hence with a . . . fixed determination to do it better this next year than it has ever been done before.

After delivering his speech, he sat down and slumped forward—dead from a massive heart attack.

Pinkley's men decided to complete the three-day conference anyway and sat for a formal photograph taken with his empty chair in the middle. Then they conducted his funeral service, not in a church, but on the grounds of his beloved Casa Grande Ruins National Monument.

They were sure "The Boss" would have wanted it that way.

Our national heritage is richer than just scenic features; the realization is coming that perhaps our greatest national heritage is nature itself, with all its complexity and its abundance of life, which, when combined with great scenic beauty as it is in the national parks, becomes of unlimited value.

This is what we would attain in the national parks.

GEORGE MELENDEZ WRIGHT

During her emotional return to the valley taken from her people, one of Totuya's escorts, chosen because he was fluent in Spanish, was a young Park Service employee named George Melendez Wright, who only recently had joined the Yosemite staff as assistant park naturalist.

He had been born into a wealthy San Francisco family, the son of a ship's captain and a mother from one of El Salvador's most prominent dynasties. After the premature deaths of both parents, Wright's brothers had returned to El Salvador, while he remained in the United States under the care of an aunt who encouraged his growing fascination with the natural world. By his mid-teens, he had become an avid bird watcher and president of his local Audubon Club, and he had hiked alone from San Francisco to California's northern border.

At the University of California, Berkeley, where he studied forestry and zoology, Wright's intelligence and irrepressible enthusiasm had so impressed his mentor, the influential wildlife biologist Joseph Grinnell, that upon graduation he had been dispatched to Mount McKinley National Park. There, on a ledge one thousand feet above timberline, he had become the first person in recorded history to find and describe the nest and eggs of the rare surfbird.

Now, working at Yosemite, Wright became concerned that the parks were fulfilling only part of their purpose. By focusing so much on attracting visitors, he worried, park managers had overlooked another responsibility, which Wright called "the very heart of the national park system": preserving not just the scenery, but the wildlife in its natural state.

When [a tourist] enters the park he is looking for the same concentration of animals he saw in the paddocks of the zoological garden, the same personal safety in feeding the tamed animals, the same convenience of driving to a known place at any convenient time to see what he wants. A galaxy of bears at the garbage platform approximates this concept and he is satisfied.

Then comes a day when his heart skips a beat. Walking along a deep forest trail he comes upon a single bear eagerly peeling the bark from a log in search of fat white grubs.

This is a fresh thrill and it brings the realization that the unique charm of the animals in a national park lies in their wildness, not their tameness, in their primitive struggle to survive rather than their fat certainty of an easy living.

Though only in his mid-twenties and near the bottom of the Park Service career ladder, Wright proposed to his superiors that he undertake something that had never been done before: a scientific survey of wildlife conditions in the national parks. It took a year of persuasion, but he finally won approval for his plan, partly because of his persistence and friendly personality, but also because Wright offered to underwrite the whole thing himself, drawing on his inheritance to pay for the salaries of the three team members, their equipment and transportation, and all other costs.

In the summer of 1930, in a Buick Roadster he had purchased and customized to carry camping gear, cameras, and scientific instruments, Wright set off with Joseph Dixon and Ben Thompson on an 11,000-mile tour of the western parks. They would keep at it for four consecutive years. At each park, Wright kept a daily log of the animals he saw. He was particularly interested in birds, the "encouragement and inspiration to the man who prays," he wrote, "that the wilderness . . . will always live."

Sometimes, while I am watching these birds . . . the illusion of the untouchability of this wilderness becomes so strong that it is stronger than reality, and the polished roadway becomes the illusion, the mirage that has no substance.

Wright also gleaned information from his conversations with people in the field: park rangers and superintendents, local ranchers and hunters, old-timers who remembered what it was like in the nineteenth century—anyone with information about the state of wildlife in the parks to augment what he and his fellow researchers were observing with their own eyes.

Everywhere he went, Wright discovered disturbing evidence that in the parks the equilibrium of nature was out of kilter. Coyotes, wolves, and mountain lions—even badgers and hawks and owls—were routinely trapped or shot as unwelcome predators. Buffalo were rounded up each year and kept in corrals like domestic cows. In some parks elk, deer, and antelope herds were being fed hay in wintertime, and

WILDLIFE DEFENDER:
As a young assistant park naturalist in Yosemite, George Melendez Wright (left) proposed a revolutionary, system-wide change in National Park Service policies. Ingrained practices such as bear feedings (above), treating animals like zoo exhibits (right), killing predators that preyed on the species tourists preferred, and dozens of other activities, he argued, should be abandoned in favor of letting nature take its course in the parks.

in others they were stripping areas of natural vegetation, because their natural grazing patterns competed with cattle and sheep on nearby ranches.

At Yellowstone he learned that rangers had been ordered to go to the nesting grounds of white pelicans and stomp their eggs, because it was feared that grown pelicans deprived anglers of too many fish.

Bears, meanwhile, were treated like pets—lured to garbage dumps, where the nightly feedings had become a major tourist attraction, or encouraged to beg for handouts from tourists along the roadside, even if the "official" policy discouraged it. "It takes time to teach the visitors . . . that they are the ones who are short-sighted in feeding candy to a bear," Wright observed.

After all, the average citizen expects more intelligence from a bear than he . . . has any right to expect.

He goes on the assumption that if he feeds a bear two sticks of candy and does not want to give it a third, he is the one to say, "No, no."

And he believes that the bear is to be accused of an unforgivable breach of etiquette . . . if it takes all the candy out of his hand and takes the hand with it, perhaps.

Wright understood that many of the management decisions sprang from age-old assumptions about controlling predators as well as from a desire within the Park Service to cater to tourists who expected a friendly encounter with their favorite animals. But when he and his colleagues eventually published two reports outlining their findings, he proposed a radically new policy. Unless threatened with extinction within a park, he wrote, each native species should be left to "carry on its struggle for existence unaided." Wright also called for the end of winter feedings, closing the bear dumps, ending the stocking of streams with nonnative fish, expansion of some park boundaries to accommodate grazing habits, and changes in a multitude of practices that had become ingrained in the parks.

Wright was challenging a status quo that had been built up over the years—reminding the Park Service that the legislation creating it called for the wildlife to be preserved "unimpaired," as well as the scenery. "Am I visionary or just crazy?" Wright had written a

colleague at the start of the project. Most park managers, unconvinced about his revolutionary recommendations, had their own opinion. But Horace Albright was intrigued by the surveys and in 1933 established a new wildlife division. Then he named George Melendez Wright, only twenty-nine years old, as its chief.

If we destroy nature blindly, it is a boomerang which will be our undoing. . . . Consecration to the task of adjusting ourselves to [the] natural environment so that we secure the best values from nature without destroying it is not useless idealism; it is good hygiene for civilization.

[F]ailure would be a blow injuring the very heart of the national-park system.

GEORGE MELENDEZ WRIGHT

THE SNAKE SWAMP PARK

There are no other Everglades in the world. . . . Nothing anywhere else is like them; their vast glittering openness, wider than the enormous visible round of the horizon, the . . . sweetness of their massive winds, under the dazzling blue heights of space. . . .

The miracle of the light pours over the green and brown expanse of saw grass and water, shining and slow-moving below, the grass and water that is the meaning and central face of the Everglades of Florida.

It is a river of grass.

MARJORY STONEMAN DOUGLAS

For centuries, the unimpeded freshwaters of Lake Okeechobee had flowed slowly (only one hundred feet per day) across a vast swath of southern Florida toward the Gulf of Mexico—a seemingly endless saw grass marsh punctuated by cypress swamps and mangrove forests creating an environment unlike anything else on earth.

Its highest elevation is never more than ten feet above sea level, yet its rich landscape supports more than a thousand different species of plants, from stately royal palms and smooth-barked gumbo limbo trees to exquisitely delicate orchids and bromeliads. It is the only place on earth where alligators and crocodiles can be found living side by side. It is also a crit-

Florida politicians like Governor Napoleon Bonaparte Broward (below) made their careers partly on promises to drain the Everglades and make way for the land speculation that inevitably followed (above, right). Ernest F. Coe (middle, right) and Marjory Stoneman Douglas (bottom, right) led the fight to protect the Everglades and its unique array of birds and plants. *Overleaf*: Red mangroves sprout in the "river of grass."

BACK TO BROWARD

NAPOLEON B. BROWARD
Florida's Greatest Son

Drain the Everglades; make good on Florida's promises to the United States Government and to the people of our sister States

SAVE THE HONOR OF FLORIDA

ical breeding ground for wading birds beyond counting: egrets and ibises and herons of all sizes, roseate spoonbills, and the wood stork, the only stork native to America.

Because of its trackless impenetrability, the Everglades became something of a sanctuary for people, too. In the early 1800s, when the Seminole Indians were driven out of Florida onto the Trail of Tears, small groups escaped and found refuge instead deep in the cypress trees and saw grass, along with the Miccosukee tribe and hundreds of runaway slaves. In the 1890s, when the fashion in women's hats made the white feathers of egrets more valuable per ounce than gold, plume hunters and poachers hid out in the Everglades and slaughtered the birds there with impunity. A few Audubon Society game wardens who dared try to stop them had been killed, too.

By the start of the twentieth century, a greater threat imperiled not just the birds, but the Everglades itself. Napoleon Bonaparte Broward, elected governor in 1904 on a slogan of "Drain the Everglades," was merely one in a long series of Florida politicians and promoters who built their careers on the idea of turning the vast wetland into a developer's promised land. As mechanized dredges began digging drainage canals, real estate speculators began offering land at one dollar an acre; then twenty; then fifty—even though some of it was still underwater. Skeptics said the unsuspecting buyers were purchasing "land by the gallon."

A succession of real estate booms soon swept South Florida, turning much of the northern Ever-glades into sugarcane plantations, vegetable fields, and cattle ranches. Meanwhile, the towns sprouting up along the coastline began taking more and more land in the interior as their populations swelled.

Then, in the late 1920s in the Miami area, a small movement began, hoping to save as much of the remaining Everglades as possible. The Florida Federation of Women's Clubs had already preserved a 120-acre parcel called Royal Palms and given it to the state. That wasn't enough for Ernest F. Coe, a landscape architect who had recently moved from Connecticut to Florida and was shocked to learn that rare orchids, exotic birds, and so much else in the Everglades were being systematically destroyed. He decided to make it his life's work to create a much larger national park. Tall, scholarly, and impeccably dressed, Coe threw himself into the cause—convening meetings, firing off petitions, and pestering politicians so relentlessly that one senator finally begged the editor of a local newspaper to support the cause and "get Ernest Coe off my back."

As crucial as Coe was to the effort, Marjory Stoneman Douglas soon became the movement's most powerful public voice—even though, as she was the first to admit, she seemed an unlikely champion.

I can't say I've spent many years and months communing with the Everglades. . . . To be a friend of the Everglades is not necessarily to spend time wandering around out there. It's too buggy, too wet, too generally inhospitable. . . . The seasons of the Everglades are the mosquito season and the non-mosquito season.

I suppose you could say the Everglades and I have the kind of friendship that doesn't depend on constant physical contact. . . . I know it's out there and I know its importance.

A graduate of Wellesley College, Douglas had come to Florida in 1915 to get a divorce after a brief and unhappy marriage, then enlisted in the navy in World War I and served with the Red Cross in Europe. "I wanted my own life, in my own way," she said. She became the *Miami Herald*'s society reporter, but found herself more interested in the struggles for women's rights and racial justice, earning a reputation for her feistiness and colorful writing. When Ernest Coe turned her attention to the

It will be the only national park in which the wildlife, the crocodiles, the trees, the orchids . . . the flights and rookeries of the amazing birds . . . will be more important than the sheer geology of the country.

Perhaps . . . in a new relation of usefulness and beauty, the vast, magnificent, subtle and unique region of the Everglades may not be utterly lost.

MARJORY STONEMAN DOUGLAS

A flat landscape less than a dozen feet above sea level, the Everglades nonetheless encompasses a great diversity, visual and biological:

from saw grass and clouds (above, left), to distinctive birds like the anhinga (above, right) and exquisite, rare orchids (right) in dense cypress swamps.

Everglades, Douglas quickly agreed with him that its unique combination of water, wildlife, and plants needed federal protection.

But at the national level, many park supporters were unsure whether the Everglades—lacking dramatic mountains, waterfalls, or geysers—was worthy of being a national park. "I found mighty little that was of special interest, and absolutely nothing that was picturesque or beautiful," reported William T. Hornaday, the respected zoologist. "A swamp is a swamp," he added, and the Everglades should not be "put alongside the magnificent array of scenic wonderlands that the American people have elevated into that glorious class" of national parks.

Frederick Law Olmsted Jr. —who, like his father, had helped define the national park idea—was dispatched to Florida by the National Parks Association to study the request. "The quality of the scenery," he conceded, "is to the casual observer somewhat confused and monotonous . . . perhaps rather subtle for the average observer in search of the spectacular." Then, at the end of a long day, Olmsted found himself near the nighttime roost of thousands of ibises and egrets.

> *After dusk, flock after flock came in from their feeding grounds . . . and settled in the thickets close at hand. It was an unforgettable sight . . . [that] ranks high among the natural spectacles of America, and can be perpetuated most effectively by the creation of a National Park in this region.*

Skeptical Park Service leaders, including Horace Albright, made a series of official trips to decide whether to support the idea. So did George Melendez Wright, director of the new wildlife division. Both found it easier to conduct at least part of their investigations from the air, floating above the Everglades in the Goodyear blimp. Both were astonished by what they saw, and both became ardent supporters of adding it to the park system. Wright was particularly insistent.

> *The Everglades is perhaps the greatest remaining area for wildlife, yet is still adjacent to one of the most highly developed and sophisticated cities in the country.*

But unless this area is quickly established as a national park, the wildlife there will become extinct.

THE MARCH OF PROGRESS: A mechanical dredge works its way across the Everglades to create the Tamiami Canal.

Park proponents promised that the land to be set aside would be either donated by individuals or turned over by the state of Florida, but in May of 1934 many in Congress still opposed creating an Everglades National Park. New Jersey Congressman Frederick Lehlbach derided the idea as "the most perfect example of super-salesmanship of Florida real estate . . . that has ever yet been made public."

> *This bill is to create a snake swamp park on perfectly worthless land . . . so the fact that it would not cost the Government anything for the initial acquisition of this worthless swamp is the height of irony, but if the Government takes this and builds a road at a cost of $1,000,000 to get to it . . . and then pours countless millions into that swamp, it will do something that adds value to the surrounding real estate in Florida.*

In the end, a bill to create Everglades National Park passed Congress by a narrow margin. The bill included an amendment that prohibited the expenditure of any federal money on the new park for five years, but Ernest Coe's and Marjory Stoneman Douglas's efforts had paid off. For the first time, a national park had been created solely for the preservation of animals and plants and the environment that sustains them.

BUILDING HUMAN HAPPINESS

There is nothing so American as our national parks. The scenery and wild life are native and the fundamental idea behind the parks is native. It is, in brief, that the country belongs to the people; that what it is and what it is in the process of making is for the enrichment of the lives of all of us.

Thus the parks stand as the outward symbol of this great human principle. . . . A great recreational and educational project—one which no other country in the world has ever undertaken in such a broad way for protection of its natural and historic treasures and for the enjoyment of them by vast numbers of people.

Franklin Delano Roosevelt

In Franklin Roosevelt, the national parks had found their greatest friend in the White House since the presidency of his cousin Theodore Roosevelt a generation earlier. FDR had developed his own deep love of the outdoors during his boyhood—hunting, fishing, and hiking on his wealthy family's country estate in New York. He liked to refer to himself as a "tree farmer" and considered himself a conservationist in the mold of his famous cousin. Adding historic sites and battlefields to the national parks had been simply a first step in the larger reorganization Roosevelt contemplated.

But a much bigger issue demanded his attention. The Great Depression had thrown one out of every four American wage earners out of work. Factories shut down. Farms were foreclosed. Unemployed young men, concerned that they had become a burden to their families, roamed the countryside by the hundreds of thousands. Many Americans wondered where their next meal would come from. In some cities, animals in the zoo were shot and the meat distributed to the poor. Everyone in the United States was affected.

Among the alphabet soup of New Deal programs Roosevelt created to combat unemployment—the TVA, the PWA, the WPA, the CWA—one was especially dear to the president's heart because it incorporated his concern for conservation; he had pushed it through Congress in less than a week after taking office. The Civilian Conservation Corps put young men to work in national forests, state parks, and national parks, clearing brush and replanting forests, building visitor shelters and ranger cabins, improving campsites and trails. Horace Albright was part of the early planning, and because the Park Service already had a long list of projects ready to go, it was given a lead role in the new program. Within three months, one thousand CCC camps were up and running, with nearly 300,000 young men at work in them, sending money back home.

Among the enrollees was Juan Lujan, from the tiny West Texas town of Redford. Like so many oth-

Juan Lujan of Redford, Texas (below), was among the thousands of out-of-work young men in the 1930s for whom the CCC meant living in military-style barracks (below, right) far from home—but also a monthly check of $30, all but $5 of which was sent back to their families.

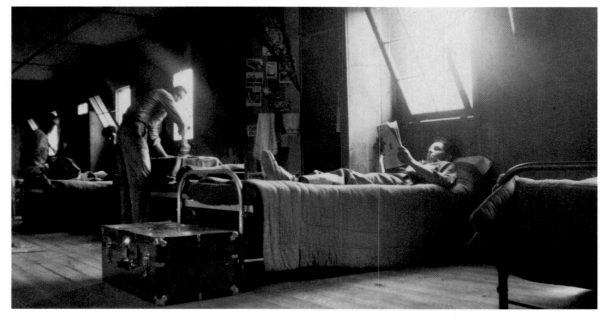

ers in the nation, his family was on "relief," receiving a regular check from the county. A social worker suggested he join the CCC. Lujan had never been to a national park. "I didn't know anything about national parks except what I read in my history books," he remembered, "that they existed somewhere." He was dispatched to a dry mountainous section of the Rio Grande, downstream from his home, at what was to become Big Bend National Park.

Like all the other camps, Big Bend's was organized along military lines. The men were housed in barracks, awakened early in the morning for calisthenics before breakfast, ate in a mess hall, and then dispersed to their duties for the day. Slackers were assigned to kitchen patrol. Lujan was put to work helping lay the foundations of new park buildings. "We got paid $30 a month, of which a whole $5 was ours," Lujan recalled. "The rest of it went home. And $25 a month seems like nothing, but it made a big difference. Money and dignity was important because, whenever you need a shirt and you buy it, if you bought it with your own money, that's a good feeling, as against having somebody give it to you."

For many of the enrollees it was their first time away from home—and their first real encounter with the natural world. At age seventeen, Burton Appleton had never traveled more than fifty miles away from his native Brooklyn, New York, and the tallest hill he had ever seen was a small bluff in Prospect Park. With no job prospects, he enrolled in the CCC and was put on a train that took him toward northwest Montana. After four days of travel, the train stopped and he looked out the window from his upper berth. Rising before him was a sight he would never forget: the mountains of Glacier National Park, covered with snow even though it was April.

Equally unforgettable was a day Appleton spent alone in the park, during time off from his work fighting forest fires, felling trees to make into telephone poles, and clearing brush from horse trails. "I was out there by myself one day with my Kodak box camera," he remembered, "and, to this day I don't believe it, a deer walked up to me within ten feet maybe. I stood stock still, couldn't believe that. And I took a picture. And as soon as I clicked the camera,

the deer turned tail and ran." Nearly seventy years later, he still had the photo, which he considered a prized possession.

Sixteen-year-old Claude Tyler, the eldest of six boys and two girls in a desperately poor farm family from Blossom, Texas, was assigned to the barren wastes of Death Valley National Monument, where he worked on a road crew, shoveling rocks near Badwater, the lowest spot in the continent. It was June, and the temperature reached 120 degrees. Next his crew was sent to Lassen Volcanic National Park in northern California, on the flank of the volcanic mountain whose peak is more than ten thousand feet above sea level. Tyler's crew had to shovel snow just to get into their barracks. Then they went to work clearing trails to the top. Tyler had never seen mountains before.

When he returned home to Blossom after his first enlistment and resumed school, his parents still had not gotten back on their feet financially. So Tyler reupped with the CCC and was sent to Arizona, then Oregon, then Wyoming, where he built log cabins near the east entrance to Yellowstone. He spent the five dollars a month he was allowed to keep on Baby Ruth candy bars and RC Cola; the $25 a month that was sent back to Texas helped his family survive the Depression.

The man all the CCC enrollees respected the most was the president who had proposed the program in the first place: Franklin Delano Roosevelt. "We almost thought he was God," Juan Lujan said. "There was progress, there was work, there was money circulated in the community."

The president reciprocated the affection toward his "CCC boys." Visiting a camp in Virginia's Shenandoah National Park, he told reporters, "I wish that I could take a couple of months off from the White House and come down here and live with them, because I know I'd get full of health the way they have." At another camp at Glacier, Roosevelt grew even more expansive.

Here, under trained leadership, we are helping these men help themselves and their families and at the same time we are making the parks more available and more useful for the average citizen. . . .

Brooklyn's Burton Appleton (top) discovered a love of nature at Glacier National Park. He recorded his CCC experiences in photographs (right, also the barracks photo on page 281) and in a letter home to his mother, extolling Glacier's scenery, but including a list of supplies he needed. Claude Tyler of tiny Blossom, Texas (above), saw much of the West moving from one CCC camp to the next: Death Valley and Lassen Volcanic in California, then Arizona, Oregon, and the east entrance of Yellowstone in Wyoming.

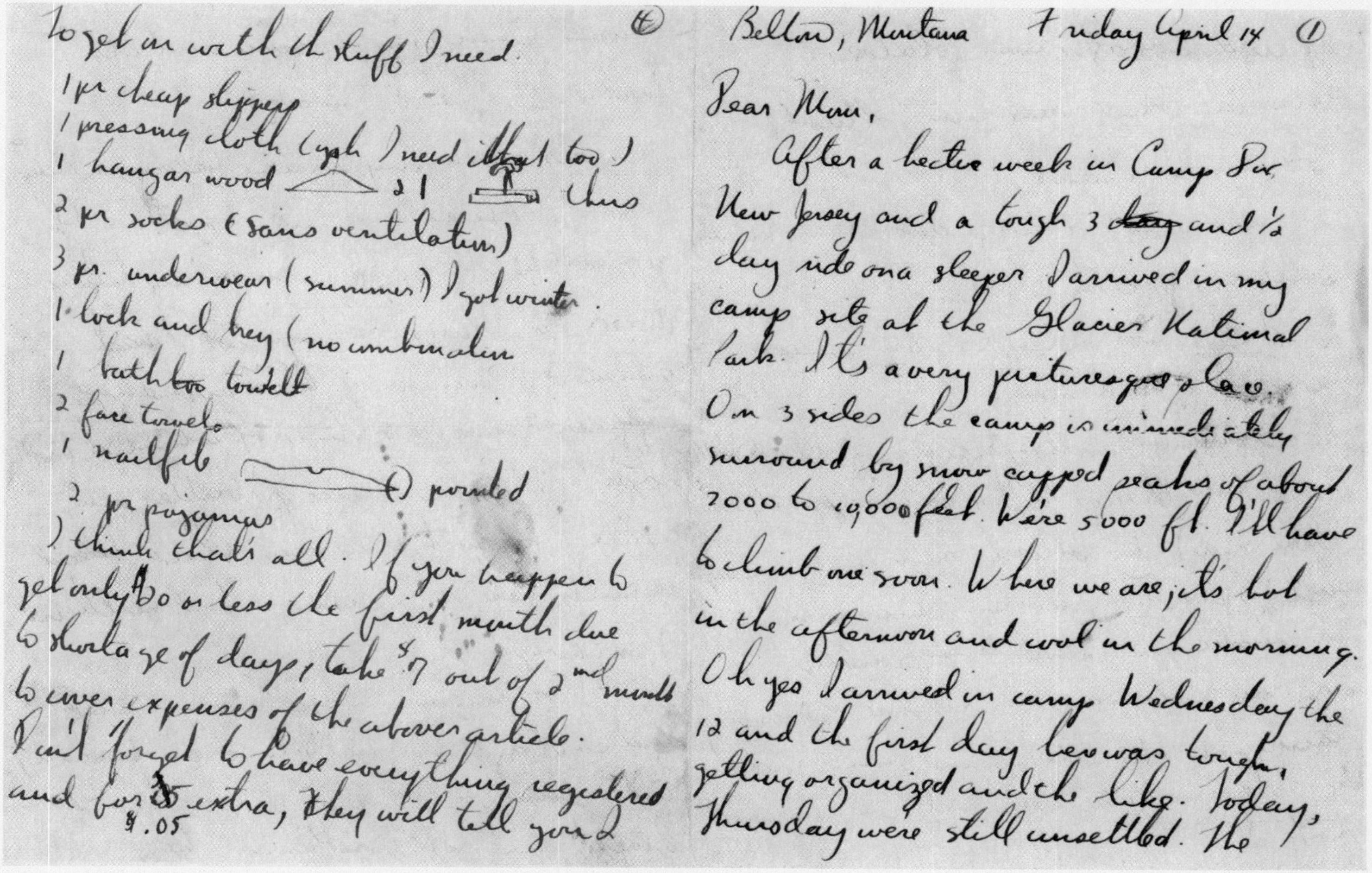

to get me with the stuff I need.

1 pr cheap slippers
1 pressing cloth (yeh I need that too)
1 hangar wood 2 1 thus
2 pr socks (sans ventilation)
3 pr. underwear (summer) I got winter.
1 lock and key (no combination
1 bath too towell
2 face towels
1 nailfile pointed
2 pr pajamas

I think that's all. If you happen to get only $30 or less the first month due to shortage of days, take $7 out of 2nd month to cover expenses of the above articles. Don't forget to have everything registered and box it extra, they will tell you &
$.05

Belton, Montana Friday April 14 (1)

Dear Mom,

After a hectic week in Camp Dix, New Jersey and a tough 3 ~~day~~ and ½ day ride on a sleeper I arrived in my camp site at the Glacier National Park. It's a very picturesque place. On 3 sides the camp is immediately surround by snow capped peaks of about 7000 to 10,000 feet. We're 5000 ft. I'll have to climb one soon. Where we are, it's hot in the afternoon and cool in the morning. Oh yes I arrived in camp Wednesday the 12 and the first day here was tough, getting organized and the like. Today, Thursday we're still unsettled. The

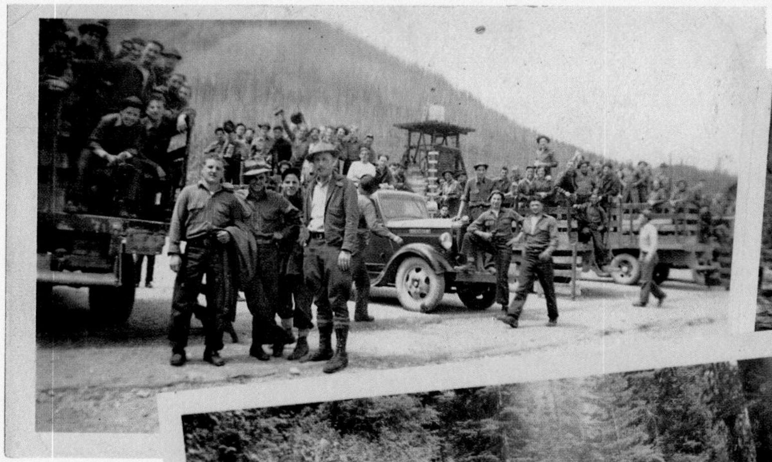

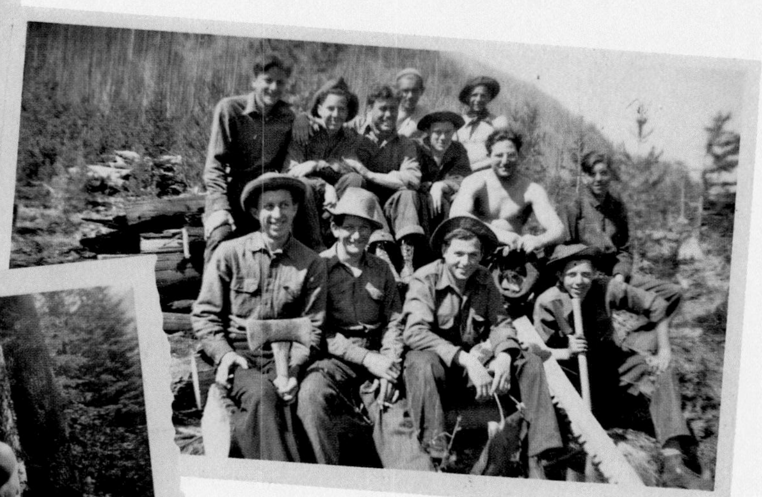

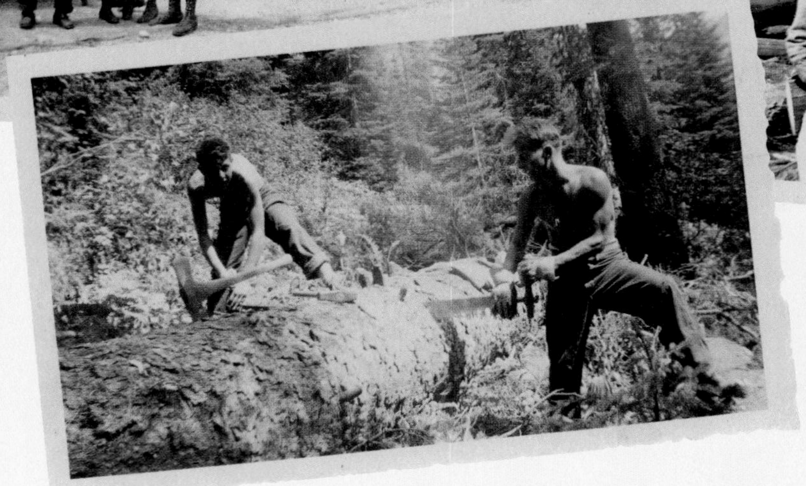

We are definitely in an era of building, the best kind of building—the building of great public projects for the benefit of the public and with the definite objective of building human happiness.

Besides the conservation work they did for the money they sent home every month, the enrollees participated in organized sports, hobby clubs, discussion groups, and classes meant to prepare them for getting jobs once they left the camps. Juan Lujan, fluent in both Spanish and English, became a guide at the park's museum—and was also put to work teaching his less educated colleagues in the camp. He would eventually go on to college, something his mother always wanted him to do, and ultimately earn a doctoral degree and continue teaching others for the rest of his life. Burton Appleton would credit his time in Glacier National Park with advancing his education—and his future—as well.

I was not a very good high school student, my grades were not all that good. And I am con-vinced to this day that the only reason I was able to matriculate at the New York State College of Forestry was that I convinced the, the registrar or the Dean of Admissions, of my experience in the CCC. That's what the CCC did for me.

It gave, it gave this young man an apprecia-tion of the vastness of this country, and the scenic beauty that one, living in Brooklyn would never get to see. He'd see the ocean and he'd see the sky-line, and he'd see the beaches, but he wouldn't see anything like Glacier Park.

Over the course of the Depression, more than three million men would find work at one time or another with the Civilian Conservation Corps. They would build more than 97,000 miles of fire roads in national forests, combat soil erosion on 84 million acres of farmland, and plant three billion trees—more than one half the total reforestation accomplished in the nation's history. During that time, some $218 million would be pumped into projects solely within the national parks—including trails and buildings that remain to this day.

THE SPIRIT OF FIGHTERS

Early in Franklin Roosevelt's first term, Horace Albright decided it was time to move on. He was only forty-three years old, but anxious to provide for his growing family, and he accepted a new job in private industry that would pay him more than twice his government salary. He promised to stay involved in the issues he and Stephen Mather had championed.

As his final act, he wrote a farewell message to his colleagues in the National Park Service:

Do not let the service become "just another Government bureau"; keep it youthful, vigorous, clean and strong. We are not here to simply protect what we have been given so far; we are here to try to be the future guardians . . . as man and his industrial world expand and encroach on the last bastions of wilderness.

Our National Park Service uniform which we wear with pride does command the respect of our fellow citizens.

We have the spirit of fighters, not as a destructive force, but as a power of good. With this spirit each of us is an integral part of the preservation of the magnificent heritage we have been given, so that centuries from now people of our world, or perhaps of other worlds, may see and understand what is unique to our earth, never changing, eternal.

Meanwhile, the wildlife division Albright had authorized and placed under the charge of George Melendez Wright was thriving. (Wright was still helping subsidize the new effort with personal funds.) By 1936, the division had twenty-seven biologists working for it, promoting Wright's vision that park policies had to take the animals and plants into account, not just the tourists. "In the end," Wright said, "the [Park] Service either will be praised for intelligently conserving the last fragments of primitive America or condemned for failure to hold to the real purpose."

Wright himself was married, with a family of his own, and busier with his work than ever. His personal interest in Yellowstone's trumpeter swans—the largest and rarest of American waterfowl, which had been reduced to a mere handful of breeding pairs—had turned into a personal crusade to save them from extinction. Wright solicited the help of local rod and gun clubs, lobbied state fish and game commissions and other federal agencies, and donated some of his own money to create a special wildlife refuge for them that ultimately brought the swans back from the brink.

Despite his youth, the Park Service increasingly saw him as an effective advocate for enlarging the system.

I no longer worry as I used to for fear the National Park System will be loaded with inferior areas. . . . What if a substandard area should slip in? This would not be calamitous. The failure to save Mount Olympus' forests, the Kings River Canyon . . . and a host of others just as valuable would be the real calamity.

Let the friends of our national parks leave it to the National Park Service to safeguard itself against intrusion of trash areas and devote their energies instead to completing the parks system while there is still time to do it.

Shame upon any standard bearer so narrowly dogmatic as to stand in the way of the perpetua-

George Melendez Wright's wife, Bee, who accompanied him on some of his wildlife surveys, admires a young trumpeter swan, a species Wright helped save from extinction.

Another New Deal agency during the Depression, the Works Progress Administration (WPA), in turn funded the Federal Art Project, which put talented artists to work. The two posters at left came from WPA artists; the one above—with George Melendez Wright's beloved trumpeter swan—was designed by Dorothy Waugh, employed as art supervisor for the National Park Service in the 1930s.

The new concept involves an appreciation of the characteristics of a real wild animal, notably, that each wild animal is the embodied story of natural forces which have been operative for millions of years and is therefore a priceless creation, a living embodiment of the past, a presentiment of the future.

It teaches the new joy of seeking out the wild creatures where they are leading their own fascinating lives.

GEORGE MELENDEZ WRIGHT

His Mexican counterparts on a joint commission studying the possibilities of an international park along the Big Bend of the Rio Grande in 1936 gave Wright (center, right) the nickname "Chapo," a term of friendly affection for a short person.

tion of any one of these last precious bits of our primeval American heritage.

The logical answer is more, not less, park area.

When part of the island of St. John in the tropical paradise of the Virgin Islands was under consideration for a new national park, Wright was sent with a team to investigate—and wholeheartedly endorsed the idea. Then he was off to the newly authorized Big Bend National Park in southwest Texas, where the Chisos Mountains rise out of the Chihuahuan Desert and the Rio Grande cuts through a series of dramatic canyons, separating the United States from Mexico. With Roger Toll, another rising star within the Park Service, Wright was part of a two-nation commission studying the possibility of an international park straddling both sides of the border. His fluency in Spanish and his outgoing disposition helped him make friends with his Mexican counterparts, who gave him the nickname "Chapo," a term of endearment for a short person.

After the meeting, Wright and Toll headed for home. But near Deming, New Mexico, an oncoming car blew a tire and crashed head-on into their vehicle. Both men were killed. George Melendez Wright was thirty-one. Without him, the Park Service's interest in wildlife waned. By the end of the decade, of the twenty-seven biologists who had once been under his supervision, only nine were left.

I am very keen about travel, not only person-ally—you know that, but also travel for as many Americans as can possibly afford it because those Americans will be fulfilling a very desirable objec-tive of our citizenship, getting to know their own country better, and the more they see of it, the more they will realize the privileges which God and nature have given to the American people.

FRANKLIN DELANO ROOSEVELT

Throughout the Depression, President Roosevelt made a number of well-publicized visits to the national parks, glorying in the chance to be outdoors in the midst of such stunning landscapes, even if the polio that had destroyed his legs confined him to the back seat of his touring car. He cheerfully encour-aged his fellow citizens to follow his example. During a visit to Glacier National Park, the president gave a nationwide radio address from one of the mountain chalets, in which he mentioned that the Secretary of the Interior had declared 1934 as "National Parks Year." Enthused by the scenery he had seen along the Going-to-the-Sun Road, Roosevelt upped the ante.

I decided today that every year ought to be "National Parks Year." That is why, with all the earnestness at my command, I express to you the hope that each and every one of you who can pos-sibly find the means and opportunity for so doing will visit our national parks and use them as they

are intended to be used. They are not for the rich alone.

Despite hard times, the number of park visitors continued to rise during the 1930s—from roughly three million a year at the start of the decade to 15.5 million in 1939. Roosevelt was intent on setting aside more places for them to visit. He provided the federal money that had made the crucial difference in creating Great Smoky Mountains National Park; saw to it that Shenandoah National Park, authorized before his presidency, finally got established; and played a role in the Everglades of Florida and Texas's Big Bend becoming national parks.

Roosevelt then turned his attention to the northwestern corner of Lake Superior, off the coast of Minnesota and Michigan, and the remote island called Isle Royale. The isolated archipelago, forty-five miles long by nine miles wide, was formed by the combined forces of one of the world's largest lava flows followed by the sculpting powers of an ice sheet more than two miles thick. A person standing on Ryan Island on Isle Royale's Siskiwit Lake would be standing on the largest island on the largest lake on the largest island on the largest freshwater lake on earth. Congress had authorized a national park there five years earlier, but stipulated that no federal money could be spent in acquiring the lands necessary for it. Private donors and the state of Michigan had done their best, but in the midst of the Depression had not been able to secure enough of the island to create the park. Ignoring the congressional restriction, Roosevelt steered $705,000 in emergency funds for land acquisition. When the purchases were done, he supported and signed a bill for a newly complete Isle Royale National Park.

He also used his authority as president to create national monuments that would eventually be elevated to park status:

- Joshua Tree National Monument in southern California, named for the distinctive plants the explorer John C. Frémont called "the most repulsive trees in the vegetable kingdom" but that later Mormon pioneers believed looked in silhouette like the prophet Joshua, raising his arms to beckon them forward.

Agave cactus on a mountain rim, Big Bend National Park

- The Dry Tortugas, a remote cluster of seven tiny islands seventy miles off the southernmost tip of Florida. On one island sits the largest brick fortification in the world: Fort Jefferson, used during the Civil War as a prison for Union Army deserters and afterward for Dr. Samuel Mudd, who was exiled there for treating the broken leg of John Wilkes Booth, the assassin of President Lincoln.

- Capitol Reef in Utah, where a one-hundred-mile, exposed wrinkle in the earth's crust, the Waterpocket Fold, exposes a panoply of differently colored rock formations the Navajo Indians called the "Land of the Sleeping Rainbow."

- And off the coast of Santa Barbara, California, the Channel Islands, home to the largest seal and sea lion breeding colonies in the nation, as well as more than a hundred uniquely native species, including the California brown pelican, whose nesting grounds had virtually disappeared everywhere else in the western United States—an oasis of undeveloped land just a few miles from the explosive urban growth of greater Los Angeles.

None of it was easy to accomplish. "We should remember," Roosevelt said, "that the development of our national park system over a period of many years has not been a simple bed of roses."

> *It has been a long and fierce fight against many private interests which were entrenched in political and economic power. So, too, it has been a constant struggle to protect the public interest once cleared from private exploitation at the hands of the selfish few.*

No one was more willing to take on entrenched interests than the president's irascible Secretary of the Interior, Harold Ickes, the self-described "old curmudgeon." A Chicago lawyer and former Republican stalwart known equally for his explosive temper and his fierce devotion to New Deal policies, he had become one of Roosevelt's closest—and most controversial—advisers: "the meanest man who ever sat in a Cabinet office in Washington," Horace Albright said, "and the best Secretary of the Interior we ever had."

Roosevelt also protected Utah's Capitol Reef, including its colorful Waterpocket Fold (left), and, seventy miles south of Key West, the Dry Tortugas, home of Fort Jefferson (above), used as a prison in the Civil War. Later, both became national parks.

No other country in the world has ever undertaken in such a broad way for protection of its natural and historic treasures and for the enjoyment of them by vast numbers of people.

It is not unkind to say from the standpoint of scenery alone that if many and indeed most of our American national parks were to be set down anywhere on the continent of Europe, thousands of Americans would journey all the way across the ocean in order to see their beauties.

FRANKLIN DELANO ROOSEVELT

MISSION DEFENDER

I consider historic shrines of inestimable worth. . . . If people—especially children—can actually see the door through which some noble man or woman passed, or some object he or she touched, they'll be impressed, they'll remember. . . . Inevitably, they'll be filled with high ideals, the desire to emulate.

ADINA DE ZAVALA

When Horace Albright persuaded President Franklin Roosevelt that preserving parts of America's past could be as important as preserving special parts of America's landscape, he was pursuing an individual passion for history. But it was hardly a new idea. No person and no place made that more clear than Adina De Zavala and the old Spanish missions of San Antonio, Texas.

De Zavala's family history and Texas history were intimately intertwined: her grandfather Lorenzo, who had served Mexico as minister to France in 1833, had emigrated to Texas in 1835, where he quickly became a leader of the independence movement, then one of the authors of the Texas constitution, designer of the new republic's flag, and elected interim vice president during its early years.

Born in 1861, "Miss Adina," as she was called, received a teacher's certificate from Sam Houston Normal Institute in 1879 and taught in San Antonio schools for twenty years. In the 1880s she formed the first women's group in Texas dedicated to preserving structures dating from the state's early Spanish, Mexican, and Anglo eras. Its purpose, she said, was simple:

To keep green the memories of the heroes, founders and pioneers of Texas; to formulate methods of arousing the dormant patriotism of the majority of their fellow-citizens; to devise ways of inculcating and disseminating a wider knowledge of the history of Texas; and of instilling a love and proper pride in town, city, county and State; acting on belief that patriotism, like charity, begins at home.

A few years later, when the Daughters of the Republic of Texas, DRT, was formed, her group was incorporated into it as the De Zavala Chapter—and launched a campaign to restore the dilapidated eighteenth-century Spanish missions of San Antonio. Adina traveled door-to-door in a horse-drawn wagon to the city's businesses, collecting donations—sacks of cement, fence posts, barrels of sand, and money to pay workmen to fill cracks in mission walls, replace fallen stones, and enclose the historic structures with protective fencing.

Top of their list was the Mission San Antonio de Valero, better known as the Alamo, the site of the battle that had galvanized Texas's fight for independence in 1836. Adina wanted not just the chapel but the original mission convent grounds surrounding it—where the fighting had actually occurred—properly restored and protected. She and her group lobbied the state legislature to appropriate $65,000 for the cause and to name the Daughters of the Republic of Texas as custodians. To speed things along, Adina wrote the bill herself.

But the De Zavala Chapter soon had a falling-out with the statewide DRT over control of the shrine to Texas independence, a schism that erupted into a public fight in 1908 when Adina learned that the DRT planned to "beautify" the Alamo grounds by removing the convent entirely and focus instead on the mission chapel.

My lawyers on whom I depended were out of the city; but I had heard that possession is nine points of the law. Something had to be done and quickly. So I took possession, and engaged three men to guard the old mission-fortress night and day.

At dusk, just as I was giving them some last instructions, the raid was made. The agents of [the DRT] threw my men out bodily, expecting to take possession. They did not know I was in an inner room; and when I hurried out to confront them, demanding by what right they invaded the historic building, consternation reigned. They withdrew outside the building for whispered consultation.

The instant they stepped out, I closed the doors and barred them. That's all. There was nothing else for me to do but hold the fort. So I did.

Taking her cue from the Alamo's original defenders, De Zavala refused to surrender—and just like them, made sure the rest of Texas was made aware of her cause. To newspaper reporters writing about the woman who had locked herself into the Alamo, she loved to quote Davy Crockett: "Be sure you're right, then go ahead."

After three days, the state took possession of property and Adina left, but public opinion had been aroused. The governor himself proclaimed he would not permit the convent walls to be torn down. The second battle of the Alamo was over, and Adina De Zavala had won it.

Now she turned her attention to the other four Spanish missions in San Antonio: Concepción, San José, San Juan Capistrano, and Espada. Other groups joined the effort, and in 1935 Congressman Maury Maverick of San Antonio gave it—and all similar efforts—a national boost by introducing and passing the Historic Sites Act, the first national policy for historic preservation. In 1941, Mission San José was officially designated a national historic site; forty-two years later, in 1983, the other three missions would join it as San Antonio Missions National Historical Park.

Adina would never lose her fierce dedication to Texas history. She wrote hundreds of articles for the state's newspapers about the rich Spanish and Mexican heritage of the Lone Star State; founded other organizations to preserve other important landmarks; and personally placed thirty-eight markers at historic sites.

In the spring of 1955, at age ninety-three, she fell and injured her hip, slipped into a coma, and died—a few hours before the dawn of her favorite holiday, Texas Independence Day.

Adina De Zavala stands behind her cadre of young Alamo Defenders (below) in 1908, outside the shrine she had rescued from the wrecking ball. As an older woman (left), she expanded her preservation efforts to include four more Spanish missions in San Antonio, now part of a national historical park, as well as other landmarks of Texas's heritage.

Ickes fought battles on every front. One of his first acts was to abolish the department's segregated lunchrooms. Then he told the national parks in the South to simply ignore local Jim Crow laws requiring separate facilities for blacks. At Virginia's Shenandoah National Park, signs segregating campgrounds or picnic areas were quietly taken down.

Ickes made more enemies by repeatedly proposing the creation of a Department of Conservation that would put national parks, national forests, and all other natural resources under the same administrative control: his. Congress repeatedly refused, but he continued to have Roosevelt's ear and trust, and was tirelessly effective in advocating new parks.

In 1937, Roosevelt and Ickes entered into a park controversy that had been raging for thirty years. On the Olympic Peninsula west of Seattle, majestic mountains trap the moist Pacific winds, which drop 160 inches of rain a year, nurturing verdant rain forests that contain the largest specimens of Douglas fir, red cedar, Sitka spruce, and western hemlock in the world.

In 1909, during the final forty-eight hours of his presidency, Theodore Roosevelt had used the Antiquities Act to set aside 615,000 acres as Mount Olympus National Monument. Six years later, responding to pressures from timber and mining interests, President Woodrow Wilson had cut the acreage in half. Since then, more than ten different bills had been introduced in Congress to make the area a national park and enlarge its boundaries. Each one was defeated, caught in a seemingly endless battle between the Forest Service and the Park Service.

Meanwhile, loggers were approaching the last virgin stands of rain forest. Left to the care of the Forest Service, Harold Ickes contended, such places suffered the same fate as a pig in the stockyards: "All that is left," he said, "is the squeal."

The president decided to have a look for himself. But his visit was arranged by the Forest Service and its allies in the lumber and pulp mill industries, all of them intent on convincing Roosevelt that a national park would ruin an already suffering local economy. No detail had been overlooked. They excluded any Park Service official—even the superintendent of the national monument—from the invitation list. They scheduled a massive logging train to rumble past the

president's lodge during his breakfast, a reminder of the jobs at stake. And they moved a sign marking the national forest boundary, giving the impression that a heavily logged area, now several square miles of burned stumps, was not on federal land. "I hope the son-of-a-bitch who is responsible for this is roasting in hell," Roosevelt said when he saw the devastation, not realizing that he was looking at a national forest and his guide was the forest supervisor.

But the deception backfired. Roosevelt had been warned by a park supporter that an attempt might be made to give him just one side of the story, so he insisted that Park Service officials be summoned to his room for a personal briefing. Every time a forester later tried to dispense partial information, he found himself corrected by the President of the United States. And when Roosevelt learned from another anonymous tip about the Forest Service's shifting boundary marker, it only increased his commitment to protect the forest.

On June 29, 1938, with the president's passionate support, Congress converted the national monument to Olympic National Park and gave Roosevelt the authority to further expand its boundaries—which he soon did, saving two of the most threatened valleys by stripping an additional 187,000 acres away from the Forest Service.

THE "OLD CURMUDGEON": FDR's Interior Secretary, Harold Ickes (below), was renowned for taking on tough fights, whether it was ending segregated facilities in national parks in the South (bottom) or battling the powerful timber interests to create Olympic National Park (right) in Washington.

HOLY MOUNTAIN

*When the weekend comes around I get restless. At
night I bring maps of Mount Rainier [into bed
with me] and fall asleep looking at them. Even
when it's time to depart for a trip, I cannot stay in
bed any longer and get up before anyone else. . . .*

I can't wait to go hiking again.

IWAO MATSUSHITA

Among the millions of people who took President
Roosevelt's advice to visit national parks were Iwao
Matsushita and his wife, Hanaye, Japanese citizens
who had moved to Seattle in 1919. There, Matsushita
had helped start the Seattle Camera Club, a predominantly Japanese group of talented hobbyists whose
work was displayed in competitions and salons
around the world. Each Sunday, the club organized
outings to nearby Mount Rainier National Park,
where Matsushita not only took still photographs
but also created homemade movies and kept a small
journal to record their adventures.

*At timberline we see lots of mountain plants by
the riverside, such as Indian paintbrush and
lupine, with beautiful red, blue, and purple
blooms. The sight makes one think that fairies
might come to dance in these flower fields. Seeing
this kind of beauty is not always possible.*

*. . . Beyond these high valleys you can see the
craggly white mountains, whose peaks are showing through a thick fog. It is view worthy of a
sumi-e painting.*

*Looking to the north, you can see Mount
Rainier, appearing majestically—like our king of
mountains, Mount Fuji.*

*I sit on a patch of heather. . . . I marvel at the
speed with which clouds are changing their shape.
I crouch by a stream fed by the remaining snow to
enjoy a cold drink of water and open up my sushi.*

By the mid-1930s, Iwao and Hanaye had visited
the park more than a hundred times, drawn to the
place they called "holy mountain," because it
reminded them of Mount Fuji, the sacred mountain
of their homeland.

Iwao and Hanaye Matsushita
in the national park with the
mountain they considered
sacred: Mount Rainier

They learned to ski—and in doing so extended
their enjoyment of Mount Rainier into an extra season of the year.

*Everyone here is having a good old time and no
one had a reason to frown, like a paradise of our
own world and time. Looking up . . . I feel as
though the great snowy mountain . . . were an
affectionate mother to all the people playing on
her slopes.*

*I fell 23 times but oddly enough this didn't
deter me; I was energized.*

*I take out my camera and go to the hill on the
right-hand side. [I] gaze at Mount Rainier to my
heart's content, always a beautiful sight no matter
how many times I see it.*

Meanwhile, farther to the south, another Japanese
immigrant was finding similar joy and inspiration in
another national park. Chiura Obata had arrived in
the United States in 1903 at age seventeen, a promising young painter whose original intention was to
stay only briefly in America before going on to Paris
to continue his career. But he soon set down roots in

San Francisco, creating some of the only on-site sketches of the destruction wrought by the great 1906 earthquake, making a name for himself in the Bay Area's international art community, and co-founding the Fuji Club, the first Japanese-American baseball team on the mainland.

Then, in 1927, a visit to Yosemite and the high Sierra provided a defining moment for Obata and his art.

> In the evening, it gets very cold; the coyotes howl in the distance, in the mid sky the moon is arcing, all the trees are standing here and there, and it is very quiet. You can learn from the teachings within this quietness.
>
> . . . Some people teach by speeches, some by talking, but I think it is important that you are taught by silence.
>
> . . . Immerse yourself in nature, listen to what nature tries to tell you in its quietness, so that you can learn and grow.

For two months he and two other artist friends tramped the high country, taking in all the park had to offer, exposing Obata to what he called not just *shizen*, or "nature," but *dai-shizen*, "Great Nature." Camping near Hetch Hetchy, the valley that John Muir had fought in vain to save, Obata wrote: "I regret that I never met John Muir . . . nor heard in his own words his praise of Nature. . . . He was a man of lofty personality and untiring energy . . . the father of the movement to protect Nature." While his companions produced a handful of sketches, Obata poured forth with 150, working from sunrise to nightfall, trying to "paint with gratitude to Nature in my heart and with sincerity in my brush." Even the postcards he sent to his children were miniature watercolors. On one he wrote: "Gyo-chan— The lovely moon is gone, it went to bed early to sleep, grow big, and shine more."

Obata's Yosemite images—ultimately made into a collection of exquisitely crafted woodblock prints—drew huge crowds when they were put on exhibit, and rave reviews from the critics. "To see our native beauty spots through the eyes of a foreign artist of high rank," one of them wrote, "is to find new charm in our own land."

By the 1930s, Obata had been asked to join the art faculty at the University of California, Berkeley, and every summer he and his family would return to Yosemite, where Obata gave lectures, taught outdoor sketching classes to the tourists, and made his annual pilgrimage to Fern Spring, whose clear mountain water he collected for use in making his paints throughout the rest of the year.

> I dedicate my paintings, first, to the Great Nature of California, which, over the long years, in sad as well as in delightful times, has always given me great lessons, comfort, and nourishment. Second, to the people who share the same thoughts, as though drawing water from one river under one tree.
>
> My paintings, created by the humble brush of a mediocre man, are nothing but expressions of my wholehearted praise and gratitude.

By 1940, thanks in great part to the national parks they had come to cherish as their own, Chiura Obata and Iwao and Hanaye Matsushita had decided the United States was their home, even if its laws at the time prohibited them from becoming full-fledged citizens because they had been born in Japan.

"I enjoy my life in Seattle," Matsushita wrote, "I have so many happy memories with nice people—

For Chiura Obata, the *dai-shizen*—"Great Nature"—of Yosemite National Park provided an enduring inspiration for his life and his art.

AN OBATA SAMPLER: Color
woodblock prints from 1930
Top left: Evening Glow at
Yosemite Falls
Above: Upper Lyell Fork, near
Lyell Glacier
Left: Death's Grave Pass and
Tenaya Peak

Hanaye and Iwao Matsushita and friends at one of their many outings in Mount Rainier National Park

both Japanese and Americans. Especially I enjoy photography and mountain climbing. I have visited Mt. Rainier, my lover, more than 190 times."

When the company he worked for offered him a promotion and a substantial increase in salary to return to its office in Tokyo, Matsushita resigned. "I cannot leave Seattle when I think of the beautiful views of Mount Rainier," he wrote. The Depression would make finding a new job—even one for less money—difficult. But he and his wife wanted to stay close to the "holy mountain" they called "mother."

WHAT WE ARE FIGHTING FOR

In 1938, a book arrived at the office of Secretary of the Interior Harold Ickes. Entitled *Sierra Nevada: The John Muir Trail,* it was filled with stunning images of the mountainous Kings River Canyon region of the southern Sierra captured by an aspiring California photographer named Ansel Adams. This was his first book of landscapes, and since he knew that Ickes was interested in making the area a national park, Adams had sent it along with his personal compliments. Ickes took it to the White House

to show President Roosevelt—who quickly appropriated it for his own.

Adams was on his way to becoming the most influential photographer for the cause of national parks since William Henry Jackson's photographs of Yellowstone had helped persuade Congress to create the world's first park in 1872. "I believe photography has both a challenge and an obligation," he wrote, "to help us see more clearly and more deeply, and to reveal to others the grandeurs and potentials of the one and only world which we inhabit."

He was born the sensitive only child of a patrician San Francisco family whose fortune had been made and then lost amidst the booms and busts of the West Coast lumber business. At age fourteen, enthralled by the hyperbolic writings of James Mason Hutchings, the first promoter of Yosemite Valley, he cajoled his parents into vacationing in Yosemite National Park. There, seeing with his own eyes the great rock faces—El Capitan, the Three Brothers, Half Dome—and the waterfalls gushing over the lips of vertical cliffs, Adams was instantly transfixed. "We should not casually pass them," he wrote later, "for they are the very heart of the earth speaking to us."

"I *knew* my destiny," he added, "when I first experienced Yosemite." He began spending every summer there; credited its clean, crisp air for healing him when he contracted the influenza of 1918; joined the Sierra Club at age seventeen, becoming custodian of the organization's lodge in the park; and began taking photos that sometimes appeared in the *Sierra Club Bulletin.*

Two extended pack trips into the Kings Canyon country in the 1920s ignited in him the conviction that it was just as inspirationally spectacular as Yosemite—and equally deserving of federal protection. It was an old dream. John Muir had fought for it—and failed—in the 1890s. Then Stephen Mather had taken up the cause, with the same result. Now Adams and the Sierra Club believed they had an ally who shared the dream—and had the power to make it come true.

Harold Ickes saw in Kings Canyon his chance to create a new kind of park—a "wilderness park" in which roads, hotels, and other large developments would be banned.

If I had my way about national parks, I would create one without a road in it. I would have it impenetrable forever to automobiles, a place where man would not try to improve upon God.

He thought it should be called the John Muir–Kings Canyon Wilderness Park, and he threw himself into the fight against the forces that instead wanted dams, irrigation projects, grazing, timber harvesting, and elaborate tourist resorts. Through a series of shrewd maneuvers, he turned one private interest group against another, waged ceaseless battle against the Forest Service's efforts to retain control over the land in question, and persuaded most of the major conservation groups not to abandon their support because of the compromises he was willing to

make to further his objective. Ickes was, one opponent of the park said, "overambitious, egocentric, ruthless, unethical, and highly effective."

But even Ickes's political mastery was not quite enough—until the bill's fiercest congressional opponent, Representative Alfred Elliott, a California Democrat, made a fateful blunder at the last moment by trying to ensnare the park bill's sponsor, Republican Bud Gearhart from the adjoining congressional district, in a phony bribery scandal. The scheme backfired, and when Gearhart exposed it on the House floor, his indignant colleagues responded by rallying behind him and his bill, which now passed easily.

In the final legislative moments, the name was simplified, dropping any reference to John Muir and wilderness, and on March 4, 1940, President Roosevelt signed the law creating Kings Canyon National Park. Because it was a roadless park, and because of his disability, Roosevelt would never be able to see Kings Canyon in person. Instead, he contented himself with following John Muir's trail through the photographs of Ansel Adams.

In August of 1941, Harold Ickes decided Adams could be of even greater assistance to the national parks. He put Adams on the Interior Department's payroll at $22.22 a day, and told him to bring back inspirational photographs of *all* the parks for prominent display in the capital city.

Adams said it was "one of the best ideas ever to come out of Washington," and happily packed up his station wagon to set out on his assignment, bringing along his eight-year-old son, Michael, and his best friend. Off and on for the next eight years, supporting his journeys with a Guggenheim Fellowship and assignments from private companies when his government contract expired, he would compile thousands of images of the national parks and visit every one of them except, to his great regret, the Everglades. Along the way, Adams became one of the national parks' most eloquent advocates.

THE "OBLIGATIONS OF ART": Ansel Adams (below, at work) used his photographs to promote and protect wilderness and the parks. His book of pictures from Kings Canyon (left) helped persuade Harold Ickes and President Roosevelt to make it a national park.

The dawn wind in the High Sierra is not just a passage of cool air through forest conifers, but within the labyrinth of human consciousness becomes a stirring of some world-magic of most delicate persuasion.

The grand lift of the Tetons is more than a mechanistic fold and faulting of the earth's crust; it becomes a primal gesture of the earth beneath a greater sky.

And on the ancient Acadian coast an even more ancient Atlantic surge disputes the granite headlands. . . . Here are forces familiar with the eons of creation, and with the eons of the ending of the world.

Contemplating the flow of life and of change through living things, each of them tied to cloud, stone, and sunlight, we may make new discoveries about ourselves.

To record and interpret these qualities for others, to brighten the drab moods of cities, and build high horizons of the spirit on the edge of plain and desert—these are some of the many obligations of art.

Just a few months after Adams began his travels, the Japanese attacked Pearl Harbor, and the United States was thrust into another world war. Now Adams pursued his project with even greater passion. To those who questioned whether his artistry could be put to a better purpose in wartime, he had a simple reply. "I believe my work," he wrote, "relates most efficiently to an emotional presentation of 'what we are fighting for.' "

But like everything else in American life, the national parks now found themselves subordinated to the all-out effort to defeat Japan and Germany. The CCC camps closed down, as the men who had been working on trails and park buildings became soldiers and shipped out overseas. Park budgets were cut to a quarter of their prewar levels. In Washington, office space for the agencies overseeing the war mobilization was in such demand that temporary buildings went up in the park around the Washington Monument, and the Park Service's headquarters was given over to more pressing business while the director and his staff were transferred to Chicago.

Just as in the First World War, pressures mounted to open up the national parks to timber cutting, mining, and grazing. Newton Drury, the new Park

AN ADAMS SAMPLER:
Top left: Glacier National Park, Montana
Far left: Carlsbad Caverns National Park, New Mexico
Left: Saguaro National Park, Arizona
Above: Canyon de Chelly National Monument, Arizona

You must have certain noble areas of the world left in as close-to-primal condition as possible. You must have quietness and a certain amount of solitude.

You must be able to touch the living rock, drink the pure waters, scan the great vistas, sleep under the stars, and awaken to the cool dawn wind. Such experiences are the heritage of all people.

ANSEL ADAMS

Service director, and his boss, Harold Ickes, did their best to minimize the damage. "When World War II began there were strong pressures in many circles to close the national parks for the duration," Adams noted, "with the thought that no one needs a vacation in wartime. Ickes disagreed with this, stating that in times of national stress and sorrow the people needed precisely what the national parks could offer."

When Ickes informed Roosevelt that a proposed bombing range would endanger the breeding grounds of the rare trumpeter swan that George Wright had worked so hard to preserve, the president dashed off a quick note to his Secretary of War countermanding the decision. "The verdict is for the Trumpeter Swan and against the Army," Roosevelt wrote. "The Army must find a different nesting place!"

In 1941, the year leading up to America's entry into the war, a record 21 million people visited the national parks. The next year, the figure dropped to nine million. Then, in 1943, it dropped again—to 6.8 million. All across the system, many park rangers changed uniforms and went off to war. The Crater Lake Lodge closed for lack of business, as did hotels

in a number of other parks. At Glacier National Park, the gasoline shortage meant the boat and touring car concessions had to be curtailed; even the park's saddle horse business deferred operations. "Poor old National Park Service is in a bad way," Horace Albright wrote to his successor after being informed of all the cutbacks.

But the parks still had a role to play. At Mount Rainier, units of what would become the 10th Mountain Division were taught how to survive high altitudes and cold weather. Desert training took place in Joshua Tree National Monument. Parts of Acadia, Olympic, and Hawaii national parks were converted to defense installations monitoring the coasts. Military equipment and clothing were tested at Shenandoah, Yosemite, McKinley.

War planners also realized that national parks could provide much-needed rest and recuperation for battle-weary soldiers. The U.S. Navy took over the swank Ahwahnee Hotel in Yosemite for a convalescent center. Rest camps went up in Sequoia, Carlsbad Caverns, the Grand Canyon. And Mount McKinley National Park in Alaska, which had originally been reduced to a basic maintenance schedule at the war's outbreak, was transformed into an army

PARKS IN WARTIME: Members of the 10th Mountain Division, in white camouflage and carrying their skis (above, left), train for winter combat at Mount Rainier. In Yosemite, the Mariposa Grove's Fallen Monarch (above) provides an oversized bench for soldiers getting some rest and relaxation.

recreation camp. Soldiers stationed in the Aleutian Islands could fish, hike, ski, skate, and relax. The year prior to the war, McKinley had recorded a grand total of 1,201 visitors. Three years later, at the war's peak, six thousand to eight thousand men a month were taking advantage of the nation's most remote national park. Across the entire system, the Park Service waived entry fees for members of the armed services. In 1943, 1.6 million servicemen found momentary solace and enjoyment in a national park—one quarter of the total visitation.

That same year, Ansel Adams interrupted his photographic survey of the national parks and went to the Owens Valley of California in the eastern shadow of Mount Whitney to document something entirely different. After the surprise attack on Pearl Harbor,

President Roosevelt signed an executive order requiring all people of Japanese descent living on the West Coast—even those who were United States citizens—to be uprooted from their homes and sent to internment camps for the duration of the war.

Adams was troubled by the policy. "We must prosecute this war with all . . . ruthless efficiency," he wrote, after he had photographed the Manzanar internment camp, but "we must be certain that, as the rights of the individual are the most sacred elements of our society, we will not allow passion, vengeance, hatred, and racial antagonism to cloud the principles of universal justice and mercy." Adams's photographs of Manzanar were turned into a book. Entitled *Born Free and Equal* and published in 1944, while the war with Japan still raged, it sold poorly—viewed by many people as disloyal to the American cause.

Because he had worked for a Japanese company, Iwao Matsushita was arrested and taken away from his wife in the first hours after Pearl Harbor. Hanaye was put in a temporary detention center near Seattle, where she tried her best to boost the spirits of her husband, far away in an internment camp in western Montana.

May 6, 1942. Dear Husband,
*   After severe rain, the sky became clear and we saw Mt. Rainier over the hill yesterday for the first time. . . . Good sleep, dear.*

Sept. 27, 1942. My dear husband,
*   There will actually be a day when you'll be released and we'll be able to rest peacefully. Once in a while I dream [about] running around the base of Mount Rainier.*
*   Remember the times we hiked through the mountains together? It all seems like a dream.*
*   Lovingly yours, Hanaye*

Farther south, as the internment roundups began in California, influential friends of Chiura Obata had pleaded with the federal government that the artist posed no security threat and suggested that he be allowed to be taken instead to his beloved Yosemite. The request was denied, and along with hundreds of other Japanese, Obata and his family were taken to an internment camp in Topaz, Utah. "The sudden burst of Pearl Harbor was as if the mother earth on which we stood was swept by the terrific force of a big wave of resentment of the American people," he wrote. "Our dignity and our hopes were crushed."

To help keep his and his fellow prisoners' minds off what he called the "intolerable sin" of their incarceration, Obata opened an art school at the camp and continued his own sketching and painting. "We only hope that our art school will follow the teachings of this Great Nature," he said, "and that it will strengthen itself to endure like the mountains, and like the sun and the moon, emit its own light." One of his paintings, *Moonlight Over Topaz,* was given to the president's wife, Eleanor Roosevelt, in thanks for

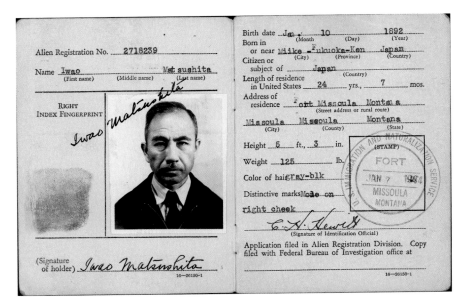

her speaking out for fair treatment of Japanese Americans.

Years later, in remembrance of his personal ordeal, Obata would paint *Glorious Struggle,* the image of a sequoia in Yosemite's high Sierra whose own struggle to survive seemed to give him strength and hope in his darkest hour.

In such times I heard the gentle but strong whisper of the Sequoia gigantean: "Hear me, you poor man. I've stood here more than three thousand and seven hundred years in rain, snow, storm,

FAR FROM NATURE: Iwao Matsushita's alien registration card (top) during his internment in World War II. Chiura Obata gave art lessons (above) to his fellow prisoners and their children at their internment camp in Utah. His watercolor *Moonlight Over Topaz* (right) was given to Eleanor Roosevelt after she spoke out for fairer treatment of Japanese Americans.

and even mountain fire still keeping my thankful attitude strongly with nature—do not cry, do not spend your time and energy worrying. You have children following. Keep up your unity; come with me."

ONE WEEPS FOR WYOMING

In the midst of the war, a letter arrived at the White House for President Roosevelt.

February 10, 1943. My dear Mr. President:

Many years ago I purchased some thirty thousand acres of land in Jackson Hole, Wyoming, on the earnest recommendation of the then Director of National Parks . . . confidently expecting that the Federal Government would gladly accept the land as a gift to be added to its National Park System.

Fifteen years have passed. The government has not accepted the property.

I have now determined to dispose of the property, selling it, if necessary, in the market to any satisfactory buyer.

. . . Because it is so uniquely beautiful an area, you will understand with what deep regret I am at length abandoning the effort to make it a place of permanent enjoyment for all the people, to which I have devoted myself so assiduously during these many years.

Very sincerely,
John D. Rockefeller Jr.

The longest-festering fight in the history of the national parks was about to erupt into a full-scale national battle.

Ever since 1926, when Horace Albright had presented his vision for a national park encompassing the entire region around the Tetons, John D. Rockefeller Jr. had been anonymously buying up ranches and homesteads in the valley with the intention of donating it all for the park's expansion. He never anticipated that purchasing the land would turn out to be much easier than giving it away.

In 1930, when Rockefeller's involvement in the land purchases was exposed—and his and Albright's plan for an enlarged Grand Teton park was publicly revealed—the uproar in Jackson Hole was so intense that a local paper supporting the idea found itself losing subscriptions and advertisers and teetering on bankruptcy, while a rival newspaper sprang up, describing Albright as a land-hungry bureaucrat and Rockefeller as a feudal lord. For the next ten years, Wyoming politicians did everything they could to thwart the expansion. The state's sole congressman even introduced a bill calling for the complete abolition of Grand Teton National Park, despite the fact that the mountains were not part of the dispute. Albright was a private citizen by now, but more determined than ever to see his dream fulfilled.

I must confess I get pretty discouraged at times in trying to understand what actuates some of the people out there. [It almost] makes one weep, not for oneself because after all what difference does it make to an individual what happens to Wyoming, but one weeps for Wyoming itself.

In 1943, with Congress still unwilling to enlarge the park, Albright and Rockefeller and Harold Ickes decided that their only hope lay in the president's authority under the Antiquities Act to create a national monument. Rockefeller's letter to Roosevelt, threatening to sell his property since the government wouldn't accept it as gift, was meant to prod the president into action.

It worked. On March 15, 1943, Roosevelt signed an executive order establishing Jackson Hole National Monument, placing 221,610 acres of public land on the eastern border of Grand Teton National Park under Park Service control. Rockefeller was elated. "I take my hat off to you," he wrote Ickes. "There was every prospect that this uniquely beautiful area . . . would have been permanently lost."

But in Wyoming, the response was a declaration of political war. The president, one senator said, had committed "a foul, sneaking Pearl Harbor blow." A journalist wrote that Roosevelt's action followed "the general lines of Adolf Hitler's seizure of Austria." Even the local newspaper that had once supported

the park expansion came out with a special edition maligning the national monument.

Wyoming's governor threatened to use state police against any national park official attempting to assume authority in the national monument. Some Forest Service employees gutted their ranger stations before turning them over to the Park Service. And hoping to provoke a confrontation and draw attention to their cause, a group of armed local ranchers—led by the aging movie star Wallace Beery—defiantly herded five hundred head of cattle across the monument without a permit.

In Washington, Wyoming's delegation pushed through a bill abolishing the national monument and turning the land back to the Forest Service. Roosevelt vetoed it. The state of Wyoming then went to court, claiming that Jackson Hole lacked the objects of scientific or historic interest necessary for national monument status. Postcards showing a ramshackle outhouse were circulated with a message saying, "These are some of the historic structures here; this is one known to have been occupied several times by Horace M. Albright." A federal judge dismissed the case, saying it was a dispute between the executive and legislative branches that the judicial branch would do well to steer clear of.

In 1945 Roosevelt died and World War II ended. But the battle of Jackson Hole roared on. Money to administer the national monument was stripped

BACKLASH: On June 23, 1943, the newspaper in Jackson, Wyoming (bottom), equated President Roosevelt with Adolf Hitler for establishing Jackson Hole National Monument. Other opponents tried humor, circulating a postcard showing an outhouse (below) they claimed was one of the "historic structures" the national monument was meant to preserve.

25, Number 52   Jackson, Teton County, Wyoming, Thursday, June 24, 1943   Price 10 Cents

Meat Committee Is ~~Nam~~ed for Teton County

Noted Columnist Likens Jackson Hole Monument to Nazi Trick

CITIZENS VOTE TO CONTINUE TO OPPOSE ICKES' LAND GRAB

Westbrook Pegler Brands Action By Ickes and Roosevelt As Typical Hitler Act

BARBARA BAKES WED TO CALIFORNIA MAN, JUNE 19

Ansel Adams's famous photograph overlooking the Snake River toward the Tetons shows part of the valley that Roosevelt, Rockefeller, and Albright were trying to save from development. *Overleaf:* The view from the valley floor at Schwabacher Landing, Grand Teton National Park

from appropriation bills. Legislation was proposed—but defeated—to void the Antiquities Act itself, retroactively. In 1947, after the Republicans had regained control of Congress for the first time in a decade, Wyoming's delegation decided the time was right to make another try at abolishing the national monument.

"Dealing with Wyoming is like dealing with the Russians," Albright complained. "You never get anywhere by trying to cooperate . . . [but] this was a battle I had to get into." He placed articles about the beauty of Jackson Hole in national publications, lobbied his Republican friends like former President

Herbert Hoover, and marshaled a campaign by major conservation groups—the Audubon Society and Sierra Club, the Boone and Crockett Club and Wilderness Society—to rally their members to tell Congress that the American public also had a stake in what happened in Wyoming. The Izaak Walton League conducted a study and published its results, showing that since the creation of the monument, retail sales taxes in Jackson Hole had doubled, real estate values had risen, and the region's overall economy had been strengthened by the boost in tourism. But the political climate remained decidedly anti-park.

LET FREEDOM RING: With the Great Emancipator seemingly watching over her shoulder, Marian Anderson sings from the steps of the Lincoln Memorial, Easter Sunday, 1939. When the Daughters of the American Revolution had refused to let Anderson perform in Constitution Hall, Eleanor Roosevelt and Harold Ickes invited her to appear instead at the memorial, one of the recent additions to the National Park System. Some seventy-five thousand people showed up.

Things remained at a standstill in 1950, when it became clear that the bitter and bruising battle would never end in unconditional surrender by either side. A compromise was worked out. Teton County would be reimbursed for lost property taxes; the migratory elk herd would be managed by both the Park Service and the state, which would be permitted to stage supervised hunts; ranchers' existing grazing rights were grandfathered in. In return, the bulk of Jackson Hole National Monument became part of an enlarged Grand Teton National Park, now three times its original size. Included in it was the thirty thousand acres John D. Rockefeller Jr. had been trying so hard to give away. "The project," Rockefeller told Albright with typical understatement, "has taken much longer to work out than either of us dreamed." It had been a quarter century.

Tucked away in the compromise that finally ended the battle of Jackson Hole was another concession. According to this provision, future United States presidents are barred from ever again using executive action to establish new national monuments in the state of Wyoming, except by the express permission of Congress. Wyoming—the state with the distinction of having the world's first national park, Yellowstone, and the first national monument, Devils Tower, now had another distinction: the only state where the Antiquities Act is null and void.

The Great Depression was over; World War II had ended. But there were still difficult issues for the nation—and the parks—to face: wrestling with tensions between the local and the national, exploitation and preservation; redefining the value of nature; and trying to come to terms with lingering issues from America's past.

In the midst of Franklin Roosevelt's presidency, the world-renowned contralto Marian Anderson had been denied the opportunity to perform in Constitution Hall, the four-thousand-seat auditorium controlled by the Daughters of the American Revolution, because of the color of her skin. At the urging of Eleanor Roosevelt, Harold Ickes, who had once been the head of the NAACP in Chicago,

quickly issued Anderson permission to sing at a different venue: the Lincoln Memorial, a recent addition to the National Park system.

The concert was free, and drew a crowd of 75,000 of all races and creeds. Ickes had the honor of introducing Anderson.

In this great auditorium under the sky, all of us are free. When God gave us this wonderful outdoors and the sun, the moon and the stars he made no distinction of race or creed or color. And 130 years ago, He sent to us one of His truly great in order that he might restore freedom to those from whom we had disregardfully taken it.

In carrying out this great task, Abraham Lincoln laid down his life, and so it as appropriate as it is fortunate that today we stand reverently and humbly at the base of this memorial to the Great Emancipator, while a glorious tribute is rendered to his memory by a daughter of the race from which he struck the chains of slavery.

Ickes noted that yet another addition to the national parks was already under construction nearby, this one a memorial for Thomas Jefferson, "who proclaimed that principle of equality of opportunity which Abraham Lincoln believed in so exquisitely and took so seriously." "In our own time," Ickes continued, "too many came near a lip service to these twin planets in our democratic heaven. There are those even in this great capital of our democratic republic who are either too timid or too indifferent to lift up the light that Jefferson and Lincoln carried along."

Then, to thunderous applause, Marian Anderson stepped to the microphone and began her program. Her first song was "America." In light of the events that had brought her to the steps of the Lincoln Memorial, Anderson made two changes to the words. Instead of, "My country 'tis of thee, sweet land of liberty, *of* thee I sing," Anderson substituted "*to* thee I sing," subtly altering the context from simple praise into an appeal to the nation's higher ideals. And she thought the final phrase of the first verse so important, she sang it a second time: "From every mountainside, let freedom ring."

DEMOCRACY AT ITS BEST

Journalist and activist Juanita Greene. *Right:* Sunset at Biscayne National Park

As a reporter for The Miami Herald, *Juanita Greene covered many stories, but none so passionately as the controversies in the 1960s over the fate of Biscayne Bay. Like the feisty Marjory Stoneman Douglas before her, Greene eventually made the transition from journalism to populist activism on behalf of South Florida's environment.*

Despite the difference in their ages, the two journalists-turned-crusaders became good friends. Greene eventually became a leader of Friends of the Everglades, the organization founded by Douglas to protect what was left of the "river of grass" that had become her life's cause.

Marjory Stoneman Douglas doesn't seem to fit the stereotype of an environmental activist.

She wouldn't voluntarily say, "Well, let's go have a picnic in the Everglades." Or "let's go boating in the Everglades." She just wasn't

that much of an outdoor person, really. But she would go into the Everglades when she had to, and she became its most ardent defender, too. And she taught people about the Everglades. She would go anywhere, anytime, to make a speech about the Everglades—and she didn't drive, and didn't own a car. But she sure got around in explaining the Everglades to the public. She taught people what a valuable resource we had right in the middle of the state of Florida that we should protect and cherish and love.

She was one of the most fascinating people I ever knew. She was a great yarn spinner. She could tell you tales and keep you entertained all day long. And she was one of the most intelligent women I ever knew, and one of the bravest. She never did fit the mold.

What about the man who got her involved in Everglades activism, Ernest Coe?

His passion was the Everglades. And he could see that it was being invaded by real estate speculators and by the dredgers and the drainers. He was a man fixated on the Everglades, and as Marjory Stoneman Douglas once said, he was a big pest and he would drive you crazy. That was all he would ever talk about.

But the big advantage he had was what he said was true. He was right. He was a visionary, and he could see that if we didn't save a goodly part of the Everglades and put it in a national park, that it would disappear under development.

There seems to be a tradition in South Florida of unforgettable and unlikely characters involving themselves in grassroots crusades to save special places. Ruth Bryan Owen for the Everglades and Lancelot Jones for Biscayne Bay are part of that collection.

Ruth Bryan Owen, who was our representative in Congress, was conducting a hearing one day on the establishment of Everglades National Park. She was sitting, there was a big table in front of her, and one of the opponents of the park approached her and laid a great big snake in front of her on the table. And she reached over and took the snake and draped it over her shoulder. That's the kind of woman Ruth Bryan Owen was.

Lancelot Jones seemed like a perfectly happy guy living out there by himself. I mean he knew a lot of people. A lot of important people would stop by and visit him when they went down there, including all these big shots that belonged to that private club, the Cocolobo. He knew where all the fish were and where everything else was, too, down there. I guess he had a right to know that because he was born in a boat on Biscayne Bay. His parents lost the race to a doctor on the mainland.

But he was not one of these greedy people who was waiting for the developers to come pay him big bucks for his land. He just liked things the way they were and was willing to help other people have an opportunity to enjoy the islands, to enable other people to enjoy the same things that made his life so rich. So I think that Lancelot Jones had a good life.

What emerges from these stories—and from so many others in the history of almost any national park—is that while the federal government ultimately has to create a park, it's usually only after a single person or a small group of people crusaded for it.

I think it's the people that pressure the government to do the things that benefit them. I don't think most politicians sit there and say, "Now what's the best thing I can do for the people today?" But they hear from their constituents and that's what makes up their minds. And the people really love their parks. There's an emotional bond there, and they'll fight for them.

I think the thing about the national parks is that they're an example of democracy. In other parts of the world, there are certain areas that are preserved that need to be preserved, but that's because some rich nobleman out of the goodness of his heart decided to decree it. But in the United States you don't have to be dependent on some rich guy being generous to you.

The great thing about national parks is they belong to everybody. To me, that's what national parks mean. It's a symbol of democracy—democracy when it works well, at its best.

What makes the Everglades and Biscayne Bay so special to you?

We used to spend every weekend down at Flamingo, which is right on Florida Bay. It's right at the end of the park where the bay begins. And the thing about Florida Bay was the birds that you would see in it, standing in the shallow water, fishing. And it would be just beautiful, this blue water with the white birds standing in what looked like a mirror. It was an enchanted spot. To me, that was the closest thing to heaven on earth, and I spent almost every weekend down in a little bitty boat, cruising Florida Bay and looking at the birds. We didn't fish. We didn't speed around in a boat. We just floated around and felt like we were all part of it: us and the birds—and the fish that we could see on the bottom, the water was so clear.

I think that's what a national park is all about. It gives people breathing room. It gives people a tranquil atmosphere. It gives them an opportunity to be a part of nature. You're just part of it all.

CHAPTER SIX

THE MORNING OF CREATION

I N THE SPRING OF 1945, as Yellowstone National Park prepared to open, everyone was anticipating another slow tourist season at the world's first national park. Nazi Germany had just surrendered to the Allies in Europe, but World War II still raged in the South Pacific, where American troops were preparing for the anticipated long and bloody invasion of the Japanese home islands.

Before the attack on Pearl Harbor in 1941 plunged the United States into the war, more than half a million people a year had visited Yellowstone. But now, with gasoline rationing in effect and restrictions placed on railroad travel, that number had dropped to 61,696, the lowest attendance in a generation.

Facing yet another season of financial losses, Yellowstone's concessionaires once more asked the federal government to officially close the park because so few customers were expected. Once more, Secretary of the Interior Harold Ickes refused. Keeping the national parks open, even with much diminished staffing, seemed to him important, if only as a symbol of the majestic land and democracy American soldiers were still fighting and dying for.

Just as predicted, only a trickle of tourists arrived when Yellowstone's 1945 season began. But in June, park officials noticed things picking up; and by the end of July, business had already topped the previous year's total. Then, in mid-August, the Japanese suddenly surrendered and four long years of war at last came to an end. Within a month, Yellowstone's attendance doubled again.

Before September, the Park Service resorted to issuing a press release aimed at discouraging more people from setting out for the park. Yellowstone's facilities, it said, were not prepared for such a late-season rush.

In 1946, gasoline rationing and travel restrictions were lifted. Yellowstone's attendance quadrupled from 189,000 to 807,000. Two years later, it would cross the one million mark for the first time and never turn back. A new era in the history of the national parks was dawning.

Preceding pages: Translucent icebergs in Muir Inlet, Glacier Bay National Park
Right: Tourists sitting on Park Service benches watch the nightly bear feeding in Yellowstone, 1946.

The beginning of man was in nature, his only home. Without a basically favorable environment he could not have endured. He now remembers, deep in his psyche, his beginnings, the experience of the mountains, deserts, forests, and still or rushing waters.

Now, in our present fateful age, we have a choice: to exploit and destroy, or to respect our legacy, to use it wisely and to hold it in trust, inviolate, for the many generations to come.

ANSEL ADAMS

Since its beginnings in the mid-nineteenth century, the national park idea had embraced two equally important, yet apparently contradictory, thoughts: that the parks should preserve America's special places in their natural conditions forever; and that they should be accessible for the enjoyment of all Americans. Early park leaders had glossed over any paradox, arguing that the best way to protect the parks was to build public support for them by encouraging more and more visitors.

But with the end of World War II, as the park idea neared its one hundredth birthday and an increasingly affluent and mobile nation placed demands on the parks as never before, the balancing act between preservation and use would be severely tested.

And just when it seemed as if there were no pristine places left to set aside as national parks, a new one would be created in the backyard of one of the nation's fastest-growing cities; while far to the north, in the nation's "last frontier," the park idea would be reinvigorated for a new generation.

A BLESSED WILDERNESS

It was just like being in heaven, being in there. In those days there was no road, the park was all a blessed wilderness, and I have often thought since what a wonderful people we would have been if we had wanted to keep it that way.

ADOLPH MURIE

Back in the summer of 1922, a college student from Moorhead, Minnesota, named Adolph Murie arrived in Mount McKinley National Park in Alaska. The park had been established five years earlier, but Congress had only recently appropriated any money for

Mount McKinley National Park would change the life of young Adolph Murie (above left); then he would change it by proposing that its wolves be protected instead of persecuted, stirring up a storm of controversy (below right).

its protection and development—$8,000, used to hire a superintendent and one assistant, who were instructed to patrol 2,200 square miles, an area half the size of Connecticut. They were also expected to keep poachers away from the wildlife and prepare the park for the tourists that promoters hoped would soon be coming to see the highest mountain in North America.

That year, a total of seven showed up. One of them was Murie, who was there to help his older half brother Olaus, a biologist, conduct a study on caribou migrations. Murie was twenty-two years old, and this was his first time away from Minnesota.

For five weeks, Murie and his brother tramped for miles across the tundra, following game trails and the braided gravel beds of glacial rivers, exulting in the notion that they seemingly had the park entirely to themselves—at least until they encountered a survey crew planning a new road into the heart of the park. "We had a feeling it was too bad a road had to come into this wilderness," Murie recalled.

Later, he came across the lone footprint of a grizzly bear.

In innocent wonder I gazed at the imprint. It was a symbol, more poetic than seeing the bear himself—a delicate and profound approach to the spirit of the Alaska wilderness.

We come [here] to catch a glimpse of the primeval. We come close to the tundra flowers, the lichens, and the animal life. Each of us will take some inspiration home; a touch of tundra will enter our lives—and deep inside, make of us all poets and kindred spirits.

Murie's trip to Alaska inspired him to get a doctoral degree in biology, and George Melendez Wright recruited him for the Park Service's newly formed Wildlife Division. By the 1940s, Murie had made a name for himself as a top-rated field biologist—and as an iconoclast whose views on the direction of park policies often got him in trouble with his superiors.

At Olympic National Park, where wolves had been hunted to extinction years earlier, he called for their reintroduction. His suggestion was ignored. At Isle Royale in Lake Superior, the moose population had grown "so plentiful" because of a lack of natural predators, he wrote, that the park looked like "a prosperous barnyard." He opposed fire suppression, preferring to let nature take its course, and even argued against developing too many hiking trails in a park he considered unique because of its high percentage of wilderness. At Yellowstone, Murie objected to plans to build a golf course and opposed a proposal to drain a wetlands around the Old Faithful Lodge in order to reduce the number of mosquitoes bothering the tourists there.

Wolf Trouble in Alaska
By RUSSELL ANNABEL

This Alaskan authority believes the situation is serious.

Old Tex, however, had his own way of handling these savage predators

"True wilderness," he wrote, "is more marvelous (and harder to retain) than the grandiose spectacular features of our outstanding parks."

Let us leave a few wilderness shrines. . . . Let there be a few outstanding scenes which can be viewed without the attendant chatter of the idly curious.

Like his mentor, George Wright, he believed Yellowstone's bears had lost their natural wildness because tourists still hand-fed them along the roadsides and garbage dumps provided them with an easy living. And like Wright, he believed many assumptions about predators needed to be scientifically tested.

For years, Yellowstone's rangers and superintendents had been poisoning, trapping, and shooting coyotes in the belief it helped the elk, deer, antelope, and bighorn herds that people enjoyed seeing. After spending two years studying the park's coyotes, Murie produced a report that flatly contradicted that notion: "The problem of the big game species in Yellowstone is not one of predation, but of inadequate winter range." And the solution, he said, was not killing more coyotes but changing park policies.

Yellowstone's superintendent was so upset, he shelved the report and nearly got Murie fired. Now one of only three biologists left in the Wildlife Division, Murie was dispatched to the nation's most remote and least visited park, Mount McKinley in Alaska, the park that had made such a profound impression on him years earlier. There he embarked on the first in-depth study of wolves ever undertaken. And once again he would find himself on the unpopular side of a raging controversy.

Americans had been killing wolves for centuries. Despite a Park Service policy against the extermination of any animal species, they had been systematically eliminated at Grand Canyon, Crater Lake, Death Valley, Grand Teton, Mount Rainier, Olympic, Rocky Mountain, and, after the death of two wolf pups in 1926, Yellowstone National Park.

Alaska was now virtually the only place left in the United States where wolves still existed—a condition most Alaskans viewed with both embarrassment and alarm. The wolf, a member of the Alaska Game Commission said, is "the master killer of all

Wolves were blamed for a decline in the numbers of Dall sheep (top left) at Mount McKinley, but Murie (above, photographing wolf tracks) came to a different conclusion after studying them more intensely than anyone ever had: wolf predation focused on the weak, thereby strengthening the herds. As part of his research, he adopted a wolf pup he named Wags (below right, with Murie's daughter Gail) and monitored its growth.

wildlife . . . the villain in Alaska's pageant of wildlife." Residents who relied on wild game for their food saw wolves as a threat to their subsistence; sportsmen saw them as competition; some politicians saw them as symbols that Alaska was still too backward to achieve statehood. The territorial legislature gladly paid bounties of $50 for every wolf that was killed.

At Mount McKinley National Park, when the park's herd of distinctive Dall sheep seemed to decline, people automatically blamed the wolves and argued that they were hurting the tourist business. Alaskans began to view the park as an incubator for animals everyone considered a scourge. Even some of the park's strongest supporters agreed. "The sheep constitute about the only interesting thing for the tourist to see in this park when the mountain is enveloped in clouds, as it often is," said former director Horace Albright. "Why should we take any chances on having our magnificent display of sheep lost to the public?"

Murie was asked to apply scientific research to the politically charged issue. It was a dream assignment. His first season, he walked more than 1,700 miles crisscrossing the park, gathering data and whenever possible taking photographs and home movies to augment his extensive field notes. He analyzed more than a thousand samples of wolf droppings to determine their eating habits; collected 829 skulls of Dall sheep to study their teeth and understand the age and health of the animals when they died. His second year, he discovered a wolf den. In the space of two months, he spent nearly two hundred hours observing the pack, sometimes all night and once for thirty-three hours straight.

He would continue his study for nearly a decade, moving his wife and two children to a remote cabin in the park and temporarily adopting a wolf pup he named Wags, so he could monitor its development as it grew from a nursling to full size. Over time, Murie would get to know wolves better than any scientist ever had—as well as the majestic park they called home. He witnessed the seasonal migrations of caribou and watched how wolf packs worked together to systematically weed out a weak calf from the herd to feed their families. He collected and analyzed 201 samples of bear scat and once watched a mother grizzly and her cub foraging for blueberries for eight hours straight. He investigated sixteen different eagle nests, studying the bones and droppings in and around them to conclude that the birds preyed mostly on ground squirrels. In monitoring the Dall sheep, he observed firsthand the heavy toll deep snows could take on a herd; came across lambs crippled by falling off ledges and old rams limping from injuries; and one time had to fend off an angry ewe with his tripod because she thought he was too close to her offspring.

He had come to study wolves, and the report he produced would become a landmark in understanding the species. But his vision had expanded to consider the entire web of life preserved in the park.

Here . . . in the wilderness of Denali . . . we have an opportunity to learn . . . how animals react to their environment, to each other, and what steps may be necessary to insure the perpetuation of the Alaskan fauna, the most striking and valuable wildlife assemblage on the continent.

Murie's conclusions—that a series of hard winters was the principal cause of the decline in Dall sheep; and that wolves actually strengthened the sheep and

caribou herds by culling out the sick and the weak—were denounced by hunting groups across the entire nation as "a piece of pro-wolf propaganda from start to finish." William N. Beach of the Camp Fire Club, a prestigious New York conservation group that had championed creation of the park back in 1917, mocked the notion of letting nature balance itself by comparing wolves to America's wartime enemies.

It would appear to me that if the wolf has a place in the animal kingdom then certainly Hitler, Hirohito, Mussolini and their ilk should be protected, for eventually there would be a balance reached, and by the same line of reasoning we should refrain from the prosecution of murderers.

As private bounty hunters and federal Fish and Wildlife Service officers initiated a campaign of poisoning and shooting wolves throughout the rest of Alaska, pressure mounted for the park to eradicate its wolves, too. The park, a writer named Israel Putnam Callison complained, was "the most colossal example of wanton waste in wildlife management ever recorded." It was "turned over to the Park Service teeming with wild game" but was now a "howling wilderness."

In response, the park agreed to a limited wolf-control program. But the person selected to oversee it was none other than Adolph Murie, who kept the number of kills to the barest minimum, thinning out only elderly wolves near the end of their natural lives. When the sheep herd rebounded as Murie had predicted and the furor subsided, the Park Service quietly instituted a permanent ban on wolf killing. It was the first time in history the species everyone seemed to hate found protection from any government agency.

"The goal," Murie wrote, "is to have the minimum of manipulation in our parks, to allow, where at all possible, the existing ecological factors to operate naturally. Let us be guardians rather than gardeners."

The national park idea is one of the bright spots in our culture . . . for here we raise our thoughts above the average, and enter a sphere in which intangible values of the human heart and spirit take precedence.

The idealism in the park concept has made every American visiting the national parks feel just a little more worthy. Our generosity to all creatures in the national parks, this reverence for life, is a basic tradition, [and is] fundamental to the survival of park idealism.

McKinley's wolves had survived. And the park had become a sanctuary not only for them, but for a park ideal George Melendez Wright and Adolph Murie had nurtured and kept alive.

THE MOST DANGEROUS SPECIES

With so many friends, it is difficult to understand why parks are so bedeviled by threats, and seem always to be fighting for their very existence.

The story is an old one. There are frequent occasions when people see nothing wrong with harming, hurting, marring, or spoiling when there are valuable resources of water, power, timber, oil, or minerals to be exploited within Park boundaries.

. . . Greatest of all threats to the Parks today is the pressure to build dams.

ALFRED A. KNOPF

By 1950, Americans who needed dams for irrigation, city water supplies, and hydropower had been in conflict for half a century with other Americans who wanted national parks kept off limits from any development. John Muir had fought and lost the first battle, when the city of San Francisco used its political muscle to win federal approval for building a dam at Hetch Hetchy.

The defeat had galvanized the nascent conservation movement into pushing for creation of the National Park Service in 1916, on the grounds that a federal agency specifically charged with protecting parks would never let something like Hetch Hetchy happen again. The specter of it had haunted Stephen Mather and Horace Albright throughout the 1920s and 1930s, when they repeatedly found themselves fending off attempts to build dams in western parks.

The Green River wraps around Steamboat Rock, the most distinctive feature of Echo Park in Dinosaur National Monument.

Now, in the aftermath of World War II, as the populations of states in the arid West began to sky-rocket, the pressure for more dams only intensified. With the enthusiastic backing of virtually every elected official in the region, the Bureau of Reclamation and Army Corps of Engineers drew up plans for $9 billion worth of dam projects. A few of them were inside national parks—Kings Canyon in California, Glacier in Montana, and Big Bend National Park in Texas—and were ultimately defeated.

The biggest fight of all then centered on a remote corner of Utah and Colorado, where the Green and Yampa rivers converge in the midst of winding sandstone canyons—a place known as Echo Park. To hydraulic engineers it was the perfect location for a pair of dams, not simply because of the terrain, but also because so few people lived there and therefore would not be affected by the huge reservoirs that would be created. But Echo Park was also the site of Dinosaur National Monument, first set aside in 1915 to safeguard an important discovery of prehistoric bones, and then expanded in the 1930s to include the dramatic canyon lands upstream.

Few people had ever visited the monument or paddled through its network of canyons. But the handful who had, like the author and historian Wallace Stegner, considered it almost sacred.

This . . . is a country as grand and beautiful as any America can boast . . . a wilderness that is the property of all Americans, a 325-square-mile preserve that is part school room and part playground and part—the best part—sanctuary from a world paved with concrete, jet-propelled, smog-blanketed, sterilized, over-insured, aseptic; a world mass-produced with interchangeable parts, and with every natural beautiful thing endangered by the raw engineering power of the twentieth century.

Even though President Harry Truman and his Interior Secretary both supported the plan for the dam at Echo Park, Park Service director Newton Drury came out against it in 1950—and was soon eased out of his job. His successor, Conrad Wirth, also opposed the dam, but it quickly became clear that the Park Service itself would not be able to stop the powerful political forces amassed in favor of turning a place few Americans had ever heard of—and even fewer had ever seen—into a massive reservoir in the middle of nowhere. It was Hetch Hetchy all over again.

Harold Bradley, a retired chemistry professor, had grown up hearing tales about Hetch Hetchy's ruination. His father had been a founding member of the

whether you are perceptive or not to the intangibles that lie beyond a price tag.

Back home in California, Bradley embarked on what he called a "one-man crusade" to save Echo Park. He showed his home movie to anyone who would watch, especially at local Sierra Club meetings, and announced in the club newsletter that he would lead a larger outing the next summer through Dinosaur. The demand was so great that two extra trips had to be scheduled.

Among those who joined him that second summer was David Brower, the new executive director of John Muir's Sierra Club, young and brash, with a flair for public relations. The club's leadership was already on record against the dam, but his firsthand look with Harold Bradley energized Brower to make stopping it a top priority.

Brower began running articles with photographs of Echo Park in the club magazine to show members who were more accustomed to pictures of Sierra peaks and alpine lakes that other landscapes were also worth fighting for. He organized more Sierra Club outings through Dinosaur's canyons and invited influential Easterners to join them. Alfred A. Knopf, the New York publisher, emerged from one so impressed that he commissioned a handsome book of photographs and essays to reach a wider audience. Knopf even wrote one of the essays himself and made sure every member of Congress received a copy of the book.

Borrowing from Harold Bradley's model, Brower produced a more professional film, with narration and a specially composed musical score, that was soon being distributed to conservation groups all across the United States—the Appalachian Mountain Club in Boston, the American Alpine Club in New York City, the National Parks Association in Washington, fishing clubs in Chicago and Denver, and in Ithaca, New York, where Richard Bradley, a physics professor at Cornell and one of Harold's sons, showed it sixteen times to packed houses.

Bernard DeVoto, one of the nation's leading writers, weighed in on the pages of the country's most popular magazine, *The Saturday Evening Post*:

Thirty-two million [Americans] visited the National Parks [last year]. More will visit them

Harold Bradley (top left, with his son Richard) assumed a place named Dinosaur would be merely an arid collection of ancient bones (far left). But when his family floated the Yampa River through the national monument in 1952 (above), he discovered a world of beauty—threatened by proposals for two dams. Bradley showed his home movies to David Brower of the Sierra Club (bottom left), whose fight against the dams is considered the beginning of the modern environmental movement.

Sierra Club; John Muir had been a family friend. Like his father, Bradley became an outdoors enthusiast—hiker, camper, canoeist. And like his father, he had instilled those same passions in his seven sons.

When one of them came back from a kayaking adventure in Dinosaur National Monument, extolling its beauty and bemoaning the prospect that it would soon be entombed under a reservoir, the seventy-three-year-old Bradley decided he had to see it for himself. In 1952, with two of his sons and their families, Bradley made a week-long trip down the Yampa River, snapping photographs and taking home movies as they traveled. He had imagined that a desert region named Dinosaur would be "little more than an arid desolate boneyard"; instead he found a world of stunning beauty.

The experience threading our way through this superb gallery of matchless pictures displayed in ever-changing vistas, left us aghast at the thought that Bureau of Reclamation engineers are calmly planning the destruction of [Dinosaur] Monument.

[Attaching a dollar value to it] would be like trying to arrive at the value of a great painting by adding the cost of the canvas, the paint and wages of the painter. Whether it be very great or very small will depend on your scale of values—

this year. The attendance will keep on increasing as long as they are worth visiting, but a good many of them will not be worth visiting if engineers are let loose on them.

No one will ever drive 2000 miles to row a boat [on a reservoir]. . . . The only reason why anyone would ever go to Dinosaur National Monument is to see what the Bureau of Reclamation proposes to destroy.

More organizations sprang into action, hoping to mobilize public opinion and kill the project in Congress, though approval there seemed almost certain. The Wilderness Society (where Olaus Murie, Adolph's brother, was now director) helped lead the charge. The Izaak Walton League informed its members that the reservoir would degrade fishing opportunities on the rivers. And the American Planning and Civic Association, headed by Ulysses S. Grant III, a former general himself in the Corps of Engineers and grandson of the president who had signed the law creating the first national park, argued that other sites—outside the national monument—would be just as suitable for the dam projects.

Harold Bradley's sons also threw themselves into the fight. Charles Bradley gave speeches pointing out that the number of wilderness acres in America was now equaled by the number of acres that had been paved over. Richard Bradley helped Brower and the Sierra Club develop statistics that challenged the Bureau of Reclamation's assumptions on how much water would be lost to evaporation in the reservoirs. Another Bradley brother, David, joined Brower in testifying before Congress. "If we heed the lesson learned from the tragedy of the misplaced dam in Hetch Hetchy," they told a Senate hearing, "we can prevent a far more disastrous stumble in Dinosaur National Monument."

Harold Bradley took the case to a different constituency. He helped persuade the Garden Club of America to oppose the dam and send leaflets to its members encouraging them to write their congressmen about it; the General Federation of Women's Clubs did the same thing.

When mail began pouring into Congress at a ratio of eighty to one against the Echo Park dam, the Speaker of the House reluctantly delayed considera-

HIGH WATER LINE

LOW WATER LINE

A PRECIOUS GEM NEEDS A SETTING. ECHO PARK HAS BOTH   Martin Litton

Hetch Hetchy – Once Is Too Often

In Yosemite we learned a costly lesson—a lesson it is imperative to heed in Dinosaur National Monument, threatened by another misplaced dam.

MEASURING THE DAMAGE: A Sierra Club booklet (left) graphically demonstrates what a dam would do to Steamboat Rock—and connects the battle of Echo Park to the fight John Muir had lost at Hetch Hetchy fifty years earlier.

tion of its approval. Authorization for the larger string of dams and reclamation would eventually pass, but without the ones in Dinosaur National Monument. Public opinion had been felt, and, as Stegner noted, a new national environmental movement had been born.

Sometimes we have withheld our power to destroy, and have left a threatened species like the buffalo, a threatened beauty spot like Yosemite or Yellowstone or Dinosaur, scrupulously alone.

We are the most dangerous species of life on the planet, and every other species, even the earth itself, has cause to fear our power to exterminate. But we are also the only species which, when it chooses to do so, will go to great effort to save what it might destroy.

LOVED TO DEATH

In 1954—just as Yellowstone, Rocky Mountain, Great Smoky Mountains, and Shenandoah national parks had before it—Grand Teton National Park attracted more than a million visitors for the first time in its history. That same year, Yosemite National

Park also crossed the million-visit threshold. Within four more years, Grand Canyon, Mount Rainier, and Olympic national parks would do the same. The 32 million Americans who had crowded into their national parks in 1949 had suddenly become nearly 62 million before the 1950s were even halfway through. Ninety-eight percent of them arrived by car.

The parks weren't ready for them. "Conditions in the major parks are appalling," Charles Stevenson reported in *Reader's Digest* after an eight-thousand-mile inspection tour.

> Drive to Yellowstone, as my wife and I did late last summer, and the moment you enter you are in a big-city traffic jam. . . . Pause to look at sights you've come thousands of miles to see, and cars pile up bumper-to-bumper a quarter of a mile behind you. . . .
>
> Tourists must compete for food and sleeping accommodations in congested centers. . . . You buy a ticket to stand in line at the restaurant of Yellowstone's Old Faithful Inn. . . .
>
> [At Yellowstone Lake], the cabins . . . are actually shacks, overpriced at $1.50 per night for two persons if they bring their own bedding, up to $4.75 if they don't. Deployed around a central toilet house, they form slum-like city-block groups. . . . Many still in use were condemned before World War II as unfit for human habitation. . . .
>
> For a shower you stand in line to buy a 25-cent ticket, then await your turn at a bathhouse open between 4 P.M. and 7 P.M.
>
> Nevertheless some of these colonies are normally sold out by mid-morning. . . .
>
> Out of 16,435 weary tourists who arrived at Yellowstone [the same day we did], some 6,000 had no choice but to sleep in their cars or drive back out of the park.
>
> There are not enough Rangers to police the crowds, which at the peak of the season pour into Yellowstone at the rate of nearly half a million a month. There were only 116 of these uniformed men for most of last summer—20 fewer than in 1931. . . .
>
> Because there is nobody to stop them or to teach them to respect the park, some visitors use the craters of geysers as trash cans. . . . Shrubbery is mutilated. Vandalism and petty crime are rampant.

"The people," a park official said, "are wearing out the scenery." The situation was the same in every

CROWDS EVERYWHERE: A long line forms for a single outhouse in Yosemite (below left), while campers searching for places to pitch a tent are forced to ignore the sign (below right) saying they can't.

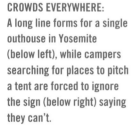

park. Yosemite Valley, Stevenson warned his readers, "has become a city festering with commercialism and ugliness. This spot, which Theodore Roosevelt once called the most beautiful in the world, now boasts three acres of burning dump." Meadows had been paved for parking lots; warehouses and stores obstructed scenic views; campgrounds squeezed in nearly a hundred people per acre; and "campers," he added, "line up 15 deep for the toilets." To make matters worse, all across the system, staff levels and budgets were no bigger—and sometimes lower—than they had been during the Depression.

Congress, Bernard DeVoto complained in the pages of *Harper's Magazine,* was requiring the Park Service to run a big industry "on a hot-dog-stand budget" and "much of the priceless heritage which the Service must safeguard is beginning to go to hell." Too many tourists, he wrote, "seem to assume that a park ranger, a road, [and] a comfort station . . . are just like the waterfalls, provided by nature at no expense." To dramatize his point, DeVoto made a sarcastic proposal in a widely read article: "Let's Close the National Parks."

The national park system must be temporarily reduced to a size for which Congress is willing to pay. Let us, as a beginning, close Yellowstone, Yosemite, Rocky Mountain, and Grand Canyon National Parks—close and seal them, assign the Army to patrol them, and so hold them secure till they can be reopened.

. . . Additional areas could be temporarily closed and sealed, held in trust for a more enlightened future—say Zion, Big Bend, Great Smoky, Shenandoah, Everglades, and Gettysburg.

Meanwhile letters from constituents unable to visit Old Faithful . . . and Bright Angel Trail would bring a nationally disgraceful situation to the really serious attention of the Congress which is responsible for it.

Park Service Director Conrad Wirth, however, had come up with his own solution. President Dwight D. Eisenhower was pushing through Congress the biggest public works program in history to date—$25 billion over ten years to build an interstate highway system. Wirth proposed a similar ten-year plan for the parks, timing its completion with the

agency's upcoming fiftieth anniversary in 1966. He named the ambitious project Mission 66 and called for spending $787 million, more than half for new construction and the rest for repairs, better maintenance, and more staff.

The national parks were "in danger of being 'loved to death,' " Wirth said, and without the infusion of funds, the Park Service faced "the destruction of what it is charged with saving." The president enthusiastically agreed to his proposal, and with Congress's approval, work began almost immediately—fixing roads, modernizing water and sewer systems, improving campgrounds and adding new ones, doubling the parks' lodging capacity. Museums, restrooms, and information offices were consolidated into a single, modern structure strategically located to intercept large numbers of people arriving by car, prepare them for their park experience through a series of displays and presentations, and send them on their way. Wirth called them "visitor centers." Before Mission 66 was through, 110 of them would be built.

For Wirth and his planners, the answer to bigger crowds would be improving what was called "visitor flow"—reducing their impact by moving them through the park more efficiently. Seeking to discourage anyone but campers from staying overnight in some parks, he advocated that the aging Paradise Inn at Mount Rainier be removed and argued against building any overnight accommodations in the Ever-

Meant to enable the parks to handle the tidal wave of Americans arriving by car in the 1950s—and encourage even more visitors to come—Mission 66 was promoted by oil companies (top right) and criticized by others for focusing too much on road construction (right). But it also instituted a new way of informing and guiding the public about what to expect in each park: the visitor center. During Mission 66, more than a hundred were built, including at Mount Rushmore (below) and Carlsbad Caverns (below right).

glades. His chief planner even suggested many of the buildings in Yosemite should be relocated outside the valley. Concessionaires and local politicians were outraged at the notion and forced Wirth to reverse course.

Restricting the number of park visitors through imposed limits or daily quotas was rejected as an option. "The principle which is guiding Mission 66," Wirth said, "is that the parks belong to the people, and they have a right to use them." Ever since the founding years of Stephen Mather, the Park Service had operated on the assumption that drawing more visitors meant creating more support for the parks; that the lesson of Hetch Hetchy had been that an unvisited park or portion of a park was the most vulnerable to exploitation; that the best way to protect and preserve the parks from their many enemies was for the public to use them.

But now, many of the parks' oldest allies became Mission 66's harshest critics. The modern design of the new buildings—so different from the "rustic" style of the past—often came under fire as not "harmonizing" with their surroundings. Some visitor centers seemed too much like the new shopping centers that were springing up in suburbs across the nation. Olaus Murie of the Wilderness Society called them "monstrosities." A new motel and marina in the Everglades was compared to a fishing resort "of the kind that is a dime a dozen in Florida."

Though supporting much of Mission 66, the National Parks Association worried that what it called "park standards" were being compromised in favor of catering to tourist demands for "amusement attractions" like swimming pools, tennis courts, golf courses, speed boating, and ski lifts. "They have the undesirable effect of drawing people not primarily interested in the parks," an association official wrote. "They are abundantly available elsewhere, and are as out of place in a national park as a roller skating rink in the National Gallery of Art would be."

But the loudest complaints focused on the road-work—and questioned the entire premise that helping more people visit the parks was a good idea. Ansel Adams, whose photographs had helped popularize the image of national parks and their scenic wonders, became one of the most vocal opponents.

One activity begets another. One facility encourages another. "Visitation" increases. . . . Increase of visitors means more cars; more cars mean more and wider roads . . . and more acres of parking space. More people of the resort-seeking type demand more comfort, more luxury . . . and push-button conveniences.

The symbol of Mission 66, Adams suggested, was a bulldozer—and it was now headed toward a beloved spot in his favorite park: Yosemite's Tenaya Lake on the Tioga Road, connecting the valley with the high Sierra.

Back in 1909, while John Muir was still alive, the Sierra Club had advocated improving the old wagon road, in accordance with the club's stated mission "to explore, enjoy, and render accessible the mountain regions of the Pacific Coast." In 1915, Stephen Mather had put up half the money to buy the road from its private owner, open it to automobiles, and turn it over to the park. In the 1930s and 1940s, special committees of the Sierra Club had voted their approval of reconstructing the road, beginning with the easiest parts at both ends. By the 1950s, all that remained for improvement was the rugged middle section, including a stretch across a long escarpment of gray granite, polished smooth by the last glaciers and skirting the shores of scenic Tenaya Lake. Mission 66 aimed to finish the job and widen the road.

Some of the Sierra Club's most influential leaders set out to stop the project. Among them were Adams, David Brower, and the club's newly elected president, Harold Bradley. "Park roads determine park history," Bradley had written in the club's newsletter. He wanted the stretch of road left in its primitive state—a form of "voluntary screening," he said, that had kept traffic past Tenaya Lake and the

The Park Service's plan to make the old Tioga Road into a paved highway along the edges of Tenaya Lake in Yosemite (left) caused a split with its usual ally, the Sierra Club, which now questioned the wisdom of encouraging more people to visit.

higher alpine meadows in the tens of thousands while Yosemite Valley was recording a million visits a year.

Reflecting the new direction Brower, Bradley, and the others hoped to take, they had already changed the Sierra Club's bylaws, replacing the phrase "*render accessible* the mountain regions of the Pacific Coast" to "*preserve* the Sierra Nevada and other scenic resources of the United States." John Muir's and Stephen Mather's notion that in order to make people value and save their national parks, people needed to experience them firsthand was now seen as a double-edged sword. "Yosemite," Adams argued, "possesses a 'fatal beauty' which invites self-destruction unless we make a strenuous effort to control visitation and use."

We can compare Yosemite with a great musical performance. We can fill all the seats and perhaps sell some standing room without destroying the quality of what we experience.

But we cannot sell lap room; in other words, we cannot permit a greater attendance than the event justifies for its own quality protection.

In the end, the road got built. "The bulldozers of bureaucracy have bypassed the gentle persuasions and advice of our conservation spokesmen," an outraged Ansel Adams wrote. From now on, the emerging environmental movement would be as likely to confront the National Park Service as to support it.

NEW FRONTIERS

As the 1960s dawned, heralding a decade of turbulent change in America, nearly 80 million people a year were visiting the national parks. Stewart Udall, a former Arizona congressman, became Secretary of the Interior during President John F. Kennedy's "New Frontier," followed by President Lyndon B. Johnson's "Great Society," and embarked on the most ambitious program of creating new parks since the time of Franklin Roosevelt. The pace of population growth and development in the United States, particularly in the West, gave Udall a sense of urgency. "What we save now," he said, "may be all we save." By the end of Udall's tenure, park visitation would skyrocket to 150 million a year.

He joined forces with the Sierra Club to press for creation of Redwood National Park, along the northern coast of California, home to the tallest trees in the world—the coastal redwoods, which over a lifetime spanning two millennia can grow three hundred feet high, requiring an environment of rainfall, fog, and soil found only in a narrow band of land a few hundred miles long. By the 1960s, logging had cleared 85 percent of the original redwood forest. The national park saved half of what remains.

In West Texas, the Guadalupe Mountains, the ancient remains of an ocean reef rising out of the desert, had once been the home of grizzly bears, wolves, and buffalo, as well as the Mescalero Apaches, who used the mountain oasis as a refuge until they, too, were driven out. "My Lord," Udall said when he first saw it, "what a paradise that place is." Then he got Congress to save it as a national park.

He also supported North Cascades National Park, a roadless wilderness park on the border of Washington and Canada containing 318 glaciers in its jumble of mountains—nearly a third of all the remaining glaciers in the Lower 48 states.

And in the stark desert of eastern Utah, where the Green River meets the Colorado amidst a seemingly

Stewart Udall at Rainbow Bridge National Monument
Right: Guadalupe Mountains National Park in Texas

Above: Mount Shuksan reflected in Picture Lake, North Cascades National Park

Left: The Lady Bird Johnson Grove in Redwood National Park, named in honor of the First Lady, who was a great champion of the parks

For every devoted individual who donates money to save a redwood grove, there are fifty who would . . . cut it down for profit.

Special lands may be set aside, as in the past, as national parks, wildlife refuges, seashores, lakeshores. But we are running out of the raw material for such reservations, and there is no more where it came from.

WALLACE STEGNER

Each generation has its own rendezvous with the land, for despite our fee titles and claims of ownership, we are all brief tenants on this planet. By choice, or by default, we will carve out a land legacy for our heirs.

We can misuse the land and diminish the usefulness of resources, or we can create a world in which physical affluence and affluence of the spirit go hand in hand.

STEWART UDALL

Mesa Arch at Island in the Sky,
Canyonlands National Park

endless maze of meandering canyons, is a place John Wesley Powell had first described in 1869 as a "wilderness of rocks" and a "world of grandeur." Powell had given the features he saw names like Cataract Canyon, the Dirty Devil, the Labyrinth. A hundred years later, Udall helped give it all another name: Canyonlands National Park.

But it wasn't just places with canyons and glaciers and tall trees Udall wanted to save. He persuaded Congress to set aside other parts of the American landscape and place them under the Park Service's protection:

- National seashores: from Cape Cod in Massachusetts to Padre Island in Texas to Point Reyes in California.
- National lakeshores, such as Indiana Dunes and Pictured Rocks in the Great Lakes.
- The Ozark National Scenic Riverways in southwestern Missouri, the first in a string of rivers that would have portions kept in their free-flowing, natural conditions.

- National trails, such as the Appalachian Trail, extending 2,100 miles from Georgia to Maine.
- And national recreation areas, often reservoirs behind the dams being built all over the West.

To help him push through such a dramatic expansion, Udall turned to George Hartzog as the new Park Service director, who brought to the job the same energy and backslapping political skills Stephen Mather had used so successfully fifty years earlier. Hartzog had grown up in South Carolina in a farm family where, he said, "poverty clung to us like a sweat-soaked shirt." He had tried his hand as a Methodist preacher while still a teenager, learned the law as a stenographer in an attorney's office and passed the bar exam, and then got a degree in business at age thirty-three before joining the Park Service. Most recently, Hartzog had supervised the construction of the stunning Gateway Arch at the national historic site in St. Louis, commemorating America's westward expansion. Now, to "bring the parks to the people," he would push the Park Service

A father and son canoe in the Ozark National Scenic Riverways, one of the many new types of additions to the park system Udall pushed through to preserve more of the American landscape.

GOD BLESS MR. ROCKEFELLER

By the 1950s, no single American had donated more to the national parks than John D. Rockefeller Jr. His gifts of land and money—nearly $45 million by some accountings—had helped create Acadia National Park in Maine, Great Smoky Mountains National Park in Tennessee and North Carolina, and Grand Teton National Park in Wyoming. Other donations had helped clean up the roadsides in Yellowstone, build museums in Yosemite and Mesa Verde.

"I have no favorite parks," he once said. "Like your children you love each of them for different reasons."

Rockefeller passed along his passion for the parks to all of his sons, but his fourth-born, Laurance, seemed to follow most closely in his father's footsteps.

In 1956, the younger Rockefeller paid $1.75 million for five thousand acres of land in the U.S. Virgin Islands—half of St. John Island, with its sparkling white sand beaches, coral reefs, and subtropical forests—and then deeded it over to the National Park Service.

Horace Albright, who had worked for many years with the family on parks projects, wrote the old man, now in his eighties, about the ceremony:

> His work in establishing our twenty-ninth national park on St. John gives him great prestige as a conservationist. I wish you could have seen him in action the day he turned over the lands to Secretary of the Interior . . . and the latter declared the park in being.
>
> The many natives standing near the official party spontaneously cried out, "God bless Mr. Rockefeller!" when Laurance rose to speak, thus eloquently and poignantly expressing the hope they felt that at last the island has a future.

John D. Rockefeller Jr. died four years later, on May 11, 1960. For the next forty years, Laurance would lead the family's philanthropic interests in national parks. He gave the initial $1 million to launch the National Park Foundation, an organization dedicated to encouraging more Americans to contribute to their parks; provided funds for the expansion of dozens of parks and battlefields; and donated a farm in

Laurance Rockefeller (above) carried on his father's tradition of philanthropy to the parks. In 1956 he donated half of the island of St. John to create Virgin Islands National Park (below).

Woodstock, Vermont, as a historic site. Shortly before his own death in 2004, he bequeathed a scenic ranch property in the Tetons to the federal government—and in doing so enlarged the park his father had done so much to protect.

And in the great cultural and historical areas we stand in the presence of great historical events and great personages reflective of the courage and creativity of the people who founded this nation and established the values that we prize today as a part of the American way of life. And in reviewing those episodes of our history, we're able to reestablish a sense of community in our society. Those stories are important in understanding the American heritage. And they need to be preserved and they need to be told.

Hartzog had been given a vivid personal lesson in the power of historical sites when his father made his only trip from his native South Carolina to visit Hartzog in Washington, D.C. Hartzog had planned on an extensive sightseeing tour of the capital region, but his father wanted to see only one place: the Lincoln Memorial. "Abraham Lincoln was not a favorite historical personage in the low country of South Carolina when I was a boy growing up," Hartzog remembered, so he was surprised by his father's choice—and equally surprised when his father insisted on visiting the memorial alone.

And I sat there and watched him walk those steps. And he got there and stopped and faced Lincoln, and turned to the right and went around that memorial and read every saying of Lincoln's, and came back and got in the car. Tears were welling in his eyes, although they were not running. And he said to me, "I'm now ready to go home." That's what they mean.

On August 28, 1963, Hartzog witnessed a much larger crowd at the Lincoln Memorial, when a quarter of a million people converged on the National Mall as part of the March on Washington to protest the Jim Crow laws that still discriminated against African Americans in the South and to call on Congress to pass a civil rights bill to bring them to an end.

There, a young minister named Martin Luther King Jr.—who had recently been jailed in Birmingham, Alabama; who the director of the FBI considered a communist sympathizer; and whose life was in constant danger from people who hated the color of his skin and everything he stood for—gave a speech

As director of the Park Service in the 1960s, George Hartzog (above, at the Jefferson Memorial) wanted to "bring the parks to the people" with more units—especially historic sites—in the nation's big cities.

to have a greater presence in urban areas—such as Gateway National Recreation Area in New York City and Golden Gate National Recreation Area in San Francisco—and to increase its number of cultural and historic sites.

To Hartzog, the park system's role in preserving and interpreting American history was just as crucial as protecting the large, natural parks, because, he believed, in combination they represent the "delicate strands of nature and culture that bond generation to generation":

National parks are exemplars of our heritage. The natural areas reflect the continent as aboriginal people knew it, and they preserve those areas in a pristine condition, the way it was when the Europeans came here. It's there that we come to understand that there's one web of life, and that we're a part of it. And it's in our relationship to all the other creatures that we find our own identity and the meaning of our lives.

that would be considered a turning point in American history. "I have a dream," he said, "that my four little children will one day live in a nation where they will not be judged by the color of their skin but by the content of their character." In his speech, Dr. King also quoted from "America," the same song Marian Anderson had sung on the memorial's steps a generation earlier.

Like millions of other Americans, Hartzog was electrified by the speech—one of those "everlasting moments," he said, "that stay with you and influence your life, all your life. . . . Of the same dimension as the first time I stood on the South Rim of the Grand Canyon and looked at that magnificent canyon in front of me."

That the massive protest took place in the national park system seemed especially meaningful to Hartzog. "What higher purpose can a national park serve?" he said. "That's the institution of free people, so why shouldn't they come to that institution to raise their concerns about the current social condition? I thought it was a perfectly ideal and marvelous place for that great speech." He was particu-

larly proud that on the steps next to Dr. King were two park rangers.

Five years later, Dr. King would be assassinated. Twelve years after that, his birthplace in Atlanta, Georgia, would be dedicated as a historic site, part of the national park system.

THE VOICE OF WILDERNESS

We were approaching [our] cabin one stormy night; it was snowing and getting dark. . . . Out of the storm came music, the long-drawn, mournful call of a wolf.

It started low, moved slowly up the scale with increased volume—at the high point a slight break in the voice, then a deepening of the tone as it became a little more throaty and gradually descended the scale and the soft voice trailed off to blend with the storm.

We waited to hear again the voice of wilderness in the storm. But the performer, with artistic restraint, was silent.

ADOLPH MURIE

The postwar stampede of tourists to national parks had not yet reached the interior of Alaska and Mount McKinley. While many of the bigger parks in the Lower 48 were now experiencing a million visits a year, the park around the continent's tallest mountain rarely got more than twenty thousand.

But a new highway being built from Anchorage to Fairbanks would pass by the east edge of the park, holding out the prospect that tourists would soon be arriving by car instead of by train—and in much greater numbers. Through its Mission 66 program, the Park Service intended to accommodate them.

Plans called for an expanded hotel near the park entrance; more campgrounds and a visitor center halfway into the park's interior; then another show-

case hotel near the shores of tranquil Wonder Lake. To reach it, the ninety-mile rough and narrow gravel road that provided the only access would be widened, paved, and made ready for the modern, traveling public. This was the model the Park Service had followed in virtually every major park in the Lower 48, and it was precisely the model Adolph Murie opposed for the Alaska park he had grown to love. "I am afraid," he wrote a friend, that they "will try to make McKinley into another Yellowstone or Yosemite." "We have the opportunity here," he added, "for some planning along idealistic lines."

When the Mission 66 plans were unveiled in 1956, he had submitted a detailed, fourteen-page analysis to the park superintendent outlining his concerns.

Mount McKinley, seen across the waters of Wonder Lake. Adolph Murie opposed plans to build a highway to the lake and a fancy hotel near its shores.

Prompted by Adolph Murie's persistent objections, George Hartzog called an end to many of the Mission 66 plans for Mount McKinley National Park, including construction of a paved highway (left) to Wonder Lake. At Yosemite, Hartzog also terminated the immensely popular "firefall" from Glacier point (top right) and at Yellowstone finally enforced the paper policy against feeding bears.

The wilderness standards in McKinley must be maintained on a higher level than anything we have attempted in the States. Because McKinley is a wilderness within a vast northern wilderness, the ill effect of any intrusion will here be proportionately greater; and any "dressing up" will be more incongruous.

Our big task is to preserve this wilderness spirit.

The point in all planning for McKinley is not to think up things to intrude in the park, but ways of preventing any intrusions. . . . We have a sacred area. Let us touch it as little as possible.

"They were not interested in my views," Murie confided, and "my efforts were not appreciated." For the next two years, he was reassigned to Grand Teton National Park in Wyoming, where he was told to catch up on writing about his studies of McKinley's birds, mammals, and flowers.

When he was finally allowed to return to continue his research, Murie was dismayed at what he found. The first thirteen miles of park road had been exca-vated and paved, and at Mile 65 a visitor center was being constructed that looked, he said, like a Dairy Queen. The work, he wrote in his journal, makes "one think of a blacksmith repairing wrist watches with his horseshoeing implements."

Murie now saw the road improvements as the key threat to what made the park so special. A paved highway would make inevitable other services—a hotel, restaurants, gas stations, stores—in the park's pristine interior. The increased traffic on such a road, he believed, would also quickly drive away the unique array of wildlife—the very things that fasci-nated McKinley's visitors—to more remote parts of the park.

Rather than trying to "bring accommodations into the midst of the scenery," he advocated "a sim-ple and delicate approach from the edge of things." And instead of planning an improved road, he said, "it would be far better to begin opposing it."

I could list many management suggestions that I personally have opposed, such as wolf control, coy-ote control, insect control, lodgepole blister rust control, excessive fire control, mosquito control (in Yellowstone), wildlife salting, exposed garbage dumps in bear country, etc. etc.

This may seem like a negative attitude, but in a national park opposition to unnecessary management can more correctly be termed a positive attitude.

CAMP CURRY'S FIRE FALL.

Murie could be passionately persuasive one on one with the people he encountered in the park, and relentless in making his superiors aware of what he considered a mistaken policy. "It was really an obsession with him," his wife, Louise, remembered. "I guess he felt as though he had to protect it himself." But he was uncomfortable before large groups, and his job with the Park Service placed other constraints on how public he could be with his criticisms.

To stop further construction on the road, Murie turned to his older brother for help. As director of the Wilderness Society, Olaus Murie was much more accustomed to waging public campaigns and in a much better position to openly challenge the Park Service. With Adolph providing him with the information, Olaus gladly took up the cause and con-

vinced other groups, such as the National Parks Association, to join in. This time, the Park Service director listened to their arguments.

George Hartzog shelved most of the Mission 66 plans for McKinley. There would be no hotel and tourist services in the interior. The roadwork was stopped where it was: thirteen miles widened and paved, another seventeen widened but unpaved, and the remaining sixty miles to be kept in more or less the condition Adolph Murie had suggested—a narrow gravel pathway where, he said, "the feeling one gets is that the road passes through a wilderness that comes up to the road." It is still that way today.

In the Lower 48, George Hartzog also brought an end to two traditions that had become ingrained as part of the national park experience. For nearly a hundred years, one of the biggest attractions in Yosemite Valley had been what one magazine described as a "man-made spectacle [that] rivaled the natural glories" of the park—the dramatic "firefall." Every evening in the summer season, as throngs gathered to watch, a huge bonfire would be built on Glacier Point, then pushed over the edge, to cascade down toward the valley floor. Hartzog ordered a stop to it in 1968. "It was an absolutely spectacular sight," he admitted, and wildly popular. "But it was about as appropriate for the silent tranquility and beauty of that great valley as horns on a rabbit."

At Yellowstone, Hartzog also enforced what George Wright, Adolph Murie, and many other biologists had advocated years earlier: not just a paper policy against feeding the bears, which tourists and park officials had routinely ignored, but a concerted effort at weaning the bears from human food—along the roadside or at garbage dumps.

Following the recommendations of a report commissioned by Secretary Udall, new Park Service policies called for placing scientific research as the basis for management decisions, emphasizing that the complex ecology of each park be restored to what it had once been, and stating that "a national park should represent a vignette of primitive America." Slowly, in the tension between preservation and use, parks as nature's sanctuaries and parks as tourist resorts, the trend had begun to shift a little back in nature's direction. George Melendez Wright's old vision was finally being taken seriously.

ISLANDIA

I like the quiet out here. I'm not pestered or bothered by a lot of people. . . . I am alone, but I am not lonely. When you have plenty of interests, like the water and the woods, the birds and the fish, you don't get lonely.

LANCELOT JONES

By the 1960s, no one knew Biscayne Bay, off the southeastern tip of Florida, better than Lancelot Jones. He had been born in the bottom of a small boat there in 1898, while his father was frantically sailing his pregnant mother toward a hospital in Miami. From that time on, the bay had been his home.

His father, Israel Lafayette Jones, had risen up from slavery in North Carolina, migrated to Florida after the Civil War, and steadily improved life for himself and his Bahamian wife through a series of jobs in the Miami area: handyman at a hotel in Coconut Grove, caretaker of a lighthouse, foreman at a pineapple farm. Eventually, he had managed to buy three of the small uninhabited islands that separate Biscayne Bay from the Atlantic Ocean and began a profitable business growing key limes. In honor of his favorite story, the Knights of the Round Table, he had proudly named his two sons King Arthur Jones and Sir Lancelot Jones—hoping "perhaps," Lancelot later said, "that by giving us great names we would become great men."

But three years after his father's death, the Hurricane of 1935 had laid waste to the family's lime crops and forced Lancelot into a new line of work: as a fishing guide for the many wealthy visitors to Biscayne Bay. Just across a small channel from Jones's home on Porgy Key was the Cocolobo Club, an exclusive retreat for some of the multimillionaires who wintered at Miami Beach; men with names like Firestone, Maytag, Honeywell, and Hertz. Lancelot Jones became the favorite fishing guide for them and their politically well-connected friends.

But other millionaires had other plans for the bay and its chain of more than three dozen pristine islands—the only remaining group of undeveloped Florida keys from Miami to Key West. In 1961, a shipping magnate from Connecticut paid $8 million for 18,000 acres of bayside land and announced he intended to construct a deep-water port, an oil refinery, and an industrial complex called Seadade on it, once he dredged a deeper channel through the shallow bay eight miles out to the ocean. At the same time, a group of developers decided to build a causeway linking the mainland to the islands, to do with them what had already happened at Miami Beach and Key Biscayne: a series of high-rise hotels, retail shopping centers, and private beachfront properties.

The organizers convinced Dade County authorities to create the city of "Islandia" and ferried a voting machine to Elliott Key, the largest island, where they staged an election attended by fourteen of the eighteen registered voters—all of them absentee landowners hoping to cash in on the anticipated real estate boom. Lancelot Jones, one of only two full-time residents of the new "Islandia," was not among them. He was against their plans—and had also turned down offers from the refinery developer to buy Porgy Key. "I always felt this land was not right for development," he said, "that it should stay as it is."

Meanwhile, a small group had formed to fight both proposals. Lloyd Miller, a midlevel manager for an airline based in Miami, was an avid fisherman and founder of the local chapter of the Izaak Walton League who believed the refinery and seaport would turn Biscayne Bay—one of Florida's most fertile fish-breeding grounds—into a stagnant pool of oily water.

Juanita Greene, an enterprising young writer for *The Miami Herald,* worried that the considerable financial interests behind both developments were steamrolling the plans toward hasty approval—her own newspaper supported the refinery—and that the public was not only being shut out of the decision, but would also be denied access to precious water-front once everything was completed. It would become, she warned, a "rich man's paradise." "I could see that for the average Joe who wanted to go to the beach on Sunday afternoon, there were fewer and fewer places to go," Greene remembered. "I didn't think that that was fair, that only people who could live in fancy hotels or condominiums had access to the beach."

At a meeting held around her dining room table, Greene, Miller, and another friend, Art Marshall, decided that the only way to stop the refinery and commercial development of the islands was to make it a national park. Miller took time off from work to give speeches to any local group that would provide an audience—sometimes three a day for weeks at a time. Greene persuaded her newspaper to at least cover the budding opposition movement—and to allow her to write occasional opinion pieces advocating her point of view. In one, she called Islandia a "freak city with a lot of power and no people."

As the public leader of the opposition, Miller found his car sprayed with paint. People suggested that his employer fire him. His pet dog was killed—followed by an anonymous call that he or a member of his family might be next.

Despite the threats and being vastly outspent by the developers, Miller and Greene's movement slowly gained strength. In elections for the county commission, a slate of anti-refinery candidates was swept into office—and quickly rescinded permission to dredge a new channel in Biscayne Bay, effectively killing the plan. Later, local political leaders also withdrew their support for a causeway to Islandia. And after visiting the bay and viewing its undeveloped islands, Secretary of the Interior Stewart Udall came out in favor of protecting it as a national monument, as a step toward it becoming a national park. In October of 1968, Lloyd Miller was peering over the shoulder of President Lyndon Johnson as he created Biscayne National Monument—protecting forever 173,000 acres of the bay, coral reefs, and islands.

The first private landowner to sell his land to the federal government for the new national monument was Lancelot Jones—277 acres on three islands on the condition that he be allowed to live out his life in the family home on Porgy Key.

The exclusive Cocolobo Club (top left) symbolized the "rich man's paradise" the string of islands in Florida's Biscayne Bay might have become. But Lancelot Jones (bottom left) and Juanita Greene and Lloyd Miller (below, standing, second from right) fought instead to have the islands preserved as a national monument, then a national park.

All in all, the monument is a good thing. Some people would have liked to make this place the No. 2 Miami Beach, but I think it's good for people to have somewhere that they can go to leave the hustle and bustle behind and get out into the quietude of nature.

I like the name "monument." It means that things here are going to stay pretty much as they are today.

Long after Congress changed the monument to Biscayne National Park, Jones was still there—able to look out on the undisturbed waters where he had been born nearly a century earlier. His favorite pastime was teaching small groups of schoolchildren about the bay's fish and sponges whenever the Park Service brought them to Porgy Key. The only compensation he asked for was a key lime pie.

LAST CHANCE TO DO IT RIGHT

The national park idea, the best idea we ever had, was inevitable as soon as Americans learned to confront the wild continent not with fear and cupidity but with delight, wonder, and awe.

Once started, it grew like the backfire it truly was, burning back upwind against the current of claim and grab and raid . . . [proving] that our rapacious society could hold its hand, at least in

the presence of stupendous scenery, and learn to respect the earth for something besides its economic value.

WALLACE STEGNER

On March 1, 1972, Yellowstone, the world's first national park, celebrated its centennial. During its hundred years of existence, the park had seen its wildlife wantonly slaughtered by poachers and then protected by law. Yellowstone had been guarded by cavalrymen and park rangers; defended by poets and studied by scientists; endlessly painted and photographed by professionals and amateurs alike; toured by one American president after another, seeking everything from exhilarating inspiration to simple relaxation. (Gerald Ford, still a Michigan congressman in 1972, had found work there one summer as a young man.) Yellowstone had been the site of everything from Indian wars to bitter fights over the limits of commercial exploitation, battles over the value of nature and a continuing argument over how Americans could enjoy its treasure-house of wonders without ruining it for the next generation.

Along the way, Yellowstone had also become one of the most recognizable symbols of America itself. In 1972, Old Faithful—still spouting as regularly as it did when it got its name a century earlier—would thrill 2.2 million people. They were but a fraction of the 165 million visitors who came that year to a national park system that now had a presence in virtually every state in the Union—thirty-eight national parks, and roughly two hundred historic sites, national monuments, and other places Americans had set aside for posterity.

In 1972, Yellowstone hosted a world conference on national parks. Delegates arrived from eighty other nations, representing more than 1,200 parks and reserves referred to as "Yellowstone's children." The park idea had spread from Yellowstone all the way around the world—ultimately becoming, like the idea of freedom itself, one of America's greatest exports.

Within the boundaries of the United States, however, the age of adding large natural areas to the park system seemed to be winding down. A handful of places previously set aside as national monuments—Arches and Capitol Reef in Utah, the Badlands of

Left: Kabetogama Lake in Voyageurs National Park, Minnesota
Right: Cedar Creek in Congaree National Park, South Carolina
Below: A cascading stream in Cuyahoga Valley National Park, Ohio

South Dakota, and Theodore Roosevelt National Memorial in North Dakota—would be elevated to national park status.

The Congaree Swamp in South Carolina—the biggest remaining old-growth floodplain forest, home to the largest water hickory, deciduous holly, overcup oak, and loblolly pine in the nation—would be saved as a national monument, as would a twenty-two-mile stretch of the Cuyahoga River in northeastern Ohio, set aside as a national recreation area. Both would eventually become national parks. And on Minnesota's remote northern border, an entirely new park was created, encompassing more than thirty lakes and nine hundred islands—a canoeist's paradise named Voyageurs National Park in memory of the French-Canadian trappers who had once paddled and portaged their way through it. But now, in the farthest corner of the nation, the park idea was about to be dramatically reborn.

Before retiring from the Park Service in 1965, Adolph Murie had joined with a group of other park lovers in urging that Mount McKinley National Park's boundaries be expanded to provide greater protection to the habitat of its diverse array of wildlife. "In our thinking of McKinley let us not have puny thoughts," he wrote. "Let us . . . think on a greater scale. Let us not have those of the future decry our smallness of concept and lack of foresight."

George Hartzog and Stewart Udall were thinking along the same lines—not just for McKinley, but for other parts of Alaska as well. They drew up a list of seven national monument proclamations, covering millions of acres, for President Johnson to issue using his sole authority under the Antiquities Act. It would be, they told him, his "parting gift to future generations." But at the last minute, Johnson had balked, fearing Congress would revolt at such a huge exercise of presidential authority. McKinley remained Alaska's only national park.

Following his retirement, Adolph Murie and his wife, Louise, returned to visit for six more summers. Now seen as something of an elder statesman, Murie would travel the park's gravel road observing the wildlife, preaching to anyone he met his gospel of preserving nature in the national parks and how Alaska could play an important part in that idea.

[Here] all the plants and animals enjoy a natural and normal life without human restrictions. Freedom prevails . . . [even] the "bad" wolf seeks an honest living as of yore; he is a respected citizen, morally on a par with everyone else. . . . No species of plant is favored above the rest, and they grow together, quietly competing. . . .

Our task is to perpetuate this freedom and purity of nature, this ebb and flow of life—first, by insuring ample park boundaries so that the region is large enough to maintain the natural relationships, and secondly, to hold man's intrusions to the minimum.

Let us remember that the very existence of Alaska is recreation for everyone who has ever heard of Alaska, whether or not he has ever seen it. To these millions, Alaska will spell recreation to the imagination, if it is preserved.

BROTHERS IN THE CAUSE: Both Adolph Murie (right) and his older half brother Olaus (left) were champions of protecting wide swaths of Alaska from exploitation. Adolph worked from inside the National Park Service; Olaus as director of the Wilderness Society.

In 1970, when he left the park for the last time, Murie's health was failing and he needed help getting onto the train that would take him away. Four years later, shortly before his seventy-fifth birthday, he died. In recognition of all that he had done, along the road he had worked so hard to keep from becoming a highway, the Park Service named one of the scenic vistas the Plains of Murie.

By this time, although it had achieved statehood in 1959, Alaska was still sparsely populated and still open for homesteading. Its official nickname was "America's Last Frontier," the one place left in the

United States where the conquest of wilderness that had marked the nation's march from the Atlantic to the Pacific during the nineteenth century might be reenacted. What was no longer certain was whether or not Americans agreed that history in fact should be repeated.

A federal law had been passed to settle the claims of Alaska's native peoples, including the Inupiaq and the Tlingit, the Aleut and the Athabascan. The federally owned land was to be divided up: some for the state to control and open for development if it wished; some for the tribes; and a portion to be withheld forever in the "national interest" for all Americans.

As the discovery of vast oil deposits on the North Slope and the construction of the Trans Alaska Pipeline demonstrated, the stakes were enormous. The fight over what to do with the federal lands would consume a decade and would quickly become a national battle, waged in the halls of Congress. On one side were commercial and industrial groups capable of spending millions of dollars in advertising and lobbying. On the other was the Alaska Coalition, a collection of fifty environmental groups with members in every state, which quickly mushroomed to 1,500 organizations, representing ten million members, most of whom had never set foot in Alaska. It was the largest grassroots conservation effort in American history.

With bipartisan support, conservationists had been steadily winning victories for nearly a decade:

When John Cook arrived in Alaska to represent the Park Service after President Jimmy Carter unilaterally set aside 56 million acres as national monuments, he was the "third least popular person in Alaska." The top two, Carter and his Interior Secretary, Cecil Andrus, were safely back in Washington.

the Wilderness Act, the Wild and Scenic Rivers Act, the Clean Air Act, the Clean Water Act. In Alaska they saw the opportunity to set aside parcels of land on a scale unimagined in the Lower 48—the possibility for parks embracing entire ecosystems in ways that Yellowstone, the Grand Canyon, or the Everglades, big as they were, did not. Alaska, the coalition contended, was America's "last chance to do it right."

Congressman Morris Udall of Arizona, the brother of Stewart Udall, sponsored a bill setting aside 110 million acres of "national interest" land as national parks, wildlife refuges, and wilderness. In May of 1978, Udall's bill passed overwhelmingly in the House, 277 to 31. But in the Senate, even though a clear majority favored Udall's proposal, a threatened filibuster by Alaska Senator Mike Gravel tied things up, preventing a vote before Congress adjourned for the session. With the statutory deadline for action only a few weeks away, it appeared that the big dreams for preserving large sections of Alaska would come to nothing.

Then President Jimmy Carter, acting on the recommendation of his Secretary of the Interior, Cecil Andrus, decided to bypass Congress and invoke the Antiquities Act, a tool presidents had been using in the name of conservation since Theodore Roosevelt. On December 1, 1978, Carter took out his pen and signed executive orders creating seventeen national monuments, covering 56 million acres of the most critical areas in Udall's bill.

In Alaska, all hell broke loose. Many Alaskans felt that outsiders from the more populated parts of the nation, with little understanding of the state and its way of life, were trying to impose needless restrictions on what Alaskans could do with the land they considered their own. Carter and the federal government were accused of trying to "lock up" the state's vast natural resources. Angry protests were staged. The president was burned in effigy. Park Service property was destroyed. There were occasional threats of personal violence against anyone who might try to carry out Carter's proclamations.

To handle the volatile situation on the ground while they worked to reach a legislative solution, the administration chose John Cook, a Westerner who had earned a reputation as a tough problem solver.

National parks were in his blood: his grandfather had worked at Grand Canyon National Park when it was first established; his father had done the same. Cook had joined the Park Service the day he graduated from high school and steadily worked his way up the ladder. He'd been a mule skinner, maintenance worker, park ranger, interpreter, and administrator.

Cook arrived at his new posting, he remembered, as the "third least popular person in Alaska," behind President Carter and Interior Secretary Andrus. Outside the buildings in some small towns where he held public hearings, there would be a mock tombstone with his name on it. But he set about trying his best to explain what were called the "Carter Monuments" to the locals, trying to dispel the rampant rumors about federal intentions to ignore citizens' rights.

On the Kenai Peninsula, at the head of Resurrection Bay, was the small town of Seward, named for Secretary of State William Seward, who, in 1867, had first made Alaska part of the United States by purchasing it from Russia for $7.2 million—prompting many Americans at the time to call the remote territory "Seward's Folly." The town's economy revolved around fish harvesting and processing; the ups and downs of the timber business; and a commercial port that had briefly boomed with activity during the oil pipeline's construction. Nearby was the Harding Icefield—a sheet of ice seven hundred square miles wide and one mile thick, spawning more than thirty glaciers, many of which descend directly to sea level, where they have carved a series of deep coastal fjords. Their waters teem with wildlife—sea lions, harbor seals, whales, and birds of all kinds.

Carter's proclamation created a 570,000-acre Kenai Fjords National Monument in hopes it all would eventually become a national park. John Cook sent a two-person team there with the instructions, "Whatever you do, never lie to the people.

SIGNS OF PROTEST: In Eagle, Alaska (above), a warning to Park Service employees and anyone supporting them; at left, President Carter is burned in effigy before a cheering crowd.

Don't whitewash anything. Always play it straight." Cook and the governor, meanwhile, came up with a term they hoped would soften the widespread opposition to the new national monuments, promising they would be Alaska's "permanent pipeline," a source of tourist revenue that would still be flowing long after the oil ran out. Nonetheless, the sentiment in Seward—as in the rest of Alaska—was dead set against the monument. Twice, the City Council passed resolutions condemning the idea.

While John Cook tried to dampen the local hostility to Carter's proclamations, the Alaska Coalition prepared for another congressional battle aimed at settling all the Alaska land issues once and for all. In May of 1979, the House again overwhelmingly passed Morris Udall's Alaska lands bill, this time 360 to 65. Opponents in the Senate, though still a minority, managed to delay action there for another year and a half, when a watered-down version finally passed—stripping away millions of acres of proposed wilderness; providing for potential oil and gas exploration in the Arctic National Wildlife Refuge and for mining in other refuges; and carving off some of the land proposed for national parks into "national preserves" instead, where hunting and other nonpark activities would be permitted.

On December 2, 1980, a month before leaving office, Carter signed the Alaska National Interest Lands Conservation Act into law. It wasn't everything he and the Alaska Coalition had once hoped for, but it was still the largest single expansion of protected conservation lands in world history—creating four national forests, ten national preserves, sixteen national wildlife refuges, and seven brand-new national parks. The national park system, with 47 million acres added to its care, had suddenly more than doubled in size.

Glacier Bay—the place John Muir had called "Nature's own reservation" a hundred years earlier—was now a national park. The solid sheet of glacial ice that once covered the entire bay had retreated sixty-five miles, exposing new inlets and glaciers, including ones named for Muir.

Wrangell-St. Elias National Park, containing the greatest array of mountain peaks higher than 16,000 feet on the continent, covers 8.3 million acres, by far the nation's largest national park. A single glacier within its vastness is the size of Yellowstone. With an adjacent national preserve of 4.8 million additional acres, Wrangell-St. Elias protects an area three times the size of New Jersey.

Lake Clark National Park, where three distinct mountain ranges collide, encompasses two active volcanoes and twenty glacial lakes, including Lake Clark itself, stretching forty miles along the fault line between the Pacific and North American tectonic plates.

Katmai National Park first caught the nation's attention in 1912, when an immense volcanic eruption dirtied the skies as far away as Virginia and Europe. Closer to the eruption, volcanic ash covered three thousand square miles and buried a ten-mile river valley with pumice hundreds of feet deep. It was still smoldering when a scientific expedition finally reached it four years later and named it the Valley of Ten Thousand Smokes. In another part of the park, at Brooks Falls, scores of Alaskan brown bears rendezvous each year to troll the clear waters and feast on the salmon struggling upstream.

Farther north, Gates of the Arctic National Park—at 7.5 million acres nearly as immense as Wrangell-St. Elias—lies entirely above the Arctic Circle. With virtually all of it officially set aside as wilderness and therefore without any maintained roads or trails, it is accessible only by air taxi, by foot,

Wrangell–St. Elias National Park

Left: The Arrigetch Peaks in Gates of the Arctic National Park
Right: Caribou migration in Kobuk Valley National Park
Below: Turquoise Lake in Lake Clark National Park

The annual gathering of bears at Brooks Falls during the salmon run, Katmai National Park

With wilderness fast disappearing in the "first 48" states, Alaska . . . offers the last large, unspoiled outdoor laboratory for the study and appreciation of undisturbed nature. Here you may still have the experience of the frontiersmen and explorers who first gazed on unbroken prairies, unharnessed rivers and undiminished wildlife.

CELIA HUNTER

or by boat in one of its six rivers designated as wild and scenic.

Just to the west lies Kobuk Valley National Park, where the boreal forest gives way to the tundra, and fierce polar winds blowing relentlessly over ancient riverbeds created sand dunes covering five hundred square miles. Some 12,000 years ago, when the climate was not as harsh, animals and humans congregated here after traversing the Bering Land Bridge from Siberia. Inupiat hunters still gather there every fall to await the caribou herds swimming across the Kobuk River. (As part of the effort to "do it right" and learn lessons from the mistakes made when parks were created in the Lower 48, in Alaska the rights and cultures of native peoples were explicitly recognized.)

And back at Seward, the national monument at Kenai Fjords became the seventh of the new Alaska parks. Five years later, as the tourist economy in Seward began to emerge as a crucial part of the town's livelihood and the local chamber of commerce began putting the town's proximity to Kenai Fjords at the top of its marketing material, the City Council quietly—but officially—rescinded its two previous resolutions denouncing the park idea. Several years after that, they asked that the national park at their doorstep be expanded.

Mount McKinley National Park, which had been in existence since 1917, was also affected by the Alaska lands act. Its area was nearly tripled in size: 2.4 million more acres to the park itself, plus an additional 1.3 million acres in two national preserves next to it—a dramatically larger expansion than even Adolph Murie had proposed just before his retirement. The old park, surrounded by the new additions, was now officially designated a wilderness, bringing with it even greater protections to the land and animals Murie had championed.

And as if to symbolize all that had happened—at McKinley, in Alaska, and throughout the park system—the park's name was changed to reflect its deeper history. It would revert to the Athabaskan Indian name for the tremendous mountain at its core—*Denali,* "The High One."

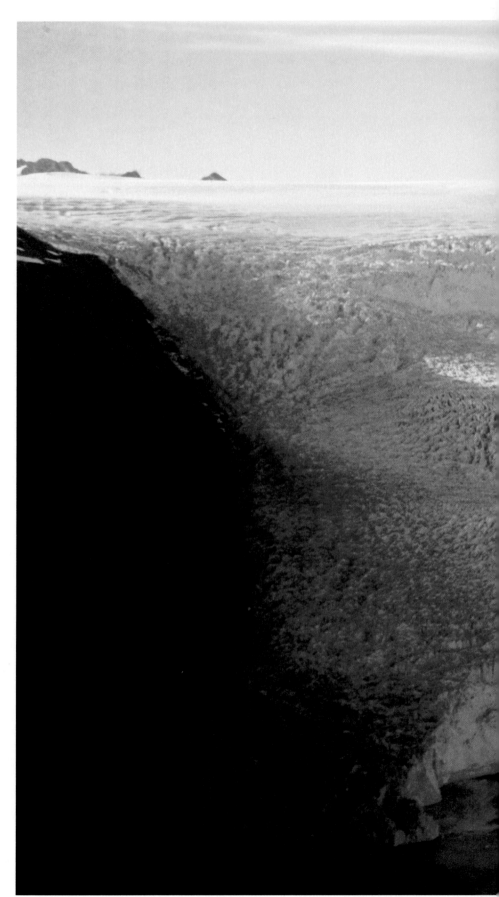

Aialik Glacier streams down to the sea from the Harding Icefield, Kenai Fjords National Park.

THE GRANDMOTHER OF THE CONSERVATION MOVEMENT

The long struggle to create new national parks and wilderness areas in Alaska in the 1970s became the largest grassroots conservation movement in American history, involving hundreds of organizations and thousands of people. But one of those who emerged as a leader was a remarkable woman who until then had preferred to work in the background.

Margaret Thomas Murie—known as Mardy—had come north with her mother as a young girl, and in 1924 became the first woman graduate of the University of Alaska at Fairbanks. That same year she married Olaus Murie, a biologist with the Fish and Wildlife Service and older half brother of Adolph Murie. For their honeymoon, Olaus and Mardy had traveled five hundred miles by dogsled while Olaus completed his research on caribou migrations.

It was just the first of many adventures she would share with her husband. She refused to be left at home while Olaus conducted his field studies, and even brought their infant children along for months at a time into Alaska's wilderness. An expedition they conducted to the northern Brooks Range—and the short advocacy movie they made about it—played a crucial role in the creation of the Arctic National Wildlife Refuge, protecting the vast migratory range of the caribou Olaus had studied so intensely. Receiving word of that designation, Mardy later remembered, was one of the few times she ever saw her husband cry.

By this time, they had settled near Jackson, Wyoming. There, the two Murie couples—Adolph and Louise, Olaus and Mardy—purchased an old dude ranch next to Grand Teton National Park. When Olaus left government service and became director of the Wilderness Society, the Murie ranch became the society's headquarters—and a principal gathering spot for conservationists from the late 1940s through the 1960s. After Olaus's death in 1963, Mardy quietly continued the environmental work they had done together and was invited to the White House Rose Garden for the signing of the Wilderness Act, for which they both had labored many years.

Then the Alaska battle began, and Mardy, now a widow in her seventies, threw herself into the effort. She was asked to return to Alaska and spend six weeks flying around the state in a small plane, helping select places to recommend as national parks, wildlife refuges, and wilderness under the "national interest" portion of the Native Claims legislation. Though she didn't like to fly, she gladly took the assignment, covering thousands of miles in the air, even gamely surviving an emergency landing on the tundra when her float plane developed engine problems deep in the wilderness.

Back in the Lower 48, she gave speeches and testified at public hearings, answering criticisms that she and other conservationists were simply "too emotional" about preserving wild lands in the "Last Frontier":

I am testifying as an emotional woman and I would like to ask you, gentlemen, what's wrong with emotion? Beauty is a resource in and of itself. Alaska must be allowed to be Alaska, that is her greatest

Mardy Murie congratulates President Carter (above) on the signing of the Alaska National Interest Lands Conservation Act. *Below:* As a much younger woman, she enjoys the wilderness she and her husband, Olaus, spent their lives defending.

economy. I hope the United States is not so rich that she can afford to let these wildernesses pass by, or so poor she cannot afford to keep them.

At the bill-signing ceremony in the East Room of the White House in December of 1980, Mardy was among those asked to speak. Less than a month earlier, President Carter had just lost his bid for reelection, and her remarks were aimed at him—as well as toward those in the state she loved who had castigated Carter for using the presidential authority of the Antiquities Act so expansively.

I firmly believe there will come a day when millions of Americans, including Alaskans, will be grateful for an act of courage, in an hour which called for courage, in saving our country's last wilderness treasure of space, beauty and freely roaming wild creatures.

People were already calling her "the grandmother of the conservation movement," but she stayed active in those issues for twenty-three more years—named an honorary park ranger by the National Park Service, awarded a Medal of Freedom by President Bill Clinton, and graciously welcoming guests who came calling at the Murie Ranch (where she lived under a life-tenancy agreement with the federal government after the property was made part of Grand Teton National Park) up to her death in 2003.

A FAMILY OF RANGERS

To date, there has been only one family in America with four generations working in the national park system: the Cooks of Arizona.

It began with John Edwin Cook at Grand Canyon, who passed on his passion to his son, John Oliver Cook (both at top left, c. 1920), who grew up to also work for the National Park Service at the canyon and then went on to become a superintendent at a number of other parks.

John Oliver's son, John E. Cook (bottom left) carried on the family tradition, joining the Park Service the day he graduated from high school and eventually holding every position from mule skinner to superintendent to regional director to associate director in Washington.

His daughter, Kayci Cook Collins (above right, with her father), is now superintendent of El Malpais and El Morro National Monuments in New Mexico. Kayci's son, Sean (below right, with his mother), already shows promise for becoming a fifth generation in the parks.

FRED'S PLACE

This has always been considered a holy place to my family. That is the reason my daddy told me to take care of the church. . . . It is a place of prayer. . . . I always make a little prayer when I go across the altar, because it is a blessed place.

FEDERICO SISNEROS

In 1792, the ancestors of Federico Sisneros had migrated north from Spanish Mexico, eventually settling near the already crumbling ruins of the Mission of San Gregorio de Abó, fifty miles south of Albuquerque.

In 1890, the family had filed the first homestead claim encompassing the ruins, and from the age of five, Federico had been assigned the task of caring for them—a job he continued after the Museum of New Mexico took over the old mission in the 1930s. He did it all for free at first; but by the 1960s Sisneros was being paid the minimum wage to lead occasional tours, help with archaeological digs, and guard against vandals.

In 1986, at age ninety-two, after the ruins had become part of Salinas Pueblo Mission National Monument, Sisneros took his first vacation—during which he nevertheless walked from his home to the church each day to open and close the monument. "I won't retire, I belong here," he said. "My retirement is going to be when I go to the other world."

By 1988, he was still working when he died, just four days shy of his ninety-fourth birthday—the nation's oldest park ranger. In accordance with his wishes, he was buried in the shade of a juniper tree overlooking the ruins he had spent his life taking care of.

Most people no longer referred to the historic site as San Gregorio de Abó; they simply called it "Fred's Place."

Federico Sisneros and his ruins

It is a better world with some buffalo left in it, a richer world with some gorgeous canyons unmarred by signboards, hot-dog stands, super highways, or high-tension lines, undrowned by power or irrigation reservoirs.

If we preserved as parks only those places that have no economic possibilities, we would have no parks. And in the decades to come, it will not be only the buffalo and the trumpeter swan who need sanctuaries.

Our own species is going to need them too. It needs them now.

WALLACE STEGNER

After Alaska, as the nation headed into a new century, Americans would continue expanding the number of national parks—and continue using them in ever-increasing numbers: from 220 million visitors in 1980 to 255 million in 1990, then edging toward 300 million a decade later.

Ten more national parks would be created, although eight of them had already been preserved as national monuments, and one as a national recreation area. (The sole exception was the new National Park of American Samoa, which set aside tropical rain forests, glistening beaches, and coral reefs on three separate islands in the South Pacific.) The greatest growth would come from the addition of more and more historic sites, including reminders of painful episodes in American history, set aside on the belief that a great nation could openly acknowledge them:

- From Kingsley Plantation in Florida, preserving not only the owner's grand home, but also the cluster of small cabins used by the slaves who made his comfortable life possible; to Central High School in Little Rock, Arkansas, where in 1957 federal troops had to escort nine African American teenagers past angry mobs to their classes, crystallizing the crisis of school desegregation.
- From Andersonville, a deadly Civil War prison camp in Georgia, to a polished slab of marble in Washington, D.C., listing the names of 58,000

Tutuila Island, National Park of American Samoa

dead and missing soldiers who served their country in Vietnam.

- From Sand Creek and Washita on the Great Plains, where Chief Black Kettle's peaceful Cheyenne villagers were massacred by American soldiers; to Manzanar in the high desert of eastern California, where American citizens of Japanese descent were kept behind barbed wire during World War II.

- From Oklahoma City, where 168 empty chairs now commemorate the men, women, and children killed in a senseless act of domestic terrorism in 1995; to a field near Shanksville, Pennsylvania, that immortalizes the sacrifices made by passengers aboard United Flight 93 on September 11, 2001.

Like the idea of America itself—filled with competing demands between local rights and those of the nation; between the impulses of idealism and exploitation, the sacred and the profitable; between the immediate desires of one generation and its obligation and promise to the next—the national park idea still found itself constantly debated, constantly threatened, and constantly evolving. "One learns," John Muir had said, "that the world, though made, is yet being made. That this is still the morning of creation."

PAINFUL REMINDERS:
As the park idea broadened further in the late twentieth century, new types of historic sites were added, so future generations could learn from them.
Top, left: The slave quarters at Kingsley Plantation in Florida
Bottom, left: Central High School in Little Rock, Arkansas, during the desegregation crisis in 1957
Top, right: The Vietnam Veterans Memorial in Washington, D.C.
Bottom, right: The Oklahoma City National Memorial in Oklahoma

RETURN TO NATURE: A transplanted wolf is released from its cage in Yellowstone in 1995 (above), the first step in reintroducing the species. They are now once more a vibrant part of the world's first national park.

In January of 1995, a convoy of trucks entered Yellowstone National Park at its northern gate, where the stone arch dedicated by Theodore Roosevelt proclaims the park's purpose: "for the benefit and enjoyment of the people." Riding in cages in the trucks were fourteen gray wolves, recently captured in western Canada. Two months later, after being kept in small pens to acclimate them to their new surroundings, the wolves were set free—in accordance with a long-range plan to reestablish the predators in their former habitat and make the world's first national park a little more representative of what it had once been.

Within only a few years, the wolves were thriving—part, once more, of the entire Yellowstone ecosystem.

Happy will be the men who, having the power and the love and the benevolent forecast to [create a park], will do it. They will not be forgotten. The trees and their lovers will sing their praises, and generations yet unborn will rise up and call them blessed.

This is true freedom, a good practical sort of immortality.

JOHN MUIR

THIS IS WHAT WE LOVED

Terry Tempest Williams grew up in Utah, where she pursued her two passions at the state university—English and environmental science—and then went on to become a renowned author, naturalist, and environmental activist. Most of her adult life has been spent as much as possible in wild lands, from the deserts of the Southwest to the Rockies to remote regions of Alaska.

Williams has served on the advisory board of the National Parks Conservation Association, the Nature Conservancy, and the Southern Utah Wilderness Alliance. Her writing has won numerous honors, and Williams herself received the Robert Marshall Award from the Wilderness Society, the group's highest honor.

Why do we need national parks? What's their value?

Our national parks are places of pilgrimage—a place where we return over and over again with family, with memories, with a desire to be still, to be contemplative. I do think they're the closest thing we have in this country in terms of sacred lands.

Our national parks are a reservoir for our spirits—memory palaces made of sandstone, granite, a sea of grass—and they spark something in us that is both uniquely and divinely human. We remember who we are, and who we are not. And we remember in our national parks where the source of our true power lies, in the land.

Not only do we save these lands, they save us. There's something about this wild continuity that gives us courage, that allows us to be the best of who we are as human beings. I think our national parks remind us that beauty is not optional, but at the very core of our being.

And it's an American idea. What's the connection to us as Americans?

I think about American ideals, and no American ideal resonates more powerfully than the national park. Equality is expressed through humility. Liberty is expressed through the simple act of wandering. The American character has been shaped by the landscapes that we live in. Wild nature is a deeply held American value, and I think our national parks reflect that.

You know, we think about the United States as being based on the individual, but the idea of the national parks is really based on the idea of the commons; the community. And they are an idea based on generosity, not just for our own species, but for all species with whom we share this planet. As a nation we have said in profoundly original terms, "We value wild nature in place. We are of this place." It is our own declaration of both independence and interdependence.

As someone who recognizes both the science and the spirituality to be found in nature, what's your view of John Muir?

When John Muir says wildness is a necessity, I think what he's saying is that we are all made of the same stuff; we are nature—body, earth—no separation. When we go into a national park we feel that this common ground.

You think about John Muir up in the top of that pine tree, waving back and forth in the middle of a snowstorm, and if that isn't speaking in tongues I don't know what is. John Muir saw the spirituality inherent in granite. His view as a scientist and his view as a deeply religious man were the same view. And I think it was this integrity of life that inspired him, fueled him toward a cause greater than himself. He had this wonderful sense of ecstasy, having been born every single day, anew, when he was in a wild, raw landscape.

Years later, another scientist—someone you knew—seemed to embody many of the same values. What's the legacy of Adolph Murie?

I often think if we were to send forth a representative of our species to meet with the animals, we would send Adolph Murie. Ade was a man who knew how to listen. He was a man who understood stillness and embodied patience. He trusted his own instincts as he was watching instincts. He listened, he observed, he waited, he watched, and then he began to see patterns that created new narratives of understanding. And more than anything, his curiosity and his extraordinary sense of science opened up the landscape in a new way for all of us. He saw the land as a set of relationships. Nothing in isolation, everything connected.

We thought wolves were the enemy. He showed us wolves were part of the connective tissue of a healthy ecosystem, that predator-prey relationships were not only natural, but essential.

Ade Murie asked us over and over and over again to think about the national parks on their terms, not ours. He reminded us that the park is *our* construction; that the wild, beautiful, magnificent country that brings us to our knees has been there for eons, and that it would behoove us to enter these landscapes with great respect and humility—to allow the land the dignity that it inherently holds.

And what about the other Muries and their legacy?

When you look at the parks in Alaska that have been set aside, you can't help but imagine the footprints of Adolph Murie in Denali, of Mardy and Olaus Murie walking the tundra in the Arctic. I think about Olaus, when he took on a graduate student, George Schaller, and George Schaller asked, "What should I do? How can I serve you?" And Murie replied, "Wear out a pair of hiking boots." Too often we stay in the car. We're on the pavement. It is our homage to

Writer and environmental activist Terry Tempest Williams, Arches National Park

the road, whereas when you look at the Muries, they sat, they stood, they walked—and they revolutionized how we think about ecology.

Mardy Murie gave us her eyes. And when she was asked by the National Park Service to fly over the state of Alaska, what she saw, her vision, became our collective vision. And that's really Mardy's legacy, that when she flew over Katmai, when she looked over Denali, when she looked over Glacier Bay, her heart opened, and, as a result, it opened the minds of the politicians to the point that President Carter could say, we are going to expand our national park system to include the legacy of a wild Alaska.

I'll never forget, when we were all testifying in Denver at one of the Alaska lands hearings, Mardy stood up—eighty-plus years of age, an elder—and she said, "I am testifying today on behalf of Alaska as an emotional woman. And I ask you, gentlemen, what's wrong with emotion?" She brought the house down as she spoke of her love for Alaska—and do we have it in us, are we big enough, to incorporate the vast beauty of Alaska into our national heritage?

You were part of the grassroots movement to add all those Alaska parks to the system. What was at stake there?

I remember at the hearing in Denver, there was a young man. He was blind. He was a piano tuner and had taken a bus ride from Austin, Texas. He stood up and he said simply this: "I will never see wild Alaska. I will never see these parks. But when I'm in Texas tuning those pianos, it will touch my heart knowing they are there."

The eyes of the future are looking back at us and they are praying for us to see beyond our own time. Alaska offers us this grace note, for the future connected to the past. Authentic wildness. Deep wildness. That's what Alaska offers us. And in that time when we as Americans were deciding, "Do we have it in us to act with restraint, to create these places of wild mercy?"—overwhelmingly the American public said yes. And we keep saying it over and over and over again every generation. The pressure to drill in the Arctic National Wildlife Refuge is relentless by shortsighted politicians. They require us to stand our ground in the places we love, repeatedly.

The connection of one generation to another keeps coming up whenever we talk about national parks.

For all the bureaucracy, for all the red tape, for all the arguments about public policy, our national parks are first and foremost places of love. I think each American can look into their own hearts and tell you, "This is *my* national park." And it might be the Great

Smokies. It might be Yosemite. For our family it's Grand Teton. This is the range of our memory. This is the silhouette of love that can never be eroded through time.

It's a generational stance. My great-grandfather brought my grandfather, who brought my father, who brought us as children. And we are bringing the next generation. Five generations. I've stood in front of the Tetons with my great-grandparents, my grandparents, my parents, and my nieces and nephews. It's where Brooke and I were married. We came and worked at the Teton Science School. It's the last place my mother came before she died. It's also the last place my brother took his family before he succumbed to lymphoma. I'll never forget, we were at the Murie Ranch and Steve and Ann and the girls were walking toward the Snake River. It was pink light, alpenglow, and Steve stopped, and you could see the reflections of the Tetons in one of the pools. And he turned to Ann and the girls and he said, "Mark this moment." And then five elk swam across the Snake River, and I watched this family of five return.

These are the stories that loom large in our imaginations. These are the stories that allow us to go home and face not only our lives, but even our deaths. That's the power of these remembered landscapes.

What lies ahead for these "remembered landscapes"?

I think our challenge as lovers of our national parks in the twenty-first century will be the challenge of restoration. We can take great courage knowing that wolves are howling once again in Yellowstone. That we have it in us to take down Hetch Hetchy Dam. That Glen Canyon can return. That the salmon will come back into the free-flowing rivers of the Pacific Northwest. I think that's the story that's yet to be told: the story of restoration.

Our national parks are not only our best idea, but our highest ideal of what it means to live with an enduring grace that will survive us. I think that every time we walk into a national park we make vows. We make vows that we will live beyond ourselves. We make vows that we will not just care about short-term gains, but long-term vistas. We remember the sacredness of life. We remember that this is the open space of democracy. And it is, as John Muir has reminded us, the beginning of creation.

And not only are our national parks a gift, I think they are a covenant. They are a covenant with the future, saying, "This is where we were, this is what we loved, and now they are in your hands. We entrust these sacred lands to you."

RANGE OF MEMORY: Grand Teton National Park, Wyoming

THE BEST DAY

On the last day of June in 1998, my wife and children and I left the tranquil shores of Lake McDonald on the west side of Glacier National Park and began the drive eastward through the heart of the park on the Going-to-the-Sun Road, the most scenic highway in America. Its power was on full display this particular summer day as we ascended steadily toward Logan Pass. The steep cliffs of the Garden Wall, alive with crystalline cascades, crowded in on our left; and to our right . . . well, to the right the world fell away. At the edge of the narrow road was a sheer drop of thousands of feet that only the strong-hearted dared contemplate for long. Fortunately, other spectacles attracted our gaze. Across the broad valley whose flank we were slowly climbing rose peaks of bare gray rock splashed with horizontal white bands of snow. From the lips of bowl-like cirques holding small glaciers, distant waterfalls plunged toward the pine forests below them, sparkling in the sun before disappearing into a green blanket. Here, in what George Bird Grinnell called the "Crown of the Continent," the diadems were freshly polished.

Dianne and I had first become enthralled by Glacier thirteen years earlier, during our courtship. Now we were back with its results: Emme (age eleven) and Will (age eight). If the scenery out the window wasn't enough to convince them that this was a special place, they knew something was different because their father kept stopping at roadside pull-offs rather than ignoring all entreaties to do so in the single-minded interest of making better time. We stopped for photographs. We stopped to splash in the waters of the Weeping Wall. We stopped to breathe deeply the crisp mountain air. Where the road cut through a massive snowdrift three times the height of the car (the final plows had opened the highway to through-traffic only a few days earlier), we stopped so the kids could throw snowballs on a day hot enough for shorts and T-shirts. And at Logan Pass, where the road crosses the Continental Divide to begin its long descent toward the Great Plains, we stopped to stretch our legs.

A trail angles up and away from the visitor center toward the broad saddle above the pass, promising a view of Hidden Lake on the other side. It sounded inviting, so we set out. But the early climb was over wet and slippery soft snow, and Emme—for whom the word "hike" was becoming a four-letter word in every respect—soon headed back to the visitor center with her mother. Many other tourists on the trail were making the same decision. Will was eager to press on, thrilled, I think, by the prospect of an adventure he could call his own, outside the shadow of his big sister. He and I

kept at it. About a mile farther, where the trail flattens across an expansive high-alpine meadow and then Hidden Lake appears off in the distance, we were the only persons left—one of those easily earned rewards to any national park visitor willing to venture a little way from the parking lot or roadside viewpoint. It was just us and a 360 degree panorama of God's own creation in all its glory. Thousands upon thousands of acres of it.

About that time, a family of mountain goats crested a turn in the trail, ambling up from the lake and heading in our direction. I hushed Will and moved with him quietly off the trail, behind a small boulder, fearful that the sight, sound, or smell of us would scatter the animals before we got a good look at them. The goats weren't fooled; but they also weren't concerned with us. Single file, as if they'd read the Park Service sign about sparing the plant life of the meadow, they kept to the trail and passed within three feet of us. Will's eyes were the size of saucers when one of the adults (male or female, I couldn't tell; both sexes sport beards and horns) paused briefly and looked him up and down before moving on, trailed by a kid goat anxious to catch up with the others. Then the parade disappeared along the route we had just taken.

In that brief moment—though it seemed a lifetime—something had changed. We were no longer visitors to a place magnificent but unfamiliar, and equally no longer representatives of a species that

Dayton Duncan, Yellowstone National Park, 1959
Left: A family of mountain goats, Hidden Lake, Glacier National Park

has steadfastly endeavored to dominate and control the planet and everything upon it. We were simply sharing the trail with the goats, and they, it seemed, with us. In that vast amphitheater of Nature, some dim memory buried deep within the DNA of all human beings was awakened. We had surrendered any notion of dominion to become part of something bigger than ourselves. Part of it all.

We must have both been holding our breath, because now we exhaled and inhaled big gulps of air, and Will began excitedly recounting the entire moment as if I hadn't been there, too. We lingered for photos at the Hidden Lake overlook and then headed back to the visitor center at a much quicker pace—it was mostly downhill, we both had some adrenaline to burn off from our goat encounter, and I realized our little excursion had now lasted more than two hours and Dianne would be beginning to worry. Will tagged along, talking all the while, gamely keeping up—the kid behind the billy goat in a hurry to get back to the nanny. I told him that in the Native American tradition of deriving a name from a significant youthful event, I was giving him a new name—in memory of the way the goats seemed interested in his presence on their turf, but also in honor of his sure-footedness along the trail and his willingness to hike into places few others ventured. From now on, I said, he would be known as Goat Boy.

That night, in the historic Many Glacier Hotel on the shores of Swiftcurrent Lake, Will got out the journal he was keeping of our trip. He was tired but had things he wanted to put down before sleeping. Once he had nodded off, I peeked at what he had written. "June 30," his entry begins in an eight-year-old's block letters. "This was the most exciting day of my life."

Nearly a century earlier and in a different national park, Theodore Roosevelt had felt the same thing and expressed the same emotion. During what was probably the most significant camping trip in American history, Roosevelt and his newfound friend, John Muir, awoke one morning under a blanket of snow on Glacier Point and descended to Yosemite Valley, where they bedded down for another night beneath the open sky, with the granite massif of El Capitan looming silently on one side and the boisterous cacophony of Bridalveil Falls on the other. "This," Roosevelt exclaimed, "has been the grandest day of my life."

Roosevelt was president of the United States at the time and a mature man—if someone continually bursting with such inexhaustible enthusiasm can be considered an adult; Mark Twain called him "the Tom Sawyer of the political world." He was hyperbolic in everything he did and said. Even without that predisposition, a few nights under the sequoias and the stars in a place as magical as Yosemite with a campfire companion like John Muir would bring out boyish superlatives from anyone. Whether Roosevelt had ever

had grander days before—or after—the point was made: a man already well acquainted with the natural world had nonetheless been especially affected by this experience; as president, he would do his utmost to give others the same opportunity. When he transferred Yosemite Valley from the lackluster care of California to the permanent protection of the federal government, Roosevelt was making his "grandest day" available to everyone, and he was stretching it to last forever.

John Muir understood this, perhaps better than anyone in our history. His first exposure to the Sierra Nevada in June of 1869 constituted, he wrote during his rambles, "the greatest of all the months of my life, the most truly, divinely free." For Muir, time spent immersed in Nature was not mere relaxation, it was ecstasy; not a luxury, but a necessity. Time, in fact, ceased to exist. The eons required for glaciers to carve a valley as exquisite as Yosemite's could suddenly conflate into a single, rapturous moment in the presence of their handiwork. Stopping just a minute to contemplate a new plant or a boulder in a running stream—to "make its acquaintance," as he put it—might just as easily transport him to embrace the endlessness of all creation. "I am a captive," he wrote. "I am bound." And yet he was set free. In those moments, in that remarkable human being, science intersected with religion. The cosmic merged with the finitely personal.

Muir invited the rest of humanity to join him in this realm of complete, unmediated connection with the natural world, which he seemed to inhabit so easily. "Climb the mountains and get their good tidings," he implored us. "Nature's peace will flow into you as sunshine flows into trees . . . while cares will drop off as autumn leaves." He makes it sound so easy. But most of us experience such transcendence rarely, if at all—and then only briefly, and only if we're lucky. We rely instead on Muir, whose command of the English language, steeped in the cadences and images of the Bible he had memorized, permitted him to express a rapture that we may have vaguely felt, but most certainly could never have put into words.

We are now in the mountains and they are in us, kindling enthusiasm, making every nerve quiver, filling every pore and cell of us. Our flesh-and-bone tabernacle seems transparent as glass to the beauty about us, neither old nor young, sick nor well, but immortal.

Somehow, there's almost no sense of hyperbole in those sentences. We take Muir at his word—or at least believe that he literally believes what he has written. He *has* ingested the mountains (just as he did the juice of sequoia cones to become "tree-wise and sequoical"). His nerves *are* quivering. And his body *is* a tabernacle of glass through which the surrounding beauty passes, making it

Dianne, Will, Dayton, and Emme Duncan, Monument Valley, Utah, 1998

immortal. Muir had already absorbed the American Transcendentalism of Emerson (his hero) and Thoreau and their friends in Concord, Massachusetts, but in the Range of Light of the Sierra Nevada, where the air is more rarefied and the scale more magnified, he found unity with a Creator for whom Walden Pond would have been a muddy street puddle. Emerson had aspired to being a "transparent eyeball"—a mystical moment in which God's presence in Nature might be sensed unfiltered by the distortions of ego and self. In Yosemite, where the trees are the largest on earth and two-thousand-foot waterfalls sing an "exulting chorus," it wasn't enough for Muir that his eyeball become transparent. He needed his entire body to take it all in.

Others have felt it, too. A multitude of voices from our past testifies to the possibility of reconnecting to something we have lost, or at least forgotten. "Contemplating the flow of life and of change through living things," Ansel Adams said, "we make new discoveries about ourselves." Then he showed us his own discoveries through stunning photographs. The painter Chiura Obata discovered more than artistic inspiration in the "Great Nature" of Yosemite: he found communion with the giant sequoias whose "strong whisper" of stoic endurance sustained him during moments of despair. Watching trumpeter swans near Yellowstone, George Melendez Wright pondered "the illusion of the untouchability of this wilderness" until it became "so strong that it is stronger than reality, and the polished roadway becomes the illusion, the mirage that has no substance." Beholding a storm raging over Longs Peak in Rocky Mountain National Park, Margaret Gehrke felt "equal to the contemplations of Divinity." Up in Alaska, Adolph Murie believed that a visit to Denali meant "a touch of tundra will enter our lives—and deep inside, make of us all poets and kindred spirits." Among the waterfowl and the fish of South Florida's Biscayne Bay, Lancelot Jones said, "I am alone, but I am not lonely."

And so, John Muir is not lonely either. He has lots of company—artists, housewives and scientists, descendants of slaves and sea captains and sodbusters who felt the same "natural beauty-hunger" and satisfied that appetite in a national park. It's just that no one seems to have done so with quite the same burning intensity as Muir. And in truth, national parks are not the only portal to such experiences. It's just that, in a national park, the door is a little wider and much easier to open.

Maybe it was because he was an immigrant, an outsider, that Muir understood Americans' complicated relationship with the land so well. Maybe it was because he had walked from the Midwest to Florida, and then walked across California's Central Valley, and then walked up and down the ramparts of the Sierras. Maybe the tuning fork of his soul simply vibrated in closer resonance with his surroundings. Whatever the reasons, despite being raised in the most crabbed and constricted Scots upbringing, Muir soaked up what our culture and land had to offer, and then generously offered back something distilled to its essence, yet much bigger. Just as he upped the ante of American Transcendentalism, he helped expand his adopted country's vision of the bountiful continent it was so busily populating. Its possibilities, he reminded us, lie beyond board feet of lumber, bushels of grain, tons of ore, kilowatts of electricity—things measured in all manners of units, but ultimately counted in dollars.

A generation earlier, another outsider, Alexis de Tocqueville, had observed that Americans, though surrounded by wild nature, seemed uninterested in it, except in their steadfast pursuit to subdue it. They "march across these wilds, draining swamps, turning the course of rivers, peopling solitudes," he wrote. "They will habitually prefer the useful to the beautiful, and they will require that the beautiful should be useful." Muir's insight into the American character was no less profound, but more succinct. "Nothing dollarable is safe," he warned. How right he was.

In 1872, as Muir was preparing to leave Yosemite and embark on a new career evangelizing through magazine articles—to "preach Nature like an apostle" and "entice people to look at Nature's loveliness"—politicians in Washington set aside Yellowstone as the world's first national park. This was a consequential moment, whether or not Congress realized it at the time. Our nation—the world—is better because of the precedent that was set. But it's worth remembering that the political impetus for Yellowstone's creation didn't come from the lyrical words of John Muir; the main engine driving it was the powerful railroad lobby. Even so, the Senate and the House had to be convinced that by creating a new park in which private ownership would be prohibited, they were not somehow being un-American. Pronounced "worthless," Yellow-

Will Duncan at Hidden Lake, Glacier National Park, 1998

stone could be saved. The real business of America could continue unaffected.

By 1890, the same year that Muir won his first political victory with the creation of three new national parks, including the high country surrounding Yosemite Valley, the Census Bureau was declaring the frontier closed. Every ten years for a century, the government had proudly marked the steady, westward march of progress by officially announcing that yet more land had been "redeemed from wilderness by the hand of man." A virgin forest, in other words, was "redeemed" when the trees were clear-cut; a wild-flowing river was "redeemed" by a dam. Miners could "redeem" mountainsides. Iron rails and barbed wire could "redeem" the vast plains from the buffalo that thrived there by the tens of millions. Now, the great forced march across the continent seemed over, and here was John Muir proclaiming the opposite point of view. Wilderness wasn't redeemed by man, he insisted, man is redeemed by wilderness.

Which is it? Are we the people who systematically drove a uniquely American animal like the buffalo to the brink of extinction? Or are we the people who created a uniquely American refuge for them in the world's first national park, where they were ultimately spared from extermination? We've never resolved that question, this tension at our core. We take our identity from the land in ways people of few other nations do, and yet, in our predilection to make the beautiful useful, we often make it ugly—or at least sullied and tawdry—and nothing and no one is redeemed in the process. We end up fouling our own nest and looking for some other last, best place in which to start the process all over again. With boundless optimism we set out to leave our mark on the world around us, but deep down there's an uneasiness, a sadness at the heart of our

exuberant energy: perhaps the world would be better off without our mark upon it.

Muir's acolyte Stephen Mather, the next great champion of the parks, didn't spend much time pondering this contradiction. His whole life embodied it in the extreme. Demonstrating a particularly American genius at public relations (*creating* a demand for a product rather than simply satisfying it) that predated the rise of Madison Avenue by a generation, Mather built a fortune extracting a mundane mineral, borax, from the dry lake beds of Death Valley and persuading the nation's housewives that their lives could be transformed using it in their kitchens and laundry rooms. Then he used his financial freedom to devote himself—utterly and completely—to the national parks and to fighting the extractive industries intent on despoiling them. His impulsive philanthropy—purchasing groves of endangered trees on the spur of the moment, buying out private inholdings, donating land—became an infectious example among the wealthy businessmen friends who called him "the eternal freshman." And his finely honed promotional skills, once placed in service of something far more transcendent than a household cleanser, transformed the entire park movement.

But as only those close to him understood, a profound insecurity, a recurrent sense of worthlessness, clung to Mather. He discovered its antidote in the parks, became their greatest salesman, declaring them "vast school rooms of Americanism," opened these national treasures to millions of his fellow citizens, and in doing so made it possible for untold generations to lift their own spirits. That, as Muir would have told him, is "a good practical sort of immortality."

Mather's life exemplifies more than the tug-of-war between exploitation and sanctification of the land that animates American history and permeates the story of the national parks. He demonstrated how the life of one person, responding to the most personal of impulses, can affect the life of the nation; how the pursuit of individual happiness can sometimes nonetheless benefit rather than diminish the common good.

He is joined by an improbable cast of fellow heroes. Less than a year after Yosemite was set aside, Frederick Law Olmsted recognized that a healthy democracy depended, in part, on making sure that its most inspirational landscapes were not walled off for the exclusive use of the rich and privileged. In the early moments of Yellowstone's existence, when the park idea was still an uncertain experiment and especially vulnerable to private interests, George Bird Grinnell pronounced it "the People's Park" and rallied defenders to protect it. Congressman John F. Lacey, the archconservative Standpatter from Standpatville, authored one revolutionary law after another that saved Yellowstone's buffalo, saved the Everglades' plumed birds, saved the fragile antiquities of the Southwest—and as a bonus, handed presidents the Antiquities Act, a tool that would thrill conservationists and bedevil Congresses far into the future.

Turn over the rock of any national park and what you inevitably discover is the story of an individual, or small group of people, working tirelessly to persuade their government to do the right thing. Virginia McClurg may have become possessive about Mesa Verde's archaeological treasures, but she was instrumental in making them a national possession. George Dorr sacrificed his inheritance—even, ultimately, the "cottage" he called home—to offer all Americans the chance to enjoy what was becoming the rarest of commodities, a scenic piece of New England shoreline. Denali had the well-connected Charles Sheldon; Biscayne Bay had Lancelot Jones, the descendant of slaves; the Tetons had John D. Rockefeller Jr., the richest man in America. Rockefeller was also instrumental in saving the Great Smokies as a national park—but equally important were George Masa, an immigrant who died penniless; Horace Kephart, a reclusive writer whose words invited the nation into his mountain sanctuary; hundreds of schoolchildren who raided their piggy banks for small change; and a president, Franklin Delano Roosevelt, who believed "there is nothing so American as our national parks." In that, he was echoing his famous older cousin and fellow president, Theodore Roosevelt, for whom the park idea was "one of the best bits of National achievement which our people have to their credit . . . noteworthy in its essential democracy."

What unites them, and all the others like them in our history, was an abiding belief in an idea as powerfully simple and yet confoundingly elusive as "all men are created equal"—that some portions of our land are so precious they have to be shared with everyone else. And in order for them to be shared, they have to be protected. Sometimes that means protected from ourselves.

It's never been easy. Consider the Grand Canyon, as self-evident a national park as any place within our borders. It would have been the world's second if the bills proposing its designation had passed in 1882, 1883, or 1886. John Muir called for it; George Bird Grinnell editorialized in favor of it. Theodore Roosevelt thundered from his bully pulpit to "leave it as it is . . . man can only mar it." If Congress had heeded him, the Grand Canyon would have become the seventh national park. But in the spirit of land "redeemed from wilderness by the hand of man," and in the fear of national interests overwhelming local desires, every repeated attempt to place it alongside Yellowstone as a protected space was beaten back until 1919, when it became the sixteenth national park. Thirty-seven years of constant struggle to decide that the grandest canyon on earth ought to be a national park. That's what defenders of the park idea have always been up against—and always will be.

There will always be someone who looks at a river flowing through a canyon and thinks, "what a perfect location for a dam." There will always be someone for whom a forest of ancient trees is a business opportunity. There will always be someone who, contemplating a magnificent mountainside, considers a housing development; or, upon entering an exquisite valley, realizes its potential for a private estate upon which to build a solitary trophy home behind a locked gate. There will always be someone whose definition of the pursuit of happiness is chasing a buffalo herd on a snowmobile, or careening across a slickrock wilderness in a dune buggy. Anyone who understands our national history, springing as it does from our national character, knows this. "The battle for conservation," as John Muir observed, "will go on endlessly."

Whether the future will generate new threats to America's best idea is not in question. The only question is whether the future will provide a fresh supply of park champions as a counterbalance. Our children and our children's children will need them. But if such champions step forward—springing as they must from the other half of our national character—Muir has already written their epitaph: "They will not be forgotten. The trees and their lovers will sing their praises, and generations yet unborn will rise up and call them blessed."

My son, Will's, "most exciting day" at Logan Pass came as part of a long family vacation visiting national parks. At Glacier, I took a picture of Emme sitting on the same stone wall with the same dramatic backdrop along the Going-to-the-Sun Road where Dianne had sat for a photograph thirteen years earlier. At Yellowstone, I had the thrill of witnessing my children encounter their first buffalo; their first coyote; their first moose; their first bear. Dianne and I enjoyed a delicately beautiful sunrise sitting on a bench at the lip of Bryce Canyon while the kids slept peacefully in a cabin nearby. At Dinosaur National Monument, we camped along the Green River, near the exact spot where my parents and sister and I had slept in sleeping bags on the sand when I was nine years old, during the only extended trip the four of us had ever taken while I was growing up—a trip in which national parks were not just the destinations, they were what made the trip possible, because we instinctively understood that as American citizens they belonged to us and, exotic as they were to a family from Iowa that didn't travel much, they were as affordable as they were accessible. At Jenny Lake in the Tetons, where the peaks lift themselves toward heaven from the shore, stark and timelessly serene, I told my children how their grandmother's eyes always got dreamy whenever she talked about our campsite there forty years earlier, offering what she remembered as the most beautiful view in the world.

I could sense memories radiating through time, backward and forward. Memories being made. Memories being awakened. I came to appreciate an unintended consequence of preserving such natural wonders as national parks. They preserve more than the increasingly rare remnants of the landscape and wildlife our nation once possessed in such abundance. They preserve memory. Not only can you have a transcendent experience in a national park, you can safely leave its memory there and know that if you return years or generations later, that place will still be the same and the memory of that experience will still be there, too, waiting for you. Name another place in America where the same can be promised. "Absolutely American, absolutely democratic, they reflect us at our best rather than our worst," wrote Wallace Stegner, the parks' most eloquent spokesman of the last half century. "They are a cure for cynicism, an exhilarating rest from the competitive avarice we call the American Way."

I've been blessed over the last ten years to get to know the parks—and their stories—better. In each one, I've tucked away a memory. I remember the song of a canyon wren in Blacktail Canyon, a side canyon of the Grand, during an eleven-day float trip down the Colorado; there was something about such a fragile sound echoing off rocks nearly two billion years old that still rings in my mind. I remember the play of sunlight on the orange-red bark of an ancient sequoia during a brief break in a February snowstorm in Sequoia National Park; flakes were still falling, but one part of the massive tree trunk was glistening. I remember watching a wolf haze three grizzlies away from her den in Denali by provoking them into chasing her in the opposite direction; I remember her triumphant howl when the job was done, answered by appreciative howls from the den. I remember the whiffs of sulphur and the hiss of waves washing over molten lava on the coast of Hawai'i Volcanoes; new land was being formed as a national park was being incrementally enlarged, without the need of congressional approval or presidential decree.

And I remember dawns . . . so many dawns, the best time in any national park. The first rays of sun penetrating the dusty ruins of Balcony House at Mesa Verde, where we had been waiting in hushed silence. The startling explosion of hundreds, perhaps thousands, of ibises and herons and egrets from their nighttime roosts in the Everglades, their silhouettes streaming across a crimson sky, as if they had overslept and were late to work. The way Yosemite's El Capitan began to glow in the early morning light; how a thick mist lifted from the Snake River and revealed the Tetons; watching the sun emerge from the Atlantic while we sat on Acadia's Cadillac Mountain, knowing that, on this day at least, we were the first in the nation to see it.

One particularly vivid dawn occurred at Glacier Bay in Alaska, the place John Muir had first made famous. We were waiting patiently for the light to allow us to begin filming Margerie Glacier. Bald eagles were everywhere and their feathers littered the shore. We had spotted a grizzly in the area the evening before and the knowledge of its presence heightened our senses. Margerie was calving into the inlet at regular intervals; we could see the distant avalanches into the icy waters seconds before their booms reached our ears. A change of wind, the slight breeze that so often signals the start of day, alerted us to get ready. Then the snowy tip of Mount Fairweather turned pink and in the next few minutes a golden light slowly descended from its summit to illuminate the river of ice winding down to the water. It was one more of what I've come to call Muir Moments. I did my best to become transparent as glass to the beauty around me, to let it fill every pore and cell and set my nerves quivering. And I could almost hear him exclaiming, as he liked to do on the hikes he led into Nature's temples, "This is the morning of creation. The whole thing is beginning now!"

Getting to know the parks—and through them, John Muir— had provided me with more than a treasure of imperishable memories left behind at some of the most stunning locations on earth. It had prepared me to anticipate the future by opening myself to the present moment. I was learning ways to connect with the natural world around me, whether it's in a national park or my backyard. In these gifts bestowed upon me—and all of us—by previous generations of Americans, I had found another gift, what Robert Frost called "the gift outright"—that once we stopped withholding ourselves from our land we "found salvation in surrender." And I had discovered an existence in which each day is fresh, and therefore you can have the grandest day of your life over and over again.

Ten years and one week after our first family trip to Glacier, we returned. We spent more nights at Many Glacier Hotel and at Lake McDonald. We took more photographs on the Going-to-the-Sun Road, newly opened by snowplows just before Independence Day. The sparkling tears of the Weeping Wall were still flowing. The views were still vertiginous. But this time Will and I didn't hike to the Hidden Lake overlook. We had more ambitious plans.

With Dianne and Emme left behind (the word "hike" was still banned from his sister's vocabulary), he and I began a 6.7-mile, 3,300-foot climb to the Sperry Chalet, where we would spend two nights. This time he led the way, an eighteen-year-old striding confidently up the trail, while I struggled to keep up, especially on the final stretch over a snowfield. Treated to a hearty supper, a soft bed, and then a hearty breakfast, the next day we set out on a day trip up over Lincoln Pass.

Word must have been passed among his cloven-hoofed brethren that the Goat Boy was back, because we encountered mountain goats at every turn. Families of goats, pairs of goats, small herds of goats, solo goats. At Lincoln Pass, I took a picture of Will with a string of goats lined up above him, stretching toward the peak five hundred feet above us. Farther on, I called a halt at a rocky promontory. To the east, Gunsight Pass looked impassable because of snow. No reason to go on, I said, so we sat down for a rest, which stretched into an hour or more of blissful solitude in the warm sun.

We were surrounded once more by Glacier's signature gray peaks striped with white. Below us to the left, maybe a thousand feet or more, Lake Ellen Wilson rested in a hanging valley. Below us to the right, but much farther down, was Lincoln Lake. Between the two, directly below us, Beaver Chief Falls dropped 1,334 feet, connecting the two lakes, a vertical ribbon of sparkling foam. Our flesh-and-bone tabernacles were becoming transparent. We were in the mountains, and the mountains were in us. We had entered a Muir Moment, part of it all.

And then, on cue, a nanny goat and her kid showed up to share our perch, as if they wanted to enjoy the moment, too. The young one came face-to-face with Will, sitting on a rock, and stared at him in curious wonder with its wide, coal-black eyes, perhaps comparing the scraggly beards they both were beginning to sprout. The mother grazed a few feet away, unconcerned. After about fifteen minutes in our midst, the two of them took turns walking out to different precipices of the promontory, to make sure we got the pictures we might want as keepsakes. Finally, they headed down the trail toward Gunsight Pass and we started back toward Sperry Chalet.

When we reached Lincoln Pass, Will announced he wanted to climb the peak above it, not so much asking my permission (he knew I was no shape to join him) as declaring his intention. I watched him scramble gleefully up the snow and loose rock, as happy to be out of my shadow as he had been a decade earlier to be free of his big sister's; saw him wave to me from the last vantage point; saw him disappear for the final assault on the peak beyond my sightline; and then, telling myself that he was a young man now and no longer a boy, and wondering if I could ever tell his mother

Will Duncan and mountain goats, Lincoln Pass, Glacier National Park, 2008

that I'd let him take off on his own to scale a 7,440-foot peak I'd never seen, I waited what seemed an eternity for him to reappear. When he finally did, just before he made an exultant jump to slide down the last snowfield on his rump, another mountain goat, a billy, showed up between the two of us. This time when I snapped a picture, the goat was at the pass and Will was higher up the trail, and when I told him about the switch in relative positions his smile was that of an eight-year-old, not a young man's.

Together, we descended across a mile of snow-covered trail to the chalet, Will talking excitedly about his adventure. We made solemn vows that we'd return to this park in another ten years. And that night, in the journal I was keeping, I wrote: "This has been the best day of my life."

DAYTON DUNCAN
Walpole, New Hampshire

ACKNOWLEDGMENTS

"When we try to pick out anything by itself," John Muir reminds us, "we find it hitched to everything else in the universe." Something similar can be said of preparing this book and the film series upon which it is based: it has been a collaborative process, spanning nearly a decade, involving scores of people, and everyone involved has been inextricably "hitched" to it. So many that thanking them all individually is an impossible task. But there are a few we'd like to mention here—in addition to the film credits that appear elsewhere—because we relied on them so heavily.

To create the film we traveled to fifty-three of the fifty-eight national parks in America, several of them more than once; shot eight hundred rolls of film (146 hours' worth); conducted fifty interviews; and collected nearly 12,000 archival photographs to help us tell a story spanning more than a century in time and more than a continent in geography. Buddy Squires, who has been Florentine Films's principal cinematographer from the beginning of its existence, did the bulk of the shooting, bringing to bear his rare combination of artistry and energy (if you saw how eagerly he wades through deep snow in the dark predawn hours of a subzero winter morning in Yellowstone just to get the perfect shot, you'd appreciate this as much as we do). Allen Moore and Lincoln Else made equal efforts with their cameras to help capture what we believe is the most stunning footage we've ever compiled. Our co-producers—Julie Dunfey, Craig Mellish, and David McMahon—managed all those shoots, located rare archival footage, organized an extensive array of music, and cheerfully took on any other task that needed to be done. Associate producers Susanna Steisel and Aileen Silverstone pored through the collections of libraries, museums, parks, and private families across the nation to amass the historical photographs. In the midst of all that activity, Pam Tubridy Baucom, the coordinating producer, somehow made sure that everything happened the way it was supposed to happen.

Then, under the steady hand of Paul Barnes, our team of editors took the material that had been gathered and crafted a film we could all be proud of. Erik Ewers and Craig Mellish joined Paul in editing two episodes each, ably assisted by Daniel J. White, Ryan Gifford, and Margaret Shepardson-Legere. Dave Mast, Meagan Frappiea, and Richard Rubin rounded out their crew. As always, and in more ways than can be enumerated, the entire Florentine Films family in Walpole, New Hampshire, was involved in this project: Brenda Heath, Patty Lawlor, Elle Carriére, and Christopher Darling. In West Virginia, Susan Shumaker proved essential in researching the multitude of stories we wanted to pursue. From New York, Geoffrey C. Ward, Lynn Novick, and Sarah Botstein took time from other projects to provide valuable advice on this one.

One of the great joys of any project we undertake is meeting new people and making new friends. In this case, we came in constant contact with the men and women of the National Park Service, the guardians of America's treasures, who invariably demonstrated a professionalism and passion that would make Stephen Mather and Horace Albright justifiably proud of the agency they founded nearly a century ago. Here, too, any attempt to list everyone deserving our thanks would be both too long and yet incomplete, but we want to mention Denis Galvin, who first established our working relationship with the National Park Service ten years ago, then became an adviser to the film upon his retirement; and the late Randy Jones, who succeeded Deny as deputy director of the Park Service. Likewise, we thank our panel of advisers for their expert guidance and the fifty people who gra-ciously agreed to be interviewed, adding immeasurably to our understanding of the parks whether or not they ended up in the final film.

As the film's narrator, Peter Coyote brought to the job an intelligence and warmth that animated the script, and in the long hours of recording he continually amazed and entertained us with his own great stories of times he has spent in national parks. We also benefited from a diverse cast of some of the nation's finest actors, who breathed vibrant life into the voices of historical characters from the past: Adam Arkin, Tom Bodett, Philip Bosco, Trina Carmody, Tim Clark, Kevin Conway, Andy Garcia, Murphy Guyer, Tom Hanks, Derek Jacobi, Gene Jones, James Kyson Lee, John Lithgow, Marcus Lovell Smith, Josh Lucas, Carl Lumbly, Amy Madigan, Carolyn McCormick, Albert McFadyen, Yumi Mizui, Campbell Scott, Lee Stetson, George Takei, John Trudell, Sho Wada, Eli Wallach, and Sam Waterston.

The multitalented Bobby Horton, working alone in his basement studio in Birmingham, Alabama, and playing nearly every instrument known to man, outdid himself on this film with arrangements and performances of traditional American tunes. We don't know what we'd do without him. The equally gifted quartet of musicians with whom we've also worked for twenty years—Jay Ungar, Molly Mason, Jacqueline Schwab, and Matt Glaser—spent two intense days in a Vermont studio with us, improvising arrangements on the spot and creating musical moments as memorable as any of the words or images on the screen.

Our film could not have been made without the financial support of our funders: General Motors, Bank of America, the Evelyn and Walter Haas, Jr. Fund, the Arthur Vining Davis Foundations, the Park Foundation, Inc., the National Park Foundation, the Peter Jay Sharp Foundation, the Pew Charitable Trusts, the Public Broadcasting Service, and the Corporation for Public Broadcasting. We are grateful to them all. We urge anyone who believes in the mission of quality, educational television to donate to their local PBS station; and those who support the mission of the parks to donate to the National Park Foundation at www.nationalparks.org. We also wish to thank our friends at our long-standing producer partner, WETA-TV in Washington, D.C.—Sharon Rockefeller, David Thompson, Dalton Delan, Karen Kenton, Craig Impink, Anne Harrington, and many others; Joe DePlasco and his team at Dan Klores Communications; and Mac Talmadge, who was instrumental in creating the signature image for the entire project.

For this book, we thank our agents, Jennifer Rudolph Walsh and Jay Mandel of William Morris and Chuck Verrill of Darhansoff, Verrill & Feldman; Sonny Mehta of Knopf, who enthusiastically agreed to publish it (continuing a deep tradition of supporting national parks begun by Alfred A. Knopf himself); Andrew Miller, who edited it; and Wendy Byrne, who designed it. And we thank Providence for somehow allowing our exploration of the parks to intersect with Tuan Luong's; his dedication to lugging his large-format camera to remote and scenic portions of all fifty-eight national parks is as inspirational as the magnificent photographs he brings back.

Finally, we wish to lovingly acknowledge our families—Julie, Sarah, Lilly, and Olivia Burns, and Dianne, Emme, and Will Duncan. As Theodore Roosevelt said, the national parks are every American's inheritance, a precious legacy that in turn has to be passed along, unimpaired, to "our children and our children's children." We hope that we have kept our part of the generational compact and that they will do the same when it's their turn.

KEN BURNS
DAYTON DUNCAN
Walpole, New Hampshire

SELECTED BIBLIOGRAPHY

For reasons of space, what follows is merely a selected bibliography, listing the principal sources used in this book and film series. Many other sources that were consulted—newspaper accounts, magazine articles, National Park Service reports and guidebooks, professional journals and notices, Web sites, and so forth—are not included.

We would like to offer special thanks to Pamela Wright Lloyd and Marian Albright Schenck for sharing unpublished materials compiled by their fathers; likewise to the University of Washington's Special Collections for the Matsushita papers, and the Nebraska State Historical Society for the rich journals of Margaret Gehrke. We are grateful to every author or editor listed below, upon whose scholarship and hard work we have built our story.

Adams, Ansel, and Mary Street Alinder. *An Autobiography.* Boston: Little, Brown, 1996.

Albright, Horace M., as told to Robert Cahn. *The Birth of the National Park Service: The Founding Years, 1913–33.* Salt Lake City: Howe Brothers, 1985.

Albright, Horace M., and Marian Albright Schenck. *Creating the National Park Service: The Missing Years.* Norman: University of Oklahoma Press, 1999.

———. *The Mather Mountain Party of 1915.* Sequoia Natural History Association, 1990.

Albright, Horace M., and Frank J. Taylor. *"Oh, Ranger!"* New York: Dodd, Mead, 1936.

Alinder, Mary Street. *Ansel Adams: A Biography.* New York: Henry Holt, 1996.

Anderson, Michael F. *Living at the Edge: Explorers, Exploiters and Settlers of the Grand Canyon Region.* Grand Canyon, Arizona: Grand Canyon Association, 1998.

———. *Polishing the Jewel: An Administrative History of Grand Canyon National Park.* Grand Canyon, Arizona: Grand Canyon Association, 2000.

Badé, William Frederic. *The Life and Letters of John Muir.* Boston: Houghton Mifflin, 1924

Bartlett, Richard A. *Yellowstone: A Wilderness Besieged.* Tucson: University of Arizona Press, 1985.

Belanger, Pamela J. *Inventing Acadia: Artists and Tourists at Mount Desert.* Rockland, Maine: Farnsworth Art Museum, 1999.

Blackburn, Fred M. *The Wetherills: Friends of Mesa Verde.* Durango, Colorado: Durango Herald Small Press, 2006.

Blackburn, Fred M., and Ray A. Williamson. *Cowboys and Cave Dwellers: Basketmaker Archaeology in Utah's Grand Gulch.* Santa Fe: School of American Research Press, 1997.

Brant, Irving. *Adventures in Conservation with Franklin D. Roosevelt.* Flagstaff, Arizona: Northland Publishing, 1988.

Brower, David, ed. *Glacier Bay: The Land and the Silence.* Anchorage: Alaska National Parks and Monuments Association, 1967.

Brown, Margaret Lynn. *The Wild East: A Biography of the Great Smoky Mountains.* Gainesville: University Press of Florida, 2000.

Brown, William E. *Denali: Symbol of the Alaskan Wild.* Denali National Park, Alaska: Alaska Natural History Association, 1993.

Browning, Peter, ed. *John Muir in His Own Words.* Lafayette, California: Great West Books, 1988.

Buchholtz, C. W. *Rocky Mountain National Park: A History.* Boulder: University Press of Colorado, 1983.

Bunnell, Lafayette Houghton. *Discovery of the Yosemite.* Yosemite National Park: Yosemite Association, 1990.

Burroughs, John. *Camping and Tramping with Roosevelt.* Boston: Houghton Mifflin, 1906.

Campbell, Carlos. *Birth of a National Park in the Great Smoky Mountains.* Knoxville: University of Tennessee Press, 1960.

Carr, Ethan. *Mission 66: Modernism and the National Park Dilemma.* Amherst: University of Massachusetts Press, 2007.

———. *Wilderness by Design: Landscape Architecture and the National Park Service.* Lincoln: University of Nebraska Press, 1998.

Collier, Sargent F. *Mount Desert Island and Acadia National Park: An Informal History.* Camden, Maine: Down East Books, 1978.

Craighead, Charles, and Bonnie Kreps. *Arctic Dance: The Mardy Murie Story.* Portland, Oregon: Graphic Arts Books, 2002.

Cutright, Paul Russell. *Theodore Roosevelt: The Making of a Conservationist.* Urbana: University of Illinois Press, 1985.

Diettert, Gerald A. *Grinnell's Glacier: George Bird Grinnell and Glacier National Park.* Missoula, Montana: Mountain Press Publishing Company, 1992.

Dilsaver, Lary M., and William C. Tweed. *Challenge of the Big Trees: A Resource History of Sequoia and Kings Canyon National Parks.* Three Rivers, California: Sequoia Natural History Association, 1990.

Dimock, Brad. *Sunk Without a Sound: The Tragic Colorado River Honeymoon of Glen and Bessie Hyde.* Flagstaff, Arizona: Fretwater Press, 2001.

Dorr, George B. *The Story of Acadia National Park.* Bar Harbor, Maine: Acadia Publishing Company, 1997.

Douglas, Marjory Stoneman. *The Everglades: River of Grass.* Sarasota: Pineapple Press, 1997.

Driesbach, Janice T., and Susan Landauer. *Obata's Yosemite: The Art and Letters of Chiura Obata from His Trip to the High Sierra in 1927.* Yosemite National Park: Yosemite Association, 1993.

Drummond, Alexander. *Enos Mills: Citizen of Nature.* Boulder: University Press of Colorado, 1995.

Ehrlich, Gretel. *John Muir: Nature's Visionary.* Washington, D.C.: National Geographic Society, 2000.

Emory, Jerry, and Pamela Wright Lloyd. "George Melendez Wright 1904–1936: A Voice on the Wing." *George Wright Forum,* Vol. 17, No. 4, 2000.

Ernst, Joseph W., ed. *Worthwhile Places: Correspondence of John D. Rockefeller, Jr., and Horace M. Albright.* Bronx, NY: Fordham University Press, 1991.

Farabee, Charles R. "Butch" Jr. *National Park Ranger: An American Icon.* Lanham, MD: Roberts Rinehart, 2003.

Fiset, Louis. *Imprisoned Apart: The World War II Correspondence of an Issei Couple.* Seattle: University of Washington Press, 1997.

Fletcher, Maurine S., ed. *The Wetherills of the Mesa Verde: Autobiography of Benjamin Alfred Wetherill.* Lincoln: University of Nebraska Press, 1977.

Fox, Stephen. *The American Conservation Movement: John Muir and His Legacy.* Madison: University of Wisconsin Press, 1981.

Franklin, Linda S. "Adolph Murie: Denali's Wilderness Conscience." Thesis presented to the University of Alaska, Fairbanks, May 2004.

Frome, Michael. *Strangers in High Places: The Story of the Great Smoky Mountains.* Knoxville: University of Tennessee Press, 1980.

Goldstein, Judith S. *Tragedies and Triumphs: The Founding of Acadia National Park.* Somesville, Maine: Port in a Storm Bookstore, 1992.

Graham, Frank Jr. *The Audubon Ark: A History of the National Audubon Society.* New York: Alfred A. Knopf, 1990.

Grunwald, Michael. *The Swamp: The Everglades, Florida, and the Politics of Paradise.* New York: Simon & Schuster, 2006.

Haines, Aubrey L. *The Yellowstone Story.* Yellowstone National Park: Yellowstone Library and Museum Association, 1977.

Hampton, H. Duane. *How the U.S. Cavalry Saved Our National Parks.* Bloomington: Indiana University Press, 1971.

Hartzog, George B. Jr. *Battling for the National Parks.* Mount Kisco, NY: Moyer Bell, 1988.

Harvey, Mark W. T. *A Symbol of Wilderness: Echo Park and the American Conservation Movement.* Albuquerque: University of New Mexico Press, 1994.

Heacox, Kim. *An American Idea: The Making of the National Parks.* Washington, D.C.: National Geographic Society, 2001.

Hill, Kimi Kodani. *Topaz Moon: Chiura Obata's Art of the Internment.* Berkeley: Heyday Books, 2000.

Hughes, J. Donald. *In the House of Stone and Light: Introduction to the Human History of Grand Canyon.* Grand Canyon, Arizona: Grand Canyon Association, 1978.

Hutchings, James Mason. *In the Heart of the Sierras.* Oakland: Pacific Press Publishing House, 1886.

———. *Scenes of Wonder and Curiosity in California.* San Francisco: Hutchings & Rosenfield, 1861.

Ise, John. *Our National Park Policy: A Critical History.* Baltimore: Johns Hopkins University Press, 1961.

Jacoby, Karl. *Crimes Against Nature: Squatters, Poachers, Thieves, and the Hidden History of American Conservation.* Berkeley: University of California Press, 2001.

Johnson, Robert Underwood. *Remembered Yesterdays.* Boston: Little, Brown, 1923.

Johnston, Hank. *Ho! For Yo-Semite: By Foot, Horseback, Horse-Stage, Horseless Carriage, Bicycle, & Steam Locomotive.* Yosemite National Park: Yosemite Association, 2000.

———. *The Yosemite Grant, 1864–1906.* Yosemite National Park: Yosemite Association, 1995.

———. *Yosemite's Yesterdays.* Yosemite, California: Flying Spur Press, 1989.

Jones, Holway R. *John Muir and the Sierra Club: The Battle for Yosemite.* San Francisco: Sierra Club, 1965.

Kaufman, Polly Welts. *National Parks and the Woman's Voice: A History.* Albuquerque: University of New Mexico Press, 1996.

Keller, Robert H., and Michael F. Turek. *American Indians and National Parks.* Tucson: University of Arizona Press, 1998.

Kephart, Horace. *Our Southern Highlanders.* Knoxville: University of Tennessee Press, 1976.

Kolb, Ellsworth L. *Through the Grand Canyon from Wyoming to Mexico.* New York: Macmillan, 1914.

Lacey, John F. *Memorial Volume.* Cedar Rapids, Iowa: Iowa Park and Forestry Association, 1915.

Langford, Nathaniel Pitt. *The Discovery of Yellowstone Park.* Lincoln: University of Nebraska Press, 1972.

Lien, Carsten. *Olympic Battleground: The Power Politics of Timber Preservation.* Seattle: Mountaineers Books, 2000.

Mackintosh, Barry. *The National Parks: Shaping the System.* Washington, D.C.: U.S. Department of the Interior, 1991.

Magoc, Chris J. *Yellowstone: The Creation and Selling of an American Landscape, 1870–1903.* Albuquerque: University of New Mexico Press, 1999.

McNitt, Frank. *Anasazi: Richard Wetherill, Pioneer Explorer of Southwestern Ruins.* Albuquerque: University of Mexico Press, 1957.

Meyerson, Harvey. *Nature's Army: When Soldiers Fought for Yosemite.* Lawrence: University Press of Kansas, 2001.

Miles, John C. *Guardians of the Parks: A History of the National Parks Conservation Association.* Washington, D.C.: Taylor & Francis, 1995.

Mills, Enos. *The Rocky Mountain Wonderland.* Lincoln: University of Nebraska Press, 1991.

———. *The Spell of the Rockies.* Lincoln: University of Nebraska Press, 1989.

Mitchell, John G. "A Man Called Bird." *Audubon Magazine,* Vol. 89, No. 2, March 1987.

Morris, Edmund. *The Rise of Theodore Roosevelt.* New York: Ballantine, 1979.

———. *Theodore Rex.* New York: Random House, 2001.

Muir, John. *My First Summer in the Sierra.* San Francisco: Sierra Club, 1988.

———. *Our National Parks.* Boston: Houghton Mifflin, 1901.

———. *The Yosemite.* New York: Modern Library, 2003.

Murie, Adolph. *Ecology of the Coyote in the Yellowstone: Fauna of the National Parks of the United States, Series No. 4.* Washington, D.C.: U.S. Government Printing Office, 1940.

———. *The Grizzlies of Mount McKinley.* Seattle: University of Washington Press, 1981.

———. *Mammals of Denali.* Anchorage: Alaska Natural History Association, 1994.

———. *A Naturalist in Alaska.* Tucson: University of Arizona Press, 1961.

———. *The Wolves of Mount McKinley: Fauna of the National Parks of the United States, Series No. 5.* Washington, D.C.: U.S. Government Printing Office, 1944.

Murie, Margaret E. *Two in the Far North.* Portland: Alaska Northwest Books, 1993.

Nabokov, Peter, and Lawrence Loendorf. *Restoring a Presence: American Indians and Yellowstone National Park.* Norman: University of Oklahoma Press, 2004.

Nash, Roderick Frazier. *Wilderness and the American Mind.* New Haven: Yale University Press, 1967.

Nixon, Edgar B., ed. *Franklin D. Roosevelt and Conservation, 1911–1945.* Hyde Park, NY: Franklin D. Roosevelt Library, 1957.

Olmsted, Frederick Law. *Yosemite and the Mariposa Grove: A Preliminary Report, 1865.* Yosemite National Park: Yosemite Association, 1995.

Pierce, Daniel S. *The Great Smokies: From Natural Habitat to National Park.* Knoxville: University of Tennessee Press, 2000.

Punke, Michael. *Last Stand: George Bird Grinnell, the Battle to Save the Buffalo, and the Birth of the New West.* New York: HarperCollins, 2007.

Pyne, Stephen J. *How the Canyon Became Grand: A Short History.* New York: Viking, 1998.

Rawson, Timothy. *Changing Tracks: Predators and Politics in Mt. McKinley National Park.* Fairbanks: University of Alaska Press, 2001.

Reiger, John F. *American Sportsmen and the Origins of Conservation.* Corvallis: Oregon State University Press, 2001.

Reiger, John F., ed. *The Passing of the Great West: Selected Papers of George Bird Grinnell.* New York: Winchester Press, 1972.

Reynolds, Judith, and David Reynolds. *Nordenskiöld of Mesa Verde.* Philadelphia: Xlibris Corporation, 2006.

Righter, Robert W. *The Battle over Hetch Hetchy: America's Most Controversial Dam and the Birth of Modern Environmentalism.* New York: Oxford University Press, 2005.

———. *Crucible for Conservation: The Struggle for Grand Teton National Park.* Moose, Wyoming: Grand Teton Natural History Association, 1982.

Roberts, Ann Rockefeller. *Mr. Rockefeller's Roads: The Untold Story of Acadia's Carriage Roads and Their Creator.* Camden, Maine: Down East Books, 1990.

Roosevelt, Theodore. *An Autobiography.* New York: Charles Scribner's Sons, 1913.

Rothman, Hal. *America's National Monuments: The Politics of Preservation.* Lawrence: University Press of Kansas, 1989.

Runte, Alfred. *Allies of the Earth: Railroads and the Soul of Preservation.* Kirksville, Missouri: Truman State University Press, 2006.

———. *National Parks: The American Experience.* Lincoln: University of Nebraska Press, 1979.

———. *Trains of Discovery: Western Railroads and the National Parks.* Boulder: Roberts Rinehart, 1990.

———. *Yosemite: The Embattled Wilderness.* Lincoln: University of Nebraska Press, 1990.

Russell, Carl Parcher. *One Hundred Years in Yosemite: The Story of a Great Park and Its Friends.* Yosemite National Park: Yosemite Association, 1992.

Sanborn, Margaret. *Yosemite: Its Discovery, Its Wonders, and Its People.* Yosemite National Park: Yosemite Association, 1989.

Sargent, Shirley. *Enchanted Childhoods: Growing Up in Yosemite, 1864–1945.* Yosemite, California: Ponderosa Press, 1993.

———. *Galen Clark: Yosemite Guardian.* Yosemite, California: Flying Spur Press, 1981.

———. *John Muir in Yosemite.* Yosemite, California: Flying Spur Press, 1971.

———. *Pioneers in Petticoats: Yosemite's Early Women, 1856–1900.* Yosemite, California: Flying Spur Press, 1966.

———. *Protecting Paradise: Yosemite Rangers, 1898–1960.* Yosemite, California: Ponderosa Press, 1998.

Sax, Joseph L. *Mountains Without Handrails: Reflections on the National Parks.* Ann Arbor: University of Michigan Press, 1980.

Schneider-Hector, Dietmar. *Sundipped Memories of Frank Pinkley.* Hillsboro, New Mexico: Percha Creek Press, 2003.

Schullery, Paul. *America's National Parks: The Spectacular Forces That Shaped Our Treasured Lands.* San Diego: Tehabi Books, 2001.

———. *Yellowstone's Ski Pioneers: Peril and Heroism on the Winter Trail.* Worland, Wyoming: High Plains Publishing, 1995.

Schullery, Paul, ed. *The Grand Canyon: Early Impressions.* Boulder: Pruett Publishing, 1989.

———. *Old Yellowstone Days.* Boulder: Colorado Associated University Press, 1979.

Sears, John F. *Sacred Places: American Tourist Attractions in the Nineteenth Century.* Amherst: University of Massachusetts Press, 1989.

Sellars, Richard West. *Preserving Nature in the National Parks: A History.* New Haven: Yale University Press, 1997.

Shaffer, Marguerite S. *See America First: Tourism and National Identity, 1880–1940.* Washington, D.C.: Smithsonian Institution Press, 2001.

Shankland, Robert. *Steve Mather of the National Parks.* New York: Alfred A. Knopf, 1970.

Sheldon, Charles. *The Wilderness of Denali.* New York: Charles Scribner's Sons, 1930.

Shellum, Brian G. *Black Cadet in a White Bastion: Charles Young at West Point.* Lincoln: University of Nebraska Press, 2006.

Smith, Duane. *Mesa Verde National Park: Shadows of the Centuries.* Boulder: University Press of Colorado, 2002.

———. *Women to the Rescue: Creating Mesa Verde National Park.* Durango, Colorado: Durango Herald Small Press, 2005.

Spence, Mark David. *Dispossessing the Wilderness: Indian Removal and the Making of the National Parks.* New York: Oxford University Press, 1999.

Stegner, Page, ed. *Marking the Sparrow's Fall: Wallace Stegner's American West.* New York: Henry Holt, 1998.

Stegner, Wallace, ed. *This Is Dinosaur: Echo Park Country and Its Magic Rivers.* New York: Alfred A. Knopf, 1955.

Stetson, Lee, ed. *The Wild John Muir.* Yosemite National Park: Yosemite Association, 1994.

Sutter, Paul S. *Driven Wild: How the Fight Against Automobiles Launched the Modern Wilderness Movement.* Seattle: University of Washington Press, 2002.

Swain, Donald C. *Wilderness Defender: Horace M. Albright and Conservation.* Chicago: University of Chicago Press, 1970.

Tebeau, Charles W. *Man in the Everglades: 2000 Years of Human History in the Everglades National Park.* Miami: University of Miami Press, 1968.

Tilden, Freeman. *The National Parks.* New York: Alfred A. Knopf, 1968.

Turner, Frederick. *Rediscovering America: John Muir in His Time and Ours.* New York: Viking Penguin, 1985.

INDEX

Grand Teton National Park, Wyoming

Bridge Mountain Arch, Zion National
Park, Utah

Taft Point, Yosemite National Park, California

ILLUSTRATION CREDITS

Quang-Tuan Luong at work in Kings Canyon National Park. His photographs of all fifty-eight national parks can be found on his Web site: terragalleria.com.

When there is more than one image for a page, the images will be listed clockwise from top left.

ABBREVIATIONS KEY

ALBRIGHT: Marian Albright Schenck and The Collections of Horace Albright
BANC: The Bancroft Library, University of California, Berkeley
CLINE: Cline Library, Special Collections, Northern Arizona University
HF: Harpers Ferry Center, Historic Photo Collection
GCNP: Grand Canyon National Park Museum Collection
HAYNES: Haynes Foundation Collection, Montana Historical Society Research Center, Photo Archives
HUNTNC: Hunter Library, Western Carolina University, Cullowhee, NC
KOLB: Emery Kolb Collection, Cline Library, Special Collections, Northern Arizona University
LOC: Library of Congress, Prints and Photographs Division
MHS: Montana Historical Society Research Center, Photo Archives
NEB: Nebraska State Historical Society
NARA: National Archives and Records Administration
QTL: QT Luong / terragalleria.com
SEQNP: Sequoia and Kings Canyon National Parks
UAF: University of Alaska Fairbanks, Archives
UPMUIR: John Muir Papers, Holt-Atherton Special Collections, University of the Pacific Library
USGS: U.S. Geological Survey Photographic Archive
UW: University of Washington Libraries, Special Collections

YELLNP: Yellowstone National Park
YOSENP: Yosemite National Park Museum, Archives and Library

FRONTMATTER

i: QTL havo3698; ii-iii: Fraenkel Gallery, San Francisco; iv-v; HAYNES H-6470; vi-vii: KOLB 568-6102; viii-ix: SEQNP; x-xi: NARA 79-G-34H-1/Freelance Photographers,1930-1960/Box 34; xii-xiii: HF 631-5; xiv: UPMUIR f24-1332; xix: Ken Burns; xx-xxvii: *all* QTL deva20809; dena21043; grba8559; grca25225.

CHAPTER 1

1: QTL yose20020; 2-3: *The Valley, from the Mariposa Trail*, Photography Collection, New York Public Library; 4: LOC LC-USZ62-64273; 5: Hank Johnston Collection; BANC 1971.055:1587 STER; 6: The Haggin Museum, Stockton, CA; 7: YOSENP; UPMUIR f45-2565; 8: BANC Conness, John POR-1; 9: Fraenkel Gallery, San Francisco; 10: QTL shen20417; 12: Castellani Art Museum of Niagara University Collection; 13: Frederick Law Olmsted NHS; 14: BANC 1966.003.12:20 PIC; 15: HF 000601; 17: UPMUIR f23-1246; 18: UPMUIR Journal July 1867-Feb, 1868; Wisconsin Historical Society 4954; 20: QTL yose2160; 21: John Muir NHS E1-24; UPMUIR f05-0244; 22: UPMUIR Shone 1.3.1.3.04; 23: BANC 1962.019:36 ffALB; 24-25: QTL yello503; 26: YELLNP 36248; HF 64-41; 29: YELLNP 36782; 30: *all* YELLNP; 30-31: Lent by the Department of the Interior Museum, Smithsonian American Art Museum, Washington, DC/Art Resource, NY; 32: USGS jwh00671; 33: USGS Yell36086; NARA 57-HS-518; 36: MHS 943-404; 36: QTL yell6025; 38: MHS Stereo Collection, Calfee & Catlin 613; James Brust Collection; 39: NSIDC, Glacier Photograph Collection; 40-41: QTL glbao281; 42: *both* UPMUIR Journal Oct-Dec. 1879; 43: Dave Bohn, courtesy Glacier Bay NP; UW 28291Z; 44: Barbara Taylor; HAYNES H-4597; 45: DeGolyer Library, Southern Methodist University, Dallas, TX; 46: HAYNES H-1052; LOC LC-USZ62-72116; 47: UPMUIR f24-1341; 48-49: QTL mora1070; 50: HF Fagersteen; 51: BANC 1962.019:36 ffALB; 52-53: UPMUIR f46-2625; 54: *all* SEQNP; 55: YOSENP RL-17,322; 56: Gerard Baker; 57: QTL thro20712; 59: Gerard Baker.

CHAPTER 2

60-61: QTL yell21262; 62-63: LOC LC-USZ62-91139; 64: LOC LC-USZ 62-59444; 65: HAYNES H-3426; 66: *both*

YELLNP 000228; 000247; 68: LOC LC-USZ62-38272; 69: *both* HAYNES H-3036; H-3261; 70: HAYNES H-3614; 71: HF HPC-000569/78-464; Karen Silliman; 72-73: UPMUIR f46-2652; 74-75: QTL meveo796; 76: Mesa Verde NP 11127, Long House; 77-78: *all* BLM, Anasazi Heritage Center, Wetherill Archives 2000.14.P.1.O; 2000.19.P.8b; 2001.2.P.17.O; 79: copy, courtesy John F. Reiger; 80-81: Burton Historical Collection, Detroit Public Library; Yellowstone Gateway Museum of Park County 14786; 83: HAYNES H-3274; YELLNP 007757; 84: The Huntington Library, San Marino, CA, photCL 352 (633); 85: UW Barnes 1995; 86-87: QTL mora1072; 88: Dartmouth College Library, Nov. 10, 1883, p. 184; 89: HF 624-1-32; Daniel Nelson Pioneer Farm, Oskaloosa, Iowa; 91: *both* LOC LC-USZC2-623; LC-USZ62-7007; 93: LOC LC-USZ62-136273; 95: HF 69-315-1; 96: LOC LC-USZ62-8672; 98: Colorado Springs Pioneers Museum; 99: Mesa Verde NP 71358/954/RHW-14; 100-101: QTL meve20137; 102: *Denver Post*, 2/24/1906; Denver Public Library, Western History Collection, *Denver Times*, 2/22/1901; 103: American Museum of Natural History Library 411947; 105: LOC LC-DIG-ppmsc-02645; HF Wa. 29; 106: HF; 107: HF Wa.7; 108: Wind Cave NP 172; 109: HF 2647; *inset* Oregon Historical Society OrHi89161; 110-113: *all* QTL crla20539; pefo25272; 114: UPMUIR f24-1299; QTLpefo5561; 115: Sagamore Hill NHS; 116-117: MHS 956-600; 118: John F. Reiger; 119: Minnesota Historical Society I.164.24; 120-121: QTL glaco561; 123: UPMUIR f25-1397; 124: Louis Lanzer; 126: HF WASO-F-451; 127: John Muir NHS A1-93; 128: Shirley A. Johnson and James O. Johnson, Jr.; 129: Ray Santos/NPS; 130: QTL Yose41040.

CHAPTER 3

132-133: *all* Enos Mills Cabin Collection 649; 1347; 910; 134-135: QTL romo20687; 136-137: Denver Public Library, Western History Collection Rh-259; 138: U.S. Borax/Rio Tinto, courtesy Death Valley NP; HF 69-551; 139: ALBRIGHT; 140: HF HPC-000354; 141: BANC Farquhar Collection brk00003721; ALBRIGHT; 142-143: *both* ALBRIGHT 145: QTL hosp38302; Florentine Films; 146: Glacier NP HPF 1950; John A. Chase; 147: MHS PAc 93-25 A4 298; 148: MHS PAc 93-25 A4 340; 149: HF 073134/14173; YELLNP 036020; 150-151: *all* QTL (clockwise) hale20915; hale25638; havo3685; havo3695; havo3701; 152-153: *both* Hawai`i Volcanoes NP HAVO-215; HAVO-555; 154-155 QTL lavo1496; Special Collections,

Meriam Library, CSU, Chico, 15020; 156: Cincinnati Art Museum, Gift of Alice Scarborough 1925.569; 157-158: Raymond Strout Collection; 159: Acadia NP 0548; 161: HF RMR-224; 162: Pennsylvania State Archives MG-85; Frederick Law Olmsted NHS; 163: ALBRIGHT; 164: Palace of the Governors Photo Archives 103023; 164-165: BNSF Railway; 166: Stephen T. Mather Family Collection; 167: Rauner Library, Dartmouth College, Belmore Browne Collection 190_4_50_b; The Karstens Library; 168: ©Myron Wright/Photographer; 169: UAF Adolph Murie Collection, Box 13, RCC13; 170: *all* NARA RG 14, US Railroad Administration, A-1 Entry 1, Misc. Records Operations, Box 93; 172-173: *both* QTL; zion21339; zion0774; 174-175: HF 85-44; 176-179: *all* QTL brca20266; arch20028; grba25209; grba6075; 180: USGS hjk00515; 181: GCNP 5305; 183: USGS arn00180; 184-185: QTL grca0698; 185: GCNP 5433; 186: GCNP 17185C; KOLB 568-2772; 187: KOLB 568-8515; 188: KOLB 568-6947; 189: GCNP 9836; 190: Rockefeller Archive Center; 191: Rockefeller Archive Center RA#1069.020; Raymond Strout Collection; 192-194: *all* QTL acad2259; acad20284; 195: Union Pacific Museum ph18b01i0515; 196: Donald Paxton; 197: QTL isr00355.

CHAPTER 4

198-199: QTL grca5506; 200-201: GCNP 12411; 202: NEB RG849-6, 99-100; 203: NEB RG849-5, 92; 204: *both* Hank Johnston Collection; 205: *both* ALBRIGHT; 206: ALBRIGHT; HF HPC-000697/101; 207: *Oregon Sunday Journal*, 11/19/1916; 208-209: SEQNP pf01467; 210: HF 86-220A; 211: HF WASO H-165 297; SEQNP 6314; ALBRIGHT; 212: *clockwise* HF; Wasson Family; HF HPC-000842; The Karstens Library; 213: HF WASO-F-850; 214: NEB RG849-9, 89-90; 215: *both* NEB RG849-9, 11; RG849-9, 123; 216: HF HPC-87; *all* Ed Rothfuss; 217: NEB RG849-12, 55; 218: HUNTNC MSS80-24/Loose Photos/p. 168/Folder 7; 218-219: QTL grsm0469; 220: Great Smoky Mountains NP III-L-4217; HUNTNC Mt. Mitchell album, p. 11; 221: HUNTNC MSS 80-29—WCU 20; NC Collection, Pack Memorial Public Library, Asheville AA-283; 222: George Ellison; 223: Great Smoky Mountains NP IV-g-6340; *Asheville Citizen-Times*, 12/8/1925; 224: Arizona Historical Society/Tucson, Portrait Collection 71233; 225: ALBRIGHT; 227: KOLB 568-5386;

CLINE NAU.PH.2001.11.6.17; CLINE NAU.PH.2001.11.6.20; 228: The Huntington Library, San Marino, CA 281199 BHGH 6; KOLB 568-5387; 229: Robert Sargent Fay; 230-231: QTL grte21278; 232: ALBRIGHT; Rockefeller Archive Center ALBUMS, Box 21, 1007 JDR 3rd; 235: Colorado Historical Society CHS.X499; Utah State Historical Society 11447; 236: Glacier NP HPF4521; 236-237: HF 770; 238: QTL maca0477; 240: Washington State Historical Society 54137; 241: Stephen T. Mather Family Collection; 242: *both* NEB RG849-13, 45; RG849-13, 100; 243: NEB RG849-13, 107; 244-245: Great Smoky Mountains NP I-A-Chim-4103; 246: Rockefeller Archive Center 1005 JDR Jr Family, Informals; *bottom:* HUNTNC Kephart; 247: HUNTNC MSS 80-29.13/WCU 103; 249: Robert Sterling Yard Papers, American Heritage Center, Univ. of WY; 250: *both* NEB RG849-3, 2; RG849-3, 78; 251: *both* NEB RG849-7, 150; NEB RG849-7, 152; 253: Paul Schullery; 254: *all* QTL yell8813; yell1838; yell1839.

CHAPTER 5

256-257: QTL ever25615; 258-259: YOSENP RL-3485; 260: Pamela Wright Lloyd; 261-267: *all* QTL caca20914; badl0583; blca20053; deva1151; sagu1233; grsa0294; 268: HF 45/169; 269: HF 71-222-2-1; 270: HF RMR-19/1702; 271: Dietmar Schneider-Hector, PhD, New Mexico State U./NPS, Intermountain Museum Services, Tucson; Casa Grande Ruins NM; 272: HF 92-26; 273: YELLNP 106403; YOSENP RL-17,167; 274: Historical Museum of Southern Florida; 275: Historical Museum of Southern Florida 5-30 Matlack; NARA 79-G-3R-8; University of Miami Libraries Special Collections, Coral Gables, Box 36, Folder 6; 276-277: QTL ever1994; 278: Clyde Butcher; 279: HF Reg No. 623; Clyde Butcher; 280: State Archives of Florida AAP-2654/Rc06610; 281: Juan Lujan; Burton Appleton; 282: Burton Appleton; Claude Tyler; 283: *all* Burton Appleton; 284: HF HPC-000969; 285: Pamela Wright Lloyd; 286: LOC LC-USZC4-2027; LOC LC-USZC4-8274; HF; 287: Pamela Wright Lloyd; 288-289: QTL bibe1420; 290: HF NPx 56-131 (46); 291-295: *all* QTL isr020404; 292: chis20522; jotr32724; care20082; drto020833; 296-297: Center for American History, UT Austin, Adina De Zavala Papers, DI_04684; DI_04683; 298: Yousuf Karsh Collection; Shenandoah NP; 299: QTL olym20645; 300: UW 28362z; 301: The Obata Family; 302: *all* The Obata Family; 303: UW

28361z; 304: NARA 79-AA-H07; 305: Sierra Club Archives, Cedric Wright Collection 0982-2; 306.1: *all* NARA 79-AA-E09; NWDNS-79-AA-N03; NWDNS-79-AA-W17; 307: NARA NWDNS-79-AA-C02; 308: Mount Rainier NP twc 3731b; 309: YOSENP 4095; 310: UW 27474; The Obata Family; 311: Franklin D. Roosevelt Presidential Library; 312: ALBRIGHT; Jackson Hole Historical Society and Museum; 313: NARA NWDNS-79-AA-G01; 314-315: QTL grte0551; 316: HF WASO-NPS 71-2; 317: Getty Images 53375133; 318: Juanita Greene Family; 319: QTL bisc25591.

CHAPTER 6

320-321: QTL glba0232; 322-323: YELLNP 27353-007; 324: UAF Adolph Murie Collection, Box 13 RCC13; 325: Dartmouth College Library, *Field and Stream*, 1947, p. 19; 326: HF *The Wolves of Mount McKinley*, Fig. 31; The Murie Center Collection 10582; 327: UAF Adolph Murie Collection, Box 16 (Assorted); 328-329: HF Waso-B-530; 330: HF; The Bradley Family; Earth Island Institute; 331: The Bradley Family; 332: Sierra Club Library, Feb. 1954, photograph by Martin Litton; 332-333: YELLNP; 333: YOSENP 3686; 334: HF 63-3113; 335: Christine Madrid French; Carlsbad Caverns NP; HF 58-JB-869; 336-337: QTL yose41088; 338: University of Arizona Library, Stewart Udall Collection; 339-342: *all* QTL guma20907; redw4284; noca20642; cany21321; 343: HF 68-OZRI-1160; QTL viis1582; 344: Getty Images 3165679; QTL viis1582; 345: George Hartzog; 346: AP Images; HF HPC-001043; 347: Bradford Washburn, Courtesy Panopticon Gallery, Boston, MA, 3454; 348: Denali NP DENA 23562; 349: YOSENP; Great Smoky Mountains NP I-E-Bear-14770; 350: *both* Historical Museum of Southern Florida; 351: AP Images; 352: QTL bisc1740; 353: *The Miami Herald*, Senior Citizens thru 1994 folder; 354-355: *all* QTL voya0430; cosw37826; cuva21332; 356: UAF Adolph Murie Collection, Box 13 RCC13; 357: John E. Cook; 358: *UAF Fairbanks Daily News – Miner*, 12/6/1978; 359: Eagle Historical Society & Museums, Eagle, Alaska; 360-367: *all* QTL wrst37087; gaar21073; kova4369; lacl1671; katm0156; katm21115; 366-377: kefj1785; 368: Jimmy Carter Library and Museum NLC18198.6; UAF 1958-1026-147; 369: *top all* Kayci Cook Collins; *bottom* HF Sisneros; 370-371: QTL npsa3782; 372: New York Historical Society 48163; Corbis BE051606;

373: Meutia Chaerani; Ken McCown; 374: YNP 15376; 374-375: Jess Lee Photos MG0188; 377: Terry Tempest Williams; 378-379: QTL grte21280.

BACKMATTER

380: QTL glac0566; 381-387: *all* The Duncan Family; 392: Milwaukee Public Museum, Matteson Collection MPM 41557; 395: Zion NP; 396-401: *all* QTL yose40016; kefj36706; kica39817.

FILM CREDITS

A Film by
KEN BURNS

Written by
DAYTON DUNCAN

Produced by
DAYTON DUNCAN
KEN BURNS

Supervising Film Editor
PAUL BARNES, A.C.E.

Episode Editors
PAUL BARNES
CRAIG MELLISH
ERIK EWERS

Cinematography
BUDDY SQUIRES
with
ALLEN MOORE
LINCOLN ELSE
KEN BURNS

Co-Producers
CRAIG MELLISH
JULIE DUNFEY
DAVID McMAHON

Associate Producers
SUSANNA STEISEL
AILEEN SILVERSTONE

Coordinating Producer
PAM TUBRIDY BAUCOM

Narrated by
PETER COYOTE

Voices
ADAM ARKIN
TOM BODETT
PHILIP BOSCO
TRINA CARMODY
TIM CLARK
KEVIN CONWAY
ANDY GARCIA
MURPHY GUYER
TOM HANKS
DEREK JACOBI
GENE JONES
JAMES KYSON LEE
JOHN LITHGOW
MARCUS LOVELL SMITH
JOSH LUCAS
CARL LUMBLY
AMY MADIGAN
CAROLYN McCORMICK
YUMI MIZUI
ALBERT McFADYEN
CAMPBELL SCOTT
LEE STETSON
GEORGE TAKEI

JOHN TRUDELL
SHO WADA
ELI WALLACH
SAM WATERSTON

Assistant Editors
DANIEL J. WHITE
MARGARET SHEPARDSON-
LEGERE
RYAN GIFFORD

Technical Director
DAVE MAST

Program Advisors
GERARD BAKER
NEVADA BARR
SARAH BOTSTEIN
GEORGE BRISTOL
TIM CLARK
WALLACE COLE
JERRYNE COLE
WILLIAM CRONON
TOM DURANT
DENIS GALVIN
JUANITA GREENE
KIM HEACOX
SHELTON JOHNSON
WILLIAM E.
LEUCHTENBURG
LYNN NOVICK
ALFRED RUNTE
PAUL SCHULLERY
GEOFFREY C. WARD
BERNARD WEISBERGER

Chief Financial Officer
BRENDA HEATH

Associate Financial Officer
PATTY LAWLOR

Assistant to the Director
ELLE CARRIÈRE

Administrative Assistant
CHRISTOPHER DARLING

Apprentice Editors
MEAGAN FRAPPIEA
RICHARD RUBIN

Assistant Camera
LINCOLN ELSE
ROGER HAYDOCK
ANTHONY SAVINI
NATE CLAPP
TONY ROSSI
JAMIE FITZGERALD
PAUL MARBURY
GARRETT GUIDERA
TRACY LITWIN
PATRICK KELLY
DICKEY GALVIN

Research Associate
SUSAN SHUMAKER

Research Assistants
MIKE HILL
KIRK CARAPEZZA

PAM TUBRIDY BAUCOM
NANCY LORY
DARRYL THOMPSON
LINDA FRANKLIN
KIMBERLY HAMLIN
BETH MAGURA
JOAN MURPHY

Production Assistants
WILL DUNCAN
KERSTIN PARK-LABELLA
CHRISTOPHER BENNETT
ALEX WILLIAMS
TONY BRAVE
AMBER MONTILEAUX
JOSHUA NELSON
MICHAEL DePERSIO
KYLE McCAFFERTY
JEFF ATKINS
SOPHIE MOORE

Supervising Sound Editor
ERIK EWERS

Dialogue Editors
CRAIG MELLISH
RYAN GIFFORD
ERIK EWERS

Sound Effects Editors
ERIK EWERS
DAVE MAST
RYAN GIFFORD

Music Editor
JACOB RIBICOFF

Assistant Sound Editors
MARGARET SHEPARDSON-
LEGERE
MEAGAN FRAPPIEA

Sound Post-Production
SOUND ONE

Re-Recording Mixer
DOMINICK TAVELLA

Voice-Over Recording
LOU VERRICO
FULL HOUSE PRODUCTIONS

Sound Recording
CRAIG MELLISH
JOHN OSBORNE
JIM GALLUP
ERIC BURGE
GEORGE SHAFNACKER
BOB POLHEMUS
JOHN HAPTAS
BOB SILVERTHORNE
CHAZ NEWMAN
LEN SCHMITZ
MICHAEL BECKER

Digital Image Restoration
DANIEL J. WHITE

Digital Animation
RICHARD RUBIN

Animated Maps
DANIEL J. WHITE
RICHARD RUBIN

Digital Finishing Service
GOLDCREST POST
PRODUCTIONS
TIM SPITZER, Project
Supervisor

2K Online Editor
PETER HEADY

IQ Pablo 2K Color Grading
JOHN J. DOWDELL III

Film Processing
DUART FILM LABS

Legal Services
ROBERT N. GOLD
VALERIE MARCUS

**Instrumentalist and
Studio Arrangements**
BOBBY HORTON

Traditional Music
JACQUELINE SCHWAB, piano
MOLLY MASON, guitar, bass
MATT GLASER, violin
JAY UNGAR, violin, banjo,
mandolin

Music Recorded at
SOUNDESIGN. Brattleboro,
Vermont

Music Engineers
BILLY SHAW
ALAN STOCKWELL

Graphic Design Consultant
MAC TALMADGE

Interns
Jessie Anderson
Kirk Ashworth
Anna Bruning
Katie Burns
Beth Cannon
Kirk Carapezza
Margaret Concannon
Jessica Correia
Christopher Darling
Edna K. Dinwiddie
Dan Ditzler
Kelly A. Doyle
Stephen Gibler
Sarah Goodno
Rebeckah Groves
Bernadette Gunn
Elizabeth Hira
Thomas Krzywicki
Reese Lester
Eli Lieberman
Laura Markiewicz
Stefanie Martin
Christopher Monahan
Kelly Morr
Debbie Pellish

Daniel Ranauro
Ted Raviv
Adam Rissolo
Lisa Romagnoli
Allison Rubin
Vasilios Sfinarolakis
Greg Stauffer
Calder Stembel
Nathan Sterner
Catherine Stryker
Michael Trapp
Kyle Turgeon
Deborah Van Fleet
Sho Wada
Lindsey Warren
Elizabeth Waybright
Alexander Williams
Stephanie Willis

Funding Provided By
General Motors
Bank of America
Evelyn & Walter Haas, Jr. Fund
Corporation for Public
Broadcasting
The Arthur Vining Davis
Foundations
Park Foundation, Inc.
Public Broadcasting Service
National Park Foundation
The Peter Jay Sharp Foundation
The Pew Charitable Trusts

A NOTE ABOUT THE AUTHORS

DAYTON DUNCAN, writer and producer of *The National Parks,* is an award-winning author and documentary filmmaker. His nine other books include, with Ken Burns, *Horatio's Drive* and *Lewis & Clark.* He has collaborated on all of Ken Burns's films for twenty years as a writer, producer, and consultant. He lives in Walpole, New Hampshire.

KEN BURNS, director and producer of *The National Parks,* founded his own documentary company, Florentine Films, in 1976. His films include *The War, Jazz, Baseball,* and *The Civil War,* which was the highest-rated series in the history of American public television. His work has won numerous prizes, including the Emmy and Peabody Awards, and two Academy Award nominations. He received a Lifetime Achievement Emmy Award in 2008. He lives in Walpole, New Hampshire.

A NOTE ON THE TYPE

This book was set in Adobe Garamond. Designed for the Adobe Corporation by Robert Slimbach, the fonts are based on types first cut by Claude Garamond (c. 1480–1561). Garamond was a pupil of Geoffroy Tory and is believed to have followed the Venetian models, although he introduced a number of important differences, and it is to him that we owe the letter we now know as "old style." He gave to his letters a certain elegance and feeling of movement that won their creator an immediate reputation and the patronage of Francis I of France.

Composed by North Market Street Graphics, Lancaster, Pennsylvania

Printed and bound by RR Donnelley, Willard, Ohio

Designed by Wendy Byrne

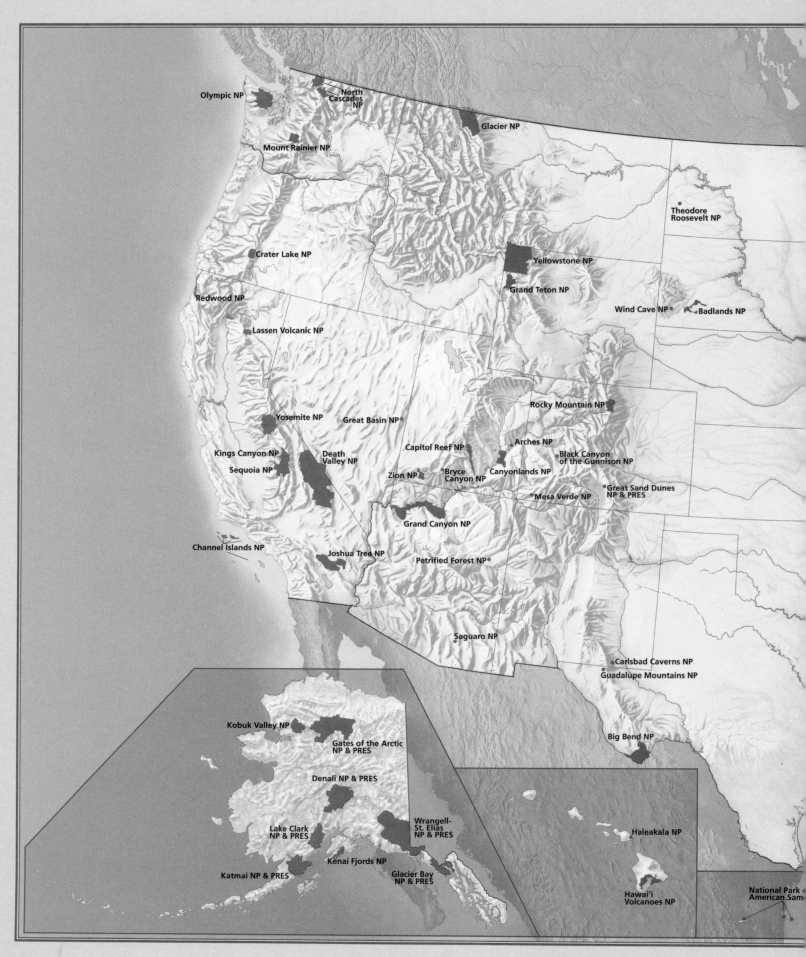

Olympic NP

North Cascades NP

Glacier NP

Mount Rainier NP

Theodore Roosevelt NP

Crater Lake NP

Yellowstone NP

Grand Teton NP

Redwood NP

Wind Cave NP • • Badlands NP

Lassen Volcanic NP

Rocky Mountain NP

Yosemite NP

Great Basin NP •

Arches NP

Capitol Reef NP

Kings Canyon NP

Death Valley NP

Black Canyon of the Gunnison NP

Sequoia NP

Bryce Canyon NP

Canyonlands NP

Zion NP

Great Sand Dunes NP & PRES

Mesa Verde NP

Channel Islands NP

Grand Canyon NP

Joshua Tree NP

Petrified Forest NP •

Saguaro NP

Carlsbad Caverns NP

Guadalupe Mountains NP

Big Bend NP

Kobuk Valley NP

Gates of the Arctic NP & PRES

Denali NP & PRES

Lake Clark NP & PRES

Wrangell-St. Elias NP & PRES

Haleakala NP

Katmai NP & PRES

Kenai Fjords NP

Glacier Bay NP & PRES

Hawai'i Volcanoes NP

National Park American Samo-